THE COLONIES IN TRANSITION

W.L. Mitchell 1970

THE NEW AMERICAN NATION SERIES

Edited by HENRY STEELE COMMAGER and
RICHARD B. MORRIS

* In preparation

THE COLONIES
IN TRANSITION
1660 ★ 1713

By WESLEY FRANK CRAVEN

ILLUSTRATED

HARPER TORCHBOOKS
Harper & Row, Publishers
New York and Evanston

FOR HELEN McDANIEL

First HARPER TORCHBOOK edition published 1968 by Harper & Row, Publishers, Incorporated, 49 East 33rd Street, New York, N.Y. 10016.

Library of Congress Catalog Card Number: 67-28805.

Contents

Illustrations

Editors' Introduction

IF the years between the Restoration of the House of Stuart in England and the Peace of Utrecht proved crucial to the shaping of the British Empire, they were alike noteworthy in the forming of society and political institutions in the English colonies on the North American mainland. During these years six of the thirteen colonies destined to become the United States of America were settled or conquered by Englishmen. Nor did the earlier colonies escape substantial transformation. Indeed, by the close of the period all the colonies were being affected by both the system of imperial control that had emerged and that ascendancy of colonial legislatures which was to become a dominant factor in constitutional development.

It is to this period that Mr. Craven devotes his specialist's talents and on which he sheds so much illumination. His is indeed a service to historical scholarship, for neither historians nor the general public have accorded to the transitional years covered by this volume the same intense devotion that has marked the treatment of the founding of Jamestown, Plymouth, and Boston, or the close study of the years of passionate controversy that preceded the American Revolution. Mr. Craven makes amends for much of this neglect. As he shows, the years he examines lacked nothing of the drama associated with the earlier or the later periods. Insurrections and violence swept the colonies from end to end. In the

South, Bacon's and Culpeper's rebellions erupted. In Massachusetts, New York, and Maryland, powerful echoes of the Revolution of 1688 resounded. And at Salem witches were hanged. Bloody Indian wars were waged during the beginning of this period and the second of two world wars came to a close as the period ends.

Less dramatic but equally significant is the social transformation that marks these years. New families, Mr. Craven tells us, are thrusting themselves forward. Large landed estates are in the process of accumulation and new fortunes derived from trade are being acquired. Special forms of compulsory labor are evolving, one form for white servants, another for African Negroes. The emergent black codes of the tobacco and rice plantations attest to the rise of racial discrimination and the pitiless character of the slave system. The Puritan oligarchy is in retreat while the Anglican church makes substantial forward strides.

If patterns of social and economic institutions are in the process of reshaping, new leaders provide momentum for the transition. In the years immediately following the Restoration of the Stuarts, colonial leadership remained in the hands of established figures like John Winthrop the Younger in Connecticut and Sir William Berkeley in Virginia. With the rediscovery of the colonies by the home government, powerful Englishmen assumed responsibility for the direction of colonization and the shape that the new colonies were to take, men like the First Earl of Shaftesbury and, greatest of all, William Penn. As the period ends a new type of colonial entrepreneur, as exemplified by Scottish adventurers like Robert Livingston and Samuel Vetch, seems to be pressing for influence. To the author we are indebted for shrewd and penetrating portraits of the vivid personalities that contest in these pages for wealth and power.

Mr. Craven has shown a fine discernment in asking pertinent questions, and his analyses of the moot issues of the period draw on his scholarship and balanced judgment. Was Nathaniel Bacon an opportunist, basically exploiting apprehension over Indian troubles, or was he a torchbearer of the Revolution seeking a broader degree of political and social democracy? Did racial discrimination trigger slavery, or was it the other way around? Were the Navigation Acts beneficent measures providing reciprocal advantages to the colonies, as twentieth-century Imperial historians have insisted, or is there ground for the vigorous and continuing opposition to them, particularly in the tobacco colonies? Were the Indians innocent victims of the white man's unrestrained land hunger or was misunderstanding grounded in no small part on differences in culture? To these and other difficult questions, the book provides guidelines, if not necessarily dogmatic answers, offering the reader at the same time new insights into an understanding of such basic documents as the Duke's Laws, the Concessions and Agreement of the Lords Proprietors of New Jersey, and the Fundamental Constitutions of the Carolinas.

Mr. Craven uncovers the roots of the Americanization of Englishmen in the years he treats in this volume. The colonists took measured steps along the road to becoming Americans, while at the same time, as he reminds us by way of conclusion, they were more reconciled to remaining within the British Empire at the end of the period under review than they were at the beginning. They had learned how to fashion and exploit political institutions within the colonies and to cajole or manipulate British agencies of imperial control three thousand miles away.

The Colonies in Transition, 1660–1713 is one of three volumes dealing with the founding and institutional development of the American colonies which are part of *The New American Nation Series*—a comprehensive and co-operative survey of the history of the area now embraced in the United States. The years of founding down to 1660 are to be covered by John E. Pomfret, and Jack Greene will complete the trilogy with an account of the years of maturity, 1713–63. Exploration, western expansion, and cultural changes are separately treated in this series, while other volumes are devoted to the Spanish and French empires in America.

HENRY STEELE COMMAGER
RICHARD B. MORRIS

Preface

LET me, first of all, remind the reader of the following pages that many topics he might expect to receive attention there have been covered, with great authority, in an earlier volume of this same series: Louis B. Wright, *The Cultural Life of the American Colonies, 1607-1763*.

The present volume, one of those belonging to that part of the series which follows a chronological pattern of organization, undertakes to provide a more general history of the colonies for the period extending from the English Restoration of 1660 to the end of the War of Spanish Succession—Queen Anne's War as it commonly was known among the colonists. The choice of 1713 as the terminal date was fixed, of course, by the Treaty of Utrecht. Except for the fact that no war actually is ended until a formal treaty of peace is accepted by the contending parties, the choice of date might just as well have been 1711, when for all practical purposes hostilities, in both Europe and America, reached their end. If this history seems to come to a somewhat uncertain ending, either with 1711 or 1713 according to the subject in hand, such too was the ending of the war which has been given, I believe rightly, the climactic position in the story told below.

The word "story" is used deliberately, for I have attempted to write a comprehensive narrative of what I consider to be the more significant developments in the history of the North American colonies at this time, in the hope that it might provide a helpful view of one of the more complex chapters of our entire history, one that has been much more often considered for the significance of its several parts than as a whole. Obviously, my choice of subject, or emphasis, will differ from that another historian might make, but I hope that he still may find my reading of the story helpful in his own attempt to gain the right perspective.

I apologize to authors whose books or articles fail here to receive citation. Such were the limitations of the space assigned that I early had to choose between comprehensive citations to a very full literature and citation only to that part of the literature upon which I chiefly depended for the argument.

Among the scholars I have leaned upon heavily, by no means least are my students, past and present, and especially John Shy, Eugene Sirmans, John Hemphill, Gary Nash, Kenneth Lockridge, David Jordan, and Richard Dunn. Each of them has taught me much about early America and has saved me from errors I might otherwise have made. Mr. Shy was good enough to read and comment helpfully upon the full text.

The financial help I have received from the Council of the Humanities at Princeton University and from the University's Research Fund is much appreciated, as is also the continuing assistance provided by the staff of the Firestone Library and by the secretarial staff of the Department of History. Howard Rice, William Scheide, and Mina Bryan have been generous with their aid in the choice of illustrations. To Richard B. Morris, one of the general editors of the series, I am indebted both for his tolerance and for his informed comments upon the text.

WESLEY FRANK CRAVEN

June 15, 1967

CHAPTER 1

The Restoration and the
North American Colonies

THE year 1660 marks one of the more significant turning points in the history of the English-speaking people. Cromwell was dead—as in America were Winthrop, Cotton, Hooker, and Bradford —and Cromwell's own soldiers, under the leadership of General Monk, had become the instrument effecting a "restoration" of king, lords, and commons to their traditional roles in the government of England. An era in which Puritanism promised to establish the rule of God's elect had reached its end in failure and reaction. The exiled Charles II landed at Dover in May, 1660, and before another year had passed it became all too evident that a restrictive type of Anglicanism controlled the re-established Church of England. Much of Puritanism was destined to survive the shock of the Restoration in the form, and the spirit, of English nonconformity, but never again would the saints hold political power—except, of course, in America.

Even in New England, where Winthrop and his associates had undertaken thirty years before to build a model Puritan commonwealth, there were signs that the heroic age of Puritanism was passing. The work of the fathers, as the founders were now beginning to be known, had stood the test of time remarkably well. Only in Rhode Island, whose disputatious people were a small fragment of the whole, had separatism and independency taken root. In the more extensive and populous jurisdictions of Massachusetts, Connecticut, New Haven, and Plymouth, an orthodox "New England way" prevailed, supported as much by the will of the people as by the authority of government. The people remained, by and large, a God-fearing and pious folk, their conduct bearing daily testimony to the continuing influence of a dedicated clergy. And yet, much of the old zeal had been lost, as may be seen in the controversy over a question of baptism which sharply divided New England at the time of the Restoration.

Membership in the New England church had been restricted to professing Christians, those who publicly could "own the covenant" in testimony of a special religious experience, and baptism had been restricted to the children of church members. It had been assumed by the founders that these children, when they reached maturity, would own the covenant for themselves, and so qualify for what may be described perhaps as full membership in the church. In other words, it had been expected that the religious revival on which the Puritan church had been built would be a continuing revival. Instead, by the 1650's an increasing number of parents, themselves baptized children of church members but having yet to qualify as communicants of the church, wished to have their own children baptized. To agree that they could have this privilege would be to take a decided step toward making membership in the church a right acquired simply by birth. No longer would the church be a body of saints, but to refuse would be to turn the children out of the church. In 1662, after years of debate, a synod of Puritan leaders agreed to extend the right of baptism to the children of parents who, in effect, reaffirmed their obedience to the church by "owning the baptismal covenant."[1] This, as its opponents contemptuously dubbed it, was the "half-way covenant."

Contrary to the assumption of some historians,[2] this famous compromise represented no victory for a restless laity arrayed against the clergy. Actually, laymen showed greater resistance to the change than did their ministers, the large majority of whom in the

[1] See especially Perry Miller, "The Half-Way Covenant," *New England Quarterly*, VI (1933), 676–715, and Edmund S. Morgan, *Visible Saints: The History of a Puritan Idea* (New York, 1963), pp. 113–138; also John G. Palfrey, *History of New England* (5 vols., Boston, 1858–90), II, 486–493; III, 81–88.

[2] Notably, James T. Adams in *The Founding of New England* (Boston, 1921), p. 263.

end rejected a solution of the problem that might leave "the bigger half of the people in this country . . . in a little time . . . unbaptized."[3] The logic that shaped the final decision was summed up by Increase Mather in a single question: "Have we for our poor Childrens sake in special, left a dear and pleasant Land, and ventured our Lives upon the great waters, and encountered with the difficulties and miseries of a wilderness, and doth it at last come to this, that they have no more Advantages as to any *Church care* about them, then the *Indians* and Infidels amongst whom we live?"[4]

Mather's emphasis on the claim of the children to the protective care of the church has a special significance. The original Puritan settlers had hoped through their great adventure not only to save their children but to redeem England itself. They had dared even to hope that the whole of Protestantism might turn from unprofitable controversy to follow the example they set in their "City upon a Hill." Instead, the New England Puritans had become increasingly a peculiar people, their example and their admonitions unheeded even by their fellow Puritans in England. The triumph of Anglicanism in the Restoration settlement completed their isolation, and left for them no other immediate mission than that of saving the remnant of God's people who had found a refuge in the New World—a cause worthy enough but one lacking the grandeur of the earlier mission.

The experience seems to have stimulated a new love among the Puritan settlers for the place in which they had found their refuge.[5] Indeed, it may not be too much to suggest that they took now a significant step toward becoming Americans. But they were still Englishmen, and they knew that in time they would have to come to terms with whatever government established itself in England. None other than the Puritan Cromwell had taught them, by forcing the submission of the "rebellious" colonists in Virginia and Barbados in 1652 and by the military conquest of Jamaica in 1655, that

---

3 Miller, "Half-Way Covenant," p. 712.

4 *Ibid.*, p. 713.

5 See Michael Wigglesworth's "God's Controversy with New England" (1662), especially the line, "Ah dear New England! dearest land to me!" Perry Miller (ed.), *The American Puritans: Their Prose and Poetry* (Garden City, N.Y., 1956), pp. 294–300. Also in 1668 the description by the freemen in Charlestown of themselves as "the most happy people that they knew of in the world." Palfrey, *History of New England*, III, 67.

the government in London could make its power felt in America. Moreover, the prosperity of New England depended in critical ways on its connections with London. American historians have often paid tribute to the skill and self-reliance with which the first generation of New England settlers developed their fishing industry and opened up an increasingly profitable trade with the West Indies, but modern scholarship has demonstrated that London played a leading role in these developments by providing much of the capital and the shipping upon which the New Englanders at first depended.[6] There is little loss for the traditional view of Yankee ingenuity in saying that only with time did New England acquire the strength to become free in any real sense of this dependence upon London. Meanwhile, a natural desire to keep New England safe as the sanctuary of the true church argued for the greatest possible isolation from a contaminated world, but the interest of an increasingly influential group of merchants demanded the maintenance of a variety of close ties with England. Upon this inherent conflict of interest would turn much of New England's history for the quarter century which followed the Restoration.

Rhode Island was the first of the New England plantations to proclaim the king. The smallest of them all, and made doubly weak by the hostility of its orthodox neighbors, Rhode Island issued its proclamation in October 1660 and promptly sued for his majesty's protection by confirmation of the colony's title and govenment.[7] For the furtherance of that hope, Dr. John Clarke was asked to act as the colony's agent in London.

The delay in other provinces should not be viewed as the result wholly of wishful thinking. Through the course of twenty years of political instability at home, the New Englanders had learned that no constitutional settlement was necessarily permanent. Perhaps time would bring better news. With some, and notably in New Haven, devotion to commonwealth principles had its part to play.[8]

6 See especially Bernard Bailyn, *The New England Merchants in the Seventeenth Century* (Cambridge, Mass., 1955), pp. 45–111; also Richard Pares, *Yankees and Creoles: The Trade between North America and the West Indies before the American Revolution* (Cambridge, Mass., 1956), pp. 4 ff.

7 Charles M. Andrews, *The Colonial Period of American History* (4 vols., New Haven, 1934–38), II, 37–42.

8 It was New Haven which gave final refuge to the regicides Goffe and Whalley; see Isabel M. Calder, *The New Haven Colony* (New Haven, 1934), pp. 216–226. The two gentlemen had been well received in Boston in July, 1660, but in February, 1661, they were allowed to escape to New Haven.

Finally, there was a now well-established tradition of dealing cautiously with the government of England lest that government be conceded a right to interfere with New England's divinely appointed task.[9] Not one of the confederated New England colonies had proclaimed either Cromwell or his son Richard.[10]

Unhappily, as each fresh advice came from England, the news got no better. Especially disturbing was a report reaching Boston in the late fall of 1660 that the king might appoint a governor-general over the whole of New England.[11] The threat was one to which the New England plantations were all too vulnerable. Only Massachusetts had a charter lending the sanction of royal authority to its government, and the Bay Colony long since had extended its jurisdiction well beyond the bounds fixed by that charter. When the original Puritan settlers moved out from their first base on Massachusetts Bay to lay claim to the more attractive parts of New England and adjacent Long Island, they had moved as men who were confident of God's favor but were unable to claim the support of a friendly government in England. In consequence, they had done much to justify Thomas Hutchinson's sad comment in 1764 "that they thought themselves at full liberty, without any charter from the crown, to establish such sort of government as they thought proper, and to form a new state as full to all intents and purposes as if they had been in a state of nature, and were making their first entrance into civil society."[12]

Plymouth had never possessed anything more than a land patent from the New England Council, a body long since defunct.[13] Connecticut had only a dubious claim to the transfer of another patent (itself of doubtful legality, if indeed it ever existed) for a part of its territory.[14] New Haven had merely a title purchased from the

9 See especially the introductory section of Richard S. Dunn, *Puritans and Yankees: The Winthrop Dynasty of New England, 1630–1717* (Princeton, 1962).

10 Palfrey, *History of New England*, II, 447.

11 *Ibid.*, II, 448. Among petitioners against Massachusetts were Quakers, two of whose coreligionists had been executed by the Boston government in October, 1659, and another in June, 1660. A fourth was executed in March, 1661. For details, see *ibid.*, II, 478–481.

12 Thomas Hutchinson, *The History of the Colony and Province of Massachusetts Bay*, Lawrence S. Mayo, ed. (3 vols., Cambridge, Mass., 1936), I, 38–39.

13 Andrews, *Colonial Period*, I, 290–296. George D. Langdon, Jr., *Pilgrim Colony: A History of New Plymouth, 1620–1691* (New Haven, 1966), has recently and helpfully filled a surprising gap in the bibliography.

14 Andrews, *Colonial Period*, II, 120–122, 128–130; also R. V. Coleman, *The Old Patent of Connecticut* (Westport, Conn., privately printed, 1936).

Indians, and, whatever satisfaction its holders may have found in the thought that God approved such a title above all others, it could not be expected to carry much weight in Restoration London.

Connecticut was the first after Rhode Island to yield. Having proclaimed the king in March, 1661, the Hartford government in the following July sent John Winthrop, Jr., son of the great Puritan leader and since 1657 governor of the province, to London in quest of a royal charter.[15] Plymouth proclaimed the king in June, but sent no agent to London and merely petitioned for royal favor. At the time of Plymouth's submission, the leading men of the Boston government were drafting a formal statement of the rights belonging to the Bay colonists under their charter of 1629, and of the duties they rightfully owed the new king. In effect, the document proposed that Massachusetts should continue to enjoy the full rights of self-government it had held since 1630, and that in return for London's recognition of these rights the colony would acknowledge its allegiance to Charles II and agree to defend its territories in his name against all foreign princes. It is hard to say what practical hope the Bay leaders had of making good these conditions, but the paper gave signal enough that Boston's proclamation of the king, which followed on August 7, was not intended to be an unconditional surrender.[16] The New Haven settlers, in many ways the most puritanical of all the Puritans, were considering a move out of the king's reach. They had entered into negotiation during the preceding spring with the Dutch at New Amsterdam for settlement in the area soon to be known as New Jersey. A possibility that Winthrop's mission might serve to protect the interests of New Haven as well as those of Connecticut led to a decision to proclaim the king on August 22. In becoming thus the last of the Puritan settlements to acknowledge Charles II, New Haven continued its negotiations with the Dutch for a possible move across the Hudson.[17]

With Massachusetts electing to stand on its charter and the uncertain promise of a conditional surrender to Charles II, the younger John Winthrop became New England's chief representative in London. When he sailed from New Amsterdam, through the

---

15 Dunn, *Puritans and Yankees,* pp. 120–125.
16 Palfrey, *History of New England,* pp. 514–518.
17 Calder, *New Haven,* pp. 217–221; also Andrews, *Colonial Period,* II, 144–194.

courtesy of Peter Stuyvesant, in July, 1661, he had been an influential leader in the Puritan community for almost thirty years. Since his migration to Massachusetts at the age of twenty-five in 1631, he had founded three towns (Ipswich, Saybrook, and New London), had held the office of an assistant in the Massachusetts government from 1632 through 1650, and had been elected to the same office in Connecticut each year from 1651 until his acceptance of the governorship of that jurisdiction in 1657. More important, perhaps, he had assumed the lead in a variety of industrial experiments looking to the production of iron, lead, and salt, the most ambitious of them being the ironworks established with the backing of London investors at Lynn on the Saugus River in the 1640's. Winthrop had been disappointed in all these ventures, but the experience had given him unusual opportunities to know at first hand the peculiar problems of New England's economy, and so to understand its continuing dependence on London.[18]

As the governor of Connecticut and the owner of extensive properties in the neighborhood of New London, he was especially alert to the needs of the Puritan towns for which Long Island Sound was the main avenue of communication. His properties included Fisher's Island at the eastern entrance to the Sound. He had lived briefly in New Haven, and undoubtedly had some firsthand acquaintance with the difficulties that community had experienced in attempts to extend its commercial activities westward to the Delaware.[19] At the time of his sailing, Winthrop was one of several partners in a speculative venture seeking possession of Indian lands along the western shore of Narragansett Bay, an area claimed by Rhode Island. He was probably too much of a realist to expect all that his commission empowered him to seek—boundaries reaching eastward across Narragansett Bay and the Rhode Island towns to Plymouth Colony, northward to the Massachusetts line, and westward as far as Delaware Bay—but in any case his instructions were broad enough to permit him to capitalize upon whatever

---

[18] For an excellent short biography, see S. E. Morison, *Builders of the Bay Colony* (Boston and New York, 1930), pp. 269–288; and for fuller discussions, Dunn, *Puritans and Yankees,* pp. 59–187, and Robert C. Black III, *The Younger John Winthrop* (New York, 1966).

[19] The best summary is Andrews, *Colonial Period,* II, 144–194.

opportunities the situation in London might afford.[20] A gentle, informed, and lovable person, whose company was prized throughout New England, Winthrop would soon demonstrate that he also had the sterner qualities of an empire builder.

He was almost as much at home in London, where he arrived in September, 1661, as he was in New London, Hartford, or Boston. As a young man he had been enrolled at one of the Inns of Court, and after his migration to Massachusetts he had returned "home" for two extended visits, the first reaching from 1634 into 1635 and the second from 1641 to 1643. On this his third and final trip to England, he found many of his former associates missing from their accustomed haunts. There was a welcome reunion with his eldest son Fitz-John, lately a captain in Cromwell's army, but his brother, Colonel Stephen Winthrop, had died in 1658. The Reverend Hugh Peter, Mrs. Winthrop's stepfather and formerly minister at Salem in Massachusetts, had been hung, drawn, and quartered in October, 1660, for his political sins as an unusually zealous Cromwellian.[21] Sir Harry Vane, who had journeyed to Boston with Winthrop in 1635 and had held the governorship of the Bay Colony for two years, awaited the trial that would end with his beheading in June, 1662. But there were others more fortunate, some of them in a position to speed Winthrop's mission. Among these was Lord Saye and Sele, who in 1635 had headed a group of Puritan lords and gentlemen vainly seeking through Winthrop's agency the control of the Connecticut River Valley. Saye and Sele put Winthrop in touch with another old Puritan, the Earl of Manchester and currently the Lord Chamberlain.[22] Winthrop may also have had the advice and assistance of his cousin, Sir George Downing, a member of Harvard's first graduating class who had risen high in Cromwell's service and who now had great influence in the councils of Charles II, especially on questions of economic and foreign policy.[23] Win-

[20] Richard S. Dunn, "John Winthrop, Jr. and the Narragansett Country," *William and Mary Quarterly*, 3d ser., XIII (1956), 68–86. See also below, p. 47.

[21] On Peter's colorful career, see Raymond P. Stearns, *The Strenuous Puritan: Hugh Peter, 1598-1660* (Urbana, Ill., 1954).

[22] Dunn, *Puritans and Yankees*, pp. 125–126, 128–129.

[23] George Louis Beer, *The Old Colonial System* (2 parts, New York, 1912), I, 9–11, and Lawrence A. Harper, *The English Navigation Laws* (New York, 1939), pp. 56–60, both credit Downing with an especially significant influence on the Restoration trade acts. Downing is best remembered for giving his name to

throp on the way to London saw Downing in Holland, where he was then serving as envoy extraordinary for the king.

Fortunately, Winthrop was by no means wholly dependent upon family relations and the associations of Puritanism. From an early age he had shown an active interest in science. The library of a thousand volumes he carried to Massachusetts in 1631 seems to have been heavily weighted in favor of scientific subjects, and his interest had grown with the years.[24] He corresponded with a number of English gentlemen having similar interests, among them Samuel Hartlib, Sir William Brereton, and Sir Kenelm Digby.[25] His standing in these circles is indicated by his election while in London to the newly chartered Royal Society, of which he thus became the first American fellow.[26] For one of the "Godly people," as the Puritans were wont to describe themselves, Winthrop was unusually well qualified to make his way in Restoration London.

Puritanism had enjoyed only a limited influence in the Chesapeake colonies of Virginia and Maryland. The Virginia colony, established at a time when the differences within the Church of England were not yet irreconcilable, had adopted as a matter of course the prescribed form of worship in Cranmer's Book of Common Prayer. To that decision all but a few Virginians had remained loyal, and those few had for the most part migrated to Maryland in the late 1640's in response to Lord Baltimore's broadly tolerant policy.[27] There they became a new irritant in the life of an already sorely divided province. The divisions were only partly those which separated Protestant from Catholic, but in the age of Cromwell that division was fundamental enough to help the Puritans, though a decided minority, to gain control of the colony in 1655. They ruled Maryland as a commonwealth for better than two years, and then in 1658 the Catholic proprietor re-established his control as the result of a settlement negotiated with the colonists in 1657. In 1660 the

---

Downing Street. The only biography is John Beresford, *The Godfather of Downing Street: Sir George Downing, 1623–1684* (Boston and New York, 1925).

24 Morison, *Builders of the Bay Colony*, pp. 272–273.

25 Dunn, *Puritans and Yankees*, pp. 129–131.

26 Raymond P. Stearns, "Colonial Fellows of the Royal Society of London, 1661–1788," *William and Mary Quarterly*, 3d ser., III, 208–268.

27 Settling chiefly in Anne Arundel County, of which Annapolis became in time the economic and political center. The migration from Virginia may have reached a total of 400 persons.

•

Puritans made their last bid for power, but this time, it seems, as only one of several dissident groups co-operating in opposition to the proprietor.

It is impossible to give the story in detail, because after the Restoration all records of the provincial government from March to November, 1660, were by order destroyed. One can report with certainty only the beginning of the trouble, in a bid by the legislative assembly early in March to make its own authority paramount. To that demand the lord proprietor's governor, Josias Fendall, strangely agreed and, if we may trust fragmentary local records, he thereafter governed in the name of the king. Any conclusion must rest largely on conjecture, but there is reason for believing that the Maryland assembly sought to take advantage of the collapse of Cromwell's regime, which had sanctioned the agreement of 1657, in order to rid the colony of its proprietor. But Lord Baltimore had the distinct advantage of being in London, and whatever proposal the Maryland assembly may have had in mind, its action, from London's point of view, could have been regarded as an attempt to perpetuate the accursed principles of Oliver Cromwell. The proprietor's chartered rights were promptly confirmed by Charles II. Aided by the desire of most Englishmen to have done with political uncertainty and by a liberal grant of amnesty, the lord proprietor re-established his control of Maryland with ease in the fall of 1660. The king was proclaimed in November.[28]

In Virginia, a royal colony after 1624, the colonists had condemned the execution of Charles I in 1649 and proclaimed their allegiance to his son Charles II. From that position the leaders of the colony sensibly retreated in 1652 by way of a negotiated settlement with commissioners sent by Cromwell. Under this settlement Virginia became in effect a self-governing commonwealth, and so it remained for eight years, with the power residing in the general assembly. Adaptation to commonwealth practices was not difficult for a people who had learned of necessity to manage their own affairs through many years of royal neglect, and whose established leaders, with only a few exceptions, continued now in office. In March, 1660, the assembly took notice of the absence of any

28 Wesley Frank Craven, *The Southern Colonies in the Seventeenth Century, 1607–1689* (Baton Rouge, 1949), pp. 297–299.

"absolute and generally confessed power in England," proclaimed itself the supreme power in the government of the colony until "such a command and commission come out of England as shall be by the Assembly adjudged lawfull," and elected to the governor's office Sir William Berkeley, who had served as the royal governor of Virginia from 1642 to 1652. By September 1660 he held once again the king's commission, and proclaimed for the people in every county a joyful day of celebration.[29]

It was natural that the Virginia colonists should have looked hopefully to the "restored" government of the king. The speed with which he confirmed Lord Baltimore's rights undoubtedly caused some concern, for the Maryland grant had ever been a reminder of the risk that Virginia too might acquire a proprietor. Since the annulment of the Virginia Company's charter in 1624, land titles in Virginia had lacked the protection that a royal charter could have provided, and as recently as 1649 Charles II had granted to seven gentlemen, in compensation for their sacrifices in the king's cause, the proprietorship of the more northern part of the colony—a grant destined ultimately to be converted, over the protests of the colonists, into the famous Fairfax proprietorship of the Northern Neck.[30] Still more disturbing was the promptness with which the Restoration parliament re-enacted the restrictive provisions of Cromwell's Navigation Act of 1651, a measure designed, among other ends, to give English merchants a monopoly of the Chesapeake tobacco trade. But there were also grounds for optimism. Virginia had a record of loyalty to king and church. Even while accommodating itself to the hard fact of Cromwell's power, the colony had provided a refuge for not a few of the king's supporters.[31] In Sir William Berkeley, moreover, Virginia had a leader admirably fitted by his English connections and his full identification with the colony to represent it in Westminster. On commission from the general assembly, he sailed for London in the spring of 1661.

Born in 1606 of a leading Somerset family, Berkeley had been educated at Oxford, where he took the B.A. in 1624 and qualified for the M.A. in 1629. Quickly he won a place for himself at the

29 *Ibid.*, pp. 262–265.
30 Andrews, *Colonial Period*, II, 234 ff.
31 On this vexed subject the latest word is that of Richard L. Morton, *Colonial Virginia* (2 vols., Chapel Hill, N.C., 1960) , I, 166–168.

court of Charles I, who knighted him at Berwick in 1639. His talents were further displayed in the writing of a play, published that same year as *The Lost Lady,* a piece with enough merit to be included later in Dodsley's standard collection of *Old English Plays.*[32] After assuming the governor's post in Virginia, Sir William quickly won the confidence of the colonists by his vigorous leadership in the Indian wars which followed the massacre of 1644. The strong hold he thus acquired on the colony's affections was destined to endure for almost thirty years. Even in the surrender of 1652 to Oliver Cromwell, the colonists seem to have been guided by Berkeley's advice,[33] and although he refused thereafter to accept office until his election in 1660, he remained a resident of the colony throughout the Interregnum. Living only a few miles from Jamestown in his famous house at Green Spring, which often has been described as the first of the great houses in Virginia,[34] Sir William directed his attention to experimental ventures promising a helpful diversification of the colony's economy. He had taken a lead in the encouragement of such ventures, and over the course of many years he undertook to produce hemp, flax, wine, silk, and rice on his own estate. By no means least of the hopes he carried to London in 1661 was that he might find badly needed financial support for a continuing effort to free Virginia from its unhealthy dependence upon tobacco.[35]

Sir William Berkeley, it must be understood, was by 1661 as much a Virginian as was the younger John Winthrop a New Englander. The king's commission can be misleading, if it be allowed to suggest a parallel with royal governors of later date whose identification with Virginia was limited, or very nearly so, to the office they held and the term during which they held it. For Berkeley, like

---

[32] W. Carew Hazlitt (ed.) (4th ed., London, 1875), XII, 537–627. Brief lives by Philip A. Bruce may be consulted in the *Dictionary of American Biography* and in *The Virginia Plutarch* (2 vols., Chapel Hill, N.C., 1929), I, 71–101.

[33] Craven, *Southern Colonies,* pp. 254–255.

[34] Actually, it seems to have been a rather modest dwelling by later standards and not to be confused with the larger mansion subsequently occupying the site. See Louis R. Caywood, *Excavations at Green Spring Plantation* (Yorktown, 1955), and Ivor Noel Hume, *Here Lies Virginia: An Archaeologist's View of Colonial Life and History* (New York, 1963), pp. 138–145.

[35] In 1663 Berkeley claimed to have lost £1,000 in attempts to produce hemp and flax; see Lewis C. Gray, *History of Agriculture in the Southern United States to 1860* (2 vols. Washington, 1933) I, 181. See also Craven, *Southern Colonies,* pp. 245, 251–253, 314.

Winthrop, had left England many years before to seek his fortune in America, and, however tentative may have been the original commitment, for Sir William there now was to be no turning back, even though his older brother, John Lord Berkeley, enjoyed an influence after 1660 that could have been helpful to him along new paths of endeavor.

It might have been expected, in 1661, that the Puritan Winthrop would face the greater difficulty in accomplishing his mission. Actually, the very reverse was to be the case. But before that story is told, it may be helpful to look more closely at the Chesapeake and New England communities, the two centers of English settlement in North America for which Berkeley and Winthrop had become the chief spokesmen in Restoration London.

It has become a commonplace of American history to distinguish sharply between the New England colonies and the tobacco plantations of the Chesapeake. That there were significant differences no one will question, but one can also suspect that the long shadow of the American Civil War too often has persuaded historians to look for contrasts when fundamental similarities have offered more profitable lines of inquiry. Even in the field of religion, the differences were by no means so marked as at first glance might be supposed.

The New England church represented an extreme form of Protestantism, one which rejected on principle the episcopal scheme of church government and much else that was traditional in the Christian church. Each congregation was a self-governing unit, with the power to call its own minister and to fix by contract the terms on which he would serve.[36] Actually, the contract with the minister was usually negotiated by the town, a fact suggestive of the expanded influence belonging to the laity. There was no place in the reformed church of New England for the ecclesiastical courts which in England continued to exercise a jurisdiction broad enough, for example, to include the probate of wills. Instead, the civil courts of the Puritan colonies enjoyed an undisputed monopoly of judicial activity. Even the institution of marriage became with the Puritan, in his rejection of most of the traditional sacraments of the Christian church, a civil institution wholly outside the jurisdiction of the

36 Morgan's *Visible Saints* is a recent and especially valuable study. See also Ola Elizabeth Winslow, *Meetinghouse Hill, 1630–1783* (New York, 1952).

church.[37] In contrast to New England's church, the Anglican Church of Virginia can be described as somewhat less vigorously Protestant, but there was no bishop of that church, not even one in England, who bothered to assert his jurisdiction over it.[38] Consequently, such episcopal powers as were exercised in the colony, as in the induction of a clergyman, belonged to the governor. As a matter of practical necessity, and simply because it was too much to expect that an ancient ecclesiastical structure, in all its complexity, could be reproduced under the primitive conditions of colonial life, the civil courts had assumed jurisdictions which in England belonged to church courts. In each parish, moreover, a vestry of local laymen held the ultimate power; indeed, the Puritan clergyman of New England, once inducted into office, enjoyed much more security of tenure than did the representative Anglican minister of Virginia. At the time of the Restoration, the marriage license, issued by civil authority, had become an established feature of Virginia's law and practice, with the result that marriage was well on the way to becoming, as in New England, basically a civil institution.[39] Already, the very concept of marriage as a civil contract between two parties had enlarged significantly the legal capacity of women before the American courts.[40]

[37] George L. Haskins, *Law and Authority in Early Massachusetts, a Study in Tradition and Design* (New York, 1960) , pp. 63, 194–195, and Chilton L. Powell, "Marriage in Early New England," *New England Quarterly,* I (1928) , 323–334.

[38] Tradition has assumed that the jurisdiction belonged to the Bishop of London, but prior to the elevation of Henry Compton to that office in 1675, the bishops were remarkably indifferent. Wilbur L. Cross, *The Anglican Episcopate and the American Colonies* (New York, 1902) , pp. 1–24; Philip S. Haffenden, "The Anglican Church in Restoration Colonial Policy," in James M. Smith (ed.) , *Seventeenth-Century America: Essays in Colonial History* (Chapel Hill, N.C., 1959) , pp. 166–191; J. H. Bennett, "English Bishops and Imperial Jurisdiction, 1660–1725," *Historical Magazine of the Protestant Episcopal Church,* XXXII (1963) , 175–188.

[39] Craven, *Southern Colonies,* pp. 273–274. Fullest and most sympathetic of modern studies of the Virginia church is George M. Brydon, *Virginia's Mother Church* (2 vols., Richmond, 1947) . See also William H. Seiler, "The Anglican Parish in Virginia," in Smith, *Seventeenth-Century America,* pp. 119–142; pertinent chapters in Philp A. Bruce, *Institutional History of Virginia in the Seventeenth Century* (2 vols., New York, 1910) , and Elizabeth H. Davidson, *The Establishment of the English Church in the Continental American Colonies* (Durham, N.C., 1936) .

[40] Richard B. Morris, *Studies in the History of American Law, with Special Reference to the Seventeenth and Eighteenth Centuries* (New York, 1930) , pp.

After long years of struggle Virginia finally had become the largest, as well as the oldest, of the English plantations in North America. Statistics on colonial population at this time are a very uncertain quantity. Contemporary estimates, upon which modern scholars necessarily have leaned heavily, were usually intended to serve some promotional purpose, and so may be suspected of exaggeration.[41] The fragmentary character of the record has discouraged analytical study of the problem, but where the attempt has been made the results argue for a significant reduction in time-honored assumptions. Thus, a recent study for Maryland calls into question the relatively modest estimate of 8,000 for that province in 1660.[42] Similarly, the persuasive conclusions of a study for New England suggest that the combined total for all the Puritan colonies, including Rhode Island, in 1660 was probably little, if at all, above 25,000—a figure not too far over that at times given for Massachusetts alone.[43] In these results there is warning enough for students of Virginia's history who have been inclined to accept the figure of 40,000 that was used by Sir William Berkeley for several

---

126 ff. If anyone wonders where Maryland fits into the discussion immediately above, it will be enough here perhaps to say simply that the governing considerations were Lord Baltimore's policy of religious tolerance, the sharp religious division among the colonists, and the absence of any religious establishment before the closing years of the century.

[41] An especially useful compilation is Evarts B. Greene and Virginia D. Harrington, *American Population before the Federal Census of 1790* (New York, 1932).

[42] Arthur E. Karinen, "Maryland Population, 1631–1730," *Maryland Historical Magazine, LIV* (1959), 365–407, which suggests that 6,000 may be nearer the fact. For comparison, it may be noted that J. Hall Pleasants and Louis D. Scisco in their introduction to Vol. LIII of the *Archives of Maryland* (1936), lviii, suggested a total of 11,000.

[43] Richard L. Bowen, *Early Rehoboth* (Rehoboth, Mass., 1945), I, 1–24, uses military levies agreed to by the United Colonies in 1653, 1675, and 1690 as a check on other available statistics, with the following results:

	Mass.	Conn.	Plymouth	Total
1653	13,986	4,494	2,520	21,000
1675	16,290	9,737	4,884	30,911
1690	33,700	20,210	10,105	64,015

Palfrey (*History of New England,* II, 362; III, 35), whose estimates seem generally to have been high, calculated that Rhode Island in 1655 had a population of 1,200 and in 1665 of 3,000. The extent of the revision proposed is indicated by Dixon R. Fox's assumption, in *Yankees and Yorkers* (New York, 1940), p. 33, that New England had a population by 1664 in excess of 50,000.

years after the Restoration to emphasize the injury sustained by the Virginia colonists from recent restrictions on the Chesapeake tobacco trade.[44] Even so, there is good reason to believe that Virginia's population by 1660 was equal to, and probably greater than, the combined total for all New England. Although immigration is but a single factor in the problem, the population of Virginia had been greatly augmented over the course of the preceding quarter century by newly arriving immigrants, at a time when emigration from England to New England after 1640 had come virtually to a stop.[45] One hesitates to accept Berkeley's figure of 40,000 even as the combined total for Virginia and Maryland, which in all probability was what he had in mind,[46] but an over-all total of 35,000, with Virginia's population approaching the figure of 30,000, does not seem to be exaggerated.[47]

From the original base on the James River the Chesapeake planters had taken advantage of a fabulous system of inland waterways to occupy fertile farmland opening upon the York, the Rappahannock, and the Potomac, and below the mouth of the James on the Elizabeth and the Nansemond. Led on by the Nansemond, and pulled perhaps by the mystery of Raleigh's lost colonists of 1587, a small number of Virginians had established themselves on Albemarle Sound, as it soon would be known in

[44] First in *A Discourse and View of Virginia,* a pamphlet usually assigned to 1663 but undoubtedly written in 1662. See below, p. 39 n.

[45] Thomas J. Wertenbaker, *The Planters of Colonial Virginia* (Princeton, 1922) pp. 34–41, indicates that immigration, mainly of indentured servants, could have been maintained at an annual average of between 1,500 and 2,000. William L. Sachse, "The Migration of New Englanders to England, 1640–1660," *American Historical Review,* LIII (1947–48), 251–278, suggests that more people left Massachusetts for England during these years than migrated thence into the colony.

[46] Note that this is the assumption of Philip A. Bruce, *Economic History of Virginia in the Seventeenth Century* (2 vols., New York, 1895; reprinted 1935), I, 391.

[47] This is close to the estimate given by Stella H. Sutherland in *Historical Statistics of the United States, Colonial Times to 1957* (Washington, 1961), p. 756. It should be noted, however, that she estimates the total for New England at 33,000, which is higher than the figure given in the text above. Miss Sutherland's *Population Distribution in Colonial America* (New York, 1936) is an especially useful study. Sara K. Gilliam, *Virginia's People, a Study of the Growth and Distribution of the Population of Virginia from 1607 to 1943* (Richmond, 1944), follows *A Century of Population Growth* (Washington, 1909), which estimated the population of Virginia in 1660 as 33,000 and of Maryland as 8,000.

honor of General Monk, newly created Duke of Albemarle.[48] Across the Chesapeake on the Eastern Shore, the Virginia colony had been extended northward from Cape Charles to cover two counties. In Maryland, Lord Baltimore's colonists had moved westward from St. Mary's, original site of their settlement off the Potomac, into Charles County and northward along the western shore of the bay as far as the recently established Baltimore County. From Kent Island, where Claiborne's Virginians had disputed Baltimore's claim to the upper Chesapeake, the Marylanders had crossed over to the Eastern Shore, where they were now spreading out, northward and southward, at a rate promising soon to draw a full ring about the great bay.[49] It would be a few years yet before the ring was closed, but only a few.

Nowhere did one find a continuous line of settlement. Generous land policies, the ease of water transport, and the general inability of the native Indian to pose a sustained challenge to the European's ambition, all combined to encourage men to seek out the more inviting spots. The isolated farmhouse, separated from other houses by unbroken reaches of forest, already had become a familiar landmark. The traveler usually came upon the house by water, for the farmer was inclined to build his dwelling, however humble, with a view onto the water, as later his descendants would build facing other highways. Only recently had settlement, even in the older areas of occupancy, penetrated far enough back from the river or bay to make the maintenance of roadways a problem of public concern.

The characteristic feature of New England's settlement continued to be the town, but the village communities in which the Puritan colonists lived, close at hand to the meetinghouse, were as widely scattered by 1660 as were the people living on the Chesapeake. From the initial settlements on Massachusetts Bay, the New Englanders had moved southward into Narragansett Bay and westward along the Connecticut shore of Long Island Sound as far as Greenwich. They had crossed the Sound to build a dozen towns on Long Island, of which Gravesend, the most westerly, lay almost within

[48] William P. Cumming, *The Southeast in Early Maps, with an Annotated Check List of Printed and Manuscript Regional and Local Maps of Southeastern North America during the Colonial Period* (Princeton, 1958), pp. 20–24.
[49] Craven, *Southern Colonies*, pp. 269–270, 303.

sight of Manhattan itself. Up the Connecticut River, past the original "plantations" at Hartford, Wethersfield, and Windsor, one came to Springfield, chief of the settlements in western Massachusetts. The four towns of New Hampshire—Hampton, Dover, Exeter, and Portsmouth—had been brought under the jurisdiction of Massachusetts almost twenty years before, as more recently had been the scattering of settlers along the coast of Maine who in 1652 were incorporated into the County of York.[50] As on the Chesapeake, settlement generally had followed the waterways and communications depended very largely upon water transportation.

The economy of the English colonies, north and south, rested basically upon agriculture. With London's assistance, New England had developed a profitable fishing industry and a growing trade into several parts of the Atlantic, with advantages which included the stimulation of local shipbuilding. But it must not be forgotten that most New Englanders drew their sustenance directly from the soil—indeed, that a chief item of New England's export trade was the surplus produce of its thrifty farmers. The typical New England town was a farming village. The farmer might turn to the cooper's trade in the winter as a supplement to the summer's farming, and his neighbors might include a craftsman who lived largely by his trade, restricting his farming to what may be described perhaps as an enlarged garden plot. One of the more prosperous men of the town might own a boat or two, large enough to participate in the coastal or river trade by which the provisions and pipestaves shipped out of Boston to Barbados were collected, and by which the supplies brought into Boston from London were distributed.[51] But outside Boston, now a town of possibly 3,000 souls,[52] subsistence farming was so basic to all other activity that even the minister at times had to be found in the field.

---

[50] Still useful is Lois K. Mathews, *The Expansion of New England* (Boston and New York, 1909).

[51] Leonard W. Labaree, *Milford, Connecticut: The Early Development of a Town as Shown in Its Land Records* (New Haven, 1938) is especially helpful. See also Darrett B. Rutman, "Governor Winthrop's Garden Crop: The Significance of Agriculture in the Early Commerce of Massachusetts Bay," *William and Mary Quarterly*, 3d. ser., XX (1963), 396–415.

[52] This is the estimate of Carl Bridenbaugh, *Cities in the Wilderness* (New York, 1938), p. 6. Perhaps an exception should also be made for Newport, which had now a possible 700 people.

As the relative positions of trade and agriculture in the economy of New England should not be reversed, so in the study of the Chesapeake community at this time one must be careful not to be misled by references to a "one-crop economy." It is true enough that the prosperity of the Chesapeake planters depended upon the export of tobacco in annual exchange for European goods and European servants, who for some time to come continued to provide the chief recruitment for the area's labor force.[53] A better understanding of the total economy can be had, however, by thinking of tobacco, to use another familiar term, as "the money crop." It was that quite literally, for tobacco served not only as the export staple but also as a medium of exchange and the common unit of accounting. The Chesapeake planter put a disproportionate part of his effort into the production of tobacco, but the demands of subsistence farming also engaged much of his attention. For food he grew chiefly Indian corn, enough to provide a surplus for export, and several European grains, usually wheat. As any number of wills testify, he counted his wealth very largely by the number of cattle he owned. More often than not, the meat on his table was a dish of pork, for the hog, if he could not be left entirely to "root for himself," at least had the virtues of multiplying rapidly and maturing in a remarkably short time. In this period, pork was hardly the less a staple of New England's diet.

There were marked differences of practice in the two areas. On the Chesapeake an improvident way of letting the stock roam for itself was invited by a climate more favorable than that of New England, where the cattle usually grazed through the day, often under the supervision of a herdsman, on land still held in common by the town, and where provision for shelter during the winter was mandatory. Although the Virginia farmer might hold land in several different places, he was likely to be cultivating at any one time a piece of land that the modern student would recognize as an

---

53 Bruce, *Economic History of Virginia*, remains standard. Arthur P. Middleton, *Tobacco Coast: A Maritime History of Chesapeake Bay in the Colonial Era* (Newport News, Va., 1953), is more helpful for the eighteenth century than for the seventeenth. Abbot E. Smith, *Colonists in Bondage: White Servitude and Convict Labor in America, 1607–1776* (Chapel Hill, N.C., 1947), is admirable on the trade in servants. Although there were several hundred Negroes in the Chesapeake at this time, the colonists did not come to depend chiefly upon Negro labor until much later. See below, p. 290.

American type of farm, generally a small farm, much of it still uncleared. In New England the farmer usually tilled, according to his fortune in a series of land divisions agreed upon by the town, several scattered strips lying outside the village.[54]

Another generation would pass before the large plantation, with its heavy dependence upon Negro labor, began to displace the small farm as the representative unit of the Chesapeake economy.[55] Moreover, many of the more prosperous of the Chesapeake colonists obviously owed much of their prosperity to some form of commercial activity, whether they acted as factors for London merchants, provisioners of ships belonging to the annual tobacco fleet, storekeepers offering European imports for sale in exchange for their neighbors' crops, Indian traders, or speculators in landed properties and the labor force required for their development.[56] Indeed, more than one of the great families of later date owed their fortunes in significant measure to trade. But the Chesapeake settler, at the time of the Restoration, already showed a marked tendency to invest the returns from trade in land, and while so doing to adjust his aspirations to the virtually limitless opportunities he found for the acquisition of undeveloped properties. If as yet the limitations imposed upon other resources at his command, and especially the labor available to him, discouraged the accumulation of what could be only an unwieldy estate, the very wastefulness of his agricultural methods also argued a need to anticipate the future requirements of his family.[57] In commenting thus upon influences encouraging the acquisition of larger holdings, it should be noted that not a few of the more recent immigrants—some of them bearing such names as Lee, Carter, Randolph, Mason, and Page—had reached the Chesa-

---

[54] See again Labaree's *Milford*.

[55] See especially Wertenbaker, *Planters of Colonial Virginia, passim;* also Vertrees J. Wyckoff, "The Sizes of Plantations in Seventeenth-Century Maryland," *Maryland Historical Magazine,* XXXII (1937), 331–339; Susie M. Ames, *Studies of the Virginia Eastern Shore in the Seventeenth Century* (Richmond, 1940), pp. 16 ff.

[56] According to Wertenbaker *(Planters of Colonial Virginia,* pp. 41–50), speculators trading in newly imported servants and the headrights, of fifty acres each, awarded for their importation account for most of the impressively large land grants made in Virginia at midcentury.

[57] See especially Avery O. Craven, *Soil Exhaustion as a Factor in the Agricultural History of Virginia and Maryland, 1606–1860* (Urbana, Ill., 1926).

peake with enough of a stake to permit them to start at a level well above that fixed by the average of their new neighbors.[58]

A comparable adjustment of ambition to a new scale of opportunity was occurring at this time in New England. By 1660 many of the towns there had completed second or even third divisions of land. The new dividends might be of common lands theretofore left undivided, or of some additional acreage purchased by the town for the purpose.[59] A part of the expansion was required to accommodate children who, having reached the age of marriage, wished to establish their own families in the community, but much of it seems to reflect simply a desire by those who had land for more land. Nor was the acquisition of land restricted to acreages intended for the immediate expansion of an established town, for the younger Winthrop was by no means alone in his response to opportunities for speculative ventures in unoccupied and well-situated farmland.[60] To Winthrop in 1664, Roger Williams expressed his fear "that God Land will be as great a God with us English as God Gold was with the Spaniard."[61] "Land! Land! hath been the idol of New-England," cried Increase Mather in 1676, as he looked back from the desolation wrought by the Indians in King Philip's War. The sons of men who had been content with twenty acres had engrossed hundreds, "nay thousands of Acres," Mather continued, "and they that profess themselves Christians, have forsaken Churches, and Ordinances, and all for land and elbow room enough in the world."[62] Even when allowance is made for the customary exaggerations of the pulpit, it is evident that Mather was commenting upon a significant development in the life of his people.

In the quest for "elbow room," whether in New England or on the Chesapeake, a simplified system of landholding greatly facili-

---

[58] And according to Bernard Bailyn (Smith, *Seventeenth-Century America*, pp. 98–100), not always under the necessity of taking undeveloped properties. See also Morton, *Colonial Virginia*, I, 166–168.

[59] Again, see Labaree, *Milford*. Also Philip J. Greven, Jr., "Old Patterns in the New World: The Distribution of Land in 17th Century Andover," *Essex Institute Historical Collections*, CI (1965), 133–148, for evidence of the effect upon the town itself as a compact unit of settlement.

[60] A topic developed in Dunn's *Puritans and Yankees*.

[61] Quoted in Alan Simpson, *Puritanism in Old and New England* (Chicago, 1955), p. 59.

[62] Quoted in Perry Miller, *The New England Mind: From Colony to Province* (Cambridge, Mass., 1953), p. 37.

tated the effort. Although institutional transfers from England included a variety of the technicalities and complexities of ancient forms of tenure, circumstances had favored a marked tendency toward freer titles and easier procedures for the transfer of titles. The original grants from the king normally were made, whether to a company of adventurers or to proprietors, with only a minimum of conditions, no doubt for the encouragement of men engaging to undertake a hazardous enterprise. Usually, the grant was in "free and common socage," which is to say, one of the simpler forms of tenure known to English law. The grantee thus could confer, and usually did, an equally free title upon the prospective settler.[63] Bankrupted at an early date by its heroic efforts on the James, the Virginia Company had turned to a quitrent of 2s. per 100 acres as the most likely source of a continuing revenue, and this had survived the collapse of the company, as the chief condition imposed upon land grants in Virginia.[64] In Maryland, Lord Baltimore had assumed that a feudal pattern of settlement would interpose between the proprietor and the majority of his people a variety of tenurial relationships, but his plan for the development of manorial jurisdictions had fallen down and most of the inhabitants held their land by freehold tenure of the lord proprietor himself. The conditions included the traditional right of the lord to escheats and after 1658 a fine of one year's rent for every alienation of the property, but the chief condition, as in Virginia, was the annual payment of a fixed quitrent.[65] Over most of New England the land was held free even of a quitrent, and subject only to such limitations as were dictated by the larger interests of the community.[66] There were exceptions, chiefly in New Hampshire

[63] See especially Viola F. Barnes, "Land Tenure in English Colonial Charters of the Seventeenth Century," in *Essays in Colonial History Presented to Charles McLean Andrews by His Students* (New Haven, 1931), pp. 4–40. Marshall Harris, *Origin of the Land Tenure System in the United States* (Ames, Iowa, 1953), has brought together under one cover a vast amount of information pertinent to the general subject.

[64] Craven, *Southern Colonies*, pp. 127–128, 176. On the general subject of quitrents, see Beverley W. Bond, *The Quit-rent System in the American Colonies* (New Haven, 1919).

[65] Newton D. Mereness, *Maryland as a Proprietary Province* (New York, 1901), pp. 49 ff.

[66] Thus no full right of alienation existed, for the purchaser of property in a given town might need approval by the town. In addition to Labaree's *Milford*, see Haskins, *Law and Authority in Early Massachusetts*, pp. 68–72.

and Maine, but John Adams could justly boast on the eve of the American Revolution that the original Puritan settlers had "transmitted to their posterity a very general contempt and detestation of holdings by quit-rents."[67]

By 1660, significant steps had also been taken toward the development of the familiar American practice of maintaining a public registry of titles, usually by a conveniently situated local court. In Virginia and Maryland, as yet, the law did not give priority of claim to the recorded deed, as already was the case in New England, but in all colonies men were coming to depend upon the public record for evidence of title.[68] One result was to facilitate transfers of title, which made it easier to put a mortgage on the land and so to make the land provide the credit needed for its own development.

When one turns to the political organization of the English colonies at the time of the Restoration, it is not surprising, in view of the scattered pattern of settlement, to discover a heavy emphasis on local rights of self-government. In Virginia local government depended basically upon borrowings from the English county and more especially the English office of justice of the peace. In each county the governor commissioned a number of leading residents for the performance of magisterial duties in their several neighborhoods, on the understanding that they would meet together periodically to form a court for the entire county. That court was no mere judicial body. It had an extensive jurisdiction over civil cases and the lesser criminal offenses, but it also held very broad authority in the field of local administration, including the power to tax and to enact its own bylaws and ordinances. Its competence had been repeatedly expanded over the preceding two decades by legislation which strongly suggests that representation in the general assembly was valued primarily for the opportunity it gave to enlarge the capacity of the local courts.[69] In Maryland, Lord Baltimore had expected that a feudal scheme of settlement would

67 In "A Dissertation on the Canon and Feudal Law," Charles F. Adams (ed.), *The Works of John Adams* (Boston, 1850–56), III, 447–464.

68 Morris, *History of American Law*, pp. 69–73; Craven, *Southern Colonies*, pp. 278–280; Haskins, *Law and Authority in Early Massachusetts*, pp. 172–174; Joseph N. Beale, Jr., "The Origin of the System of Recording Deeds in America," *The Green Bag*, III (1907), 335–339.

69 Craven, *Southern Colonies*, pp. 269–95; Bruce, *Institutional History of Virginia*, I, 484–646.

leave many of the responsibilities for local administration in the hands of manor lords. Instead, with the failure of manorial jurisdiction to undergo any significant development,[70] the responsibility had fallen to justices of the peace, serving individually as local magistrates and collectively as a court for the entire county, much as in the case of Virginia.[71]

In New England the town, rather than the county, bore the main burden of local government. The town meeting, which might take more than one form,[72] was basically a general assembly of the town's inhabitants for the settlement of questions of common concern. Drawing heavily upon the conventions of the congregational form of church government and the traditions of the English parish as an agency of local administration, the town had developed by 1660 into a remarkably self-sufficient unit. In its meeting, the members of the town chose their selectmen, officers in whom the community might have enough confidence to assure for them full control of local affairs between meetings that often gathered only once a year. Here the town also chose its clerk, its constable, and such other officers as were deemed necessary. As in any self-governing community, the town had a right to spend money and to apportion the costs among its inhabitants.[73] And as with most self-governing communities, there were obligations imposed upon the town by superior authority—for example, those requiring the maintenance of schools in keeping with the standards set by the provincial laws of Massachusetts, Connecticut, and New Haven. In Plymouth and Rhode Island the towns enjoyed more freedom and the children less schooling.[74]

It should not be assumed, however, that the New England town had the entire field of local government to itself. This was true

---

[70] *Archives of Maryland,* LIII, contains records of a manorial court for St. Clement's Manor, possibly the only one functioning at this time.

[71] Craven, *Southern Colonies,* pp. 201–204, 302–309.

[72] Thus, in addition to the general meeting for purely local purposes, there was the meeting of freemen qualified to vote in provincial elections.

[73] John F. Sly, *Town Government in Massachusetts, 1620–1930* (Cambridge, Mass., 1930); Haskins, *Law and Authority in Early Mass.,* pp. 72–77; Kenneth A. Lockridge and Alan Kreider, "The Evolution of Massachusetts Town Government, 1640–1740," *William and Mary Quarterly,* 3d ser., XXIII (1966), 549–574.

[74] S. E. Morison, *The Puritan Pronaos: Studies in the Intellectual Life of New England in the Seventeenth Century* (New York, 1936), pp. 63–67.

enough in Rhode Island, New Haven, Plymouth, and Connecticut at the time of the Restoration, but in Massachusetts the county had been established as early as 1642 and the county court can be traced back to an even earlier date. In each of the counties, of which there were four originally, the resident magistrates (a term reserved in early Massachusetts for the governor's assistants, or chief advisers) were empowered to act together as a local court.[75] That court did not have to assume the full responsibility imposed upon the county court in Virginia, and consequently its functions were more largely judicial. But in its criminal and civil jurisdiction, in its work as a probate court, in its care for the poor, in its superintendence of highways, and in its regulation of tavern keepers and others in a position to gouge the public, there was much to remind us of the county court in the Chesapeake area. Moreover, in the designation by special commission of other residents to assist the magistrates in the fulfillment of their obligations to local administration, whether on the county level or for the purpose of providing an inferior court in each community, Massachusetts had adopted the office of justice of the peace in every essential but the name.[76]

At the provincial level the ultimate authority—administrative, legislative, and judicial[77]—belonged in the Chesapeake colonies to a general assembly, in New England to the general court. The two institutions, though differing in important particulars, were basically very much the same. Each of them brought elected representatives of the local units of government into formal consultation on public issues with the governor and his chief advisers, who were the members of the council in the Chesapeake plantations and in New

[75] Herbert L. Osgood, *The American Colonies in the Seventeenth Century*, (3 vols., New York, 1904–7), I, 190–191; Zechariah Chafee, Jr., *Records of the Suffolk County Court, 1671–1680*, in *Publications of the Colonial Society of Massachusetts*, XXIX (Boston, 1933), xvii–xx; Joseph H. Smith (ed.), *Colonial Justice in Western Massachusetts (1639–1702) : The Pynchon Court Record* (Cambridge, Mass., 1961), pp. 69–79. In Virginia, too, members of the governor's council originally served as local magistrates and heads of the county courts. See Craven, *Southern Colonies*, pp. 169–170, 288.

[76] Connecticut would be divided into counties in 1666, and with the county came a county court patterned after that of Massachusetts. Palfrey, *Hisory of New England*, III, 58.

[77] For a summary discussion of the judicial functions of the older assemblies, see Mary P. Clarke, *Parliamentary Privilege in the American Colonies* (New Haven 1943), pp. 14–60.

England the assistants, or magistrates. Once more the governor and council in Virginia held commissions from the king, and in Maryland from the lord proprietor, whereas in every New England plantation the governor and magistrates were subject to annual election by the general court. But the significance of this difference can be exaggerated. John Winthrop would serve as the governor of Connecticut by annual re-election for almost exactly the same term after the Restoration as did Governor Berkeley on royal commission in Virginia.[78]

Whether choosing selectmen, magistrates, or a governor, the colonists were guided by long-established traditions of the homeland which equated social position with political power. The experience of all the colonies demonstrates that it was far easier to borrow the institutional forms of the English government than it was to transfer to America the supporting social structure.[79] At each level of administration, and especially the local, there could be difficulty in finding men who fully met the traditional tests;[80] but everywhere the governor and his immediate advisers presumably were the great men of the province, men whose right to rule was in large measure predetermined by considerations other than those which can be described as strictly political.[81]

The early representative assembly is best described as a consultative body in which the governor and his immediate advisers, who carried a continuing responsibility for the colony's administration and who also served as its high court, periodically took counsel with the elected delegates of county or town. In other words, the elected element had as its primary function the yielding of its assent to proposals submitted by the acknowledged leaders of the colony. Lord Baltimore's instructions to his son Charles in 1661 helpfully make the point in contemporary phrasing. Assemblies were to be called "for the giving of the advice, assent and approbation by the freemen to such laws and acts as shall be by us att any time ordayned

78 Actually, Winthrop served from his first election in 1657 to his death in 1676, and so had an administration exceeding in length either of the two terms served by Governor Berkeley.

79 A point suggestively developed in Bernard Bailyn's "Politics and Social Structure in Virginia," Smith, Seventeenth-Century America, pp. 90–115.

80 For example, Craven, Southern Colonies, pp. 287–289.

81 The term "social" should not be too narrowly defined, for in the Puritan colonies religious considerations undoubtedly counted heavily.

made and enacted."[82] Let it be said at once that this is too clean-cut a definition for exact description of the way in which the assembly at this date actually functioned, and nowhere more so than in Maryland. The right of the elected delegates to initiate proposals of their own was generally recognized, and only in Maryland had there been a prolonged struggle over the issue.[83] In any of the provinces by this time, the legislative process might involve on occasion not a little negotiation. Nevertheless, there can be no doubt that the normal function of the elected element in the seventeenth-century assembly was to yield its "advice, assent and approbation," not to take the lead.

Originally, all of the assemblies had been unicameral in organization. Thus, the governor, his advisers, and the elected representatives sat together, with obvious advantages for the leadership the governor sought to exercise. The appearance at midcentury of a bicameral organization in Virginia, Maryland, and Massachusetts marks a significant step in the development of the American assembly. But it must not be forgotten, as perhaps too often it is, that the general court in the Plymouth colony was never divided, and that the division into two houses in Rhode Island and Connecticut came only in 1696 and 1698 respectively.[84] Nor should the immediate effect of the bicameral structure in the other colonies be exaggerated. Neither in Sir William Berkeley's Virginia before 1676 nor in Puritan Massachusetts does one find much evidence that the established leadership as yet faced serious embarrassment in accomplishing its purposes. Even in Maryland, Charles Calvert, who would succeed to the proprietorship as the third Lord Baltimore in 1675, enjoyed, for almost a decade after the Restoration, a relatively quiet government.[85]

There can be no doubt that the peculiar circumstances of the Interregnum had contributed significantly to the development of the bicameral form of assembly in the Chesapeake colonies.[86]

[82] Quoted in Andrews, *Colonial Period*, II, 326.

[83] *Ibid.*, II, 300–302.

[84] Osgood, *American Colonies in the Seventeenth Century*, I, 298; Samuel G. Arnold, *History of the State of Rhode Island and Providence Plantations* (2 vols., Providence, 1894) , I, 533; Palfrey, *History of New England*, IV, 228, 236.

[85] Craven, *Southern Colonies*, pp. 300–302.

[86] But not in Massachusetts, where the division had occurred as early as 1644 over an old issue of the negative voice claimed by the governor and assistants. See Andrews, *Colonial Period*, I, 451–452.

Perhaps, too, commonwealth sentiment should be credited with legislation of 1656 which extended the franchise in Virginia to all freemen, but it must be noted that in Maryland this was the condition originally stipulated in the proprietary charter.[87] In Massachusetts and New Haven the exercise of the franchise continued to be limited to church members, a restriction which now may have disfranchised a larger number of men than in the past, simply because fewer of the inhabitants had qualified as communicants of the church. In Connecticut, Plymouth, and Rhode Island the electorate had a somewhat broader base, and nowhere in New England was the practice quite so "undemocratic" as twentieth-century historians at times have assumed.[88] Indeed, there is evidence that not a few of those who could have qualified for exercise of the franchise failed to take the formal action necessary to establish their qualification. In other words, the franchise at this time could be viewed as an obligation to be avoided rather than as a privilege to be sought.

It was already the standard practice for the elected members of the assembly to be residents of the constituencies they represented, perhaps because originally they were viewed as deputies bearing the proxies of other men entitled to attend.[89] Already, too, it was the general practice to compensate these deputies for their service, though more as a return of expenses incurred than as a salary. The total cost might rank among the heavier charges for the conduct of the provincial government, so much so that in Virginia, at least, lengthy or too frequent sessions of the legislative body could be viewed as a potential grievance of the people.[90] Even so, it had be-

[87] Craven, *Southern Colonies*, p. 263; Andrews, *Colonial Period*, II, 341.

[88] See especially Morison, *Builders of the Bay Colony*, pp. 340–341; B. Katherine Brown, "Freemanship in Puritan Massachusetts," *American Historical Review*, LIX (1954), 865–883; David H. Fowler, "Connecticut's Freemen: The First Forty Years," *William and Mary Quarterly*, 3d. ser., XV (1958), 312–333; George D. Langdon, Jr., "The Franchise and Political Democracy in Plymouth Colony," *ibid.*, XX (1963), 513–526.

[89] Andrew C. McLaughlin, *The Foundations of American Constitutionalism* (New York, 1932), pp. 52–55.

[90] See William W. Hening, *The Statutes at Large; Being a Collection of All the Laws of Virginia, from the First Session of the Legislature, in the Year 1619* (13 vols., Richmond and Philadelphia, 1819–23), II, 24, 31–32, where the assembly sought to effect a saving by authorizing the governor and council for a time to impose the provincial levy within a limit of twenty pounds of tobacco per poll.

come normal practice for the legislative body to assemble at least once a year, and in New England twice a year, with the spring election court an especially well-attended session. The concept of government by consent, however much it may have been limited at first by traditional notions as to those who properly were entitled to govern, has a very deep rootage in the American experience.

To talk of the taxing power belonging to the early assembly is to run the risk of seriously misrepresenting the fact, especially if it be implied that a parallel existed with the later political use to which the power was put by the assemblymen in quite a different political context from that obtaining at the time of the Restoration. At that time, and for some years thereafter, the question was much more one of how best to keep the burden to a minimum and to see that it was fairly apportioned. The assessment of the provincial levy, or rate as it was now commonly known in New England, could become almost a routine part of the session's business, however alert all those present may have been to the need for keeping down the cost.[91] Moreover, if Virginia's experience may be considered as representative, by far the heaviest burden of taxation carried by the colonists was normally that imposed by local rather than provincial agencies of government.[92]

The burden of taxation owed much to the fact that taxes usually were paid in the produce of the country, with the result that their collection, storing, and marketing added substantially to the cost. Accordingly, the colonists sought other means for the support of government services, the most common being the fee for a specific service rendered the individual.[93] Salaries were few but the fees were many, and the assemblymen correspondingly alert to the need for their regulation. Other devices included the exemption from

91 For New England, see Osgood, *American Colonies,* I, 468–495; for Virginia, Percy S. Flippin, *The Royal Government in Virginia, 1624–1775* (New York, 1919), pp. 230 ff.; for Maryland, Mereness, *Maryland as a Proprietary Province,* pp. 339 ff.

92 Thus William H. Seiler in a discussion of the Virginia parish (Smith, *Seventeenth-Century America,* p. 137) suggests that of the average of 100 lbs. of tobacco per poll collected annually in the colony, 15–20 lbs. would be for the provincial tax, 35–40 lbs. for the county, and up to 45 lbs. for the parish. In this connection, it should be noted that the county bore the cost of its representation in the assembly.

93 An especially illuminating study is Donnell M. Owings, *His Lordship's Patronage: Offices of Profit in Colonial Maryland* (Baltimore, 1953).

taxation, within specified limits, awarded for public service, as with members of the council in Virginia, and the percentages allowed for the collection of taxes. New England seems to have made more use of salaries, at times supplemented by fees, than did the other colonies. In New England the governments depended chiefly upon a combination of general property, poll, and excise taxes. The Chesapeake colonies relied mainly upon the administratively simple poll tax. Virginia supplemented the revenues from this source in 1658 by a duty of 2s. per hogshead of tobacco exported from the colony, and more than one of the New England provinces relied partly upon import or export duties.

Charges for defense, which included the cost of attempts to maintain at least minimum fortifications at key points along the coast as well as expenditures for security against the Indians, ranked among the heaviest charges upon provincial revenues. But military costs in all of the colonies were kept to a minimum by a basic dependence upon the militia, an ancient institution then passing into disuse in the Old World but finding in English-speaking America a new vitality. Although general observations are made at the risk of ignoring variations from time to time and place to place, the militia at this time is perhaps best described as a system of universal military training. The obligation fell upon every able-bodied free male between the ages of sixteen and sixty. Each man was required to provide his own weapon, and to participate in more or less regular musters and drills. Rarely would the full company with which a man drilled be called into service as a unit. Instead, volunteers or levies drawn from the several units would be given in time of trouble whatever organization and command the circumstances might dictate.[94] Only in the case of the New England Confederation, uniting Massachusetts, Connecticut, New Haven, and Plymouth, did there exist formal arrangements for intercolonial co-operation in time of war.

One final observation needs to be made on a point that too often

[94] For New England, see especially Douglas E. Leach, *Flintlock and Tomahawk: New England in King Philip's War* (New York, 1958); and for Virginia, Bruce, *Institutional History*, II, 3–226, is the most complete discussion. John Shy, "A New Look at Colonial Militia," *William and Mary Quarterly*, 3d. ser., XX (1963), 175–185, challenges the view that the militia system was one and the same everywhere and at all times.

has been overlooked, or simply taken for granted, and that is that every able free male inhabitant of an English settlement in North America was armed. He had never known what it was to live in a colony depending upon a garrison, except where it was understood that every able-bodied male belonged to the garrison, as in the early years of Virginia. Having committed himself to a remarkably dispersed pattern of settlement, he accepted a responsibility for service in defense of the community as an indispensable condition for his own survival and that of his family. But the emphasis should not fall wholly on defense. The defensive weapon he possessed, in addition to certain economic advantages it provided, also gave him power of far-reaching political consequence. The implications for the political life of his own province are well enough suggested by Governor Berkeley's lament, at the time of Bacon's Rebellion, for the fate that had brought him to rule in a country where six men out of seven were "Poore Endebted Discontented and Armed."[95] And on the larger scene, one thinks immediately of Peter Stuyvesant, who in New Amsterdam had a garrison paid by the Dutch West India Company, but who lived through many years in dread fear of the overwhelming force of ambitious militiamen New England might throw against him.

---

[95] Quoted in Wilcomb E. Washburn, *The Governor and the Rebel: A History of Bacon's Rebellion in Virginia* (Chapel Hill, N.C., 1957), p. 31.

CHAPTER 2

Navigation Acts and Royal Charters

I T is especially instructive to observe the sharply contrasting experiences of Sir William Berkeley and John Winthrop, Jr., on their respective missions to London in 1661. Sir William, Anglican and royalist, returned home in the following year emptyhanded and embittered. In that same year the Puritan Winthrop won a royal charter for Connecticut which conferred upon its people, in addition to generous bounds, such full rights of self-government that their descendants at the time of the American Revolution saw no need to substitute another frame of government. Indeed, the independent state of Connecticut would continue to be governed by its colonial charter until 1818.

There is little difficulty in explaining Sir William's disappointment. He had come to London primarily for the purpose of winning a major revision in the Navigation Act of 1660, a law destined actually to serve as the foundation for England's colonial policy through almost two centuries thereafter. He had hoped too that substantial assistance for Virginia's church might be had, but the religious establishment to which he necessarily looked for that assistance was dominated by followers of the late Archbishop Laud whose attention was focused on an effort to consolidate the victory they were winning in England over Presbyterianism and Independency—so much so that they were as indifferent to the needs of fellow Anglicans in America as they were to favors which the government might show to Puritans safely removed from England.[1] Almost a generation was destined to pass before the Church of England awakened to the opportunities presented by the colonies as a field for missionary endeavor. Finally, Sir William's appeal for financial aid to the diversification of Virginia's economy had to be made to a government notoriously hard pressed for funds.

The Navigation Act of 1660 had taken its shape from a variety of pressures, some of them representing private interests, others the needs of the state. Any attempt to catalogue specific provisions according to considerations of public and private interests would be misleading, for the two repeatedly coincided. Similarly, it is advisable to avoid too much dependence upon such broad terms as "England's trade," for Englishmen traded with many different places and by no means did the law assist all branches of their commerce.[2] Nor is there much point in talking at length of mercantilism. The act fits well enough into the patterns of mercantilist thought, with its concern for the promotion of national self-sufficiency, but mercantilist theory had a way of convincing the men who lived at that time very largely because it fitted the hard facts of a practical situation.

The interest most obviously served by the act was that of English shipping, an interest, incidentally, often at variance with the merchant's concern to find the cheapest freight. The act thus took its place in a long line of legislative enactments and administrative decrees designed to build up the English merchant marine.[3] Of these the most recent was Cromwell's Navigation Act of 1651, a statute requiring that all the products of Asia, Africa, and America reaching England, Ireland, or the colonies be carried in English ships, and stipulating that European goods could be imported into England, Ireland, and the colonies only in English ships or in

[1] On the dominant influence in the Restoration establishment, see especially Robert S. Bosher, *The Making of the Restoration Settlement: The Influence of the Laudians, 1649–1662* (London, 1951). On Berkeley's objectives, see Craven, *Southern Colonies,* pp. 291–292, and below, pp. 39–42.

[2] A helpful short summary of England's trade at this time is found in David Ogg, *England in the Reign of Charles II* (2 vols., Oxford, 1955), I, 219–251. See also G. D. Ramsay, *English Overseas Trade during the Centuries of Emergence: Studies in Some Modern Origins of the English-Speaking World* (London, 1957).

[3] See especially Lawrence A. Harper, *The English Navigation Laws* (New York, 1939).

shipping that belonged to the country producing the goods.[4] The statute was directed principally against the Dutch, who then plied the most flourishing entrepôt trade in all Europe and who threatened to dominate Europe's trade with Asia, Africa, and America.

Because no legislation of the Interregnum could be viewed as valid after the Restoration, the government had either to abandon Cromwell's policy or re-enact his statute. The very promptness with which the parliament moved indicates that no real consideration was given to the former course. Although the English had fought from 1652 to 1654 the first of three wars they would fight with Holland in a period of twenty-two years, and although the enforcement of the Act of 1651 had been by no means so ineffective as sometimes has been assumed,[5] the Dutch still held a lead which excited both fear and envy among Englishmen.[6] The Dutch position was by no means entirely one of strength. In America, for example, the Dutch West India Company recently had been expelled from its Brazilian bases, and in New Netherland it had failed dismally in the effort to build up a population numerous enough to resist encroachment by the more populous settlements of its English neighbors. But such evidences of weakness, when combined with the challenge posed by Dutch success on the continent of Europe, in the Baltic, in the Mediterranean, on the coast of Africa, in the Spice Islands, and even in the herring fisheries off Britain's own shores, served only to strengthen the demand of Englishmen for action by their government. Among those holding great influence in the government were several gentlemen who were to show during the next few years an extraordinary interest in the promotion of trade and colonization—among them James, Duke of York, the younger brother of the king, heir apparent to the throne, and lord high admiral, and Edward Hyde, Earl of Clarendon, lord chancellor, and for several years after the Restoration the most powerful of the king's ministers. At the instance of influential London merchants, two special councils, one for trade and one for

[4] George L. Beer, *The Origins of the British Colonial System, 1578–1660* (New York, 1908) , pp. 384–387.

[5] Harper, *English Navigation Laws*, pp. 50–51.

[6] See Charles M. Andrews' discussion of the Anglo-Dutch rivalry in his *Colonial Period*, IV, 22–49; and, of more recent date, Charles Wilson, *Profit and Power: A Study of England and the Dutch Wars* (London, 1957) .

plantations, were established, with representation for the merchants, to advise on policy in these closely related areas.[7] Simultaneously, Sir George Downing, an inveterate foe of the Dutch, guided through Parliament the new navigation act.[8]

That law, as had Cromwell's statute before it, dealt with much broader problems than those merely of trade with the American colonies. Restrictions imposed by the act of 1651 on the trades with Europe, Africa, Asia, and America were re-enacted without fundamental change.[9] Provisions more particularly affecting the American plantations may be quickly summarized. No goods could be imported into or exported from the colonies save in English ships—English built, English owned, and English manned. In other words, English shipping was given an unqualified monopoly of all trade with the colonies, except that the act specifically entitled colonial shipping and seamen to enjoy the full benefit of its exclusive provisions. Second, the statute incorporated a requirement, new to legislation though often enforced during the preceding forty years by administrative decree, that certain colonial products, which were enumerated by name, could be shipped only to England, Ireland, or another of the English plantations. The first enumerated commodities—a list lengthened by subsequent legislation—were sugar, tobacco, cotton, indigo, ginger, fustic, and other dyewoods. All of these were West Indian products or, in the case of tobacco, the produce of the Chesapeake plantations. It should be noted also that, while foreigners were rigidly excluded from trade with the English colonies, no bar was put in the way of colonists who might wish to trade in their own shipping with foreign plantations, provided they did not violate the enumerated commodity clause. And within the limits imposed by the same proviso, colonial ships were free to trade with European countries other than England.[10]

A purpose obviously suggested by the provisions of the act was to stimulate those branches of England's trade which depended upon the long haul rather than the short haul—the trade with India,

---

[7] Charles M. Andrews, *British Committees, Commissions, and Councils of Trade and Plantations, 1622–1675* (Baltimore, 1908), pp. 61–79.

[8] Harper, *English Navigation Laws*, pp. 57–58.

[9] But see *ibid.*, pp. 54–55, with reference to Section IV of the act.

[10] In addition to Harper, see Beer, *Old Colonial System*, I, 58–77; Andrews, *Colonial Period*, IV, 59–107; and E. Lipson, *The Economic History of England* (3 vols., London, 1920–31), III, 116–153.

with Africa, and with America rather than the exchange with nearby Europe which traditionally had been the main dependence for the marketing of England's woolen staples—and to gain for England the diverse advantages of serving as an entrepôt in the trade between Europe and the more remote parts of the world.[11] In other words, the new restrictions imposed upon the commerce of the colonies were intended to accomplish more than merely to exclude the Dutch from trades that could be viewed as properly belonging to English merchants, or to make England self-sufficient in her supply of New World commodities. The sugar of Barbados or the tobacco of the Chesapeake, to mention but two of the enumerated commodities, might give to English merchants the means to command other profitable markets in an increasingly complex pattern of world trade. That the act ultimately achieved this end is indicated by a study showing that, whereas in 1640 woolens still represented up to 90 per cent of London's exports, 30 per cent of the kingdom's exports at the end of the century were re-exports, chiefly of American and Eastern commodities.[12] In short, the Navigation Acts help to mark, as they undoubtedly helped to stimulate, one of the more significant developments in the long history of England's economy.

It must be remembered, however, that this development was stretched out over the course of approximately half a century.[13] The farsightedness of those who enacted the legislation can be exaggerated. Although the example of Holland's great entrepôt trade undoubtedly helped to fix English objectives, there were other considerations which probably carried more immediate weight, some of them rather negative in character, some of them reflecting the urgent needs of the state. One can explain the enumeration of tobacco, which had the effect of glutting the English market with a surplus in excess of its current needs, whether for sale at home or

---

11 Ogg, *England in the Reign of Charles II*, 1, 241–242.

12 Ralph Davis, "English Foreign Trade, 1660–1700," *Economic History Review*, 2d. ser., VII (1954), 150–166. The comparison, of course, is not perfect, for the first figure is for London, at a time when the national percentage is apparently not available, and the second for the entire kingdom.

13 An especially helpful study is Jacob M. Price, *The Tobacco Adventure to Russia: Enterprise, Politics, and Diplomacy in the Quest for a Northern Market for English Colonial Tobacco, 1676–1722*, Transactions of the American Philosophical Society, new ser., LI, Pt. 1 (1961).

abroad, as basically a punitive measure intended to deny Holland the well-known advantages she enjoyed by trading with Virginia tobacco in many different places. That the duties paid by tobacco on its entry into England were a prime consideration is shown by a report to the king in 1661 that American tobacco produced "more custom to his majesty than the East Indies four times over." Other considerations of state are suggested by the further observation that the American plantations "are his majesty's Indies, without charge to him raised and supported by the English subjects, who employ above two hundred sail of good ships every year, breed abundance of mariners, and begin to grow into commodities of great value and esteem."[14] One lingers a moment over this last phrase, for it carries an unmistakable reference to the low esteem in which tobacco long had been held and to the hope for a more diversified economy in the colonies that was stimulated in part by a recent shift from tobacco to sugar in the West Indian plantations. It is even possible, for that moment at least, to wonder if the enumeration of tobacco may have been partly intended to place the Chesapeake farmer at such a disadvantage as to force him, at no cost to the king, to co-operate with Sir William Berkeley in the development of commodities having, for all, more esteem and profit.

We can be certain only that the interests and motives which gave shape to this legislation were as mixed as they were varied. The needs of the royal treasury are no more evident than are considerations affecting the strength of the Royal Navy, at a time when the latter's strength depended much more heavily than it does in modern days upon the health of the merchant marine. Concern for the prosperity of the English shipbuilders, as important for the navy as it was for the merchant marine, was balanced by the encouragement given to shipbuilding in the colonies, where the supply of suitable timber was much more plentiful than it was in England. It is a serious error to assume that the act can be judged by standards appropriate to a purely economic measure. As its preamble affirmed, the purpose was to promote "the wealth, safety, and strength of this kingdom." With good reason, a distinguished English authority has declared that "the argument in favour of the Navigation Act was primarily political."[15]

14 Quoted in Lipson, *Economic History of England,* III, 156.
15 *Ibid.,* III, 136.

In 1663, the year following Berkeley's return to his post at Jamestown, Parliament rounded out the basic legislation governing colonial trade for many years thereafter by prohibiting the importation of European goods into the colonies unless the goods first had been landed in England, and had been shipped thence in lawful English shipping. Thus did the Navigation Act of 1663 undertake to make England, with the allowance of only a few exceptions, the staple in any trade that might develop between European countries and the English colonies. The exceptions made were for the salt that the Newfoundland and New England fisheries required; for the servants, horses, and provisions from Scotland and Ireland needed especially by the West Indian sugar planters; and for the wine from Madeira and the Azores, possessions of Portugal, where the king recently had found a wife. Although the legislation was intended primarily to protect the colonial market for English goods against foreign competition, the statute also placed still another barrier in the path of foreign ships seeking a trade with the English colonists.[16] As had the act of 1660, the law required that all colonial governors be sworn to its enforcement on penalty of removal from office.

Twentieth-century American historians have shown a remarkably sympathetic attitude toward the policies established by the Navigation Acts. Because of the influence especially of George Louis Beer, the leading student of England's early colonial policy, the emphasis has been placed on the reciprocal advantages belonging to mother country and colony. For such a view, of course, there is much supporting evidence. If England after 1660 held a monopoly of colonial tobacco, the colonists in turn were given, through preferential tariffs and other devices, a virtual monopoly of the English market for tobacco. It is true, moreover, that the colonies enjoyed additional compensations for the restrictions imposed upon their trade, among them the encouragement provided by the law for the development of their own merchant marines. But this emphasis upon the reciprocal advantages in the policy has all too often encouraged a tendency to discount the significance of immediate, vigorous, and continuing protests by the colonists.[17]

[16] Beer, *Old Colonial System*, I, 77–79; Andrews, *Colonial Period*, IV, 108–115.
[17] See especially Beer, *Old Colonial System*, II, 104–119. It is interesting that English scholars have taken these protests more seriously, as in Lipson, *Economic*

These protests, as would be expected, came chiefly from the colonies producing enumerated commodities. New England for some time yet would suffer no adverse effects from the legislation, but in Virginia and Barbados the story is different. At a time of expanding production, and after years of relatively free trade with the Dutch,[18] the West Indian and Chesapeake colonists faced the prospect of being rigidly limited to an English market incapable of absorbing their full crops at favorable prices. It is true enough that the surplus over England's own needs could be exported, and that policy provided in such cases for a rebate of much of the customs previously paid at the entry of the product·into England, but this rebate failed to cover the additional costs incurred for warehousing, insurance, freight, and commission.[19] Nor did it compensate for the depressed prices paid for colonial tobacco through many years.

In a memorial presenting Virginia's case in 1662, printed as *A Discourse and View of Virginia*,[20] Sir William bitterly complained that the king's customs doubled "the first purchase" of Virginia tobacco, that "the merchant buyes it for one penny the pound, and we pay two pence for the custom of that which they are not pleased to take from us." He protested "that forty thousand people should be impoverished to enrich little more than forty merchants, who being the only buyers of our Tobacco, give us what they please for it, and after it is here, sell it how they please; and indeed have forty

---

History of England, III, 172; Ogg, *England in the Reign of Charles II*, I, 243–244; and Vincent T. Harlow, *A History of Barbados, 1625–1685* (Oxford, 1926) , pp. 168–173. But see Harper, *English Navigation Laws*, p. 245; also his comment on the act of 1663, p. 59.

18 That Dutch merchants traded as freely with Virginia after 1651 as before seems unlikely, but the evidence argues also that after the war of 1652–54 they regained a substantial share in the Chesapeake trade. See Bruce, *Economic History of Virginia*, I, 350–359.

19 Lipson, *Economic History of England*, III, 173–176.

20 Although the pamphlet is both unsigned and undated, there can be no doubt as to Berkeley's authorship and little if any doubt as to when it was written. It may have been printed in 1663, the year to which it is usually assigned by standard bibliographical references, but the internal evidence argues strongly that it was written in 1662, and probably well ahead of the instructions of September 12 given to Berkeley on the eve of his departure for Virginia. Sister Joan de Lourdes Leonard, "Operation Checkmate: The Birth and Death of a Virginia Blueprint for Progress, 1660–1676," *William and Mary Quarterly*, 3d. ser., XXIV (1967) , 44–74, carries helpful detail on both the pamphlet and the governor's mission.

thousand servants in us at cheaper rates, then any other men have slaves." But it is evident, from the beginning to the end of his memorial, that Berkeley had been forced into a defensive attitude because of Virginia's unhealthy dependence upon tobacco. His protests over the low price of tobacco obviously had been met by suggestions that the colony should diversify its economy, and so make itself both useful and prosperous in the supply of England's need for a wide variety of commodities. Accordingly, Sir William devoted most of his space to a lengthy apology for the colony's past failures, and to an effort to demonstrate that Virginia was ready and able to accomplish within a short span of time all that was desired of it. The principal difficulty, he explained, was a want of skilled workmen and "a publick stock" to meet the cost of providing them and to offset other charges incidental to the experimental stage of new projects.

For remedy the governor proposed that the king add a penny to the customs on tobacco, the resulting revenue to be placed at the disposal of the colony. If this proposal was not acceptable, it was suggested that His Majesty might increase by one or two shillings the colony's 2s. per hogshead export duty. Berkeley also asked, for the encouragement of shipbuilding in Virginia, that all ships built there be allowed a free right of trade with any port of choice. But these pleas were of no avail. By late summer, when preparations for Berkeley's return to Virginia were in hand, his hopes had come to be pinned on a petition for a grant of £500 from the royal treasury; this too was denied in a decision, one of the more important of the Restoration era, that Virginia must bear its own full charges.[21] Final instructions for Berkeley, dated September 12, authorized the colony to increase the 2s. duty if it so desired, but offered no other assistance except the assurance that Lord Baltimore would co-operate in efforts to get an agreement with Maryland on a plan to limit the Chesapeake tobacco crop.[22] In short, Sir William returned home toward the end of 1662 with nothing more than suggestions

---

[21] *Calendar of State Papers, Colonial, 1661–1668,* Nos. 332, 333, 334, 341, 345.
[22] *Virginia Magazine of History and Biography,* III (1895–96) , 15–20. Even the governor's salary of £1,000 was left a charge against the revenues from the 2s. duty instead of being charged to royal customs collected in England, as had been the practice before the Civil War. See Flippin, *Royal Government in Virginia,* pp. 74–76.

and admonitions as to the ways in which Virginia might help itself out of its own difficulties. He brought not even a penny for the benefit of the colony's church.

For this final disappointment the governor could blame, in part at least, an Anglican clergyman recently returned to England from a ten-year exile in Virginia who wrote an especially interesting pamphlet that was printed in London during the fall of 1662 under the title of *Virginia's Cure*. Because the pamphlet carried only the author's initials, R.G., the name of the man is uncertain. The initials may stand for a Robert Gray, if the attribution by standard bibliographical references can be trusted, but there is good reason for believing that the pamphlet actually was written by one Roger Green.[23] Whatever may have been the author's identity, *Virginia's Cure* cannot be overlooked by those who would understand fully the course of Restoration policies toward the colonies. The document records the author's appearance as an agent of the Virginia Assembly before Bishop Gilbert Sheldon of London. Whether R.G. acted on a commission directly received from the Virginia Assembly, as he implies, or in lieu of the Reverend Philip Mallory, who had accompanied Berkeley to London and had died soon after reaching the metropolis, matters little. The point is that the author of *Virginia's Cure*, in submitting the colony's petitions for financial assistance, advised the bishop that favorable action could do no more than provide a mere palliative for the serious ills besetting the colonial church. To this suggestion the bishop seems to have

---

23 R.G., *Virginia's Cure: Or An Advisive Narrative Concerning Virginia* (London, 1662). The copy belonging to the McCormick collection of the Princeton University Library is attributed to Robert Gray in a penciled notation on a blank leaf, and this attribution finds support in such standard references as the catalogues of the Church Collection, the John Carter Brown Library, and Donald Wing's *Short-Title Catalogue . . . of English Books . . . 1641–1700* (New York, 1948). But Brydon, *Virginia's Mother Church*, I, 138, 176, 180, 483–484, attributes the pamphlet to Roger Green, as also does William H. Seiler in his helpful studies of the parish in Virginia. The strongest argument for following these close students of the Virginia church is that there was a Roger Green who was active as a clergyman during the Interregnum in Virginia, and who possibly returned to London in 1661 with Governor Berkeley and the Reverend Philip Mallory. See Edward L. Goodwin, *The Colonial Church in Virginia* (Milwaukee, 1927), pp. 274–275, 291. It is difficult to find any certain evidence of the existence of an Anglican clergyman by the name of Robert Gray in Virginia at this time. I am indebted to Professor Seiler for a very helpful response to an inquiry addressed to him on this question.

been quite receptive, for he encourged the agent, according to the latter's account, to submit his own proposals.

According to the author of *Virginia's Cure,* the fundamental cause for the unhappy state of the English church in the colony was to be found in the failure of Virginians "so to unite their Habitations in Societies in Towns and Villages, as may best convenience them constantly to attend upon the publique ministery of God's Word, Sacraments and Worship." The author proposed that the bishop sponsor collections in the churches throughout the three kingdoms for the purpose of sending over workmen to build towns in Virginia. Unhappily, this proposal apparently had no other result than a provision in Berkeley's instructions requiring the colonists, at their own cost, to build a town on each of their great rivers.[24] For Sir William the last straw must have been the citation to the admirable example of the people of New England, "who have in few years raised that colony to breed wealth, reputation, and security."

Because Sir William was one of the eight "true and absolute lords proprietors" to whom Charles II, on March 24, 1663, granted the vast territory of Carolina, it has been assumed that Berkeley scored at least one triumph on his mission to London. Indeed, he often has been credited with a large share in the initiation of the project.[25] But on this point there is room for doubt—enough, in fact, to make it possible that the Carolina charter represents one more of Sir William's disappointments.

It may well be true, though it is by no means certain, that Berkeley during his stay in London had consulted with some of the later proprietors regarding plans for a new settlement in the Carolina region.[26] It is quite conceivable that he showed an

[24] Legislation for this purpose was enacted after Berkeley's return to the colony by an assembly which also struggled unsuccessfully with the problem of crop control by agreement with Maryland. See Craven, *Southern Colonies,* pp. 312–314.

[25] Louise F. Brown, *The First Earl of Shaftesbury* (New York, 1933), pp. 151–152; Andrews, *Colonial Period,* III, 183–187 Craven, *Southern Colonies,* pp. 321–322.

[26] The letter announcing the winning of the charter to Berkeley is none too helpful. It begins: "Since you left us we have endeavored to procure and at length have obtained his Majestie's charter for the province of Carolina." *Colonial Records of North Carolina,* I, 52.

interest in proposals by Barbadian adventurers for settlement in the more southerly parts of Carolina, and that the proprietors' long-sustained hope for the production there of a wide variety of staples owed much originally to advice given by him while in London.[27] But all such assumptions are merely assumptions, depending for their force upon evidence that at best is circumstantial. On the other hand, the record establishes several pertinent and incontrovertible facts which argue for another interpretation. At all times after 1660 Sir William showed a loyalty to Virginia that could have been second only to his loyalty to the king, if second it was. Virginia's territorial claims, under the 1609 charter of the Virginia Company, extended southward from Point Comfort for 200 miles and so comfortably included Albemarle Sound, where Virginians had been settling on grants from Virginia's government as early as 1660, and probably well before that.[28] While in England Berkeley had sharply condemned the conflicting grant of Carolina in 1629 to Sir Robert Heath (which served as the basis for the new proprietary charter) on the ground that Heath's patent, like that of Lord Baltimore to Maryland, weakened Virginia politically, militarily, and economically.[29] He continued to issue Virginia titles for substantial acreages in the Albemarle area as late as September 1663, when apparently he first heard of the new charter.[30] He seems to have been reluctant at that time to act on the request of his fellow proprietors that he appoint a governor for the settlers living on Albemarle Sound. William Drummond, a Scotsman whom Berkeley later would find a special satisfaction in executing for his complicity in Bacon's Rebellion, did not take office as the first governor of the Albemarle settlement until October 1664.[31] Finally, when Berkeley died in 1677, and the question of the claims his estate might have under the Carolina charter had to be met, his

[27] That Berkeley knew in 1662 of the Barbadians' interest in the mainland is suggested in *Discourse and View of Virginia*, p. 12.

[28] Cumming, *The Southeast in Early Maps*, pp. 21–24; Craven, *Southern Colonies*, pp. 317–318.

[29] *Discourse and View of Virginia*, p. 6.

[30] *Colonial Records of North Carolina*, I, 59–67.

[31] *Ibid.*, I, xii–xiii; Hugh T. Lefler and Albert R. Newsome, *The History of a Southern State: North Carolina* (Chapel Hill, N.C., 1954), p. 33.

fellow proprietors made it a matter of record that he had not contributed a single penny to the enterprise.[32]

No less revealing than the failure of Sir William Berkeley's mission to London is the marked success simultaneously attending the efforts of John Winthrop of Connecticut. Perhaps Winthrop enjoyed some advantage from the relative insignificance of the community he represented. At a time when the government's attention was focused sharply upon the need to establish effective con-:rols over the trade of the West Indian and Chesapeake plantations, no one in power was likely to be greatly disturbed by concessions to Connecticut. Perhaps the emphasis belongs rather to Winthrop's unmistakable talents as a negotiator, for it is evident that he won the confidence of Lord Chancellor Clarendon, who above all of the king's ministers was in a position to aid Winthrop's cause. Still more pertinent, however, may be the generally favorable attitude initially displayed by the Restoration government toward New England.

The government had shown a brief concern over reports that some of the regicides had found a refuge there, as indeed two of them had.[33] It listened to complaints from men who had quarreled in one way or another with the leaders of the Puritan community, and especially of Massachusetts.[34] It even entertained protests in behalf of the persecuted Quakers, four of whom were executed by Massachusetts between 1659 and 1661.[35] It most certainly was determined that each of the Puritan colonies must make a due acknowledgment of the king's right to rule, as was only to be expected of a government which, for all its claims to legitimacy, knew that it actually held office through still another turn of the wheel of fortune in an age of revolution. The demand for an appropriate submission, destined to pose the key issue between the king and Massachusetts through many years to come, was all the

[32] Saunders, *Colonial Records of North Carolina*, I, 337–338. It is interesting to note that there was a proposed, but evidently ineffective, agreement of 1672 for assignment of the Albemarle region to Berkeley in return for his surrender of all other claims under the charter. See M. Eugene Sirmans, *Colonial South Carolina: A Political History, 1663–1763* (Chapel Hill, N.C., 1966), p. 25.

[33] Goffe and Whalley. See Dunn, *Puritans and Yankees*, pp. 119–120.

[34] *Calendar of State Papers, Colonial, 1661–1668*, Nos. 45, 50, 51, 53, 80.

[35] *Ibid.*, Nos. 89, 90; Osgood, *American Colonies in the Seventeenth Century*, I, 285–286.

more necessary, of course, because New England was Puritan. But there is no reason for believing that the Restoration government had any intention of punishing the Puritan colonies for their Puritanism, or even of disturbing them in the exercise of their peculiar rituals.

On the contrary, the new government at Whitehall showed both an extraordinary tolerance for New England's religious practices and a marked regard for the more material achievements of its people. Several years would pass before the king and his ministers had cause for quarrel with New England on economic grounds. Her expanding commercial activity was now essentially complementary to the interests the Navigation Acts were intended to promote, not in conflict with them, as so often has been assumed.[36] Especially was this true of the trade with the West Indian plantations, where the foodstuffs supplied by New England shipping permitted larger transfers of land to the production of sugar.

Even in the case of Massachusetts, the delaying and evasive tactics of negotiation which the colony quickly adopted, and for which it was destined to win no small fame over the years, were met at first by a remarkably lenient response. After special agents from the colony had reached London in March, 1662, with a letter of submission that contained no real concession beyond the most general acknowledgment of allegiance to the king, and with instruction to parry all demands for something more specific by the argument that they had no instruction and therefore no power, the king's advisers drafted a reply which came very close to ignoring all the plain facts in the exchange. Dated in June, 1662, the royal letter sent back to Boston expressed the king's great pleasure on receiving Boston's expression of loyalty, announced the confirmation of the charter his father had issued to the Massachusetts Bay Company, and in the same breath offered to renew it in order that the people of Massachusetts Bay might "freely enjoy all their privileges and liberties." In return, the king asked that legislation derogatory to his government be repealed, that the oaths of allegiance be observed, that justice be administered in his name, that any of his subjects who might desire to worship according to the Book of Common Prayer be allowed to do so without prejudice to any other

[36] Bailyn, *New England Merchants*, pp. 126–134.

of their rights, and that, for the protection of these rights, the franchise be based on property rather than upon membership in the Puritan church.[37] From Boston's point of view, this was asking for more than could be rightly or safely given. But from Whitehall's point of view, the conditions proposed in no way outmeasured the concessions offered.

Where a proper submission to the king had been made, his government could be still more generous, as the Connecticut charter had already amply demonstrated. Having passed the final seal on May 10, 1662, this charter created in Connecticut a completely self-governing corporation after the model provided by the earlier Massachusetts Bay charter.[38] Indeed, the charter called for no substantial change in the government of the colony as it had been conducted since the adoption of Connecticut's famous Fundamental Orders of 1639. The governor, the deputy governor, and the assistants would continue to be elected by the general court. Nothing more was required than that all writs run in the name of the king, that all officers of the province take the oath of supremacy, and that no laws be enacted that were contrary to the laws of England. The document is as interesting for what it did not say as for what it did say. It made no provision, and established no agency, for the enforcement of the restrictions mentioned above. It said nothing about the franchise. It included no reference to Connecticut's ecclesiastical system, not even a provision that Anglicans be allowed freedom of worship. Obviously, when one considers the extraordinarily full rights of self-government that were conceded, the orthodox Puritans of Connecticut were left full freedom to pursue their own restrictive religious policies.

Comparably generous were the provisions bounding the colony. On the east Connecticut would extend to Narragansett Bay (not across the bay to Plymouth as in Winthrop's instructions), on the north to the Massachusetts line, on the south to "the Sea," a phrasing interpreted by Connecticut to include Long Island, and

---

[37] *Calendar of State Papers, Colonial, 1661–1668*, No. 314.

[38] Francis N. Thorpe, *Federal and State Constitutions, Colonial Charters, and Other Organic Laws* . . . (7 vols. Washington, 1909), I, 529–536. On the procurement of the charter, see Black, *Younger John Winthrop*, pp. 206–226; Dunn, *Puritans and Yankees*, pp. 127–136; Andrews, *Colonial Period*, II, 132–142; Albert C. Bates, *The Charter of Connecticut* (Hartford, 1932), pp. 5–28.

on the west all the way to the South Seas—or, as we would say, to the Pacific. The Hartford government thus acquired title to the whole of the New Haven jurisdiction, and to the Narragansett lands in which Winthrop was a speculative adventurer and which Rhode Island also claimed under its parliamentary patent of 1644. More than that, Hartford had secured a pretentious title to a substantial part of Dutch New Netherland. Or would some other word than pretentious be more fitting? Connecticut itself was the result of a steady encroachment by the New England Puritans upon the prior claims of the Dutch West India Company in New Netherland, and it is by no means inconceivable that Conneticut, with the aid of its colleagues in the New England Confederation, might in time have overthrown the Dutch at New Amsterdam. The sea-to-sea provision of the Connecticut charter has an easy explanation in the colony's argument that such were the bounds established by the so-called Warwick patent of 1632, a copy of which Winthrop vainly sought to find in London in keeping with his instructions to secure from the king a confirmation of all it presumably had conveyed.[39] Even so, one is entitled to comment briefly on the possible significance of the Connecticut charter as a further item documenting the extent to which the policy of the Restoration government was shaped by hostility toward the Dutch.

But perhaps it is best not to talk at all about policy in the context of actions by the Restoration government which affected the American colonies. The term, of course, is almost unavoidable, and its use is easily justified. It is easy, as one reviews the sum total of actions taken by king and Parliament during the five years immediately following the Restoration, to state, and to state helpfully, the main features of what may be described as an emerging colonial policy. The government of England, which theretofore had given only fitful attention to the colonies, obviously now had come to place a higher value upon them. They were valued chiefly for their trade, for the contribution they could make, directly or indirectly, to the strength of England's position with reference to an increasingly complex scheme of world trade and, more particularly, to the trade of the Atlantic basin. They were prized all the more because they

---

[39] As previously noted on p. 5 above, this document may never have existed and, if it did, its legality is very questionable.

had been acquired at no cost to the government, and because it could be expected that in the future the advantages they offered might be enjoyed at a comparably cheap rate. Not only Sir William Berkeley's Virginia but the other colonies as well were expected to bear their own full charges. In return, they might expect to enjoy generous concessions of self-government within their own bounds, so long as they made an appropriate acknowledgment of their submission to the king. Whether viewed as parts of the king's dominions or as possessions of the nation (and on this point the phrasing employed is more than a little mixed), it was considered that the colonies lay outside the realm of England. One consequence was that the king's government found itself free to pursue policies in the colonies that were in direct conflict with its policies at home. Thus, and thanks very largely to the indifference of the Church of England to questions not directly affecting its authority within the realm, the Restoration era, known in England for religious persecution, was to be remembered in America for the great progress Englishmen made toward realizing the ideal of religious freedom. In short, one can point to a number of policies that were followed by the Restoration government of Charles II, some of them destined to have an enduring influence upon the history of what became in time an empire, but strictly speaking the government at this time had no colonial policy.

It was a government that was very poorly organized and equipped for the purpose of defining such a policy. There was no colonial office to provide assurance of informed and co-ordinated action by different branches of the government, hardly even the faintest beginnings of such an office. The councils of trade and plantations which functioned, on and off, during the course of fifteen years after the Restoration had no archives worth mentioning, no staff of bureaucratic experts to guide them. The membership was at times cumbersomely large, and might vary according to the fortunes experienced by politicians in contests over other and more important questions.[40] Representatives of the trading and shipping interests were usually respectfully heard, as were the representations of the royal treasury or Navy, and so there was a certain

---

[40] Andrews, *British Committees*, records their history to 1675; for a short summary, see Andrews, *Colonial Period*, IV, 56–58.

consistency in the advice offered to the government, but the opinions expressed by the councils were purely advisory. The power to act belonged to the king, to the privy council, to Parliament, or to such men as happened to enjoy a significant advantage of position in the royal court. This last was the place where agents from the colonies normally had to make their suits for favor, and during the first years of the Restoration the man to see at court was the Earl of Clarendon. It makes a great deal more sense for this period to talk of Clarendon's colonial policy than to talk of the policy of either England or Charles II.[41] The historian who finds in the actions taken by the early Restoration government a delineation of the course imperial policy was destined to take finds also a gap of several years after Clarendon's fall from power in 1667 before policy seems to be well enough back on course.

Clarendon had an interest in the colonies. He invested in properties in Cromwell's Jamaica, and he became one of the proprietors of Carolina.[42] His loyalty to the king and to the king's cause was attested by long years of exile and sacrifice for that cause, and yet he was something of a Puritan, which may have been a help to John Winthrop of Connecticut. Certainly, Clarendon gave his trust to Winthrop, for it is obvious that the governor determined the main provisions of the Connecticut charter. Equally obvious, however, is the fact that Winthrop overplayed his hand, with the result that Clarendon's view of Puritan New England became progressively less favorable than it had been.

Hardly had the Connecticut charter passed the final seal before Dr. John Clarke, Rhode Island's agent, protested that the document "injuriously swallowed up the one half of our Colonie."[43] He asked for a review by the king of the whole question. Clarendon granted the request for a hearing, though apparently without losing full confidence in Winthrop, who in July was allowed to forward the new charter to Hartford, an action greatly to Connecticut's advantage. Discussions continued without agreement into the winter of

[41] A still useful summary is found in Percy L. Kaye, *English Colonial Administration under Lord Clarendon, 1660–1667* (Baltimore, 1905).

[42] Andrews, *Colonial Period*, III, 186.

[43] Andrews, *Colonial Period*, II, 44. Clarke had entered an earlier petition for a charter that would have included in Rhode Island the Narragansett tract lying west of the bay that now had been given to Connecticut. On Clarke and his mission, see *ibid.*, II, 39–49.

1662–63, when protests reaching London from New Haven brought fresh complications.[44]

Had not the quarrel with Rhode Island's agent delayed Winthrop's return to New England, there might have been little or no serious difficulty between Connecticut and New Haven. Disappointed in the high hopes for commercial success with which it originally had been founded, New Haven headed a jurisdiction that was now both poor and divided. It had no agency of its own in London, had entered no petition for a separate charter, and had no prospect of assistance in the protection of its interests there except such as might be given by John Winthrop of Connecticut. Winthrop seems to have anticipated that with patience and diplomacy the New Haven towns could be persuaded to accept union with the Hartford government, under the extraordinarily liberal terms of its new charter, as the best protection of their interest to be had in the circumstances. Whether this might have happened no one can say, but Winthrop had many friends in New Haven, as elsewhere in New England, and there can be no question as to his very great gifts as a diplomat. Unhappily, the Hartford government, upon receiving its new charter, most undiplomatically issued a peremptory demand that the New Haven towns surrender to its authority. By the end of 1662 all save three of the towns had complied, either because of some discontent with New Haven's leadership or because they saw no other course open to them, but New Haven, Milford, and Branford stoutly refused to yield. Indeed, they persisted until the issue had divided the entire Puritan community. When New Haven appealed to the commissioners of the New England Confederation in September, 1663, she won the backing of both Massachusetts and Plymouth. Encouraged thus, New Haven continued her bitter resistance for another year and more, through which time Connecticut remained also stubbornly uncompromising.[45] In the end, Connecticut was to win, but at the cost of having helped persuade Lord Clarendon that he needed to look somewhat more closely, and critically, into the affairs of New England.

More immediately, the quarrel with New Haven had added to

[44] Especially helpful are Dunn, *Puritans and Yankees*, pp. 122–124, 136–141, and Black, *Younger John Winthrop*, pp. 226–239.

[45] Andrews, Colonial Period, II, 187–191; Calder, *The New Haven Colony*, pp. 231–252.

Winthrop's difficulties in the continuing negotiations with Dr. Clarke and Lord Clarendon for settlement of the dispute with Rhode Island. The task was made no easier by the meddling of John Scott, an adventurer of vaulting ambition who had been in London when the Connecticut charter passed the final seal. He then had hurried back to New England, where he offered his assistance, on a return trip to London, both to New Haven and to the Narragansett proprietors, who were fearful that their colleague Winthrop might concede Rhode Island's territorial claims. Indeed, they were so fearful, and so taken in by Colonel Scott that they took him into their own company. John Scott was hardly the man to prevail in an argument with John Winthrop before Lord Clarendon, but his presence in London after February, 1663, and the news he brought were hardly the less embarrassing.[46] After the dispute had been submitted to arbitration, an agreement with Clarke was reached in April, when finally Winthrop sailed for New England.

Everything considered, it had been an extraordinarily successful mission. After reaching the agreement with Clarke, Winthrop had loyally supported the former's petition, and so he has been credited with a significant role in the winning of the Rhode Island charter, a remarkable document that was destined to have an even longer life than did the Connecticut charter. And yet, it is doubtful that Winthrop's thoughts, as he listened at night to the groaning timbers of his ship, were entirely self-congratulatory. He had been warned by Clarendon of a purpose to investigate more fully the problems of New England.[47] He knew much of the bitter divisions his own achievement had caused there. Nor was there any reason for him to assume that the end was in sight, if only because of the agreement he had made with Clarke.

The Rhode Island charter, which cleared the final seal on July 8, 1663, fixed the western boundary of the province at the Pawcatuck River.[48] In other words, the disputed Narrangansett territory was awarded to Rhode Island. In an attempt to avoid the complications

---

46 On Scott's career, see especially Wilbur C. Abbott, *"Colonel" John Scott of Long Island, 1634?–1696* (New Haven, 1918). Lilian T. Mowrer attempts to rescue his reputation in *The Indomitable John Scott* (New York, 1960). For the discussion above, see especially Dunn, *Puritans and Yankees*, pp. 138–141.

47 Dunn, *Puritans and Yankees*, p. 142.

48 Thorpe, *Federal and State Constitutions*, VI, 3211–3222.

to be expected from the resulting conflict with the Connecticut charter, it was stipulated in the Rhode Island charter that wherever in the Connecticut charter reference was made to the "Narragansett River" (the terms river and bay had there been used interchangeably), it was to be understood that the Narragansett was the Pawcatuck, which was to say that the Pawcatuck River was Narragansett Bay, a somewhat more impressive body of water. There was also a clause confirming the grant to Rhode Island, "anything to the contrary notwithstanding" in the Connecticut charter. It was a brave effort, but it failed, partly because Winthrop had an understanding with Clarke, not written into the charter, that his fellow proprietors were to have a free choice of the jurisdiction to which they would belong, and they promptly chose Connecticut.[49] The quarrel over the boundary between the two provinces reached a final settlement, in favor of Rhode Island and according to the terms of its own charter, only in 1727.

The charter of the Rhode Island and Providence Plantations, to use the proper name of the province, is best remembered, of course, for its provisions regarding religion. No other document speaks quite so emphatically of the willingness of the Restoration government to endorse religious policies in the colonies that were in sharp contrast with its own policy for England. Having noted the existence of distinctive religious principles among the colonists, the charter expressed His Majesty's belief that a concession in this regard, "by reason of the remote distances of those places," need bring no breach of the religious uniformity "established in this nation." The phrasing, let it be noted, is that of a broad and general statement of policy. As for the specific concessions made to Rhode Island, not even Roger Williams could have asked for more. The charter declared that "noe person within the said colonie, at any time hereafter shall be in any wise molested, punished, disquieted or called in question for any differences in opinions in matters of religion" so long as he did not "actually disturb the civill peace" of the colony.[50] For further assurance it was affirmed that no "usage or custome of this realme, to the contrary hereof" could affect the rights thus established.

[49] Dunn, *Puritans and Yankees,* pp. 141, 146–147; Black, *Younger John Winthrop,* pp. 239–243.
[50] Thorpe, *Federal and State Constitutions,* VI, 3212–3213.

It is unfortunate that the fame of these provisions of the Rhode Island charter has depended so largely upon their uniqueness. The modern American has found in them an expression of his own belief as to the limits which should be placed upon the power of the state to interfere with the individual conscience. So spontaneous has been his response that he often has failed to give the subject the second thought it deserves. He has credited Roger Williams as the author of Rhode Island's policy of separating the church and the state. If well read in history, he has assigned credit also to Dr. Clarke and to John Winthrop for the assistance he gave to Clarke. He may even have assigned a measure of credit, with some puzzlement, to the Restoration government for having at least once gotten itself onto the right track. What he usually has failed to understand is the attitude of that government with regard to religion in the colonies. It was an attitude based upon the assumption that each colony might safely be allowed to follow its own inclinations, however peculiar. If Rhode Island was the only colony to receive a grant of religious freedom in terms the modern American easily grasps, it was because only Rhode Island would have wanted such a grant. Actually, Rhode Island received no more than had Connecticut the year before, which was a guarantee that the colony might continue to follow its own religious policies. The grant in one case was positive; in the other it must be found in the negative, the silent parts of the Connecticut charter, but the effect was the same.

One more assurance on this main point for Rhode Islanders was provided by the charter's guarantee of rights of self-government as generous as those recently given to Connecticut. Several changes were made in the government the colony had established by its own orders of 1647, with the result that practices thereafter conformed more closely to the standard New England model. For a president there was now substituted a governor, elected annually by the general assembly, as were also a deputy governor and ten assistants to the governor. The assembly, of representatives from the several towns, was to sit in May and October of each year, and at such other times as might be necessary. The laws of the province, except on questions of religion, were required to conform with English usage, but again no provision was made for review in England of the legislation enacted. Perhaps a provision establishing the privilege for inhabitants of the Rhode Island towns of free movement for lawful purposes through any other of His Majesty's dominions deserves also special mention. All said, the Rhode Island towns had lost some of the autonomy they formerly had held, but collectively they had gained much.[51] Rhode Island would remain a place where men were free to dispute their differences.

The transition from the Rhode Island charter back to the Carolina charter of March, 1663, is easier than one might assume at first glance.[52] Carolina's charter immediately calls our attention away from the liberal concessions the Restoration government made to communities of Englishmen already established in America for consideration of the government's interest in expanding English holdings there. Rhode Island's charter created a self-governing corporation in New England, after the models provided by the Massachusetts and Connecticut charters, and with little regard for the need any authority in old England might have to interfere. The Carolina charter established a multiple proprietorship that was in no legal sense a corporation, and gave to the palatine court of the lords proprietors in England the power to override the governing agencies of the colony. The pattern was found in Lord Baltimore's Maryland charter, not excluding its Bishop of Durham clause.[53] In other words, the prototype must be sought in the feudal lord of earlier years, not the modern corporation. The grant of land, and of jurisdiction over all those who might occupy the land, was of the type that soon would be made to the Duke of York in the charter commonly known as the New York charter, that would be held by Berkeley and Carteret as the proprietors of New Jersey, and by William Penn as the proprietor of Pennsylvania. The Carolina charter emphasizes the leading role assumed by the landed gentlemen of England during the later phase of English colonization in North America; the Rhode Island charter harks back to an earlier period when institutional forms were more commonly borrowed from the usages of England's mercantile community. And yet, when

[51] Andrews, *Colonial Period*, II, 47–49.

[52] For the charter, see Mattie Erma Edwards Parker (ed.), *North Carolina Charters and Constitutions, 1578–1698* (Raleigh, 1963), pp. 76–89.

[53] This stipulated that the jurisdictional rights of the proprietor were to be equal to those held at any time theretofore by the bishop, whose power as the head of a princely palatine jurisdiction had reached its peak in the fifteenth century. See Andrews, *Colonial Period*, II, 282–283.

one considers the beginning of the Carolina project and the very limited responsibility the lords proprietors were willing to assume, the transition from the one document to the other is easily made. It is to be found in the extraordinary dependence after the Restoration of a reviving interest in colonization upon the ambition and enterprise of Englishmen already living in America.

There is good reason for believing that the Carolina venture had its origins in Barbados. For a generation past Englishmen settled in the West Indies had moved from island to island of the Lesser Antilles in a bewildering pattern of settlement that reminds us of nothing quite so much as it does of the way in which the Puritans moved around in New England, or in which the Chesapeake settlers spread out along the rivers emptying into the great bay. As the islands filled up, it was natural that some of the settlers should have been attracted by the unoccupied lands of a not too distant mainland, and more particularly by the Carolina area, which had a long-standing identification with England's challenge to the pretentious claims of Spain in the New World. The English plantations in the West Indies represented an especially significant stage in the development of that challenge, and Cromwell's Western Design for seizure of the whole of the West Indies, though a failure except for the conquest of Jamaica, recently had provided fresh stimulation to an old spirit of rivalry. Additional encouragement to the interest in Carolina came from the economic revolution through which Barbados was passing at midcentury. As the economy shifted its base from tobacco to sugar, and larger units of cultivation employing Negro labor proved increasingly to be the more profitable, many of the English planters found their opportunities limited. A turbulent political situation and the adverse effect of the Navigation Acts upon prices also deserve mention. In 1667 it was reported that 12,000 men had left Barbados for other plantations since 1643.[54] Some of these had gone to Surinam, others to Jamaica, which as one of the Greater Antilles might well have absorbed all of the Barbadian capital and labor available for new enterprises had not the

54 Vincent T. Harlow, *History of Barbados*, p. 309, and, for the period, pp. 93–153. See also Beer, *Old Colonial System*, II, 9 ff.; Arthur P. Newton, *The European Nations in the West Indies, 1493–1688* (London, 1933) , pp. 194–199; Andrews, *Colonial Period*, II, 241–273; and A. P. Thornton, *West-India Policy under the Restoration* (Oxford, 1956) , pp. 22 ff.

recent conquest of that island been based upon Barbados, with a resulting accumulation of irritations. For several influential planters, Carolina seemed to offer a more attractive field of endeavour.

Sir John Colleton, who had fought for the king, who subsequently had settled in Barbados, and who had returned to London shortly after the Restoration, has been credited with initiating the Carolina project.[55] In the Duke of Albemarle, formerly Cromwell's General Monk, Colleton had a powerfully placed kinsman. His associates also included Sir Anthony Ashley Cooper, an earlier investor in Barbadian property who currently was active in the councils of trade and plantations. One of the shrewder politicians of the era, he later would become the Earl of Shaftesbury.[56] John Lord Berkeley was closely associated with the Duke of York. It was probably he who was responsible for the inclusion of his brother, Sir William Berkeley of Virginia.[57] Lord Chancellor Clarendon; William Craven, Earl of Craven, a staunch royalist who was to win still other rewards for his loyalty; and Sir George Carteret, to whom the king was heavily indebted for valiant services duing the Civil War, brought the total to eight proprietors. It was a powerful combination, so powerful as to make it unnecessary to go beyond that fact for an explanation of the king's decision to make the grant.

Let it be noted also that five of the proprietors held membership on the councils established in 1660 for trade and for plantations; that three of them had been leaders in organizing that same year the Company of Royal Adventurers Trading to Africa; that two of them soon would have an active part in planning the conquest of Dutch New Netherland and subsequent thereto would become the original proprietors of New Jersey; that five of them, plus Colleton's son and heir, Peter, would become in 1670 the first proprietors of the Bahama Islands; and that four of them, plus Peter Colleton, in 1670, also would be among the founders of the Hudson's Bay Company[58] Had the Duke of York, his cousin Prince Rupert, and

---

[55] Andrews, *Colonial Period*, III, 183–187; Craven, *Southern Colonies*, p. 321.
[56] For his exceptionally significant career, see again Louise T. Brown, *First Earl of Shaftesbury*.
[57] See above, p. 42–44.
[58] Craven, *Southern Colonies*, pp. 322–323.

William Penn been numbered among the Carolina proprietors, the modern student could find in one place a remarkably complete list of those who during the reign of Charles II held the leadership in efforts to expand English interests in the Atlantic basin.

It is all too evident that the Carolina proprietors planned themselves to make no more than a very limited investment in the enterprise. An accounting in 1666 of expenditures over a three-year period, from a fund depending upon an assessment of £75 each, indicates that the chief costs to the proprietors had been for the procurement of their two charters,[59] for the purchase of a great seal, and for arms and ammunition contributed to a projected settlement by Barbadian adventurers at Port Royal.[60] No proposals for a significant migration from England had been made, or for many years yet would be made. The plan, rather, was to recruit settlers from the West Indies, from Virginia, from New England, from the Bermudas—experienced colonists who presumably were ready to migrate at their own costs to Carolina in exchange for a good English title to whatever lands they might occupy there, and for the generous concessions of self-government and religious freedom the proprietors were prepared to offer.[61] Having won their original charter in the spring of 1663, the lords proprietors, in addition to sending instructions to Governor Berkeley for the establishment of a government on Albemarle Sound, promptly entered into correspondence with a group of New Englanders who had expressed an interest in Carolina, possibly associates of the New Englanders who that same spring undertook a quickly abandoned settlement near the mouth of the Cape Fear River. Through Colleton, the proprietors also kept in touch with interested Barbadians, who in August, at their own charge, sent William Hilton on a hopeful exploration of the coast below Cape Fear.[62] Such was the beginning of the proprietors' effort to accomplish the settlement of Carolina.

[59] The second charter of 1665 (Parker, *North Carolina Charters*, pp. 91–104) extended the proprietary bounds northward from 36 degrees by half a degree, the better to incorporate the Albemarle settlements, and southward from 31 degrees to a point 100 miles below the modern boundary of Georgia and Florida.

[60] Craven, *Southern Colonies*, p. 333.

[61] See below, pp. 88–92.

[62] For a discussion of the early activity of the proprietors, and their ideas, see Craven, *Southern Colonies*, pp. 318–320, 324–330.

One is struck immediately by the sharp contrast with the heavy responsibilities assumed by the original promoters of English settlement in America. They had been forced to carry the full burden of recruiting and directing, initially at considerable charge to themselves, a costly transatlantic migration. But of the great men who assumed the leadership in the post-Restoration phase of English colonization in North America, only William Penn, in the Quaker settlement of the Delaware Valley after 1675, was to sponsor a significant migration from England. The others placed no obstacle in the way of Englishmen who might wish to migrate to the new proprietorships. Indeed, the early publication in London of two promotional tracts advertising the attractions of Carolina, the earliest in 1664, strongly suggests that the proprietors undertook to encourage such an emigration.[63] Not until 1669, however, would they dispatch an expedition of their own from England, and even then it carried hardly more than a hundred prospective settlers.[64] Prior to the 1680's the hopes which sustained the Carolina venture continued to depend chiefly upon the migration of settlers from the older colonies, and especially from the West Indies.

A changing attitude in England toward emigration to the colonies may well have influenced the proprietors. Although earlier colonial ventures had been encouraged by the prevailing opinion that colonization by Englishmen strengthened the kingdom, emigration from the homeland was now coming to be viewed as actually a drain upon national resources.[65] But it is not necessary to bring in theoretical considerations in order to explain the promotional policies of the Carolina proprietors. Men who were accustomed to count wealth in terms of landed property, men who from the vantage point of the offices they held had observed the remarkable tendencies toward expansion in every community of Englishmen previously established in America, they are best understood as gentlemen who responded to an apparent opportunity to

[63] The first being an account of Hilton's explorations; the second, of uncertain authorship, was printed in 1666. Both may be consulted in Alexander S. Salley, Jr. (ed.), *Narratives of Early Carolina, 1650–1708* (New York, 1911), pp. 37–73.
[64] See below, pp. 97–99.
[65] Mildred Campbell, "The Conflict of Opinion on Population in Its Relation to Emigration," in William A. Aiken and Basil D. Hening (eds.), *Conflict in Stuart England: Essays in Honour of Wallace Notestein* (London, 1960), pp. 169–201.

extend their personal estates into the New World at a minimum cost to their Old World estates.[66] In so doing, they saw themselves also as servants of the state.

In no other of the post-Restoration ventures did the interests of the state figure quite so prominently as they did in the hastily concocted plans of 1664 for the conquest of Dutch New Netherland. The story is thinly documented and full of puzzles. In telling it the historian finds, on more than one occasion, that conjecture must take the place of well-authenticated fact.

To say this, however, is not to say that there is cause for puzzlement as to why the English undertook the venture. The Navigation Acts of 1660 and 1663 had been adopted with a view primarily to the competition England faced from the Dutch. New Netherland, advantageously situated for the purposes of trade with all of the English colonies, challenged every hope that their trade might be a monopoly of English shipping. The conquest of New Netherland, in short, can be viewed as a logical consequence of decisions on questions of national policy previously taken by the English Parliament.

Nor is there cause for surprise in the leadership that was assumed by the Duke of York. Since 1660 he had been notably active in efforts to expand England's trade at the expense of the Dutch. As lord high admiral and leading adventurer of the Company of Royal Adventurers Trading to Africa, forerunner of the Royal African Company,[67] he more than once had been a party to especially aggressive action against Dutch shipping and fortifications on the coast of West Africa. The peak of the effort there came in the winter of 1663–64, when an English fleet commanded by Captain Robert Holmes did such damage that the Dutch sent their great admiral, De Ruyter, to recoup the loss.[68] During that winter, also, John Lord Berkeley, Sir George Carteret, and William Coventry,

[66] Wesley Frank Craven, *New Jersey and the English Colonization of North America* (Princeton, 1964), provides a more general discussion.

[67] See George F. Zook, *The Company of Royal Adventurers Trading to Africa* (Lancaster, Pa., 1919), and the more recent work of Kenneth G. Davies, *The Royal African Company* (London, 1957).

[68] J. K. Laughton's article on Holmes in the *Dictionary of National Biography* is helpful. It should be noted that Holmes did not participate, as American writers often have assumed, in the expedition against New Amsterdam. See also Wilson, *Profit and Power*, pp. 112–115.

close associates of York in the administration of the Navy, sat as a special committee of the Council for Foreign Plantations, of which Berkeley was then president, for review of complaints against the Dutch in New Amsterdam.[69] The committee's report, submitted late in January, 1664, concluded that three of the king's ships and 300 soldiers, augmented by 1,300 to 1,400 men recruited in New England, would be a sufficient force for the reduction of New Netherland.[70] Before the year had reached its end, events would prove that the estimate had erred only in the assumption that substantial assistance from New England would be needed.

It would be difficult for the historian to exaggerate the feebleness of the Dutch grip on New Netherland. Although modern scholars apparently have overestimated the population of the New England settlements, the contrast with the Dutch community is nonetheless impressive. The largest center of population was New Amsterdam, where perhaps 1,500 people lived.[71] In all New Netherland, not counting the English on Long Island and in Westchester, whose lack of loyalty to the Dutch regime constituted a major cause of its weakness, there were probably few if any more than 5,000 European inhabitants, and these were widely scattered.[72] Some of them lived on the western end of Long Island and a few across the Hudson from Manhattan on Staten Island and in Bergen. The Hudson River Valley was virtually unoccupied, except for a handful of settlers at the mouth of the Esopus (Kingston), and for the trading and farming community adjoining Fort Orange near the juncture of the Mohawk and the Hudson. The remainder of the population lived far removed on the west bank of the lower Delaware River. There were found perhaps 600 Swedes and Finns, remaining from the Swedish colony conquered by Stuyvesant in 1655, and a comparable number of Dutch settlers, mostly recent immigrants.[73]

[69] Andrews, *Colonial Period*, III, 53–57; Ogg, *England in the Reign of Charles II*, I, 257–259.

[70] *Calendar of State Papers, Colonial, 1661–1668*, No. 647.

[71] This is the figure given by Stuyvesant at the time of the surrender. J. Franklin Jameson (ed.), *Narratives of New Netherland, 1609–1664* (New York, 1909), pp. 452, 464. For New England, see above, p. 14.

[72] If Stuyvesant's estimate for New Amsterdam is correct, it is difficult to arrive at any higher figure. Certainly, this is much closer to the truth than the 7,000–10,000 commonly given.

[73] The best summary of the history of the Delaware settlements is found in John E. Pomfret, *The Province of West Jersey, 1609–1702* (Princeton, 1956), pp.

The Dutch West India Company had not been wholly indifferent to the need to build up the population of its colony. As early as 1629, it had offered generous land grants, much as did contemporary English promoters of colonization, to investors who would undertake to settle a specified number of colonists on the land received. Several patroons, as the recipients of such grants were described, had responded to the offer, but after thirty years only one patroonship had undergone any real development. That was Rensselaerswyck, property of the Van Rensselaer family of Amsterdam, which was located in the neighborhood of Fort Orange. The patroonship had boasted some eighteen farms in the 1650's, but the number seems to have fallen by the time of the English conquest. Indeed, the Van Rensselaers, true Dutchmen, actually had given more attention to opportunities for trade with the northern Indians than to the development of their extensive land grant.[74] Howeve. much the seventeenth-century Dutchman may have excelled in other areas, his record as a colonizer is not impressive.

The West India Company, ever more interested in the trade of Africa and in plundering expeditions against Spaniards than it was in New Netherland, was now virtually bankrupt. After being expelled from its possessions on the Brazilian coast in 1654, it had managed to meet the costs of Stuyvesant's conquest of New Sweden in the following year only by transferring the area south of Fort Christina (Wilmington) to the City of Amsterdam in payment of the debt incurred. The city thereafter undertook a surprisingly vigorous effort to build up that part of New Netherland, sending out several hundred colonists, but this was the work of the city, not the company, which by the end of 1663 had transferred the whole of the Delaware Valley from Stuyvesant's jurisdiction to Amsterdam's control.[75] On the eve of the conquest, the company's mood was to cut its responsibilities and its losses in New Netherland. It had given up the attempt to maintain a monopoly of the fur trade there

3–52. See also Philip L. White, *The Beekmans of New York, 1647–1877* (New York, 1956), pp. 33–50.

[74] A story told in detail by S. G. Nissenson, *The Patroon's Domain* (New York, 1937).

[75] Pomfret, *Province of West Jersey*, pp. 41–43; a recent and realistic discussion of the colony's fortunes is that of Henry H. Kessler and Eugene Rachlis, *Peter Stuyvesant and His New York* (New York, 1959).

as early as 1639, and even had quit trading on its own account in 1644.[76]

Compounding the difficulties of Stuyvesant at New Amsterdam was the continuing aggressiveness of the New England Puritans, especially on Long Island. Indeed, by 1664 the long-standing quarrel there between the Dutch and the English, it almost might be said, had given place to quarrels among the long-since-victorious English. Once more, Colonel John Scott enters the picture. He seems to have been the one who first brought from England to New England the news that an attack upon New Amsterdam was planned. His information may have rested upon nothing more than the gossip of London, but he posed as an advance agent for the Duke of York. His purpose, it soon became evident, was to establish a personal control over Long Island that might persuade the duke to reward him with its proprietorship. In the circumstances, Connecticut, too, had an interest in making complete its control of the island; although it had a claim to full possession under its recent charter, the claim was disputed not only by the Dutch towns in the western part of the island but as well by some of the English towns. Scott won a commission from Connecticut for the purpose of forcing these towns, Dutch and English, to submit to her jurisdiction. Having made progress toward the accomplishment of this mission, he negotiated an agreement with the virtually helpless Stuyvesant to recognize Scott as president of the English towns of Long Island. To cut short a long and exceedingly complicated story, an aroused Connecticut government sent an armed force which seized Scott in March, 1664, and packed him off to a Hartford jail. Governor Winthrop followed up by visiting Long Island in April for the purpose of ousting Scott's magistrates and replacing them with men who acknowledged the jurisdictional rights of Connecticut.[77] In this crudely played game, Stuyvesant had been hardly more than a pawn.

While Winthrop hurried to bring the Long Island towns into line with Connecticut's ambition, in England Colonel Richard Nicolls rushed to complete the preparations for his sailing at the

[76] Allen W. Trelease, *Indian Affairs in Colonial New York: The Seventeenth Century* (Ithaca, 1960), pp. 112–113.

[77] See again the sources cited in note 46, and especially Dunn, *Puritans and Yankees*, pp. 149–150.

head of an expedition comprising three men-of-war, a transport, and troops whose number has been placed as high as 450 but was probably closer to the 300 recommended in the preceding February.[78] The soldiers were recruited in the service of the Duke of York, some at least on a promise of land grants in the area they were to conquer,[79] but the ships were the king's own. This dependence upon resources a modern person might describe as public and private was both congenial to the age and characteristic of the Restoration phase of English expansion.

The king had given sanction to the enterprise by granting to his brother on March 12, 1664, an extraordinary charter.[80] The shortest and most hastily executed of the seventeenth-century colonial charters, this instrument, though usually described as the New York charter, actually gave the Duke of York full proprietary rights over the mainland area lying between the Delaware and Connecticut rivers, with a northward extension to include Fort Orange; over Long Island, Nantucket, Martha's Vineyard, and other islands lying off New England's coast; and over the vast region beginning on the Maine coast between the Kennebec and St. Croix and extending northward to the St. Lawrence River. By fixing the western boundary of the grant on the Delaware River, the charter failed to include the Dutch and Swedish settlements in the Delaware Valley, which were situated on the west bank. On the other hand, by specifying that the proprietorship would extend eastward from the Hudson to the Connecticut and would include Long Island, the charter embraced most of the area recently deeded by royal grant to Connecticut and most of the towns assumed to be within that jurisdiction, including New Haven. The addition of Nantucket, Martha's Vineyard, and the region that perhaps can be briefly described as Maine gave to the new proprietorship the configuration of an arm reaching out to encircle Puritan New England.

These astonishing bounds present to the historian many difficult questions. A part of the explanation probably lies in the great haste with which the document was drafted and executed. The omission

---

[78] In using the total of 450, all later authorities seem to have followed John R. Brodhead, *History of the State of New York* (2 vols., New York, 1853–71), II, 20.

[79] Andrews, *Colonial Period*, III, 64 n.

[80] Thorpe, *Federal and State Constitutions*, III, 1637–1640.

of the Delaware settlements may be explained by a desire to avoid an immediate quarrel with Lord Baltimore, who claimed under his Maryland charter a boundary on the Delaware. Maine, Martha's Vineyard, and Nantucket were included, it is evident, because they were parts, with Long Island, of territories to which the Earl of Stirling held title under a patent of 1632 from the New England Council, but to say this is not to resolve the problem entirely. Whether because the duke wished to eliminate a competing English claim to Long Island, as an important segment of Dutch New Netherland, or because of his willingness to accommodate his friend Berkeley, who had purchased a half-share in the Stirling title early in 1662 and then had failed to win the royal confirmation he sought, York had acquired the Stirling title by an agreement to purchase.[81] Whatever the full facts may be in this instance, the duke had shown more regard for one competing English claim than for another and much more recent one. The encroachment on the Connecticut colony is especially puzzling. A stipulation in the Duke of York's charter that the rights there established would override all conflicting claims depending upon earlier grants seems to justify dismissal of the frequently repeated suggestion that those who processed the charter simply had forgotten Connecticut's charter. Perhaps the explanation lies, at least partly, in London's dissatisfaction with Connecticut's conduct since 1662. Perhaps it was thought that John Winthrop might be able to persuade his fellow colonists to go along with an arrangement uniting their own lands with territory they long had coveted, on the understanding that as Englishmen they could expect to enjoy a dominant influence in the new government. Perhaps the chief consideration was the need felt to establish in the Duke's charter full title to all that the Dutch had claimed theretofore, in the belief that the conflict with Connecticut's charter could be settled by negotiation. This, at any rate, is what actually occurred, for soon after the conquest Nicolls and Winthrop negotiated an agreement to fix the boundaries separating the two jurisdictions along lines very close to those dividing New York and Connecticut today.[82]

[81] A footnote in Andrews, *Colonial Period*, III, 58, provides the most succinct account. See also Isabel M. Calder, "The Earl of Stirling and the Colonization of Long Island," in *Essays . . . Presented to Charles McLean Andrews*, pp. 74–95.

[82] See below, p. 74.

The Duke of York's charter gave him all the customary proprietary rights, and more. Because the usual provision for a representative assembly was missing, he held powers more absolute than those belonging to any other of the colonial proprietors. But to a remarkable extent, by the standard set by other proprietors, the Duke of York would govern his people in the name of the king. He demanded of them no oath of fealty to himself, as did other proprietors. Instead, the inhabitants of New York would swear allegiance to the king, and in his name would run all writs. When finally the proprietor became king himself in 1685, the transition from proprietary to royal rule in New York would require only a slight adjustment in the institutional life of the province. The New York charter, the only one ever issued in behalf of a member of the royal family and to one who was himself heir to the throne, is best viewed as an exceptional development.

The beginning of military preparations for the assault upon New Amsterdam predated the issuance of the charter.[83] Nicolls' choice for the command was confirmed by the commission he received on April 2 as the proprietor's deputy. It was an uncommonly happy choice. Richard Nicolls had led a troop of the king's horse during the Civil War. Thereafter, he had added to his military experience by fighting under York's command in the French wars of the Fronde, and he had returned to London in 1660 as a member of the duke's household, being at that time about forty years of age. He would continue in the duke's service until he was killed at the Battle of Soleby in 1672, aboard ship and at the side of his patron.[84] Although the record of his career is unfortunately sparse, the four years of service he gave to the Duke of York in North America conclusively testify that his loyalty was matched by his ability.

In the spring of 1664, he faced first a twofold task: to effect the conquest of New Netherland and then to organize an English government for a people as strangely assorted as were the territories over which he was expected to govern. And to these responsibilities,

---

[83] In addition to Andrews, *Colonial Period*, III, 55–60, see Henry L. Schoolcraft, "The Capture of New Amsterdam," *English Historical Review*, XXII (1907), 674–693.

[84] Leonard W. Labaree in *Dictionary of American Biography*

heavy enough in themselves, the king added a third job. Or perhaps it should be said that Lord Clarendon added it.

Clarendon's attitude toward the proposed attack on New Amsterdam is not clearly established. He was still, nominally at least, the king's first minister, and as such sponsored continuing negotiations with the Dutch, negotiations that would continue for several months after the conquest of New Netherland, but diplomatic negotiations, as the modern American well remembers, can serve to cover a military operation. We can be certain only that Clarendon saw in the proposed departure of Colonel Nicolls for New England, the intended base of operations for the attack on New Amsterdam, an opportunity to implement his growing determination to investigate the situation in Puritan New England. On April 21, Nicolls received an appointment from the king as the head of an investigative commission. Joined with him in the commission were Sir Robert Carr, Colonel George Cartwright, and Samuel Maverick, an old enemy and especially severe critic of the orthodox leadership of Massachusetts.[85] His inclusion strongly suggests that the continuing recalcitrance of Massachusetts, rather than the quarrels between Connecticut and Rhode Island and between New Haven and Connecticut, was the governing consideration. One can wonder about York's acceptance of the proposal, for it imposed upon Nicolls the hazard that is known in modern times as a conflict of interest. He was now expected to look into the more closely guarded secrets of Puritan New England, and at the same time to seek its cooperation in the attack against the Dutch.

But on one point there can be no doubt. The commssion for the investigation of the problems presented by New England served to provide, and the record suggests intentionally, an almost perfect cover for the military operation against the prying eyes of Dutch agents in London. After the surrender of New Amsterdam, Peter Stuyvesant bitterly complained to his superiors in Holland that he had received no advance notice of the attack except the assurance from his superiors that Colonel Nicolls had no purpose other than that of reducing the Puritans of New England to the authority of the Anglican bishops.[86]

[85] N.Y. *Colonial Documents*, III, 64–65, and for the accompanying instructions, pp. 51–64.
[86] Stuyvesant's report in Jameson's *Narratives of New Netherland*, p. 461.

The instructions given the commission which Nicolls headed have an extraordinary interest for students of American history. The commissioners formed a body primarily clothed with investigative duties and so it had little power to act. Nevertheless, their instructions called for exploration of possibilities that must be described as nothing less than revolutionary in their implications. Especially significant are the "Private Instructions" intended only for communication among the commissioners.[87] It is regrettable that these instructions, at critical points, are subject to two readings. Although clearly labeled at the beginning as a document covering all the New England colonies, and accordingly phrased.in most places, a suggestion that the colonists might be persuaded to choose Nicolls as their governor, and Cartwright for the command of their militia, can be read either as applying only to Massachusetts or as a startling suggestion for the establishment of some kind of governor-general over the whole of New England. Probably, Lord Clarendon hoped immediately for nothing more than to win agreement on a proposal that the governors of the several jurisdictions should be appointed thereafter by the king from nominations submitted to him by the several general courts. Such an agreement would have settled other issues which had come into question, including the royal right to review colonial legislation and a right of appeal from colonial courts to the king. In any event, the commissioners were to demand that government in New England henceforth be conducted in the king's name, and that existing charters be surrendered for reconfirmation. Assurances to be given for the protection of established liberties included the right of the Puritan colonists to follow their own forms of worship, but on the understanding that the same liberty of conscience would be conceded to others, without prejudice to their political rights.

Richard Nicolls sailed from England for North America late in May, 1664, with baggage he no doubt viewed occasionally with a troubled eye.

[87] N.Y. *Colonial Documents*, III, 57–61.

CHAPTER 3

The Restoration Colonies

S IX of the thirteen colonies destined to form the United States of America—New York, New Jersey, Pennsylvania, Delaware, and the two Carolinas—came into the possession of Englishmen during the reign of Charles II, and of these all save Pennsylvania were occupied within the decade immediately following the Restoration.[1] No other chapter in the history of English colonization in North America has greater significance, not even those which record the earlier settlements established on the Chesapeake and in New England. Nor can there be doubt as to the story, in this later phase of England's colonial expansion, which claims the first and closest attention. It is the story of New York.

The Carolina project also significantly expanded the area of English endeavor in North America. But the history of that venture initially is one of repeated disappointment in efforts to achieve its main objective, the establishment of a colony in the more southern reaches of the grant. Not until the spring of 1670 would that end be accomplished, and for many years thereafter the colony was slow to develop. Even slower was the development of the older settlement by Virginians on Albemarle Sound.

In contrast, Richard Nicolls quickly and easily had conquered the whole of New Netherland. His victory brought into English possession an area of the greatest strategic significance, whether

[1] The fullest and most authoritative discussion of the post-Restoration colonies is found in the third volume of Andrews, *Colonial Period*.

considered for the linkage it provided between earlier English settlements on the Chesapeake and in New England, the advantage of position it offered in the pursuit of an inland fur trade, or with a view to the coming contest with the French in Canada. As for the first time an English colonial administration confronted the problem of ruling over a significant number of alien colonists, the decisions taken foretold a continuing policy of encouragement and accommodation for many other aliens whose ambitious energies would bring strength first to the English colonies and then to the United States. No less significant were Governor Nicolls' prompt efforts to strengthen England's hold upon the newly acquired territory by encouraging immigration from New England, especially into the area lying west of the Hudson. Even after the New Jersey grant had brought frustration to the governor's plans by reducing the New York jurisdiction to little more than what Stuyvesant hopelessly had sought to defend in 1664, its story continues to have a peculiarly critical importance. Recurrent assertions of jurisdictional rights depending upon the Duke of York's extraordinary charter were to be an especially troublesome factor in the history of New Jersey, and no other of the so-called middle colonies, not even Pennsylvania, has a history that is free of the need to pay attention to the strange geographical configuration of the areas over which the New York government at first presided. To mention but one other point, the special problems of New York's defense were destined eventually to cast a shadow over the relations between the English government and every English colony in North America from Virginia northward.

Given the importance of New York's early history, it is unfortunate that historians have not devoted to the subject more thoughtful attention than they have. The fault lies partly with New England's influential historians, who all too often have allowed the emphasis to fall upon New York's failure to live up to the high standard set by its Puritan neighbors, as in the failure through many years to establish a representative assembly in its government. Almost as if in response, New York's own historians, and especially those who magnificently served the state during the nineteenth century, have elected to emphasize the advantages of descent from the Dutch of the seventeenth century.

No one can fail to understand the pride New Yorkers have taken in the Dutch origins of their community. Nor can there be doubt regarding the importance of its Dutch inhabitants for the development of both colony and state. The Dutch Reformed Church remained the most influential denomination in the colony for a long time after the conquest, and still exerts a significant influence throughout the area that once was New Netherland. Despite an early tendency for the English tongue to assert its ascendancy as the language of government and of commerce, the Dutch language served for many years after 1664 as the vernacular for a large part of the population. In addition, it has bequeathed to modern American usage such popular terms as Santa Claus, boss, cooky, crib, snoop, stoop, and spook. Similarly, there have been interesting architectural survivals from the Dutch period, and the folklore of the Hudson River Valley has won a place of special favor in American letters.[2] But the tradition built upon New York's Dutch origins has also left a variety of misleading impressions. New Netherland, for example, has been presented as a much more tolerant community than it actually was.[3] The dictatorial methods of Peter Stuyvesant, New Netherland's able but narrow-minded and autocratic head, have been discounted in the attempt to enlarge the Dutch contribution to the development of self-government in America. Finally, the Hudson River aristocracy has come to be viewed popularly as a Dutch creation, whereas in fact it grew up almost wholly as the result of policies instituted by the English. In the general field of early American history there are few needs greater than that calling for a first-class study of seventeenth-century New York.[4] And when that study is made, it will begin with the expedition Colonel Nicolls led out from England in May, 1664.

[2] Henry L. Mencken, *The American Language* (4th ed., New York, 1937), pp. 108–111; Louis B. Wright, *The Cultural Life of the American Colonies* (New York, 1957), pp. 48–50; Thomas J. Wertenbaker, *The Founding of American Civilization: The Middle Colonies* (New York, 1938), pp. 29–118; and Merle Curti, *The Growth of American Thought* (New York, 1943), p. 7.

[3] See the discussion of the difficulties experienced by Lutherans, Jews, and Quakers in Kessler and Rachlis, *Peter Stuyvesant and His New York*, pp. 169–196. For an especially authoritative account of the experience of the Jewish community in New Amsterdam, earliest such community in what is now the United States, see Jacob R. Marcus, *Early American Jewry* (2 vols., 1951–53), I, 3–55.

[4] The most useful single study yet made, though marred by a strong Dutch bias, is John R. Brodhead's *History of the State of New York*, now a century old.

Nicolls' immediate objective as he approached the American coast toward the end of July was an anchorage at Gardiner's Island, in the mouth of Long Island Sound. Instead, contrary weather brought him first to Boston, where his reception was correct enough but hardly warm. Upon hearing there that all Long Island had fallen into the hands of the English, he determined to move at once against New Amsterdam.[5] On August 18 he dropped anchor in Gravesend Bay, and so came into position to blockade the entrance to the great harbor, for which purpose he also seized a Dutch gun emplacement on Staten Island. The major part of his troops were deployed on Long Island across the East River from lower Manhattan.

Governor Winthrop, to whom Nicolls had written ahead, came over from Connecticut to assist in the negotiations that were promptly opened with Peter Stuyvesant. Also present were representatives from Plymouth and New Haven, but the bulk of the auxiliary forces gathered for Nicolls' aid undoubtedly came from the English towns of Long Island. It is impossible to say how many men there were, but the number matters little. They were enough to persuade Stuyvesant that he faced a force of perhaps 2,000 men, and to remind him of the overwhelming numbers that could be brought against him should the whole of New England join in the attack.[6] More important than the soldiers were the three men-of-war, for they enabled Nicolls to follow up the blockade of the harbor by a blockade of the town itself.

On Manhattan, Peter Stuyvesant vainly sought to rally his people for the defense of New Amsterdam. Fort Orange, in response to a call for help, had pleaded its own difficulties with the Indians, which were real. Farmers living closer to New Amsterdam had refused to leave their farms, perhaps in part because, unlike English colonists, they were accustomed to depend upon a paid garrison for their defense. The people of the town itself undertook to persuade

[5] Nicoll's own account in New York *State Library Bulletin* (May, 1899), pp. 74–77. For the situation on Long Island, see above, pp. 62.

[6] Stuyvesant's report and that of town council in Jameson, *Narratives of New Netherland*, pp. 451–466. Brodhead's *History of New York*, II, 22–41, has perhaps the best over-all account of the military operation and the surrender. Nicolls had won a promise of 200 men from Massachusetts, but neither did they march nor were they needed. New York *State Library Bulletin*, pp. 77–78, 93, 100–103; Hutchinson, *History of Massachusetts Bay*, I, 199–200.

the director-general to accept the favorable terms of surrender offered by Nicolls. The unwillingness of his people to fight left Stuyvesant no choice. On August 27, New Amsterdam—and with it, for all practical purposes, New Netherland—was surrendered without a shot having been fired.[7] Fort Orange quickly yielded to Colonel Cartwright, received its English garrison, and accepted the name of Albany, one of the titles belonging to the Duke of York. Downriver, at the outlet of the Esopus, the English stationed a detachment of troops at the place henceforth to be known as Kingston, and so made complete their control of the Hudson River Valley.

Only on the Delaware at New Amstel (New Castle) did the English invaders meet resistance. This was the City of Amsterdam's main fortification, and so it guarded the most recent and successful of the Dutch colonizing ventures. When Sir Robert Carr arrived there in October with two vessels and the soldiers who could be spared from New York, its commander refused to surrender. Carr took the fort by storm, killing three men and wounding several others. He then allowed his victorious troops shamefully to plunder the inhabitants.[8] Thus did the communities to which the state of Delaware traces its origins come first under English rule.

Although the Duke of York's charter gave him a title that reached only to the Delaware River, Nicolls obviously had proceeded on the assumption that he was expected to reduce all of New Netherland and that whatever had been claimed by the Dutch would now belong to the Duke. To cover the eventuality of a protest in behalf of Lord Baltimore, who also claimed the west bank of the Delaware, Carr had been instructed to say that the place would be held for the king until "his majesty is informed and satisfied otherwise."[9] But this was a question on which Charles II seems never to have bothered to be satisfied. Despite Baltimore's protests, the Duke of York continued to hold the settlements on the west bank of the Delaware by right of conquest, and to govern them as a part of the

[7] In addition to Brodhead, see Kessler and Rachlis, *Peter Stuyvesant,* and Mrs. Schuyler van Rensselaer, *History of the City of New York in the Seventeenth Century* (2 vols., New York, 1909).

[8] Brodhead, *History of New York,* I, 743–745; Pomfret, *Province of West Jersey,* pp. 54–55.

[9] Brodhead, *History of New York,* II, 50.

New York proprietorship until he deeded the area to William Penn in 1682.

At New Amstel, as at Fort Orange and New Amsterdam, the terms of surrender were intended to encourage the inhabitants to remain as tenants of the new proprietor. Denizenship was promised for all who would take an oath of allegiance to the English king. Existing titles in property were to be confirmed. The people were guaranteed against interference with their customary forms of worship, which is to say that assurance was given for protection of the Reformed Church among the Dutch and of the Lutheran Church among the Swedes and Finns.[10] All but a very few of the settlers elected to remain, including Philip Schuyler, William Beekman, Olaff Van Cortlandt, Frederick Philipse, Jeremias Van Rensselaer, and others whose families would rise to great wealth and power in English New York. Even Peter Stuyvesant, after a visit to Holland for the purpose of clearing the record, returned to New York in 1667 for the remaining five years of his life.

There is no need for surprise that the government established by Nicolls was at first authoritarian, indeed basically military, in its character. Not only had the Dutch colonists long been accustomed to such a government,[11] but England and Holland were once more engaged in open hostilities from the spring of 1665 to the summer of 1667, when by the Treaty of Breda the Dutch first conceded the English title to New York. There followed five years of peace between the two states, but only five, and in the third Anglo-Dutch war the Dutch recaptured New York. Not until a second cession of the territory by the Treaty of Westminster in 1674 can it be said that the English title was finally cleared of all doubt.

Stuyvesant had ruled with the aid of a small council, and so did Nicolls, all of its original members being Englishmen. The seat of his government was New York City, formerly New Amsterdam, where the English garrison in 1665 numbered 200 soldiers.[12] Detachments were stationed at Albany, at Kingston, and on the

[10] New York *State Library Bulletin,* pp. 95–98, 112–114, 125–128.

[11] Although there had been occasional meetings of representatives from the several communities of the jurisdiction, called together by the director-general or assembled in protest of his actions, these had failed to give the representative principle an established place in the government of the Dutch colony. See Osgood, *American Colonies in the Seventeenth Century,* II, 95–118, 141–158.

[12] N.Y. Historical Society *Collections,* II (1869), 75.

Delaware. For the government of the remote Delaware settlements, the Dutch had developed the office of commissary, or vice-director, an office which easily served as a model for English military commanders stationed outside New York City. In the outlying villages of New Netherland local government had been entrusted to a resident magistracy of schout and schepens, the schout being something of a chief magistrate and chief constable. Originally appointed by the director-general on nominations from the inhabitants, the magistrates formed a local court to which appointments thereafter were made from nominations by the court itself. These local courts, which happily were not too different in organization and function from those the English colonies had found useful, were allowed to continue for varying periods of time after 1664 in the usage of their own law and custom. Policy, in other words, provided for a gradual transition from Dutch to English law.[13]

Nicolls was extraordinarily prompt, however, in drafting a comprehensive code of English law for the province—the so-called Duke's Laws of March 1, 1665, a remarkable document which deserves to be better remembered than it has been.[14] Proclaimed at Hempstead, on Long Island, before deputies assembled from seventeen towns, both English and Dutch, the Duke's Laws immediately had full force only in a newly created county of Yorkshire that embraced Long Island, Westchester, and Staten Island. It often has been assumed that the primary purpose of the legislation was to provide an English form of government for that part of the colony in which the population was overwhelmingly English. Certainly, this was one of the governor's aims. After he had agreed with John Winthrop late in 1664 to surrender the Duke's claim to western Connecticut in return for an undisputed title to Long Island and Westchester,[15] the areas designated as York County embraced most

13 On the general subject, see Albert E. McKinley, "The Transition from Dutch to English Rule in New York," *American Historical Review*, VI (1900–1901), 693–724; Osgood, *American Colonies in the Seventeenth Century*, II, 119 ff.

14 *Colonial Laws of New York* (Albany, 1896), I, 6–71. Morris, *History of American Law*, contains helpful comments, as does also Julius Goebel, Jr., and T. Raymond Naughton, *Law Enforcement in Colonial New York: A Study in Criminal Procedure* (New York, 1944).

15 Dunn, *Puritans and Yankees*, pp. 155–156; also his "John Winthrop, Jr., Connecticut Expansionist: The Failure of His Designs on Long Island, 1663–1675," *New England Quarterly*, XXIX (1956), 3–26.

of the English then living under New York's government. Only on Long Island, however, was there found a substantial number of English settlers. In Westchester, where the New Englanders had carried their thrust into New Netherland to its most westerly point, the European inhabitants were a mere handful.[16] Similarly, Staten Island contained no more than another handful of Europeans, although over the years past a number of Dutchmen had sought their fortunes there.[17] The very bounds assigned to York County indicate that Nicolls had a larger aim in view than merely to accommodate the existing English population. When one considers the interest he already had shown in the encouragement of further migration by New Englanders into the Duke's territories, and the great energy he would devote to that end thereafter,[18] the Duke's laws must be viewed as the single most important item in a shrewdly conceived promotional campaign. More than that, there is good reason for believing that the governor hoped to establish a standard of law and administration to which the entire province in time might be converted. This, certainly, is what in no small measure he achieved, and it was no mean achievement.[19]

It is significant that the Duke's laws are described, in the very beginning, as laws "Collected out of the Several Laws now in force in his majesties American Colonyes and Plantations."[20] Even more significant is the fact that the borrowings came chiefly from the laws of Massachusetts and Connecticut. Here and there the governor drew upon Dutch usage, as though he was conscious of the need to ease the transition to English law for the older settlers. But over all, the legislation held true to an English standard of law and government, with such modifications as had been suggested by the experience of Englishmen living in America.[21]

16 A document in Robert Bolton, *History of the Several Towns, Manors, and Patents of the County of Westchester* (3d. ed., 2 vols., New York, 1905), II, 286–287, suggests that the heads of families in 1664 may have numbered little more than seventeen.

17 Stuyvesant in 1666 described the settlers there as ten or twelve men capable of bearing arms. Henry G. Steinmeyer, *Staten Island 1524–1898* (Richmondtown, N.Y., 1950), pp. 10–11.

18 Discussed below, pp. 79–80, 82–83.

19 See below, pp. 78–79.

20 *Colonial Laws of New York*, I, 7.

21 McKinley, "Transition from Dutch to English Rule," analyzes the provisions with reference to New England, Dutch, and other origins.

The provision for local government in York County was destined
to have an especially wide and important influence upon the course
of American history. Nicolls elected to depend basically upon the
justice of the peace, an officer long familiar to all Englishmen and
one who was not too different from the resident magistrate upon
whom the Dutch had relied in New Netherland. For each of the
three ridings into which Yorkshire was to be divided, there was to
be a local Court of Sessions made up of resident magistrates
appointed by the governor. Meeting three times a year, the court
was given broad administrative powers and judicial responsibility
for issues not involving life or limb. When life or limb was at stake,
and in cases of appeal, the jurisdiction belonged to a Court of
Assizes meeting annually under the presidency of the governor, with
members of his council and justices from the local sessions in
attendance. Yorkshire was to have a high sheriff appointed by the
governor, and in each of the three ridings a deputy sheriff. At the
town or village level, the government was entrusted to eight overseers elected by the inhabitants under a rule calling for the retirement of four members each year. From the retiring members one
was to be chosen annually as constable or chief magistrate. The
franchise was based upon the ownership of property.

No less important are the provisions for the support of religious
worship. The Duke's Laws proclaimed a policy of tolerance for any
branch of the Protestant faith; at the same time, they required that
each town build and support a church of its own faith. The town
was made free in the choice of its minister, provided that he could
offer proof of ordination by a Protestant bishop or minister within
the king's dominions or within the domain of any foreign prince
belonging to the Reformed Church. No person was to be molested,
fined, or imprisoned for a difference of religious opinion. The chief
restriction left thus upon the right of the individual was the
possibility that he might be required, through the taxes he paid, to
support a church other than the one he would have chosen.[22] But
this limitation must be interpreted with due regard for the fact that
the people of Yorkshire normally lived in either a Dutch or an
English village, and so shared with their neighbors a common

[22] In *Colonial Laws of New York*, see especially I, 24–26 and 95 for an
amendment of 1672 specifying that persons of "different judgments" must contribute to the support of the minister in their town.

religious allegiance. In other words, the emphasis belongs to the freedom that was given each community to go its own way, which undoubtedly was the freedom most highly prized by the very mixed assortment of communities over which Governor Nicolls presided. His policy offered confirmation of assurances already given to the Dutch and Swedish inhabitants of the province. And for the New England Puritans who were contemplating a migration into the Duke's territories, be they orthodox or unorthodox, there was assurance that they might live there without weakening the church so many of them had come to America to build. In the broad sweep of history, religious freedom has many different meanings, and among those who have significantly advanced the cause was Governor Nicolls of New York.

Unfortunately, historians have come close to paying more attention to what the Duke's Laws did not provide than they have to what they did provide. New England's historians especially have deplored the absence of some provision for the town meeting. Actually, the laws conceded what many New Englanders certainly viewed as the most essential of the town's rights, which was the election of its local officers. Too often, it seems to have been forgotten that Nicolls had to keep in mind the Dutch village as well as the Puritan town. Too often, also, it seems to have been forgotten that the town meeting repeatedly has flourished without a heavy dependence upon permissive legislation—among other places, on Long Island after 1665. Another indictment brought against the legislation has been for its failure to establish a representative assembly. Perhaps there should have been an assembly, although Nicolls had no authority to create such an agency, even had he deemed it advisable in the unusual situation he faced. The Long Island Puritans were to find in this omission a troublemaking grievance for many years thereafter. Not until 1683 would the first representative assembly meet, and not until after the English Revolution of 1688 would the institution have a secure place in the government of the colony. It is wrong, however, to infer from this fact, as has often been done, that during the interim New York's government was wholly lacking in recognition for the principle of local representation. At the Court of Assizes, whose functions included the amendment of existing laws, justices representing local courts of sessions were in attendance, as Nicolls had decreed they should be.[23] They were not, of course, elected representatives. Their attendance, moreover, seems to have depended upon the business the court might have in hand, upon whether or not their own community was directly involved. Even so, it must be recognized that in the early government of New York there were formal and established procedures through which any community might get at least a hearing when the laws were to be changed.

To bring the entire province under a uniform system of law and administration required much more time than Richard Nicolls was to have in New York. But the transition in the predominantly non-English sections of the proprietorship to an English type of government began under his supervision, and was destined to be brought to a successful completion through policies for which he was primarily responsible. As would be expected, the beginning was made in New York City, where, also in 1665, schout, burgomasters, and schepens were replaced by a mayor, five aldermen, and a sheriff.[24] In the local court at Kingston, the changeover from Dutch law and procedure came by stages between 1669 and 1673. On the Delaware, the transition reached a significant degree of completeness as early as 1672. Although the reconquest of New York in the following year brought a brief disruption, the English laws were soon re-established. After 1674, when Sir Edmund Andros repossessed the province for England, the government of the Delaware settlements depended upon three courts of sessions: the oldest of them met at New Castle, another to the south at Whorekill, and a third above New Castle at Upland, later to be known as Chester and to become a part of Pennsylvania.[25] As these subdivisions of responsibility

23 See the proceedings of the General Court of Assizes, 1680–82, in N.Y. Historical Society *Proceedings, Collections* XLV (1912), 3–38. For examples of amendments subsequently promulgated by the Court of Assizes, see *Colonial Laws of New York*, I, 72–100.

24 McKinley, "Transition from Dutch to English Rule"; Bayrd Still, "New York's Mayoralty: The Formative Years," *New-York Historical Society Quarterly*, XLVII (1963), 239–255; and especially Richard B. Morris (ed.), *Select Cases of the Mayor's Court of New York City, 1674–1784* (Washington, 1935), pp. 40–48, which carries a very helpful discussion of the transition from Dutch to English rule in the city.

25 Goebel and Naughton, *Law Enforcement in Colonial New York*, p. 16 n.; Osgood, *American Colonies in the Seventeenth Century*, II, 125, 281–283; H. Clay Reed, "The Early New Castle Court," in *Delaware History*, IV (1951), 227–245; Leon de Valinger, Jr., *Colonial Military Organization in Delaware, 1638–1776* (Wilmington, 1938), pp. 22–25; de Valinger (ed.), *Court Records of Kent County, 1680–1705* (Washington, 1959).

suggest, the evolution was toward a county system of administration, although the formal establishment of counties in the Delaware area, as on the Hudson, did not come until the 1680's.[26] Andros in 1674 by proclamation had extended the English laws to all parts of the province, but this can be misleading. Especially at Albany, and in the much younger community of Schenectady, one finds a pronounced tendency for Dutch law and procedure to survive. As in law, so also in language and social custom, the upper Hudson River Valley would remain for many years very much of a Dutch enclave.

Governor Nicolls had been quick to fasten his highest hopes for an increase of the English population, and for rounding out New York's economy, upon the fertile lands lying between the Hudson and the Delaware. In an unusually revealing letter of July, 1665, to the Earl of Clarendon, he reported that the winter season in the Hudson River Valley was too severe for it to attract more than a few settlers, that the soil of both Connecticut and Long Island was poor, and that Nantucket, Martha's Vineyard, and Maine were of no use to the Duke's estate.[27] The most valuable part of the newly acquired possessions lay across the Hudson in what unhappily had been designated as the separate proprietorship of New Jersey. The letter was written at a time of extreme disappointment, when either he had heard for the first time of the grant the Duke had made a year earlier to John Lord Berkeley and Sir George Carteret, or else when finally he had been forced to surrender such hope as he may have had of persuading York to reconsider.[28] There is no reason for doubting, however, that the letter expressed the carefully considered judgments upon which Nicolls much earlier had based his own plans.

The first of two major grants to be made by him within the limits of New Jersey had come as early as December, 1664. Puritan promoters, mainly from Long Island, had approached the governor in the preceding September with proposals for a settlement there. He agreed on the condition that they first clear the Indian title by purchase and, having been satisfied on this point, he deeded to the

<hr />

26 See below, p. 197.

27 N.Y. Historical Society *Collections*, II (1869), 74–77.

28 According to a letter from York to Governor Lovelace in 1672, Nicolls had been notified of the New Jersey grant by letters of November 28, 1664. Aaron Leaming and Jacob Spicer, *The Grants, Concessions and Original Constitutions of the Province of New Jersey* (Philadelphia, [1752]), p. 31.

purchasers on December 1 an area reaching along the coast from the Passaic River to the Raritan, and inland for almost twice the distance. This, as it came to be known, was the Elizabethtown Grant. The grantees, and their settlers, were promised that they would enjoy "equal freedom, immunities and privileges with any of his majesties' subjects in any of his colonies in America," in return for the payment of "a certain rent according to the customary rate of the country for new plantations."[29] It should be observed that both the guarantee and the limitation were stated only in the most general terms, as though decisions upon specific details had yet to be made.

The details affecting religious and political rights were spelled out well enough in the Duke's Laws of March, 1665. There, too, were found several specific provisions governing new land grants, all of them fundamental in the development of New York's land system.[30] It was required, as the first step toward getting a new deed, that the Indian title be extinguished by purchase. It was promised that all grants would be free of fines and licenses for alienation, as also of other traditional reservations affecting the heirs' rights at the time of inheritance. But once again the question of the rent to be paid the lord proprietor was left in need of clarification, to say the least.

Unfortunately, this question of the rent, never the liveliest of subjects, has critical importance. Not only is it pertinent to an understanding of several troubled chapters in New Jersey's later history, but it bears directly upon the further question of the Duke of York's interest in his proprietorship. For all the distinctive features of that proprietorship, historians generally have assumed that the Duke of York's motivation was basically economic—that, like other proprietors, he hoped above all to find in his proprietorship a profitable extension of his own personal estate.[31] Possibly

[29] For details, see John E. Pomfret, *The Province of East Jersey, 1609–1702* (Princeton, 1962), pp. 35–37; for the quotation, Leaming and Spicer, *Grants,* p. 671.

[30] *Colonial Laws of New York,* I, 44; the best brief account of New York's land system as it developed in the seventeenth century is in Dixon Ryan Fox, *Caleb Heathcote: Gentleman Colonist, the Story of a Career in the Province of New York, 1692–1721* (New York, 1926).

[31] See especially, Andrews, *Colonial Period,* III, 99. Despite the objection that can be made on this point, Andrews' chapter remains by all odds the best discussion of the proprietorship in the literature.

this is true, but the evidence regarding quitrents in proprietary New York raises a serious doubt.

The frequently repeated statement that the Duke's Laws provided for a quitrent of 2s. 6d. per 100 acres is misleading.[32] Actually, the provision is found in an amendment to the Laws that was promulgated by the Court of Assizes in the fall of 1665.[33] When one turns back to the original Laws, he finds only this enigmatic and curiously incomplete provision: "Every Purchaser in acknowledgment of the propriety of such Lands belonging to his Royal Highness James Duke of Yorke, shall upon Sealing of the Pattent Pay unto the Governoure So much as they shall agree upon; not excceding for every hundred Acres [sic]."[34] Presumably the "acknowledgment" could have been intended as a continuing obligation, although it is not so said. If so read, two questions immediately arise, neither of which has as yet an answer. Does the omission of a stated figure indicate that no decision on the rent had been made? Or is the omission attributable to an error in transcription? Whatever may be the fact, the point that requires emphasis is that the governor's apparent purpose was to establish an outside limit on payments, not a minimum.[35] His phrasing strongly suggests that the quitrent was to be a negotiable item in all patents. And this, it

[32] Among others, by Bond, *Quit-rent System*, p. 111. The difficulty, no doubt, is partly one of terminology, for the amendments and additions to the laws given at Hempstead in March, 1665, came, altogether, to be commonly known as the Duke's Laws.

[33] *Colonial Laws of New York*, I, 81, and for the date, pp. 73, 82, where Nicolls under the date of October 30 gives formal confirmation to this and other changes made in General Assizes beginning late in September. The amendment reads: "That every Purchaser &c. shall pay for every hundred Acres as an acknowledgment two Shillings and Six pence." A further clarifying amendment came from Nicolls, under date of February 26, 1665/66, which declared: "That whereas its said in the Lawes, that implanted Lands shall pay 2s. 6d. for every Hundred Acres, as an acknowledgement to the Duke; Its to bee understood of Lands not formerly Planted" (*ibid.*, I, 88). It may be significant for the interpretation of the original document that it was there, in the paragraph immediately preceding the one quoted hereafter, that the phrase "implanted Lands" was used.

[34] *Ibid.*, I, 44. The usual citation for the statement referred to at the beginning of the paragraph above is a combination of pp. 44 and 81.

[35] This assumption would seem to be in conflict with his answer to a query of 1669, after he had retired from the governorship, which declared that the "least" rent for newly purchased lands was 2s. 6d. *Documentary History of the State of New York*, I, 59. But see the evidence cited below that the quitrent was nothing more than a formal acknowledgment.

appears, was the actual practice. An examination of surviving patents by the leading authority on the subject of quitrents in the American colonies has shown that no uniform scale of rents was followed.[36] The "acknowledgment" at times was merely nominal, as in patents specifying the payment of a peppercorn. In other instances, some more valuable consideration, such as a lamb, might be specified. Of comparable significance is the conclusion, by this same authority, that no real effort was made to collect the rents. The quitrent in proprietary New York, in other words, was more a formality, honoring tradition, than a burden actually imposed upon the settlers.

Whatever may be the full explanation, and surely the proprietor's apparent indifference must be taken into account, Governor Nicolls undoubtedly was very largely responsible.[37] It will be helpful, therefore, to consider a special problem he confronted in his persistent attempts to recruit settlers in New England. Because land had been granted free of quitrents in New Netherland, large acreages were permanently exempted from rent in New York by the confirmation of existing titles that had been promised in the conditions of surrender.[38] Obviously, it would have been difficult to collect payments from new settlers that were not demanded of the older inhabitants, and Richard Nicolls was too informed regarding the law and custom of New England not to know that its people too generally paid no rents.

Two other documents are pertinent to the discussion. The first is the so-called Monmouth Grant of April 1665, a patent which conferred title upon a group of Puritan promoters, with Long Islanders again in the lead, to the generous acreage reaching southward from the Raritan to Barnegat Bay. In addition to political and religious guarantees in keeping with the policies already set forth in the Duke's Laws, which were given here an overriding authority, the patentees and their settlers were assured that for seven years they would be free from the payment of any rents, customs, excises, taxes, or levies. Subsequently, they were to

36 Bond, *Quit-rent System*, pp. 111–113. The subject may need closer examination, especially for the period after 1674, but it seems to be doubtful that Bond's general conclusions will be greatly modified.

37 Surviving instructions to Nicolls are so largely concerned with the investigation of New England's affairs that the best evidence we have of what he may have been told to do, or not to do, is what he did.

38 Bond, *Quit-rent System*, pp. 110–111.

pay "after the same Rate, which others within this His Royal Highnesses Territories shall be obliged unto."[39] The second document is a broadside which Nicolls had printed by Samuel Green, at Cambridge, while on a hurried trip to Boston during May, 1665.[40] *The Conditions for New-Planters in the Territories of His Royal Highnes the Duke of York* directed the attention of prospective emigrants throughout New England to the general area lying westward of the Hudson, with particular mention for the valley of the Esopus, which flows from points not greatly distant from the upper Delaware Valley along a route destined much later to be followed by the Delaware and Hudson Canal. The now familiar guarantees of local self-government and religious freedom were repeated, and the land was to be deeded free of "assessments or rates" for a term of five years. Thereafter, the grantees would become liable only "to the publick Rates and Payments, according to the Custom of other Inhabitants, both English and Dutch." Rents were not even mentioned.

It is quite possible that Nicolls acted with no explicit authorization from the Duke of York. But there are difficulties that must be faced by anyone who assumes that his action was out of line with the Duke's wishes, including the fact that Nicolls obviously continued to enjoy York's favor. Indeed, there is difficulty in reaching any assumption other than that the Duke of York's primary interest, at least in the beginning, was political—that he cared for little beyond the need to get the Dutch out of North America. If there are doubts, consider the way in which he gave away New Jersey.

The Jersey grant was made, for no more than a nominal consideration, by a deed of lease and release on June 24, 1664.[41] At that time Colonel Nicolls was hardly more than halfway across the Atlantic. Two full months remained before he would accomplish the first part of his mission with the conquest of New Amsterdam. Not only did the Duke fail to wait for so much as a single report from his lieutenant, but there is no reason for believing that Nicolls had been advised previous to his departure from England of an

---

[39] Leaming and Spicer, *Grants*, pp. 661–663.

[40] *Ibid.*, pp. 667–668. The broadside bears no date, but the time can be fixed by reference to Nicolls' letter to Clarendon, in N.Y. Historical Society *Collections*, II (1869), 74–77, and to Andrews, *Colonial Period*, III, 63 n. For a reproduction of the broadside, see Illustrations, No. 15.

[41] Leaming and Spicer, *Grants*, pp. 8–11.

intent to make the grant. In fact, his own subsequent efforts to develop the New Jersey area under New York's jurisdiction, as also his continuing protests of the Duke's action, strongly argue the very opposite.[42] The deed of lease and release conferred upon Berkeley and Carteret nothing more than title to the soil, and yet York allowed them to assume full jurisdictional rights.[43] Having named the proprietorship New Caesaria, or New Jersey, after Carteret's native Isle of Jersey, the proprietors in the summer of 1665 sent out Philip Carteret, cousin to Sir George, with a commission to serve as governor. Although Governor Nicolls was in no position to challenge the authority claimed by Carteret, the legality of New Jersey's government was destined to remain in doubt for nearly forty years, and repeatedly to the serious disturbance of the colony.

Just as serious, and in some ways more so, was the effect upon New York's subsequent development. By giving away all the land lying between the Hudson and the Delaware rivers, the Duke left his own government, as also most of the people living within its jurisdiction, hemmed in between New England and New Jersey—"cooped up" was the term employed by one of Nicolls' successors.[44] The remote settlements on the far side of the Delaware could be expected to bring no more military strength to New York than they had to New Amsterdam. As for upper Maine and the islands lying off New England's coast, they served chiefly to give to the New York Colony, if that it may be called, as ridiculous a configuration as can be imagined.[45]

It is not easy to explain the Duke of York's decision. He may have been under some pressure from the royal court, where Carteret was vice-chamberlain of the household. Sir George was a famous seaman, who during the Civil Wars had seized and held the Isle of Jersey as a place of refuge for more than one royalist exile, including the prince who now was king.[46] Carteret was also trea-

[42] After returning to England, Nicolls remained hopeful that the Duke might be persuaded to reverse his decision. Pomfret, *East Jersey,* p. 102.

[43] On the technical limitations of the deed of lease and release, see especially Andrews, *Colonial Period,* III, 138 n.

[44] Thomas Dongan, quoted by Andrews, *Colonial Period,* III, 120.

[45] Also to provide an irritant in the relations of New York with the New England colonies. The main outlines can be followed conveniently in Fox, *Yankees and Yorkers.*

[46] See especially the king's promise to remember Carteret's services, quoted in Andrews, *Colonial Period,* III, 187 n. The *Dictionary of National Biography* has a helpful summary of his career.

surer of the Navy, and so closely associated with York in its administration, as was Berkeley, who long had enjoyed the Duke's favor. Both of the Jersey proprietors had participated actively in the planning of the attack upon New Netherland, and in other enterprises directed against the Dutch.[47] In Berkeley's case, some consideration has to be given to the purchase he had made of a half-interest in the Earl of Stirling's claim to Long Island and other territories included in the Duke's charter. It apparently had been necessary to extinguish this claim in order to clear the way for the New York charter, and Berkeley's half-share in New Jersey can be viewed as compensation for his half-interest in the Stirling title.[48]

Whatever the full facts may be, and the record is quite incomplete, the news of the New Jersey grant brought bitter disappointment to Richard Nicolls, who in November, 1665, asked that he might be relieved of his office.[49] Actually, he was to stay on until 1668, but the more productive period of his governorship had reached its end with the coming of the summer of 1665. Within less than the span of a year, he had conquered New Netherland, had laid the foundation for an extraordinarily successful transition there from Dutch to English rule, had drafted an enlightened code of laws which was to have an influence reaching well beyond the limits of what became the New York province, had provided the basic stimulus for a further and highly significant extension of Puritan influence in the area later identified as that of the middle colonies, and had determined in important particulars a pattern of administration that would help to join the middle colonies with their neighbors to the south and on the east in a common devotion to like principles of local self-government. For one who was allowed only a few months to make his mark in history, Richard Nicolls had done very well indeed.

Only in his capacity as the head of the commission for investigation of New England's affairs did he fail of any real achievement.[50] As previously noted, he had gone to Boston in May, 1665, but soon he rushed back to New York because he had received a report that the Dutch were sending De Ruyter for the reconquest of New

47 See above, pp. 59–60.
48 Andrews, *Colonial Period,* III, 58 n.
49 *Ibid.,* III, 107.
50 See above, pp. 66–67.

Netherland.[51] Although this report proved to be false, Nicolls devoted his chief attention for some time thereafter to the defenses of New York. For all practical purposes, the investigation, from its beginning in the winter of 1664–65 to its end a bit over a year later, was conducted by his colleagues, no one of whom was his equal. Maverick was an old and embittered enemy of the Puritan leaders of Massachusetts. Carr lacked both tact and judgment. Cartwright, ablest of the three, was no substitute for Nicolls.

The mission was a delicate one. Indeed, it might almost be described as a hopeless one, especially in the absence of Nicolls' sensible guidance. The commissioners found a friendly enough reception in Connecticut, Rhode Island, and Plymouth, which had some hope of securing a royal charter comparable to those so recently issued to the other two of these provinces. The real test, however, came in Massachusetts. There the commissioners were successful in suspending the jurisdiction of the Bay Colony over York County in Maine,[52] but they were completely frustrated on all the major issues affecting the government of Massachusetts itself. Though not without support from old friends of Maverick, other dissident elements in the population, and some of the more recently arrived merchants,[53] the commissioners failed in their attempted appeal over the head of Governor Bellingham and the magistrates to the general court.[54]

The cost of this signal victory for the Puritan leaders of the colony could have been high. Instead, the continuing demands of the Dutch war and the declining influence of Lord Clarendon combined to save Massachusetts from the penalties recommended to the government in England by the irate commissioners. In 1667, the year of Clarendon's fall from power, Massachusetts contributed some two dozen masts to the Royal Navy, reassumed its jurisdiction over York County, and congratulated itself on having preserved its

[51] Andrews, *Colonial Period*, III, 63 n., where also is found a helpful summary of the itineraries of the four commissioners.

[52] This was according to instructions drafted in behalf of the Gorges family, which claimed the territory under a grant from the old New England Council. Efforts in behalf of the claim of the Mason family to New Hampshire were less successful.

[53] Bailyn, *New England Merchants*, pp. 121–126.

[54] The fullest discussion is in Kaye, *Colonial Administration under Lord Clarendon*, pp. 75–139.

liberties intact. There can be little doubt that the memory of this success explains in part the attitude adopted by Massachusetts when it faced, after the passage of another decade, a more persistent attempt to bring the colony into line.[55]

No less marked was the failure of the commissioners to resolve in any permanent way the several boundary disputes it had been hoped they might settle. Their appointment, it is true, served to bring about the final collapse of the New Haven jurisdiction, and so to remove the most bitterly contested issue then dividing New England, but this result can hardly be attributed to the actual efforts of the commissioners. It happened this way. Massachusetts, which previously had supported New Haven in the quarrel with Connecticut,[56] decided, in the face of the pending investigation, to advise both parties to compose their differences for the sake of the common interest. In the circumstances, this brought strong pressure upon New Haven, already deserted by most of its towns, to surrender and accept membership in the Connecticut jurisdiction. Connecticut's hand was further strengthened by its boundary agreement with Governor Nicolls of New York, for the agreement tended to confirm Hartford's claim under the charter of 1662 to all the mainland between the Connecticut River and Westchester. The signs, indeed, were so clear to read that serious defections, even among its own people, quickly undermined such authority as New Haven had managed to retain. Milford, Branford, and finally, on January 7, 1665, New Haven itself surrendered. By no means the least important result of this surrender was a decision by unreconciled members of the New Haven community to migrate to New Jersey, where Robert Treat and Abraham Pierson were to build in 1666 the Puritan town that was first known as Milford and later as Newark.[57]

The New Haven Puritans had found a ready response to proposals for the accomplishment of this new settlement from Governor Philip Carteret, who was no less anxious than had been Richard Nicolls to attract settlers from New England into New Jersey. Indeed, the proprietors had no other plan for the development of

[55] Andrews, *Colonial Period*, III, 63–68.
[56] See above, p. 50.
[57] Calder, *New Haven Colony*, pp. 249–259; Andrews, *Colonial Period*, II, 192–193.

the area except one depending upon just such a migration. When Governor Carteret landed at Elizabethport in August, 1665, he was accompanied by Robert Vanquillin, a native of Caen who had been appointed as surveyor-general; by James Bollen, who soon was designated as secretary; and by thirty servants, mostly French-speaking recruits from the Channel Isles. The servants presumably provided manpower enough to implement such personal ventures as may have been planned by the governor, the surveyor-general, and the secretary,[58] who taken together suggest nothing quite so much as they do the minimum staff required for the operation of a land office. And there can be little doubt that this is what, above all else, they were intended to be.

For the promotion of the desired immigration from the older colonies, the proprietors had sent wth Philip Carteret an extraordinarily interesting statement of the conditions to be offered new settlers—"The Concessions and Agreement of the Lords Proprietors of New-Caesaria, or New Jersey, to and with all such as shall Settle or Plant there."[59] Considered simply as an announcement of policy by the Jersey proprietors, the document has great importance. But its very special significance is attributable to the fact that it originally had been drafted by the Carolina proprietors in response to a request from Barbadian adventurers for a statement of the conditions upon which they might expect to settle in Carolina. No other single paper reveals quite so much as does this one regarding the hopes and plans of English promoters of colonization during the Restoration era. It will be helpful, therefore, to turn our attention away from New Jersey, for a moment, to consider the special circumstances which first gave shape to the document.

Barbadian planters continued to hold the initiative, and to carry the major responsibility, in the development of plans for the colonization of Carolina. Although the Barbadian adventurers had a few associates in England, New England, other West Indian

---

[58] There is evidence that Carteret later claimed headrights for eighteen of the thirty servants, which could have left twelve for Vanquillin and Bollen. William A. Whitehead, *East Jersey under the Proprietary Governments* (Newark, 1875), pp. 41 n., 59; Edwin P. Tanner, *The Province of New Jersey, 1664–1738* (New York, 1908), pp. 27 n., 35, 83.

[59] Leaming and Spicer, *Grants*, pp. 12–26, and Julian P. Boyd (ed.), *Fundamental Laws and Constitutions of New Jersey, 1664–1964* (Princeton, 1964), pp. 51–66.

plantations, and Bermuda, there can be no doubt that projects for the establishment of new plantations along the Carolina coast had their home in Barbados. Hilton's explorations of 1663 had been followed in May, 1664, by the planting of a colony of Barbadians on the Cape Fear River, in modern North Carolina. An exceedingly ambitious plan called also for the establishment of still another colony at Port Royal, located well below the site of the later city of Charleston and the place at which the French Huguenots in 1562 had first challenged the Spaniard's claim to a monopoly of North America. Among the Barbadians who were active particpants in these enterprises, John Yeamans was the leader, and during the fall of 1664 his son was in England for the purpose of negotiating an agreement with the proprietors that obviously had particular importance for the projected settlement at Port Royal. The proprietors agreed to make a contribution to the defenses of Port Royal that would amount to nearly £300, the only significant financial contribution they were to make to an actual effort to plant a colony in Carolina before 1669. Through their influence at court, they contributed also a baronetcy for Yeamans, who henceforth was to be known as Sir John.[60] But chiefly they contributed "The Concessions and Agreement," which received the proprietary seal on January 7, 1665.[61]

Berkeley and Carteret, both of whom were Carolina proprietors and so in position to have influenced the original, issued the Concessions as a statement of conditions for settlement in New Jersey over the date of February 10, 1665. Only occasionally, and in relatively minor details, had they bothered to amend its provisions. For all practical purposes, the two copies are one and the same.

The most arresting single observation that comes from a reading of the Concessions, in either copy, is that it obviously had been drafted with close attention to the appeal it might have for the inhabitants of New England. Why this should be true of a paper written for the encouragement of a Barbadian adventure is an interesting question, but there is no mystery. At the very time of its drafting, the Carolina proprietors recorded their hope that New England might become a major field of recruitment for the settle-

60 Craven, *Southern Colonies*, pp. 329–331, 333.
61 Parker, *North Carolina Charters*, pp. 107–127; Saunders, *Colonial Records of North Carolina*, I, 79–92.

ment of their province.[62] The basis for this hope is not so well
documented. One thinks at once of the New England associates of
the Barbadian adventurers, of the growing trade between New
England and the West Indies, and of the earlier landing by New
Englanders, with cattle, on the Cape Fear River.[63] There are
further opportunities for speculation, including the possibility that
New Jersey's proprietors may have contributed significantly to the
Concessions with a view to the double use to which it was later put.
But of one point we can be certain and that is that the Concessions
and Agreement of 1665 offer additional testimony to the high
regard with which Englishmen interested in the colonies at the time
of the Restoration viewed the achievements of the Puritan colonists.

Some of the document's provisions are more important for an
understanding of the history of one of the ventures than they are
for the other. For example, the headright, borrowed from the usages
of Virginia and Maryland as a convenient unit of measurement for
the distribution of land among new settlers, seems to have had
slight influence on the history of New Jersey—indeed, to have been
included with a view primarily to the needs of the Carolina project.
Even so, each copy specified that land would be awarded according
to a scale of headright claims dropping down every year from the
150 acres promised each free man and woman going in the first
voyage to Port Royal, or to New Jersey, until the award leveled off
in 1667 at sixty acres. Each copy also provided that the same awards
would be made for every "able man servant" carried or sent to the
colony, and that lesser acreages would be allowed for "weaker
servants," who were described as "women, Children, and Slaves."[64]
But the question whether the Jersey proprietors made any extensive
use of this device for the distribution of land matters much less than
does the revelation these provisions offer of the essentially similar
approach by each group of proprietors to the economic problem of
colonization. In both instances, the proprietors planned to use a
liberal land grant as a subsidy for the immigration that was
fundamental to the development of the estate they had acquired by
royal or ducal grant. The land was offered in free and common
socage tenure to the grantee, his heirs, or assigns, in return for an

62 Craven, *Southern Colonies*, p. 329.
63 See above, p. 57.
64 Parker, *North Carolina Charters*, p. 120.

annual rent of half a penny per acre, the first payment falling due in 1670. There can be no mistake as to what was the primary purpose of the Carolina and New Jersey colonies. Each was intended to become, for the proprietors, their heirs, and their assigns, a rent-producing estate.[65]

To the promise of generous land grants the proprietors added political and religious guarantees that were extraordinarily liberal by any standard other than that already established by the Restoration government, and soon to be established by the Duke's Laws. In New Jersey and in each of the three widely separated Carolina settlements, existing and projected, the government was to be entrusted to a governor, council, and general assembly. The Carolina proprietors designated each of their colonies a county, the settlement on Albemarle Sound becoming thus Albemarle County, but the pattern for the government of each of the counties was actually that of a provincial administration. It was provided that as lesser, or local, units of government were established these would become the constituences for deputies representing the "Inhabitants or Freeholders" in the general assembly. That body, comprising the governor, council, and the elected delegates, was to meet annually, and to have very broad legislative authority. It was empowered to establish courts, to provide for local government, to levy taxes, to fix fees and salaries, and even to specify conditions affecting the distribution of land among the settlers. These extensive legislative powers were held subject to three comparably broad limitations: no law was to be allowed that was contrary "to the Interest of . . . the Lords Proprietors," to the laws and customs of England, or to provisions of the Concessions and Agreement.[66] Briefly stated, prospective settlers in Carolina and New Jersey were promised a voice in the conduct of provincial affairs

[65] No doubt, the question of rent collection was the primary consideration making the secretary in each colony responsible for keeping a registry of all land grants made in behalf of the proprietors, as also of all conveyances and leases "from man to man." It was stipulated that the recorded deed or lease would have priority at law over any other that might exist, a point of some significance for the history of recorded titles in the United States. See above, p. 23.

[66] It was also stipulated that laws would be in force for a year and a half unless disallowed by the proprietors, and that with their confirmation laws would continue in force until they expired by their own limitation or by an act of repeal. Parker, *North Carolina Charters*, pp. 115–116.

that was strong enough to protect also whatever rights of local self-government they might deem to be necessary.

Provisions governing religion have a special interest, and a certain complexity that demands close reading, if they are to be fully understood. The basic guarantee was that no colonist, or colonies, would be "any ways molested, punished, disquieted, or called in question for any differences in opinion or practice in matters of religious Concernment, who do not actually disturb the Civil peace. . . ."[67] Because the Carolina charter had conferred upon the grantees "the Patronage and Advowsons of all the Churches and Chapels . . . to be erected" in the proprietorship, together with power to build and found churches, "and to cause them to be Dedicated and Consecrated according to the Ecclesiastical Laws of . . . England,"[68] it was promised by the lords proprietors, for themselves, their heirs, and their assigns, that this power would never be used to infringe the "Liberty of Conscience" granted by the Concessions and Agreement. To make the promise still more binding, the proprietors gave to the general assemblies, and in the same paragraph, the "power, by act, to constitute and appoint such and so many Ministers or Preachers as they shall think fit, and to establish their maintenance; Giving Liberty besides to any person or persons to keep and maintain what preachers or ministers they please."[69]

This, of course, was essentially the religious policy Governor Nicolls shortly thereafter would announce in the Duke's Laws.[70] He too proclaimed liberty of conscience for all inhabitants, and then linked this liberty with the requirement that every town build a church and provide for the support of a minister of its own choice. The Carolina and New Jersey proprietors imposed no such obligation. Instead, their action in the grant of power to the legislative assembly was permissive, but there can be no doubt that the purpose was the same—which was to define a policy that would make allowance both for the divergences of religious opinion among the colonists and for the desire by communities of like-minded men to use the full sanction of public authority for the support of their own churches.

[67] *Ibid.*, p. 114.
[68] The best account of Albemarle County is found in the earlier pages of 1665.
[69] *Ibid.*, p. 114.
[70] See above, pp. 76–77.

Although Governor Carteret's announcement of these guarantees was quickly followed by a growing migration from New England into New Jersey, there is no way of determining how far the Concessions and Agreement can be credited with it. The movement had received its initial impulse from the efforts of Richard Nicolls. Presumably, the Concessions provided an encouraging confirmation of the political and religious assurances he had given. In other words, less liberal provisions conceivably might have brought a check to the movement, but to put the point thus is to raise the critical question of why the provision for quitrents brought no such check. The attempt to collect the rents after 1670, when they first fell due, resulted in open rebellion that kept the colony in turmoil for better than two years. Unfortunately, the story of this rebellion, the first of its kind in our history, is poorly documented. But if only for that reason, it has overshadowing importance for any discussion of New Jersey's early settlement.

When Carteret landed at Elizabethport in August, 1665, he found there four English families, and that was all. The Monmouth patentees, though holding the later of Nicolls' two grants, had moved more promptly, with the result that the towns of Middletown and Shrewsbury already were reasonably well established.[71] The governor bought out one of the Elizabeth patentees, thus becoming an associate in the project.[72] This may have been a mistake. Not only did his action tend to confirm claims held under grant from Governor Nicolls of New York, but there could have been some confusion as to the capacity in which he acted in subsequent negotiations with the New Englanders who settled at Elizabeth, Woodbridge, and Piscataway.[73] There is evidence that he was careful to protect the rights of his superiors, but the date at times also suggests that he may not have been so careful at first as experience taught him later to be.[74] Whatever the full facts, the resistance to the payment of rents after 1670 was centered mainly in the areas covered by the Elizabeth and Monmouth patents.

Trouble had come as early as 1668. When in that year the first general assembly met, the Monmouth towns refused to be repre-

71 Andrews, *Colonial Period*, III, 141–142; Whitehead, *East Jersey*, pp. 17–49.
72 Pomfret, *East Jersey*, p. 38.
73 *Ibid.*, pp. 34–55, for detailed account of the early settlements.
74 See, for example, the Woodbridge charter of 1669 in Whitehead, *East Jersey*, pp. 286–288.

sented except on an understanding that there could be no infringement of the rights they held under grant from Governor Nicolls. These conditions, of course, were unacceptable, and their delegates were not seated. Whereupon, Middletown and Shrewsbury refused payment of a tax voted by the assembly, citing their exemption for a period of seven years under the Nicolls patent. The inhabitants of Middletown, in town meeting, explained their refusal to swear allegiance to "the absolute Lords Proprietors," as was demanded, on the ground that such an oath would make them "absolute tenants." They were prepared to acknowledge the rightful authority of the proprietary government, but only insofar as they did not sacrifice their own rights under their patent.[75]

The details of the later rebellion need not long detain us. Interestingly, the stoutest resistance came this time from those holding their lands under the Elizabeth patent. An irregular assembly of May, 1672, so far defied the authority of the governor as to elect as its president James Carteret, a son of the proprietor who had stopped off in the colony while on his way to Carolina. His acceptance, to say the least, was unwise, for his co-operation with the insurgents was subsequently repudiated by his father. Governor Carteret during the summer of 1672 carried the issues to England, where he received the full backing of the proprietors. The Dutch reconquest of New York in 1673 delayed enforcement of new instructions for a general submission until Governor Carteret's return to New Jersey in 1674. In sum, these instructions stipulated that no man be allowed to participate in the government who had not secured a proprietary patent and paid the rent therein required. As backing, the proprietors had secured from the Duke of York a disallowance of the troublesome patents granted by Nicolls.[76] Quitrents were to be paid in colonial New Jersey, but only after vigorous protest. Each side in this dispute had ground upon which to stand, but the question of who technically had the better argument is less important than is another point. The American colonist, upon whose ambition and enterprise depended so largely

---

[75] Pomfret, *East Jersey*, pp. 56–59.

[76] *Ibid.*, pp. 60–81; Andrews, *Colonial Period*, III, 144–150; Bond, *Quit-rent System*, pp. 84–88. The settlers at Newark and other groups who had settled by agreement with the proprietors' agents were in a different position. In their case, the issue tended to turn on the question of how the rents were to be paid.

the promotional plans of the Restoration colonizers, had a keen sense of the contribution he himself had made, and was making, to the promotion of the English interest in North America. Out of this came a strong disinclination to pay tribute to anyone for the land he developed by his own labors, an attitude that was in fundamental conflict with proprietary aims and prerogatives.[77]

The Puritan settlers who so largely shaped the life of early New Jersey came from all parts of New England, and brought with them diverse religious opinions. At Newark the most orthodox struggled to rebuild the Zion they formerly had known in New Haven. At Piscataway, Baptists and Quakers shared the task. The town pattern of settlement was followed, though often with some adjustment to the generous acreages that could be had in New Jersey for the purposes of settlement. Perhaps, it should be said that in the very act of migration the town was becoming the township upon which the state still depends as its basic unit of local government.[78] With the town came the town meeting, which over the years ahead would share the responsibilities of local government with commissioned magistrates who functioned in ways that foretold the later adoption of a county system of administration.[79] But not all of the settlers were New Englanders. In addition to those who came with Governor Carteret, there was the small Dutch settlement in the neighborhood of Bergen (all told perhaps 200 souls in 1664), one destined to grow by further migration across the river from New York.[80] There were also a number of immigrants from Barbados, some of them destined to become very influential, and notably the founders of the Morris family of New Jersey and New York.[81]

[77] The background, and long-range implications, of this attitude are discussed in Craven, New Jersey and the English Colonization of North America.

[78] Lewis Morris in 1700 wrote that the towns there "are not like the towns of England . . . the houses built close together on a small spot of ground . . . but they include large portions of the country, of four, five, eight, ten, twelve, fifteen miles in length, and as much in breadth." Quoted in Wertenbaker, Middle Colonies, p. 135.

[79] Roughly in the 1680's, at about the same time that the New York, Delaware, and Pennsylvania settlements were so divided. See below, pp. 197, 209.

[80] It is to this postconquest migration, rather than to the Dutch period, that New Jersey owes its substantial Dutch community of the later colonial period. See Adrian C. Leiby, The Early Dutch and Swedish Settlers of New Jersey (Princeton, 1964), pp. 65 ff.

[81] See D.A.B. article on Lewis Morris (1671–1746), whose father Richard and his brother Lewis migrated from Barbados to New York in 1670. The elder

Perhaps the Barbadians were drawn to New Jersey because the opportunities there had been made known to them by the Concessions and Agreement. Perhaps it was because they shared religious convictions with some of the New England settlers.[82] Perhaps it was because the Carolina venture, upon which the Barbadians had fastened high hopes, continued to be plagued by misfortune and failure. Although it was reported in 1666 that the Barbadian settlement on the Cape Fear River had grown to approximately 800 persons,[83] the place had been completely abandoned by the end of 1667. There are a few clues, but only a few, as to what happened. It is evident that there had been trouble with the Indians, and that the colonists, who had begun their settlement before the Concessions and Agreement of 1665, were not satisfied with plans which tended to subordinate the Cape Fear project to the hope of achieving a settlement of Port Royal. Among other things, the settlers objected to the preference given the Port Royal project by the assignment to it of higher headrights than were allowed for Cape Fear. The Port Royal venture seems also to have been based in part upon the Cape Fear, and so to have imposed an unhelpful burden upon a community still struggling to establish itself. Certainly, a succession of misfortunes attending Yeamans' efforts to complete the exploration of the Port Royal region contributed to a declining zeal among Barbadians for investment in Carolina.[84] Not until the proprietors themselves had agreed to assume the responsibilities of their position would the Barbadians show a reviving interest.

Once more Albemarle Sound boasted the only settlement in Carolina, but in its lagging development there was little really of which to boast. It traced its beginnings to the restless energies of Virginia's expanding population, and presumably might have enjoyed a continuing advantage from its proximity to that colony. But those who in Virginia wished to move on found it easier to get to Maryland, where an expanding frontier of settlement is marked for

Lewis subsequently acquired extensive property in New Jersey, which was inherited by his nephew. See also Whitehead, *East Jersey,* pp. 54–55, 116–117, for a grant of 1668 that came to be known as New Barbadoes.

[82] It should be noted that Richard Morris had fought in Cromwell's army, and that his brother was a Quaker.

[83] In a promotional pamphlet. See Salley, *Narratives of Early Carolina,* p. 67.

[84] Craven, *Southern Colonies,* pp. 330–333.

us by the creation of eight new counties between 1650 and 1674, the last being Cecil at the very head of the Chesapeake.[85] From Virginia southward the overland route ran through difficult country, which included the Dismal Swamp, and the way by sea through the often dangerous waters of the upper Carolina coast. Then, as later, the Albemarle settlement was virtually landlocked, and only New England ships seem ever to have bothered to come there for trade.

An intelligently conceived promotional policy might have helped Albemarle, but from the first the proprietors favored the Cape Fear and Port Royal projects. By 1667 the headright in Albemarle had fallen from the eighty acres allowed originally by the Concessions and Agreement to forty, which compared unfavorably with Virginia's long-established fifty acres. Similarly, the halfpenny quitrent was double that demanded in either Virginia or Maryland. Although a petition from the Albemarle assembly that the inhabitants might hold their land on the same conditions as did the Virginia colonists was granted by the proprietors in 1668, legislation of the following year clearly indicates that more than this was needed. Borrowing from an earlier statute of Virginia, the assembly promised all newcomers exemption from taxes for one year after settlement plus a stay of five years in prosecutions for debts contracted outside the colony. The poverty of the community received special emphasis in another law which provided for marriage by civil officers on the ground that the colony had no minister.[86]

When the Carolina proprietors in 1669 finally bestirred themselves to assume the responsibilities of their position, they once more turned their attention away from Albemarle to Port Royal. Of the original proprietors, Lord Clarendon was now in exile, Sir John Colleton was dead, and other members of the board showed an interest in proportion only to their investment, which so far had been a small one.[87] But there was one exception, at least. Cooper, now Lord Ashley and soon to become the first earl of Shaftesbury, brought the proprietors to an agreement in the spring of 1669 that they would each subscribe £500 to a common fund for the settle-

---

85 *Ibid.,* p. 303.
86 The best account of Albemarle County is found in the earlier pages of Lefler and Newsome, *North Carolina.*
87 See above, p. 57.

ment of Port Royal. Not all responded, but a total of better than £3,000 was contributed and invested in an expedition of three ships which sailed from England for Barbados in the following August under the command of Joseph West. Although a hundred prospective settlers were carried out from England and Ireland, the basic policy of the proprietors remained unchanged, for they still planned to depend chiefly upon settlers drawn from other parts of America, and more particularly from Barbados. The new departure was that the proprietors now proposed to underwrite the actual work of settlement. They would provide shipping for the transport of settlers and their goods; the three vessels, of which only one was of any size, were to remain indefinitely in the colony's service. The proprietors promised also to advance such credit as prospective settlers might need for supplies shipped now from England or purchased subsequently in the older colonies on the proprietors' account. The interest to be charged on the advance thus made was large enough to carry a promise that the venture would be self-liquidating. But this was not a commercial venture. As Shaftesbury later explained, the proprietors aimed not "at the profit of merchants but the incouragement of landlords."[88] By underwriting the original settlement, they hoped the sooner to enjoy their rents from a profitably developed estate.

The plan for underwriting the project extended even to a substantial investment in agricultural experimentation. Thirty servants to be recruited in Ireland by West on his way to Barbados were to be used for the development of an experimental farm testing a wide variety of possible staple crops—cotton, ginger, indigo, sugar, grapes, olives, and any other such like as could be had for trial, except the tobacco already in too plentiful supply. Liberal headrights, beginning at 150 acres, were promised the settlers, together with a postponement of the first payment of rents until 1689. The rent stipulated was double the halfpenny per acre formerly demanded, no doubt in consideration of the heavy risk now assumed by the proprietors. Advertisement was to be made in Barbados that claims to land in Carolina surviving from earlier adventures would be fully honored. Nowhere was it made clearer

---

[88] Quoted in Brown, *First Earl of Shaftesbury,* p. 171. For the general discussion, see Craven, *Southern Colonies,* pp. 334 ff.

that the overriding purpose in 1669 was a revival of the Barbadian adventure than in the blank commission for the governor's post that was carried by West, together with instructions to Sir John Yeamans that he fill in his own name or that of such other person as he might choose.[89]

West reached Barbados in October, where he was delayed by a severe gale. When he finally got away, he was forced by the still stormy weather to take refuge in Bermuda. Yeamans, who had sailed with West from Barbados, at this point decided that he would not go on to Carolina, and appointed William Sayle, a septuagenarian and former governor of Bermuda, to go in his place as governor. Sayle and West reached Port Royal in April 1670, but they quickly decided to seek some more northerly site, perhaps to put a safer distance between the new colony and the Spanish fort at St. Augustine. Their choice was a place some twenty-five miles up the river destined to carry the name of Lord Ashley, and there they built their town, naming it for King Charles. Only after a decade had passed would the colonists abandon this site in favor of a location at the confluence of the Ashley with the Cooper, where Charleston stands today.[90]

Further and extraordinary testimony to the proprietors' fresh interest in their province is provided by the "Fundamental Constitutions" they agreed upon in July, 1669, and sent out with West. The copy he carried, and which subsequently was sent to Albemarle, seems to have been only a draft, for it was later revised and finally given the date of March 1, 1670.[91] Because Ashley was so obviously the leading spirit in the revival of the Carolina project, it has to be assumed that he was very largely responsible, but there is no way of establishing what he may have had to concede to his colleagues in order to get their co-operation. This last consideration is pertinent also to the intriguing and probably unanswerable question of how far the document reflects the influence of John Locke, confidant of Ashley and secretary to the proprietors from 1668 to 1675.[92] There is reason for believing that James Harring-

---

[89] The pertinent record is found chiefly in Shaftesbury's own papers, in *Collections of the South Carolina Historical Society*, V (1897).

[90] Until 1783 the name was Charles Town.

[91] For texts, see Parker, *North Carolina Charters*, pp. 128–185.

[92] Maurice Cranston, *John Locke, a Biography* (London, 1957), pp. 119–120, suggests that the influence may have been considerable. Peter Laslett, in his

ton, another of England's political philosophers of the seventeenth
century, had more influence upon the contents of the document
than did Locke, though not of course by direct participation in its
drafting.[93] The document itself, in the revised version, ran to 120
separate articles, which taken together almost defy any attempt at a
brief description. At one and the same time, the paper suggests that
the proprietors were guided by an ideal almost unbelievably ill-
suited to the American scene and also by a very hardheaded understanding of the realities of that scene. Perhaps this was precisely the
stage the attitude of Englishmen toward America, at any rate of
those who bothered at all to think of America, at this time had
reached.

The ideal was the hope that the balance between the aristocratic
and more democratic elements of society, which Harrington had
taught Englishmen of this generation to regard as a source of
strength in their own society, might be transferred to the New
World by a judicious control over the distribution of property. The
colony was to be settled in accordance with a symmetrical plan of
survey, one county at a time, calling for the division of the land in
such a way as to assure that in each county three-fifths of the land
would be held by freeholders and two-fifths in perpetuity by the
proprietors and the colony's own hereditary nobility. It should not
be overlooked that the Constitutions assumed that any one of the
lord proprietors, most of them great men in England, might elect to
transfer his residence to Carolina. If he did so, it was provided that
he would outrank any member of the Carolina peerage, for which
the distinctive titles of landgrave and cacique were established.
Each of the seigniories, baronies, and manors to be established
would have its court leet, and the freeholds would be divided for
purposes of local administration into precincts, four to a county.
The oldest lord proprietor in residence automatically would become

especially authoritative edition of the *Two Treatises of Government* (Cambridge,
Eng., 1960), pp. 29–30, concludes that we probably never will know exactly the
extent of Locke's influence and comments upon the contrast in views expressed in
the Constitutions and the later *Treatises*. But he also notes that Locke a decade
later referred to the document as though he had been responsible for it, and in
editing the text of the *Treatises* Laslett occasionally cites parallels between the
two documents. Fortunately, the question is of much more importance for
students of Locke than for students of Carolina's history.

[93] H. F. Russell Smith, *Harrington and His Oceana: A Study of a 17th Century
Utopia and Its Influence in America* (Cambridge, Eng., 1914), is suggestive.

the governor, and each of the proprietors not in residence would be represented by a deputy of his individual choice. The governor, all resident proprietors, the proprietary deputies, the landgraves, the caciques, and elected freeholders, one from each precinct, would sit together as a parliament for the enactment of laws recommended to it by a grand council comprising the great men of the province. The franchise belonged to all fifty-acre freeholders, but to qualify for election to the parliament a man must possess as much as 500 acres. In short, political power at all levels depended upon the property a man might hold.

To the modern American this elaborate attempt to transfer the standards and values of an Old World society to the New World must always seem unrealistic. The proprietors almost admitted the point when they advised the colonists to look upon the Constitutions as a guide to the ultimate goal, rather than as an objective that could be immediately achieved.[94] Resulting uncertainties as to the fundamental law which governed the colony would be troublesome for many years to come, but it should not be forgotten that the proprietors in proposing their extraordinary equation of power and property also proposed to give away the property on the most generous terms to anyone willing and able to gamble on the future of Carolina. They were particularly anxious to attract men of means, those who had capital to invest in the development of the colony, and the suggestion that such a man might become in Carolina as great as any lord in England was probably a more shrewdly conceived promotional device than the modern American can readily recognize.[95]

Several provisions remind us that the proprietors hoped especially to attract settlers from Barbados, as in the guarantee provided in the Constitutions that any settler going to Carolina would enjoy there "absolute Power and Authority over his Negro Slaves."[96] And

94 *Collections of the South Carolina Historical Society,* V (1897) , 119.

95 See Craven, *Southern Colonies,* p. 327, for the advice of Surveyor Thomas Woodward from Albemarle in 1665: "Rich men (which Albemarle stands in much need of) may perhaps take up great Tracts, but then they will endeavour to procure Tenants to helpe towards the payment of their Rent, and will at their owne charge build howseing (which poore men cannot compasse) to invite them."

96 Parker, *North Carolina Charters,* pp. 150, 164, 183. The word "Power" was added after the first draft in an obvious attempt to strengthen the provision.

this was accompanied by a provision entitling the Negro to enjoy full membership in the Christian church, but on the understanding that admission to the church would not affect his legal status as a slave.[97] It was consistent with the Carolina charter that the proprietors should require the colony's legislature, after the colony had been "sufficiently planted," to make provision for the public support of the Anglican Church, but there is some reason for believing that this requirement was intended for the assurance of Barbadians they hoped to recruit. At any rate, most of those who soon migrated from the island to Carolina later showed an inclination to identify themselves as Anglicans. There was no retreat, however, from the proprietor's firm adherence to the principle of religious liberty that had been so fundamental in the promotional efforts of all the Restoration proprietors. The Jew and even the "Heathen" were specifically protected in articles imposing no limits on their freedom other than a requirement that they "acknowledge a God, and that God is publicly and Solemnly to be worshipped." Membership in some church would be required, but any seven men would have the right to organize a church of their own, and all others were forbidden to use "any reproachful, reviling, or abusive Language" with reference to such a church. No religious test for office was established, and the colonists were "to bear Witness to Truth," each in his own way.[98] The invitation to the Quakers, who had been active in the West Indies as elsewhere, is obvious.

It is hardly necessary to add that the development of the new colony showed early and marked divergences from the great plan of its founders. A generation would pass before action was taken to establish the Anglican Church. The proprietors, in keeping with their announcement that the Constitutions represented an ultimate

---

[97] *Ibid.*, p. 183, where section 107 reads: "Since Charity obliges us to wish well to the Souls of all Men, and Religion ought to alter nothing in any Man's Civil Estate or Right, it shall be lawful for Slaves, as well as others, to Enter themselves and be of what Church or Profession any of them shall think best, and thereof be as fully Members as any Freeman. But yet, no Slave shall hereby be exempted from that Civil Dominion his Master has over him, but be in all other things in the same State and Condition he was in before." This passage acquires additional interest because it may have been written by Locke, who earlier had written an unpublished essay on toleration. See Laslett's edition of the *Two Treatises*, p. 29.

[98] Parker, *North Carolina Charters*, pp. 181–183.

rather than an immediate goal, established a provisional government which in its main outline followed rather closely the standard prevailing in other colonies. Leadership was entrusted to a governor and a council composed of the proprietary deputies and five men elected from the membership of the parliament, as the provincial legislature was at first designated. The parliament included the governor, the council, and twenty delegates elected by the freemen. Its members sat as one body and its function was limited to action upon proposals laid before it by the governor and council. Governor Sayle having died in March, 1671, he was succeeded by Joseph West and after a year by Sir John Yeamans, who remained in office until his death in 1674.[99]

Yeamans' succession to the governor's post in 1672 may be taken as a convenient mark of the rising influence of the Barbadians, who for a decade were to be by far the most numerous of the immigrants entering the colony and who found leadership in such men as Maurice Mathews, James Moore, and Arthur Middleton. For the systematic pattern of settlement proposed by the proprietors the colonists substituted a first-come, first-served occupation of lands fronting on convenient waterways. Hopes for an early discovery of a highly profitable staple, or staples, met with disappointment. But cattle brought from the older settlements flourished, and after a few years of the usual shortages and hardships, the colony began to produce a surplus of foodstuffs, meat and cereal, which found a ready market in the West Indies.[100] Still another foundation for the colony's later prosperity was laid in the opening of a trade with the Indians, but to that subject we can return on another page. The point here is that the venture launched by the proprietors in 1669 was soon winning a modest degree of success, though it would continue for many years to fall far short of the high hopes which had inspired it.

99 Sirmans, *Colonial South Carolina*, pp. 15–29.
100 Craven, *Southern Colonies*, pp. 355–358.

CHAPTER 4

The Indian Neighbor

FOR both England and the colonies, the 1670's were an especially troubled time. A third and needless war with Holland began in 1672. The growing power of Louis XIV of France argued strongly for an accommodation of Anglo-Dutch differences in the face of a threat potentially as dangerous to the overseas interests of the two states as it was to their security in Europe. But Charles II elected to gamble on an alliance with France which brought him a French subsidy for the relief of persistent financial embarrassments, and so the lot was cast for war.[1]

Nowhere did the war go very well for the English, and in North America it went very badly indeed, thanks largely to the often ungovernable fortunes of war itself. Late in 1672, Cornelius Evertsen, who was of a family famous in Dutch naval annals, sailed from Holland for America with four men-of-war and a complement of 150 marines commanded by Captain Antony Colve. In the West Indies, Evertsen joined forces with Jacob Binckes, who also had four men-of-war.[2] After destroying the English fortifications on St. Eustatius, the joint forces sailed north for a foray into the Chesapeake, where in July, 1673, they captured nine English vessels.[3] So

[1] Keith Feiling, *British Foreign Policy, 1660–1672* (London, 1930); and for a shorter discussion, G. N. Clark, *The Later Stuarts, 1660–1714* (Oxford, 1934), pp. 66–79.

[2] Van Rensselaer, *History of the City of New York*, II, 98–99.

[3] Thomas J. Wertenbaker, *Virginia under the Stuarts, 1607–1688* (Princeton, 1914), pp. 129–130.

far the Hollanders had sought only to injure their foe and to seize enough booty, as Evertsen's instructions had frugally advised, to cover the costs of the expedition. But on the way out from the Chesapeake the swollen Dutch fleet seized an English sloop on the way in from New York, thereby gaining intelligence which encouraged an attempt to recapture that place.[4] This was done at the end of July, with no great difficulty, and soon thereafter Dutch rule was re-established throughout the former province of New Netherland, except for the easternmost of the Puritan towns on Long Island.[5] When the Dutch fleet sailed for home in September, carrying a substantial part of the English garrison, Antony Colve was left behind as governor.

This disastrous turn of events naturally threw a scare into New England, where the several governments gave first thought to preparing their defenses against the prospect that Evertsen might next strike there. When the departure of the Dutch fleet brought relief from that fear, the New Englanders postponed serious thought of joint action against New Orange, as New York had been renamed, until instructions, and possibly help, came from England. Only Connecticut became involved in actual hostilities, and these were conducted for the limited objective of re-establishing its title to Long Island, where the more easterly towns, with Connecticut's support, continued to resist Governor Colve.[6] New England's decision in the end proved to be the right one, for in 1674 came the news that peace had been concluded with the Dutch on the principle of a return to the situation *ante bellum*.

For the Dutch the war quickly had become a struggle to maintain the independence of Holland itself against French armies penetrating her own borders. William of Orange, called now to the office of stadtholder traditionally belonging to his family, sought a separate peace with England while building on the continent a coalition against Louis.

For Englishmen too the war had been, at home as in America, an unhappy venture. On the very eve of hostilities Charles II had issued a Declaration of Indulgence extending religious toleration

4 Van Rensselaer, *History of the City of New York*, II, 99–100.
5 Van Rensselaer and Brodhead, *History of the State of New York*, II, 205 ff., provide full accounts of the Dutch interlude.
6 See again Dunn, "John Winthrop, Jr., Connecticut Expansionist," pp. 3–26.

both to Catholics and to Protestant dissenters. Though welcomed at first by some of the dissenters, an unfavorable reaction quickly followed. Although King Charles' subsidies from Louis XIV depended upon a secret treaty, its existence was widely suspected long before the fact became generally known. As a consequence the French alliance prompted a growing suspicion that England faced a Catholic conspiracy to strengthen royal power at the expense of Parliament, a fear that would disturb English politics for many years to come. Parliament yielded up the funds needed for the war only on the king's agreement to recall the Declaration of Indulgence and to accept the Test Act of 1673, which made adherence to the Church of England a test for the holding of any office, civil or military. With no major military achievement to offset the suspicions of his people, Charles II ultimately had to accept William's offer of peace. The Treaty of Westminster came in May, 1674.

English rule was re-established in New York during the following November, when Major Edmund Andros arrived with a contingent of 100 troops. Legal requirements arising from the Hollanders' repossession of the area had caused the king to reissue his brother's charter of 1664, without change in any of its provisions, territorial or other, and Andros bore the Duke's commission to serve as governor over all the extraordinary collection of territories originally granted by that charter.[7] One might think that the Duke of York, who as a Catholic had withdrawn from the office of Lord High Admiral after the enactment of the Test Act, and who presumably now had more time for his responsibilities as a proprietor, had reconsidered some of his former actions. But that he had is not at all certain. He promptly had reconfirmed Sir George Carteret's half-interest in New Jersey, and probably would have done the same for John Berkeley except for the fact that Berkeley, whose fortunes were in decline, sold his half-share this same year to Edward Byllynge, a Quaker acquaintance of his.[8] Byllynge's affairs were in a very tangled state, and not until 1680 would York confirm his claim to title.[9]

[7] Van Rensselaer, *History of the City of New York*, II, 124–126, 167–168; Andrews, *Colonial Period*, III, 111, 151–152; and for Andros's commission and instructions, N.Y. *Colonial Documents*, III, 215–219.

[8] Pomfret, *East Jersey*, pp. 102–103.

[9] See below, pp. 188–189, 204.

The resulting complications are almost unbelievable. In the confirmation of Carteret's title, his half-interest was defined as the upper half of New Jersey, which is to say that the Duke now gave to Carteret the entire settled area of the colony, the part destined soon to be known as East Jersey. This left for Byllynge the virtually unoccupied wilderness that was to become West Jersey and the first seat of Quaker settlement in the Delaware Valley. Henceforth, there were to be two Jersey colonies, not just one, each of them suffering through many years from uncertainty as to the legality of its government.

These difficulties in the more recently acquired of England's possessions were quickly cast in the shadow by the tragic events which in 1675 and 1676 shook to the very foundations the older of the English settlements in North America. Hardly had the fears stirred by the Dutch recapture of New York been set at rest before New England found itself engaged in the bitter struggle that is known as King Philip's War, which still has a claim to being considered the bloodiest and most costly war of our history. And hardly had the grass begun to grow upon New England's countless graves before Bacon's Rebellion pitted Virginian against Virginian in the most destructive civil war of American colonial history.

The two wars had nothing more in common, aside from the coincidence of time, than the fact that they both owed their origins to the discontent of the Indian. Bacon's Rebellion had its beginning in a quarrel among the colonists over Indian policy, a quarrel precipitated by damaging attacks upon the colony's frontier settlements in January, 1676. The attacks, certainly in very large part, had been made by roving bands of the Susquehannah Indians, who recently had been defeated by the Iroquois in a long war that ultimately forced the surviving Susquehannahs back upon the upper Chesapeake in search of a refuge they failed to find. The fear which seized the Virginians after the January attacks was intensified by the dreadful news from New England which reached Jamestown late in the winter and encouraged men to believe that they faced a conspiracy among all of the Indians, from north to south, against the English.[10] No such conspiracy existed, of course, but obviously

10 Wilcomb E. Washburn, "Governor Berkeley and King Philip's War," *New England Quarterly*, XXX (1957), 363–377.

one of the climactic moments which repeatedly have punctuated the history of relations between the American settler and the Indian had been reached.

Although the story of that relationship is complex and difficult, some attempt here at generalization may be helpful. The invitation to make the attempt is the more inviting because each of the developments just mentioned is representative of a distinct aspect of the general problem. In Virginia we see the all too familiar clash that so often occurred along the frontiers of European settlement. The part played in this particular clash by the Susquehannahs reminds us of the unsettling influences which flowed from bitter contests among the Indians themselves, for the defeat of the Susquehannahs brought to culmination a long series of Indian wars through which the Iroquois won a commanding position on the backside of the English settlements they would hold for many years to come. King Philip's War developed into a virtual war of annihilation between colonists and Indians inhabiting the same general area.

The Indians with whom the English now shared the coastal plain, from Maine southward to the upper part of Carolina, all belonged to one linguistic family.[11] They were Algonkins, who prior to the arrival of the colonists had enjoyed, or suffered, only occasional contacts with Europeans. Their economy, it is important to note, rested basically upon agriculture, which was supplemented by hunting and fishing. An eminent authority has aptly described them as "agricultural hunters."[12] The Algonkins had no concept of the state, and their many divisions, tribal and other, seriously weakened them in any contest with the Europeans.[13]

One must be on guard against any assumption that colonization had led promptly to displacement of the native inhabitants. A more accurate picture can be had by thinking of the English as having "moved in" with the Indians, on an undertaking to share with them

[11] The basic authority remains John W. Powell's map of the "Linguistic Stocks of American Indians," in *Seventh Annual Report of the Bureau of Ethnology to the Secretary of the Smithsonian Institution* (Washington, 1891). See also Clark Wissler, *The American Indian* (New York, 1917), pp. 280–283, 369–370.
[12] A. L. Kroeber, *Cultural and Natural Areas of Native North America* (Berkeley and Los Angeles, 1947), p. 150.
[13] On tribal groupings, see John R. Swanton, *The Indian Tribes of North America* (Washington, 1952).

the land and other resources of the seaboard area. Here and there, as in southern New England, where epidemic disease had carried off much of the native population on the eve of the Puritan migration, or in the lower reaches of the Virginia Peninsula, where the Indians had been driven out after the massacre of 1622, there were to be found relatively large blocks of territory almost exclusively occupied by Englishmen, but these were the exception rather than the rule. More numerous perhaps were the areas, interspersed among the habitations of the English, that were still held very largely by the natives. Were we able to draw a map for illustration, the actual displacements undoubtedly would tend to emphasize the waterways along which the English preferred to settle, but such a map would in no way alter the main point. Nowhere did the colonists live at great distance from Indian neighbors.

Two sharply contrasting cultures thus had been brought into a relatively intimate and continuing relationship. Of the two the native culture was distinctly the weaker—whether the test be that of economic, social, or political development—but it has to be remembered that the European settlers, scattered as they were over considerable distances, often had reason to see themselves in the weaker position. The most primitive type of fear could easily, and on either side, become the dominant influence.

Where the Indian had dared to challenge the European community, as in Virginia in 1622 and again in 1644, he had paid a high price for his daring. It has been estimated that the probable total of nine to ten thousand Indians living in Virginia when Jamestown was settled had been reduced by 1670 to three to four thousand, these survivors having become a subjugated people residing as "friendly" or allied Indians within, and at the mercy of, the European community.[14] On the other hand, in New England, where a brief war with the Pequots was the only serious conflict before 1675, authoritative estimates are impressively different. The Indian population of southern New England in 1675 may have been as large as 20,000, a figure to be compared with an estimate of 25,000 at the beginning of the century and a probable 35,000—

[14] This is the estimate given by Washburn, *The Governor and the Rebel*, p. 19. Swanton, *Indian Tribes of North America*, p. 71, suggests the even lower figure of 2,000.

40,000 English inhabitants on the eve of King Philip's War.[15] Whatever may be the credit that should be given these or any other such estimates, it is evident enough that the intrusion of the English settler did not consistently lead to an immediate and drastic reduction in the native population. Everywhere, however, the end result was a great tragedy, and nowhere more so than in New England.

The opportunities for misunderstanding between the two peoples were virtually limitless. For example, although both of them depended basically upon agriculture for their livelihood, there were significant differences in the concepts they had of land tenure. It is easy to exaggerate these differences, and at the same time difficult to draw an exact contrast, because of variations in practice from group to group and place to place. Generally speaking, the landholding unit among the natives was not the tribe or nationality, to use two of the designations upon which Europeans have depended for description of the larger units in which the Indians were grouped, but rather a subunit known as the band, which may be loosely described as an extended family connection of people living together in a particular area. The band's property seems usually to have had well-defined boundaries, and the concepts of trespass and permissive hunting or fishing were by no means unfamiliar to the Indian. He was familiar too with individual landholdings, especially those set aside for cultivation, and these were inheritable. In the absence of heirs, the holding might be transferred to another person or persons, but it is doubtful that the sale of land had any important place in Indian usage before the coming of the European.[16]

15 Leach, *Flintlock and Tomahawk*, p. 1; James Mooney, *The Aboriginal Population of America North of Mexico, Smithsonian Miscellaneous Collections,* LXXX, No. 7 (1928), 3. Alden T. Vaughan, *New England Frontier: Puritans and Indians, 1620–1675* (Boston, 1965), p. 28, suggests that as a result of the epidemic of 1616–17 the total population at the time of settlement was 15,000–18,000.

16 Frank G. Speck, *Territorial Subdivisions and Boundaries of the Wampanoag, Massachusetts, and Nauset Indians,* Museum of the American Indian, Heye Foundation, *Indian Notes and Monographs,* No. 44 (New York, 1928); "The Wapanachki Delawares and the English," *Pennsylvania Magazine of History and Biography,* LXVII (1943), 319–344; A. L. Kroeber, "Nature of the Land-Holding Group," *Ethnohistory,* II (1955), 303–314; Anthony F. C. Wallace, "Political Organization and Land Tenure among the Northeastern Indians, 1600–1830," *Southwestern Journal of Anthropology,* XIII (1957), 301–321; Trelease, *Indian Affairs*

To a far greater extent than most of our histories have bothered to suggest, the English colonists purchased from the Indians the land upon which they settled. This was especially true in the case of New England, but hardly more so than in New York or New Jersey.[17] In the contemporary phrase, the settler undertook to "quiet the Indian title" before taking possession, but this did not always assure him of what he understood to be a quiet possession. Something of the limitations existing in the Indian's concept of individual title is suggested by the common practice of having deeds of sale to the English carry the mark, as a substitute for the signature, of the chieftain as well as of the man or men who were understood to have a special claim to the tract involved in the transaction. Just what the Indian thought he was transferring in the way of a title, if the European term may be used, is uncertain, but it can be doubted that he thought of it as being anything quite so absolute as did the Englishman to whom he sold. No doubt, experience began to teach him an obvious lesson, but not necessarily to reconcile him to the pressure under which he might sell or to the differences in custom he might subsequently encounter. It seems to be true that his own concept of title had passed beyond the simple assumption that he held his land for use, and only for so long as he used it, but he must have been ill-prepared for ready adjustment to the growing English practice of making extensive purchases in anticipation of future need rather than for immediate use, or to purchases made only in the hope for a speculative gain by resale at a later date. Land abandoned by the more mobile members of an unfamiliar type of society, and perhaps resold at a later date to another European, might confuse the native on questions of the survival of his own rights in what for him were peculiar circumstances. The record, very largely made by the European, is less conclusive than we would like it to be, but one point is clear. There was misunderstanding, and misunderstanding bred fear and, on the English side especially, contempt. If any one doubts this, let him listen to the child

---

in Colonial New York, pp. 11–12; and Ralph M. Linton, "Land Tenure in Aboriginal America," in Oliver LaFarge (ed.), *The Changing Indian* (Norman, Okla., 1942), pp. 42–54. For an interpretation somewhat different from my own, see Vaughan, *New England Frontier*, pp. 104–107.

17 See Vaughan, *New England Frontier, passim,* and above, pp. 79–80.

at play in the street who shouts "Indian giver" after the boy whose departure with a baseball bat has ruined the game.

Athough mutually satisfactory trading relations between the two peoples had been more easily established, the end result was a tragic loss of independence for the Indian. Trade between the European and the North American Indian predated colonization by many years. Fishermen swarming to the rich waters of the North Atlantic during the sixteenth century seem to have taken the lead. Coming ashore to dry and salt their catches, the fishermen found a supplementary source of profit by trading with the natives, who offered chiefly the furs with which the region abounded. The highest value came to be attached to the beaver skin, which by the end of the sixteenth century had won a ready market among the hatmakers of Europe because of its special advantages for the manufacture of fine felt.[18] English, French, and Dutch colonizers counted heavily upon the profits of this trade to underwrite their North American settlements, and everywhere the Indian was willing enough to trade. Living in the Stone Age, he was quick to recognize the superior quality of the weapons, tools, and other implements of an Iron Age economy, whether the item be a gun, hatchet, knife, hoe, fishhook, needle, or the kettle that came to be so highly prized by the native women. The furs demanded by the European were in plentiful supply and could be had by the use of long-familiar skills. As a result the Indian found it possible to make an extraordinarily rapid transition from the Stone Age to the Iron Age, but in the process he became dangerously dependent upon the European trade. And this dependence became the more serious as he forgot some of the skills by which he formerly had lived.

The beaver is a peculiarly vulnerable animal, and the Indian could be a ruthless hunter. Soon the supply of the more marketable furs within the environs of any European settlement approached exhaustion, not so much because the settler's clearing had driven off the game, as our textbooks used to suggest, but rather because of the Indian's intensified hunting. In this situation the native quickly lost the means for maintaining an acceptable degree of economic

18 John Bartlet Brebner, *The Explorers of North America, 1492–1806* (London, 1933) , has a brief account. Especially important for the development of the trade is Harold A. Innis, *The Fur Trade in Canada* (New Haven, 1930; rev. ed., Toronto, 1956) .

independence, unless circumstances made it possible for him to become the middleman in a trade with more distantly situated Indians, or for him to seize by warfare some new hunting ground. Where neither of these alternatives was open to him, his lot could become a pathetic one.

As yet, this side of the story lacks full documentation, but where the subject has been investigated, the findings leave little room for doubt that the depressed economic status of the Indians living along the seaboard contributed significantly to the tensions affecting the security of the English colonists who also lived there. A recent and valuable study of Indian affairs in New York during the seventeenth century has revealed that by midcentury the natives living close at hand to Manhattan had become dependent upon the barter of foodstuffs, firewood, and their own labor at odd jobs for the purchase of European stores.[19] Out on Long Island some of the Indians were finding fresh opportunities for employment in a newly developing whaling industry, but generally a depressed status, economically and socially, already foretold the ultimate doom of the native inhabitants in the settled part of the province. Still more suggestive is a study of the conflict between European and Algonkin cultures in eastern Canada.[20] The Indians there had been among the first to respond to the opportunities of the fur trade, and the extent of their dependence upon the trade is suggested by the fact that in time they purchased from the French—in addition to weapons, tools, and implements—tobacco, clothing, and even foodstuffs. As the supply of beaver along the coast and in the lower St. Lawrence Valley began to be exhausted, and the advantage of location passed to the more westerly situated Hurons, the Algonkins had to accept a reduced standard of living. This, in turn, seems to have contributed to the ravages wrought by European types of disease, among which tuberculosis was the steadiest killer. Not only were the easily lost skills of an earlier way of life difficult to recover, but there seems to have been no strong incentive for doing so. With the mores of the native culture crumbling under the diverse pressures resulting from contact with a more advanced society, the

19 See Trelease, *Indian Affairs in Colonial New York*, pp. 175–203, for a chapter on "The Submergence of the Algonquian."

20 Alfred G. Bailey, *The Conflict of European and Eastern Algonkian Cultures, 1504–1700* (Saint John, New Brunswick, 1937).

response of the Indian might be either submissive despair or a heedless resort to violence.

Further documentation may be had simply by recalling the familiar history of a fur trade that too often has been studied as though it had pertinence only for the economic history of the colonies. In each area of English settlement, the trade at first tended to be a trade with local Indians, and to be conducted with so large a degree of participation by the colonists as to defeat most of the attempts that were made to establish some company, proprietary, or other form of public monopoly. But rather quickly the chief centers of the trade come to be somewhat removed from the main centers of settlement, and the trade falls largely into the hands of a relatively small number of men who presumably have brought to its organization superior capital resources and entrepreneurial skills. Such a man was William Claiborne of Virginia, who, with the backing of London investors, established an outpost of trade and settlement on Kent Island in the upper Chesapeake just on the eve of Lord Baltimore's grant to Maryland.[21] Cut off by the Marylanders from the opportunity for a profitable trade that soon was prosecuted chiefly with the Susquehannahs, who lived along the beautiful river whose name still perpetuates their memory, the Virginians turned their attention southward and westward. By midcentury Abraham Wood, trading from a fort at the falls of the Appomattox, where modern Petersburg stands, had taken the lead among Virginia's traders. He would become one of the wealthier and more powerful men in the colony. Later on, William Byrd I, from his plantation near the falls of the James, began a trade that would provide the foundation for one of the great fortunes of colonial Virginia.[22]

On the eve of Bacon's Rebellion the Virginia traders were testing the possibilities for a trade reaching westward to the mountains and far down into Carolina. Between 1670 and 1674 they conducted a remarkable series of explorations. In the first of these years, they backed the German physician William Lederer, who twice reached the Blue Ridge in western Virginia and, more important, journeyed southward along the great Appalachian barrier to a point perhaps

[21] Andrews, *Colonial Period*, II, 302–307; Craven, *Southern Colonies*, pp. 196–198.
[22] Craven, *Southern Colonies*, pp. 362, 370–372.

within the modern state of South Carolina.[23] Lederer soon left
Virginia under circumstances almost as mysterious as those which
first had brought him there, but in 1671 William Byrd himself
crossed the Blue Ridge with a considerable company. Thomas Batts
and Robert Follam, on commission from Abraham Wood, pushed
across the Allegheny Divide to point a way into Kentucky a full
century before the day of Daniel Boone. Two years later James
Needham and Gabriel Arthur followed the Indian trails leading
across the more difficult Blue Ridge of northern Carolina into the
Great Smokies, close at hand to the land of the Cherokees. Needham, after a visit to Virginia, was murdered on the way back to the
mountains. But Arthur, who did not return to Virginia until 1674,
had then many remarkable adventures to relate of travel with
Indian parties far into the south.[24] For Virginians in 1675 the
prospect for a continuingly profitable trade seemed to be as chal-
lenging as that to which the recently arrived settlers at Charles
Town already were vigorously responding.

The story of the early Indian trade in New England has a quite
different ending. For a number of years after settlement furs were
an important item of export from the region, but by 1660 the trade
was in decline, even in such places as the upper Connecticut Valley,
where the Pynchons at Springfield had been the pioneers. By the
time of King Philip's War, the Indian trade had little significance
for the economy of the Puritan community.[25] What had happened,
it appears, was precisely what had happened in Virginia: the supply
of peltry within New England itself was approaching exhaustion,
and the only opportunities for a truly profitable trade now lay
outside the area. The difference was that the New Englanders
found themselves cut off on the north by the French and on the
west by the Dutch and, more recently, the English in New York.[26]

[23] William P. Cumming (ed.) , The Discoveries of John Lederer (Charlottesville
and Winston-Salem, 1958) , which re-establishes Lederer's claim to have made
important discoveries.

[24] Clarence W. Alvord and Lee Bidgood, The First Explorations of the Trans-
Allegheny Region by the Virginians, 1650–1674 (Cleveland, 1912) .

[25] Bailyn, New England Merchants in the Seventeenth Century, especially pp.
53–60. See also Francis X. Molony, The Fur Trade in New England, 1620–1676
(Cambridge, Mass., 1931) .

[26] For a discussion of efforts by New Englanders to cut in on the New York
trade, the last in 1672, see Arthur H. Buffinton, "New England and the Western

In the decline of the New England trade one sees a concession by the Puritan merchants, never indifferent to any real opportunity for trade, to the superior advantages of location belonging to Montreal and to Albany.

Historians of King Philip's War have paid remarkably little attention to this decline,[27] but there can be no doubt that it must be given a place, and probably a very significant place, in any attempt to explain the dangerous psychology of the native in 1675. Nor can there be much room for doubt that the resultant effect upon the economic status of the native contributed to the generally contemptuous attitude of the European settler toward him. Even so friendly an observer as Roger Williams could describe the Indians as the "barbarous scum and offscouring of mankinde."[28]

Let it be said, at once, that such expressions of contempt do not constitute the whole story. Although the surviving record is full of evidence that the native was repeatedly and contemptuously victimized by his European neighbor, the record itself, by its very existence, bears testimony to a public conscience that was also repeatedly exerted in his behalf. Perhaps conscience is not the word to use. Perhaps instead, it should be said that the leaders of the early colonies realistically understood the grave dangers they faced if they allowed the Indian problem to go unresolved. Accordingly, they attempted especially to regulate all trade with the Indians, usually by restricting it to those who were licensed by public authority, and to guarantee for the Indian a fair share of the land upon which he, hardly less than the European settler, basically depended for his livelihood. If the one effort tended to encourage a monopoly of the trade by some of the more powerfully placed men in the community, and the other to move the colonists toward a policy depending upon the Indian reservation, the only solution the Americans were to find for the problem over the course of three hundred years of expanding settlement, there need be no surprise. What has to be remembered is that the effort, however ineffective, was made, and made in advance of the great tragedies of the 1670's.[29]

Fur Trade, 1629–1675," *Publications of the Colonial Society of Massachusetts*, XVIII (Boston, 1917), 160–192.

[27] But see Leach, *Flintlock and Tomahawk*, pp. 20–21, and Vaughan's chapter on "Commercial Relations, 1620–1675" in his *New England Frontier*.

[28] Leach, *Flintlock and Tomahawk*, p. 6.

[29] In Virginia, for example, by legislation of the 1650's and 1660's. See Craven, *Southern Colonies*, pp. 361–369.

It should also be remembered that the interest shown in Christian missions was greater than the modern American, perhaps in token of the penance he feels that he owes, has preferred to believe. Indeed, the very special tragedy of King Philip's War is that it came as a sequel to the most ambitious missionary endeavor in the early history of the English colonies.

Far too many of our recent historians have dealt slightingly, at times almost sportingly, with the work of John Eliot in New England while conceding to French and Spanish missionaries in other areas every point that can be conceded. His efforts deserve more serious attention, if only because the conditions making possible his devoted labors are suggestive as to the main cause for the relative unimportance of missionary endeavor in the larger story of English colonization. Each of the English colonies represented no more than a small part of a highly fragmented movement, and often an unsettling fragmentation of the Christian Church in England itself. No one of the colonies could have been expected out of its own resources to accomplish much more than it did in getting itself established. In other words, a successful missionary movement in English America necessarily depended upon strong and continuing support from England, of the sort French and Spanish missionaries enjoyed in Canada and Latin America. But among the early English colonies, only in New England were there missionaries who enjoyed anything like that kind of backing. The support came from the Society for Propagation of the Gospel in New England, which was organized in 1649 under the provision of an act of Parliament and whose original membership was largely drawn from prosperous Puritan merchants of London. Thanks very largely to the interest of Sir Robert Boyle, the Society survived the Restoration and, with some reorganization, even received a royal charter in 1662 as the "Company for Propagacion of the Gospell in New England and the parts adjacent in America." The New England Company, as it was commonly designated, gave financial support to Indian missions in the colonies until the colonies themselves were lost to England.[30]

The extent of this support should not be exaggerated, for the Company's resources, collected by popular subscription and invested in England, were limited. Even so, prior to the organization

30 See especially William Kellaway, *The New England Company, 1649–1776: Missionary Society to the American Indians* (New York, 1961).

in 1701 of the Anglican Society for the Propagation of the Gospel in Foreign Parts, the Company's contributions to Puritan missions in New England were greatly in excess of any other such help coming to the colonies from England. The Society's funds had made it possible to build in the 1650's the Indian College at Harvard, first of the physical monuments to the English dissenter's belief that conversion of the North American Indian depended first upon his education. It was the Society's money too which provided the printing press for publication between 1660 and 1663 of John Eliot's translation of the Bible, both the Old and the New Testaments, into the tongue of the Algonkins.[31] However misspent may have been the effort, it was a magnificent achievement.

Nor was this all that Eliot accomplished. At Natick, under the authority granted by the Massachusetts government in 1651, he had built the first of his "praying Indian" towns, a venture as significant for the attempt to fit the Indian into the pattern of a European community as for the hope of affording the native convert the protection of membership in a fixed congregation. According to Daniel Gookin, an immigrant from Virginia who had become a superintending magistrate for the converted Indians, there were fourteen such towns in 1674, when Gookin estimated that there were 1,100 Christian Indians in Massachusetts. Possibly an even larger number were to be found in Plymouth, Nantucket, and Martha's Vineyard, where Thomas Mayhew provided a shepherding care.[32]

The immediate cause of King Philip's War was the trial, conviction, and subsequent execution of three Indians for the murder of one of the "praying Indians"—a man named Sassamon, who had attended Harvard and afterward gone native and become a special confidant of Philip, and still later had rejoined the Christian

---

[31] S. E. Morison's essay on Eliot in *Builders of the Bay Colony,* pp. 289–319; also Morison's *Harvard College in the Seventeenth Century* (2 vols., Cambridge, Mass., 1936) , II, 345–359, where, additionally, the disappointing venture with an Indian college at Harvard is authoritatively disposed of. A useful summary containing much interesting data on the New England missions is Frederick L. Weiss, "The New England Company of 1649 and Its Missionary Enterprises," *Publications of the Colonial Society of Massachusetts,* XXXVIII (Boston, 1959) , 134–218.

[32] Kellaway, *New England Company,* p. 116; and for an especially full discussion of Indian missions in New England, see Vaughan, *New England Frontier.*

community. The trial, in the court at Plymouth, had been conducted according to well-established procedures, in which the verdict of an English jury received backing from an auxiliary jury of Indians, but Philip was not content.

As he bitterly recalled in a last-minute and futile conference with Rhode Island authorities, Philip was the son of Massasoit, great friend to the Pilgrim Fathers.[33] Living on the Mount Hope peninsula, southwest of the Plymouth colony, he had been the sachem of the Wampanoags since 1662. More than once he had been suspected of plotting trouble for the English, but each time he was called to account he renewed his father's alliance with the authorities at Plymouth, a traditional protection against the hostility of the Narragansetts, whose lands lay westward across Narragansett Bay from Mount Hope.

That he had undertaken to enlist other Indians in some conspiracy against the English is quite possible, even probable, but there can be no doubt that he had failed in whatever attempt he may have made to form a general conspiracy. All that he can be certainly credited with is having started the war, and having started it altogether too soon for the purposes of a well-laid plan to destroy the English.[34]

The war had its beginning on June 20, 1675, when Wampanoag warriors plundered and burned some of the outlying houses of the scattered settlement of Swansea, situated just above Mount Hope at the neck of the peninsula.[35] As the settlers sought refuge in three of the blockhouses which were standard defensive constructions in frontier towns, messengers carried a warning to Plymouth. Governor Winslow promptly called upon the nearer towns to raise a force for the rescue of Swansea, alerted the authorities in Boston and Rhode Island, and proclaimed June 24 as a day of prayer and humiliation throughout the colony. It proved to be a day of bloodshed too, for at its end nine men had been killed at Swansea and at

[33] John Easton's *Relacion*, in Charles H. Lincoln (ed.), *Narratives of the Indian Wars, 1675–1699* (New York, 1913), pp. 10–11.

[34] See especially Leach's appraisal, *Flintlock and Tomahawk*, p. 241; also pp. 48–49.

[35] The following account of the war depends upon Leach, who has written an admirable study which draws fully upon contemporary histories by Church, Hubbard, and Mather. Langdon's *Pilgrim Colony*, pp. 152–187, also carries a helpful account of the background and history of the war.

least two more were mortally wounded, some of them in attempts to rescue property from abandoned farms, one of them in the successful ambushing of a party on the way from its prayers.

The immediate problem was to keep Philip's warriors bottled up in the Mount Hope peninsula until they could be destroyed, and to make sure that other Indians did not join the fight. Massachusetts promptly sent emissaries to assure the loyalty of its western Indians, and dispatched a similar mission to the Narragansetts, who were visited also by the aging Roger Williams. Rhode Island, in addition, put boats on station in the hope of preventing Philip's escape by water. Connecticut ordered a small force to its eastern frontier,[36] and by June 26 Massachusetts had two companies of militia on the march for Swansea. The drums in Boston's streets had raised a third before the next sunrise, and soon there would be five Massachusetts companies in active service. But inexperience and some confusion in council, attributable in part to provincial jealousies, so postponed aggressive action against Philip as to permit him to escape eastward across the Taunton River into a refuge in the Pocasset swamplands, where rattlesnakes were almost as troublesome to the English as were the Indians. By the end of July clumsy and ineffective efforts to dig him out had given way to a plan, once more, for bottling him up, and once more Philip had escaped, this time into the country of the Nipmucks in western Massachusetts.

Twice the English had had an opportunity to crush Philip, and twice they had failed, with results that were nothing less than disastrous. Although Philip at the beginning may have had the assistance of a few warriors other than his own, it is evident enough that the original contest was between the English and the Wampanoags, and that other Indians were inclined to adopt a policy of watchful waiting. But when they found that the English could be defied and outwitted, many of them responded with savage delight.

As the Nipmucks joined the fight, the smoking ruins of Brook-

---

[36] It might have been larger except that Governor Andros took this occasion to visit Saybrook with a demand that the Hartford government recognize his authority over its territories west of the Connecticut River. In the face of a stubborn refusal made good by the fort at Saybrook, he soon withdrew, but at a critical point of time Connecticut had reason to fear a war on two fronts. Such is the account given by Leach, *Flintlock and Tomahawk*, pp. 59–60, but this contrasts sharply with Trelease, *Indian Affairs*, pp. 230–231, where Andros's visit is interpreted as intended for the aid of the New Englanders.

field, on the pathway linking Boston with Springfield, had to be abandoned after a bitter and famous siege. By September the flames had spread to the upper Connecticut Valley, where Northfield, Deerfield, and even Springfield were burned. An uprising of the Indians along the coast of Maine added to the terror and to the especially heavy burden that fell upon the government of Massachusetts. When the approach of winter brought some slackening of aggressive action by the Indians, the greatest fear was of the Narragansetts, who could muster perhaps a thousand warriors and whose neutrality was rightly considered to be all the more doubtful because it had been forced upon them by a show of force early in the war. A joint expedition against the Narragansetts that was led by Governor Winslow in December, in one of New England's severest winters, won the greatest single action of the war, the Great Swamp Fight. The victory cost casualties as high perhaps as 20 per cent of the English engaged, many of them more attributable to exposure in the bitter weather than to the marksmanship of the natives. It could not be said that the power of the Narragansetts had been wholly broken. Nevertheless, it was a heartening victory, helping to build the stamina that would be required to see New England through a dreadful spring.

The terror lasted from February through May. A list of the towns in Massachusetts alone which experienced the horror of an Indian ambush on its outskirts, or whose inhabitants watched from the relative security of a garrison house while the Indians burned their homes, would provide almost a complete gazeteer for the province. No longer was the conflict confined to frontier regions, for the natives brought fire and death to within twenty miles of Boston itself. In Rhode Island they burned Warwick and Providence, and only Connecticut came through substantially free of serious punishment, perhaps because its own Indians had learned their lesson in the Pequot War as early as the 1630's.

There could be no question, of course, as to which side ultimately would prevail. The English colonists were handicapped by provincial jealousies. Their famed Confederation was virtually defunct since Connecticut's absorption in 1665 of New Haven, one of the original members, except that its commissioners continued to serve, as they would until 1684, as the acknowledged agency of the New England Company for missionary affairs, and except that its organization provided some precedents for the co-operation among the colonies a desperate situation now required. The war brought something of a revival, but it also has to be said that the organization, created originally for just such an emergency, failed to meet the test.[37] It took time for New England's soldiers to learn, from bitter experience, how to fight a maddeningly mobile foe. The economic loss was by no means limited to the property destroyed. Fields went untended and crops unharvested. The surplus farm produce upon which New England's trade significantly depended now disappeared. Further injury to trade resulted from wartime interruptions of the fishing industry. But the Indian had his problems too, and fewer resources to see him through the long pull.

The Indian's mobility had been bought at the cost of abandoning vital foodstores and the fields he customarily cultivated. Moreover, the hunger which punished him through the winter was only partially relieved by the plunder he seized during the spring, for the English too were then short of supplies. By May, 1676, the native's need to fish the rivers and to plant corn in the valleys had brought to him a new vulnerability. The hostility of the Mohawks, who had driven Philip and some of his warriors from a winter encampment near Albany, discouraged thought of escape westward into New York.[38] As their situation worsened, the Indians began to return some of their prisoners, including Mrs. Rowlandson, wife to the minister at Lancaster whose narrative of her Indian captivity would set the pattern for a new and distinctively American branch of literature.[39] Pathetically, the hard-pressed native tended to gravitate toward familiar surroundings, and so it was that Philip met his death where he had begun his resistance, at Mount Hope in August, 1676, from a gunshot. And so ended King Philip's War.

No one could tell then, nor can he tell now, the full cost.[40]

[37] Though marred by a tenuous line of argument, there is useful detail in Harry M. Ward, *The United Colonies of New England, 1643–90* (New York, 1961).

[38] Trelease, *Indian Affairs in Colonial New York,* pp. 233–236, where it is noted that perhaps 200 refugees from New England were settled in New York after the war.

[39] Mrs. Rowlandson's narrative, first printed in 1682, has been many times reprinted. It is most easily consulted in Lincoln, *Narratives of the Indian Wars,* pp. 112–167.

[40] See especially Leach's concluding chapter, *Flintlock and Tomahawk,* pp. 242–250.

Several thousand persons—men, women, and children—had lost their lives, and among those who survived many were maimed and crippled for life. More than a dozen towns had been almost completely destroyed, and others had sustained heavy loss. In Massachusetts alone some 2,000 people were left dependent for a time on public relief. The United Colonies estimated their total war expenses at above £100,000.

For the Indians the cost was even higher. Many of them had been killed, or had died of exposure and privation. Although the English took prisoners throughout the war, it was largely because they could be sold as slaves in the West Indies.[41] Many of the natives surrendering at the end of hostilities were bound over as servants to colonists for aid in rebuilding what they had destroyed. The New England governments had resorted to the promise of land bounties for the encouragement of enlistments during the war, and after the war there came the veterans' insistent demand for compensation. It was the Indian, of course, who paid, and even when left with his land he found himself subject to new restrictions as to his place of residence, his freedom of movement, and his right to own arms. The fur trade, virtually gone even before the war, underwent no significant revival thereafter.

John Eliot still lived as apostle to the "praying Indians," who had been remarkably loyal in the face of suspicion and hostility that imposed the severest strain upon their loyalty.[42] But whatever hope there may have been before the war that Christian missions might save the Indian, the hope was even more slender now. The funds of the New England Company would continue to be drawn upon for missions in New England, but it is hard to see this later part of the story as anything more than an epilogue appended to a history that had its tragic ending in 1676.

Before leaving King Philip's War, it should be observed that both sides fought with guns. The point requires special emphasis because the modern American persistently clings to the romantic image of an Indian who fought only with bow, arrow, and tomahawk. All of the colonies at first had attempted to maintain a strict prohibition

41 Leach, *Flintlock and Tomahawk*, pp. 224–227.
42 *Ibid.*, pp. 145–154, for an excellent chapter on "The Problem of the 'Friendly Indians.' "

of trade in firearms with the natives, but everywhere these efforts had failed by the middle years of the seventeenth century, in no small part because of keen competition among the representatives of several European nations.[43] Prototypes of the familiar "Indian" or "trade gun" of later date—a relatively light and inexpensive weapon produced for the American market—already were in manufacture.[44] It is impossible to say how well equipped in this regard were the New England Indians at the time of the war. But there can be no doubt that the Indian's musket cost the English heavily, if only because of the bitterness with which the New England governments charged that Albany was the source of their foes' ammunition.[45]

Whether a superiority in the firearms they possessed is fundamentally responsible for the extraordinary success of the Iroquois is another and more difficult question. Strategically located in an area of the sharpest competition among French, Dutch, Swedish, and English traders, they were well armed, but so too were the Hurons over whom the Iroquois prevailed. The Susquehannahs also had firearms. Indeed, Maryland even had supplied artillery pieces for the defense of their key fortifications.[46]

Whatever may be the fact on this point, the Iroquois undoubtedly enjoyed many advantages from their location. Stretched out along and below the Mohawk Valley, the five nations of the Mohawks, the Oneidas, the Onondagas, the Cayugas, and the Senecas were in position to control the easiest route linking the eastern seaboard with the heart of the continent. They also were in position to check ambitious moves toward the west by New England's Indians, to intercept routes of trade leading from Montreal to the interior, and to frustrate the hopes of the Susquehannahs on the

[43] See for examples, George T. Hunt, *The Wars of the Iroquois: A Study in Intertribal Relations* (Madison, Wis., 1940), pp. 165–175; Trelease, *Indian Affairs*, pp. 94–102, 135–136, 190–193; and Craven, *Southern Colonies*, p. 310.

[44] Interesting data can be found in Carl P. Russell, *Guns on the Early Frontiers: A History of Firearms from Colonial Times through the Years of the Western Fur Trade* (Berkeley and Los Angeles, 1957). But notice William Byrd's warning to his commission house in London, several years later, that the Indians would not take "any gun." Craven, *Southern Colonies*, p. 371.

[45] Leach, *Flintlock and Tomahawk*, pp. 176–177; Trelease, *Indian Affairs*, pp. 231–233.

[46] A. Cadzow, *Archaeological Studies of the Susquehannock Indians of Pennsylvania* (Harrisburg, 1936), pp. 22–23.

south, who had no hope of gaining an outlet from their valley into the interior except by pushing aside the westerly situated Senecas.

During the earlier years of European settlement, the situation of the Iroquois might be described in terms almost the reverse of those just stated. It is evident that the Mohawks, who kept the most easterly of the Iroquois fires, did not command as yet the critical juncture of the Mohawk and the Hudson, which was occupied by the Mahicans, a warlike branch of the Delawares. On the west, the Senecas were hemmed in by the Neutrals, allies of the powerful Hurons in Canada. In the South the hostile Susquehannahs enjoyed the advantage of supply by Swedish, Dutch, and English traders. The Iroquois, moreover, were small in numbers, and their famed confederacy was actually a far less perfect union than tradition would have us believe. Their warriors seem at no time to have exceeded a total of 2,500.[47] Nevertheless, by 1675 a long series of successful wars, in which the Mohawks and the Senecas carried the main burden, had brought victory to the Iroquois over all their major rivals.

As early as 1629 the Mohawks had pushed aside the Mahican barrier to direct access to the Dutch traders at Fort Orange,[48] and for forty years thereafter they kept a pressure on the Mahicans that had reverberations reaching eastward to Maine. By 1649 the Iroquois had broken the Hurons and forced their dispersal. The dispersal of the Neutrals and the Eries, who lived between the Genesee River and Lake Erie, followed, and then came the turn of the Susquehannahs, with whom Lord Baltimore's colonists had entered into formal alliance in 1652. This climactic struggle extended, with the intermittent conflict so characteristic of Indian warfare, from about 1660 to 1675.[49] For the Iroquois most of the fighting was done by the Senecas, whose position at the western end of the Long House was especially vulnerable to attack by way of the Susquehanna Valley, and they had their hands more than full during most

47 Helpful short accounts are provided by Paul A. W. Wallace, "The Iroquois: A Brief Outline of Their History," *Pennsylvania History*, XXIII (1956), 15–28, and by Trelease, *Indian Affairs*, pp. 12–24.

48 Trelease, *Indian Affairs*, p. 48.

49 For an over-all account, see Hunt, *Wars of the Iroquois*. Cadzow, *Susquehannock Indians*, p. 26, fixes the probable date for the termination of this conflict as 1675. His conclusion fits well with subsequent developments on the Virginia frontier.

of the war. But in the end Maryland read the signs clearly enough, abandoned its allies, and the Susquehannahs were also broken and dispersed. On the backside of the English colonies, from New York to Virginia, there was now only one Indian power which counted for much.

The question of the motivation for these and later wars of the Iroquois has recently come into fresh discussion. For more than a generation after the publication of Charles H. McIlwain's seminal introduction to *Wraxall's Abridgment of the Indian Affairs*,[50] historians have generally accepted his suggestion that the Iroquois fought for the advantage of the middleman in a trade between the Europeans and more distantly situated tribes.[51] Faced with an early depletion of the stock of beaver in their own territories, they had avoided the fate overtaking the coastal Indians by warring upon all tribes who were in position to bid for control of the inland trade. Professor Trelease, after close study, has challenged this interpretation.[52] He insists that the motivation was only partly economic, that there is more evidence that the Iroquois fought for the possession of additional hunting grounds than for trade with other Indians, and that the wars had deep rootage in ancient rivalries, as also in the political and military usages of the North American native. Undoubtedly, it is this last reminder, based partly upon ethnological studies by scholars in other disciplines, that is Professor Trelease's chief contribution to the discussion. Whether the Iroquois fought for the advantage of the middleman or for additional hunting grounds matters less than that they fought, in part at least, to maintain the advantages of a trade with the Europeans.

The surviving Susquehannahs fell back into Maryland, where they became a problem for that province's government but not necessarily a serious menace to the settlers, either in Maryland or

---

[50] Charles H. McIlwain (ed.), *An Abridgment of the Indian Affairs . . . in the Colony of New York, from the Year 1678 to the Year 1751, by Peter Wraxall* (Cambridge, Mass., 1915).

[51] This is true of *The Fur Trade in Canada* by Innis, and especially of Hunt's *Wars of The Iroquois*, where the thesis may be somewhat overstated. Anthropologists too seem to have found the hypothesis helpful, as in Bailey's study, *Conflict of European and Eastern Algonkian Cultures*.

[52] See especially his *Indian Affairs*, pp. 119–120, and more recently his "The Iroquois and the Western Fur Trade: A Problem in Interpretation," *Mississippi Valley Historical Review*, XLIX (1962), 32–51.

Virginia. Blundering by the colonists themselves seems to have created the real trouble. The story begins in July, 1675, when a petty squabble between a Virginia planter living on the Potomac and the Doeg Indians, camping across the river in Maryland, led to the murder of the planter's herdsman. Some thirty Virginians, crossing the river for revenge, killed ten or more of the Doegs and, by an unhappy mistake of identification, fourteen Susquehannahs as well. Resulting difficulties caused Governor Berkeley to authorize the commanders of the militia in the Northern Neck to investigate, determine the guilty parties, and call out such forces as were needed to bring them to account. But the situation already was out of hand. Acting with a degree of autonomy that long had been familiar in the handling of local police actions, the northern militia crossed the Potomac in force for a juncture with 250 militiamen called up in Maryland for pacification of its own territory. The joint force, late in September, 1675, laid siege to the principal encampment of the Susquehannahs in a mood revealed by the fact that five chieftains who came out for a parley were murdered in cold blood, an act for which the Maryland commander seems to have been chiefly responsible. Then the English failed to make the siege good. In the end, the outraged Susquehannahs escaped.[53]

Whatever may have been their responsibility for previous depredations, the Susquehannahs now took to the warpath. During January, 1676, Indian raids upon the settlements located between the Potomac and the Rappahannock took the lives of thirty-six colonists, and drove survivors down upon the older areas of settlement. Scattered attacks followed, one of them as far south as the James, where Nathaniel Bacon's overseer was killed, but the evidence argues that the Susquehannahs had very largely spent their wrath in January. Thereafter, it appears, the colonists actually suffered less at the hands of the Indian than they did from the fears his retaliation had stimulated.[54]

53 Washburn, *The Governor and the Rebel*, pp. 20–25; Thomas J. Wertenbaker, *Torchbearer of the Revolution: The Story of Bacon's Rebellion and Its Leader* (Princeton, 1940), pp. 75–83.

54 It is impossible to say how many of the colonists were killed by the Indians, but there is good reason for believing that the largest number fell in January and that the grand total came nowhere near the 300 reported by the royal commissioners after the rebellion. Craven, *Southern Colonies*, p. 374 n.; Wash-

A part of the evidence supporting such a conclusion may be had merely by noting the subsequent course of events in Virginia. During the spring of that year the colony held two sessions of its general assembly, conducted between the two a general election, and in the second meeting of the assembly undertook significant reforms in its political system. Then, still disagreeing, the colonists found themselves sufficiently free of outside interference to fight a civil war of several months duration. The story leading down to Bacon's Rebellion seems best to illustrate the role that simple hysteria might assume in the lives of the colonists as a result of difficulties with the Indians.

That the news from New England, which reached Jamestown in February,[55] contributed to the hysteria is unmistakable. When the assembly meeting in the following March petitioned King Charles for assistance, it justified its appeal on the ground that the colony faced no "private grudge, but a general Combination of all [Indians] from New England hither."[56] Perhaps that assumption helps to explain the assembly's decision to accept Governor Berkeley's proposal for construction of a system of forts along the frontier to be manned by 500 men who would maintain "ranging" patrols between the forts, a scheme soon to be rejected by the colonists as too costly. Perhaps it was only that in this, the last meeting of an assembly elected as far back as 1661, the governor still held a dominant influence.[57]

For the rapid decline of Berkeley's influence thereafter, a number of explanations can be suggested. His own decisions had shown some uncertainty as to the proper course of action. Having at first commissioned Sir Henry Chicheley to lead a march in force against the offending Indians, the governor had then recalled him. The subsequently adopted plan to rely instead upon a defensive policy was open to criticism not only for its cost but also for the time it would take to put it into effect. Perhaps some of the colonists feared that the forts Sir William proposed to build at the fall line of the principal rivers would have the effect of drawing a line beyond

---

burn, *Governor and the Rebel*, p. 33; Morton, *Colonial Virginia*, I, 237, for Berkeley's report that "in April and May we lost not one man out of any plantation."

[55] Wilcomb E. Washburn, "Berkeley and King Philip's War."

[56] Washburn, *Governor and the Rebel*, p. 30.

[57] After the election of 1661, there was no general election for the assembly until that held for the assembly meeting in June, 1676.

which further expansion of the area of settlement would become difficult.[58] Certainly, the suspicion grew that Berkeley's policy was dictated by a desire to protect the Indian, a suspicion that had not a little justification. Whatever may have been his original fears, the governor apparently gained with the passage of time a more realistic view of the problem confronting the colony than most of the colonists had, as also of the aid the "friendly" Indians might provide in coping with the problem.[59] The fact that a relatively small number of men, some of them closely identified with Berkeley, now dominated the Indian trade invited the charge that he would sacrifice the security of the colony for the sake of his own interest in that trade. Although no positive evidence that Berkeley himself invested in the Indian trade has been found,[60] the belief that special interests dictated the governor's policy became widespread.

Nothing else perhaps aggravated public sentiment more than did the anticipated cost of the governor's proposals. It was rumored that the total might reach as high as a thousand pounds of tobacco per poll.[61] The Virginia farmer had had a rough time for several years past, and he was more than ordinarily sensitive on the question of taxes. Ever since the enactment of the Navigation Act of 1660, his tobacco had been sold at depressed prices, and bad weather and epidemic disease among his cattle had compounded his difficulty in recent years.[62] How far he may have been aware of the additional burden to be expected from the recent imposition of the "plantation duty" by act of Parliament in 1673 is difficult to say.[63] But certainly he had no reason whatsoever for optimism.

No one could have pleaded his cause with the authorities in

58 Proof of this frequently expressed assumption, however, seems to be wanting.

59 Washburn, *Governor and the Rebel*, pp. 33–35; also Morton, *Colonial Virginia*, I, 237, for a letter of April 1 in which Berkeley asserted that the Virginia frontier could cope with ten times the number of hostile Indians then disturbing it.

60 Washburn, *Governor and the Rebel*, p. 28; Morton, *Colonial Virginia*, I, 236; Craven, *Southern Colonies*, pp. 378–379. It should be noted that the burgesses in March had taken control of the trade from the council and given it to local magistrates.

61 Washburn, *Governor and the Rebel*, p. 40.

62 There is no dispute, of course, on the question of prices, but see Gray, *History of Agriculture in the Southern United States*; Wertenbaker, *Virginia under the Stuarts*, pp. 123–133, and *Torchbearer of the Revolution*, pp. 26–31; and Craven, *Southern Colonies*, pp. 375–376.

63 See below, p. 147. Andrews, *Colonial Period*, IV, 119–124, 138–139, discounts the early effect of the new duty.

London more vigorously and persistently than had Sir William Berkeley, but a debt for past services, especially if they be ineffective, is easily forgotten in hard times. Moreover, the governor was getting old. In 1676 he reached the age of seventy, and the irascibility he so dramatically showed during and after the Rebellion may have appeared earlier.[64] That the colonists generally were losing confidence in their leaders is made all too evident by the complaints they registered with the royal commissioners who investigated after the rebellion.[65] These complaints struck with special rancor against the county magistrates, who still imposed the heavier part of the taxes paid. In some counties ugly rumors of corrupt bargains in the building of recently constructed courthouses circulated, and the suspicion carried by such rumors offered an easy explanation for the failure of fortifications built by the colony during the second Anglo-Dutch War to keep the Dutch out during a third and very recent war.[66] It was hardly the time to propose additional construction at public expense.

However one may weigh the several factors involved, it is evident that the Virginia colonist in 1676 was in a dangerous frame of mind. He was quite capable of venting his wrath either upon the Indians who seemed further to challenge his security or upon those who seemed to deny him an opportunity to protect himself against the Indian. In time, he struck at both of them, and with the arms which in his own hands constituted the sole military strength of the colony. All that was required to bring his discontent to a head was that he find leadership.

This he found in Nathaniel Bacon, who had been a resident of the colony for only two years. Son and heir to one of the more substantial squires of England's Suffolk County, Bacon had studied at Cambridge, where he took the M.A. in 1668, had spent three years on a grand tour of the Continent, and had finished off his education with a residence at one of the Inns of Court. Obviously, it had been expected that the young man would succeed to his father's position as an influential country gentleman, perhaps in time even sit for the county in the House of Commons. But Bacon had a

[64] Morton, *Colonial Virginia*, I, 236–237; but see Washburn, *Governor and the Rebel*, pp. 34–35.
[65] See below, pp. 138, 146.
[66] Craven, *Southern Colonies*, pp. 375–379.

penchant for getting into trouble. Although his marriage to the daughter of a neighboring knight would seem to have met every test for an acceptable union, the bride's father promptly disinherited her. Later Bacon became involved in a scheme to defraud another young man of his inheritance. In 1674 his father packed him off to the plantations, with his wife and the extraordinary stake of £1,800.[67]

Virginia was selected, no doubt, because Bacon had several relatives there, including Governor Berkeley's wife and an older Nathaniel Bacon who had a seat on the governor's council. In keeping with conventions of the time, the younger Bacon was sworn to membership in the council, as early as March, 1675. Already he had bought an estate up the James, where he settled down as a neighbor of William Byrd and, like Byrd, secured a license from the governor to engage in the Indian trade.[68] Prior to the spring of 1676, Bacon seems to have devoted his attention almost exclusively to his personal affairs.

It was after the killing of his overseer that Bacon took the leadership in the opposition to the governor's Indian policy. As rumor spread the report down the James River that the Susquehannahs were concentrating above the falls, volunteers moved up the river to encamp near the juncture of the Appomattox and the James. This was in the month of May. At a later time in American history the gathering there might have been described as one of vigilantes, men ready to provide by their own efforts a remedy for the deficiencies of their government. It was no mere mob. Men of substance and position had joined the movement, and it seems to have been by prearrangement among several gentlemen, including William Byrd, that Bacon was persuaded to take the command.[69] His choice may have reflected the knowledge his neighbors had quickly acquired of a spirit reckless enough to meet the demands of the occasion. Perhaps it was only because Bacon held membership in the governor's council, and so was in a position to lend a show of legality to an unlawful act.

The volunteers' plan, made evident in a public statement, was to force the governor's hand by promising to do themselves the job

[67] Wertenbaker, *Torchbearer of the Revolution*, pp. 39–58.
[68] Washburn, *Governor and the Rebel*, pp. 18, 29.
[69] Morton, *Colonial Virginia*, I, 237–239.

they felt needed to be done—to do it the right way, to do it promptly, and to do it without cost to the colony. There was to be no more waiting on useless and expensive fortifications. It was promised that the governor's commission would be sought for Bacon, but it had been agreed that the volunteers would go ahead in any case.[70] This, of course, was mutiny, as the governor promptly charged. After a fruitless exchange between Berkeley and Bacon, the governor rode up the river with a mounted force, but only to arrive too late.

Bacon and his volunteer army had disappeared into the forest in pursuit of a report that Susquehannahs were encamped near Occaneechee Island, where the Dan and the Staunton join to form the Roanoke River. There the Occaneechees themselves agreed to take on the job of destroying a small band of Susquehannahs camping nearby and, this having been accomplished, Bacon, treacherously it seems, attacked the Occaneechees, killing men, women, and children. There is room for debate on this charge of treachery, for the accounts differ, but in any case the act was done.[71] The Occaneechees, who may have been something of a nuisance along the route of the newly developing trade with the Carolina Indians, were wiped out.[72] Of greater importance for the purposes of this discussion is the fact that, when Bacon returned to the Virginia settlements late in May, he was immediately acclaimed as the hero of the people. As the man who had marched against the Indians and killed Indians, he had won the upper hand over Berkeley.

Already, the governor had taken steps to rally popular sentiment in support of his own leadership. Before Bacon's return, Berkeley had dissolved the old assembly and called for the election of a new one. Despite a statute of 1670 which had restricted the franchise to

[70] See the report of the royal commissioners in Charles M. Andrews (ed.), *Narratives of the Insurrections* (New York, 1915), pp. 108–113; Washburn, *Governor and the Rebel*, pp. 34–37.

[71] See especially Thomas P. Abernethy's introduction to the reprint of *More News from Virginia* (Charlottesville, 1943); Washburn, *Governor and the Rebel*, pp. 40–46.

[72] Washburn may be right in viewing the Occaneechees as "friendly" Indians, but for evidence that they had made trouble for the Virginia traders, including the killing of James Needham, see Alvord and Bidgood, *Explorations of the Trans-Allegheny Region*, pp. 80, 81, 84, 124 n.; Morton, *Colonial Virginia*, I, 244.

freeholders in accordance with the English practice, all freemen were allowed to vote. Even more significant was Berkeley's invitation for the colonists to submit such grievances as they might have through their newly elected burgesses.[73] Obviously, the government's failure to respond to popular pressures for an acceptable Indian policy had brought it under attack upon a very broad front, and no one understood this better than did the governor. Among those elected as burgesses for the new assembly was Bacon, who of course had been removed from his seat on the council. The assembly meeting in June, 1676, has been known to history as Bacon's Assembly, and the statutes it enacted, including provisions for significant reforms in the government, have been described as Bacon's Laws.[74] But there is reason for believing that Bacon himself had very little to do with the work of the assembly except insofar as it related to Indian affairs—that his own primary concern was to get a commission as commander against the Indians and amnesty for what he and his followers previously had done.[75]

He was in Jamestown only twice during the assembly's session, each time briefly. On the first of these visits there occurred a public reconciliation with the governor which restored Bacon to his seat on the council, and so automatically disqualified him for a seat in the house. This reconciliation presumably depended upon some assurance that he would receive the commission he wanted, but soon Bacon fled the town, apparently in fear of his life, and then marched back with his aroused neighbors to win his commission at gunpoint. He thus was in Jamestown when the assembly completed its business and adjourned. Thereafter, Berkeley's attempts to recruit troops in Gloucester County caused Bacon to turn his attention from whatever plans he had for warfare against the Indians to the problem of making his rear secure. Berkeley's recruiting efforts having failed, the governor retired to a refuge on the Eastern Shore, and Bacon quickly had control over most of Virginia. Bacon's efforts to bind the colonists to a recognition of his own authority until the king could hear both sides of the story, his unsuccessful attempt to seize the governor, and his capture and

---

73 Wertenbaker, *Torchbearer of the Revolution,* pp. 106–107.
74 For discussion, see below, pp. 137, 138.
75 Craven, *Southern Colonies,* pp. 383–385; Washburn, *Governor and the Rebel,* pp. 48–67; and for a contrary view, Morton, *Colonial Virginia,* I, 249–255.

burning of Jamestown after Berkeley had returned there in September made of the popular leader much more of a rebel than he probably ever had intended to be. After his death in October, 1676, from exposure and exhaustion, the rebellion collapsed.[76]

Meanwhile, there had been little time for attention to the Indians. Except for a late summer attack upon the "friendly" Pamunkeys, who by retirement into difficult swampland seem to have kept their losses down to eight, Bacon's forces were otherwise engaged.[77] After the action at Occaneechee Island, the Susquehannahs simply drop out of the story. At the end of the Rebellion, the remaining Indian problem was pacification of the colony's own tributary Indians. They had been the objects of general suspicion by the colonists throughout the trouble, most of whom probably shared Bacon's expressed belief that Indians were "all alike."[78] Exposed to the gravest dangers by this suspicion, the tributary Indians may well have been guilty of some of the hostile acts with which they were charged, but it has to be remembered that their ability to make serious difficulty for the colony long since had disappeared. By a treaty of May, 1677, which the king's newly arrived commissioners had negotiated, the tributary tribes were re-established in the colony under an agreement that their chieftains held "their Crownes and Landes of the Great King of England."[79] Some of their descendants still live in Virginia on lands thus confirmed to them.

Bacon's Rebellion had given no new direction to Indian policy in the colony. If some years later the colonists, who for the first time began a significant movement of settlement beyond the fall line, faced no serious barrier to their ambitions from the natives, it was because there existed between the Iroquois in the north and the Cherokees and Tuscaroras in Carolina no tribesmen who were capable of effective resistance. Indeed, the chief risk of disturbance along Virginia's frontier came now from the Iroquois, whose bands,

[76] Wertenbaker, *Torchbearer of the Revolution*, has the most readable of the narrative accounts.

[77] Washburn, *Governor and the Rebel*, pp. 75–76; Morton, *Colonial Virginia*, I, 265–266, where the author suggests, in contrast to Washburn, that there may have been some ground for the colonists' suspicion of the Pamunkeys.

[78] Washburn, *Governor and the Rebel*, p. 58.

[79] *Ibid.*, p. 135.

for hunting or other purposes, might wander as far south as Carolina. During the later years of the seventeenth century, peace on the frontier depended chiefly upon negotiation with the Iroquois in New York and upon patrols by "rangers," first introduced in the 1680's as the sole surviving element of Berkeley's policy of 1676.[80] Their purpose was to provide some advance notice to the settlers of where trouble might be expected.

Similarly, Virginia's trade with the Indians seems to have suffered no more than a brief interruption. For many years the local Indians had counted for little in the colony's trade, and as the Virginians followed up their recent explorations, they assumed the lead in opening up the only trade which in colonial times would rival, both in its geographical reach and in its profits, the trade that had found its headquarters at Albany. It seems to have been the Virginian who set the pattern of trade through pack teams traveling far into the interior that would distinguish the southern trade for many years to come.[81] He, too, seems to have been the first among the English to discover that the skin of the deer, as common in the south as was the beaver in the north, was as valuable for the manufacture of fine leather as was the beaver's fur for the production of fine hats. But the Virginian was soon also to discover that, whether the trade be for fur or skin, the advantages of location belonged to Albany and to Charles Town, both of which were in better position to command routes reaching far into the interior of the continent.

The Carolina proprietors, for all their primary interest in the settlement of tenants upon their lands, were nowise indifferent to opportunities for trade with the natives. Their hope that this trade might be developed as a proprietary monopoly passed again through an all too familiar sequence of hope and disappointment, despite the services rendered to them by Dr. Henry Woodward, one of the more colorful adventurers ever to appear upon the frontiers of European adventure in America. Woodward had been studying the Indian as early as 1666, when he participated in the explorations of the Carolina coast sponsored by the Barbadians who hoped to settle at Port Royal. Indeed, when his colleagues departed the coast, he had remained behind to live with the Indians at Port

80 As in the treaty of 1684. Morton, *Colonial Virginia*, I, 306, 314–315.
81 Craven, *Southern Colonies*, 371–372.

Royal, whence he subsequently was carried as a prisoner by the Spaniards to St. Augustine. Rescued by an English pirate who attacked the place in 1668, he returned to the West Indies in time to join West's fleet for the final stage of its voyage to Carolina.[82] Among his associates, after the founding of the new colony, was a James Needham who probably was the same man who later was killed in Virginia as an employee of the Virginia traders by the Occaneechee Indians.[83] Still another significant chapter in the history of Anglo-Indian relations in North America had been opened.

The Indians who were destined to fill many colorful pages in this new chapter were different from those previously discussed here. For one thing, the stocks they represented were more mixed. The original inhabitants of this southeastern area seem to have belonged to the Siouan family, but subsequently they had been broken into scattered pockets by the invasion of other Indians, more familiar with the natural routes of migration than the Europeans had yet become. The Cherokees were of Iroquoian ancestry, as were the Tuscaroras, who lived in eastern Carolina, below the southward extension of the coastal Algonkins. The Casabos on the coast above Charles Town may have been related to the more westerly situated Creeks. An extraordinary mixture of minor groupings along and in the neighborhood of the Savannah River, among whom the Westos would be the most troublesome, separated the Carolina Indians, of whom the Cherokees were the dominant group, from the Muskhogean Creeks, Choctaws, and Chickasaws to the west.[84] Occupying one of the more fertile regions of North America and enjoying an especially favorable climate, the southeastern Indian depended even more heavily than did his northern brothers upon agriculture. The southern colonists would very largely adopt his seasonal diet of corn, beans, squash, and pumpkins.

[82] Verner W. Crane, *The Southern Frontier, 1670–1732* (Durham, N.C., 1928), pp. 6–7, 12–17.

[83] Alvord and Bidgood, *First Explorations of the Trans-Allegheny Region*, p. 79 n.

[84] In addition to the more general works previously cited, see John R. Swanton, *The Indians of the Southeastern United States* (Washington, 1946); Douglas L. Rights, *The American Indian in North Carolina* (Durham, N.C., 1947); Chapman J. Milling, *Red Carolinians* (Chapel Hill, N.C., 1940); and R. S. Cotterill, *The Southern Indians* (Norman, Okla., 1954).

CHAPTER 5

A Time of Trouble

ALTHOUGH Bacon's Rebellion had its origin in a dispute over Indian policy and probably would not have occurred except for that dispute, it is more significant for the revelation it provides of political unrest among the Virginia colonists than for anything else. This is true in part because the rebellion came at the beginning of an especially turbulent period in the political life of the colonies generally, and so it serves to highlight an important and complex chapter of our history. The full story, which includes the overthrow of existing regimes in several of the North American colonies at the time of the English Revolution of 1688–89, must wait for its completion in later pages. Here it will be enough to suggest that the significance of Bacon's Rebellion is by no means limited to its place in the history of Virginia.

The problem it presents to the historian is difficult. It is easy enough to demonstrate how the governor's failure to respond to popular demand for aggressive action against the Indians precipitated a major political crisis. It is also easy to determine what were the general grounds for the colonists' discontent with their government. Among the laws enacted by the June assembly of 1676, commonly designated as Bacon's Laws, were statutes returning the franchise to all freemen, re-establishing popular election for membership in the parish vestries, providing for the election of some of the "discreetest" inhabitants in each county to sit with the justices for the levying of annual taxes and the framing of local ordinances, revising the rules governing the collection of taxes, forbidding a man to hold the sheriff's office for two successive years, prohibiting certain pluralities of officeholding, attempting to establish new controls over the fees to be paid for the services rendered by a number of officers, eliminating the tax exemption formerly belonging to members of the governor's council, and denying to them a long-standing right to sit and vote with the county courts.[1] The report of the investigation conducted in the following year by royal commissioners underscores the main items in a comprehensive indictment: that the cost of government was unnecessarily high, that some men enjoyed unwarranted privileges, that there was corruption in the conduct of office, and that local authorities were less free of influence by Jamestown or Green Spring, where Governor Berkeley lived, than they ought to be.[2] There are many questions, however, that are hard to settle, and historians have been sharply divided in their interpretation of the evidence.

Until recent years the prevailing interpretation has viewed Bacon as the leader of a popular protest against oppression and tyranny, even as a forerunner of the American Revolution.[3] The argument depends, in part, upon an assumed parallel between developments in the England of Charles II and in the Virginia of Sir William Berkeley, and so draws heavily upon a Whiggish interpretation of contemporary English history. Especially helpful has been the fact that the House of Burgesses elected in 1661 continued to sit, without another general election, for almost as long as did the Cavalier Parliament elected in the same year. Helpful, too, has been the restriction of the franchise by the act of 1670, and Sir William's record of loyalty to the Stuart kings. The difficulty is that a long-popular governor has to be converted into a tyrant, and rather suddenly at that, insofar as the surviving records of his administration show.

The usual assumption, and at best it is little more than an assumption, is that Berkeley underwent a fundamental change of

[1] Hening, *Statutes*, II, 341–365.

[2] The "Grievances" for several of the counties may be consulted in *Virginia Magazine of History*, II (1894–95), 166–73, 289–292, 380–392; III (1895–96), 35–42, 132–147.

[3] A view most eloquently argued by Thomas J. Wertenbaker in his *Torchbearer of the Revolution*.

character after 1660. Perhaps he did. His conduct on several occasions during 1676 was marked by a stormy response to those who opposed his will, but it would be difficult to prove that these outbursts of temper represent anything more than the understandable irrascibility of an elderly man, long accustomed to lead, who faced an unprecedented challenge to his leadership. That there were serious complaints regarding the government he headed is unmistakable, but it has to be noted that these complaints, if one may judge by the legislation of June, 1676, were more largely directed against the county magistrates and members of the governor's council than against the governor himself. Indeed, by one of its actions the assembly expressed its full confidence in him.[4] This came early in the session, and it has been suggested that at the time Berkeley was able to dominate its proceedings.[5] Possibly he was. The governor undoubtedly enjoyed a momentary advantage from Bacon's decision to pin his own hopes upon a reconciliation with Berkeley. A more probable explanation, however, is that the burgesses, overwhelmingly sympathetic with Bacon by the governor's own admission,[6] were merely taking an elementary precaution against a charge of sedition. The line between legitimate criticism of the government and sedition had never been an easy one to draw in the colonies, and here the circumstances compounded the risks. Berkeley bore the king's own commission, and the distance from London added to the danger of misunderstanding there. Whatever may be the fact on this point, and however justified may have been the grievances expressed by the assembly, there is very little hard evidence that Berkeley's character had changed until we reach the period of the Rebellion itself. Indeed, it has to be suggested that the argument hangs very largely upon the wrathful vengeance with which he pursued his opponents after the Rebellion.[7]

Of comparable difficulty is the question of Bacon's responsibility

[4] Berkeley had asked the king that he be relieved of his post; the assembly by resolution asked that he be continued. The text is quoted in full by Washburn, *Governor and the Rebel*, p. 56.

[5] Thomas J. Wertenbaker, *Bacon's Rebellion* (Williamsburg, 1957), p. 25; also Morton, *Colonial Virginia*, I, 249.

[6] Washburn, *Governor and the Rebel*, p. 50.

[7] Although open to possible criticism for overstatement of the case for Berkeley, Washburn's *Governor and the Rebel* provides a valuable corrective to long-established assumptions.

for the reform measures adopted by Bacon's Assembly. In a very real sense, of course, his was the ultimate responsibility, for without his headstrong action in the dispute over Indian policy the burgesses would have had no such opportunity as they enjoyed in June, 1676, to record their general grievances. Moreover, he seems to have been nowise reluctant to become the symbol of the hope men had for a redress of these grievances. In his appeals for popular support, both before and after the assembly, he more than once identified his cause with that hope. At the same time, his opponents showed no hesitancy in assigning full blame for their difficulties to Bacon. As a result, there is much in the record to suggest that Bacon's Laws, in their entirety, should be credited to him. But to a remarkable extent the evidence supporting the view that he was directly responsible for the reforms they embodied is purely circumstantial.[8] As was noted in the preceding chapter, he was in Jamestown only twice during the assembly and each time briefly.[9] On the first of these visits, Bacon, the governor, and the burgesses—these last named possibly embarrassed in their own plans by the apparent reconciliation between Berkeley and Bacon that returned the latter momentarily to his seat on the council—agreed that first consideration should be given to Indian affairs. On the second visit, which significantly included the closing days of the assembly, Bacon's presence with an impressive force of armed volunteers, at the time when the more important of the laws were adopted, could have counted heavily. Once more, however, there is no conclusive proof that Bacon did more than to create circumstances favorable to the enactment of the laws. Certainly, his own primary concern continued to be the securing of a commission for his command against the Indians.[10]

There is also reason for believing that the Indian war remained the fundamental commitment of the rank and file of those who subsequently followed Bacon into full-fledged rebellion. That they turned back from this war to fight Berkeley instead is easily explained by their anger at the apparent perfidy of the governor in

[8] Nowhere is the evidence better summarized than in Morton, *Colonial Virginia,* I, 250–256; the opposing view is presented in Washburn, *Governor and the Rebel,* pp. 49–67.

[9] See above, p. 133.

[10] See especially Washburn, *Governor and the Rebel,* pp. 56–60.

trying to raise troops against men engaged in an enterprise authorized by both governor and assembly. In so turning upon the
governor they soon found themselves irrevocably committed to
another and more desperate cause, but not without the hope held
out by Bacon's assurance that if they persisted until the king could
be accurately informed, they would be fully vindicated.[11] It is in
this connection that one finds special interest in Bacon's now
famous conversation with John Goode in September of 1676. At the
time, Bacon had driven Berkeley into a second exile on the Eastern
Shore, burned Jamestown, and held most of the colony under his
own control. The weakness in his position was that Sir William all
along had been free to communicate with London. In fact, the
conversation with Goode turned upon a report that the king was
sending 2,000 troops to put down the rebellion. Bacon speculated
upon the chance he might have of holding out against these troops,
even upon the prospect that the inhabitants of neighboring Carolina and Maryland might join the Virginians in an attempt "to cast
off their governors." But there would seem to be greater significance
in Goode's warning to Bacon that his men considered themselves
committed only against the Indians and not against their king.[12]

That Bacon himself understood this is well enough indicated by
his attempt early in August to bind the leading men of the colony to
his cause by a special oath. Those taking the oath were sworn to
support Bacon, even against the king's own troops, until the king
could be acquainted "with the state of this country," to condemn
the governor's conduct as illegal, and to uphold Bacon's commission
as both "lawfull and legally obtained." Subsequently, it was demanded of the people generally that they take the same oath before
their several county courts.[13]

Still more impressive evidence that the fundamental loyalty of
the colonists as Englishmen was never at issue is found in the
relative ease with which Governor Berkeley re-established his authority after Bacon's death. The confusion overtaking Bacon's men

11 Bacon took and required that all of his followers take the oaths of allegiance
and supremacy. Wertenbaker, *Virginia under the Stuarts*, pp. 172–173.
12 The fullest account is in Wertenbaker, *Torchbearer of the Revolution*, pp.
135–137; but see also Washburn, *Governor and the Rebel*, p. 156.
13 Craven, *Southern Colonies*, pp. 387–388; Morton, *Colonial Virginia*, I,
262–263.

with their loss in October of an obviously magnetic leader helped the governor. In tracking down broken and scattered bands of rebels, Berkeley enjoyed assistance from ships which had arrived from England for the annual tobacco crop. He undoubtedly was aided by the general anxiety of the people to escape a charge of treason, an anxiety intensified by their expectation that the king would intervene. Even so, a governor whose own recent conduct repeatedly had encouraged men to court just such a risk was able to demonstrate that he could reclaim the authority of his office without the king's intervention. When over a thousand English troops arrived early in 1677 for the pacification of the colony, they found a province no longer needing to be pacified, with exceptions chiefly for an irate governor and the Indians still in hiding. Indeed, Sir William was so well entrenched in his accustomed seat as already to have been well on the way to executing more of the rebels than the total of Cromwell's followers put to death after the Restoration of 1660 in England.[14] And so ended Bacon's Rebellion.

How then, on balance, should it be viewed? Obviously, it was not an effort to gain independence of England. Nor is it to be interpreted as an early expression of American democracy. It is true that the Rebellion fed upon popular discontent, and that the cure proposed by Bacon's Laws for the colony's political ills was a wider participation by the people in the conduct of their government. But popular participation, though one of the elements of democracy, does not in itself constitute democracy. There are too many rebellions in history which enjoyed widespread popular support, without even a pretence of being democratic, for one to be mistaken on that point. To read into the story of Bacon's Rebellion the values and standards of a much later time in our history, when the doctrine of popular sovereignty had basically altered the very concept of the sources upon which depended the right to govern, is to take the story out of context. Whatever else may be debatable about Bacon's Rebellion, it belongs to the seventeenth century, and it must be interpreted according to the conventions which governed the politics of that day. What those conventions were may be suggested

14 Morton, *Colonial Virginia,* I, 273–280; Washburn, *Governor and the Rebel,* pp. 85–91. Washburn (p. 119) puts the total of executions at twenty-three, with the royal commissioners participating in the proceedings leading to nine of these.

1. John Winthrop, Governor of Connecticut

(Harvard University)

2. Sir William Berkeley, Governor of Virginia, by Sir Peter Lely

(By kind permission of the Trustees of the late Randal Thomas Mowbray, eighth Earl of Berkeley)

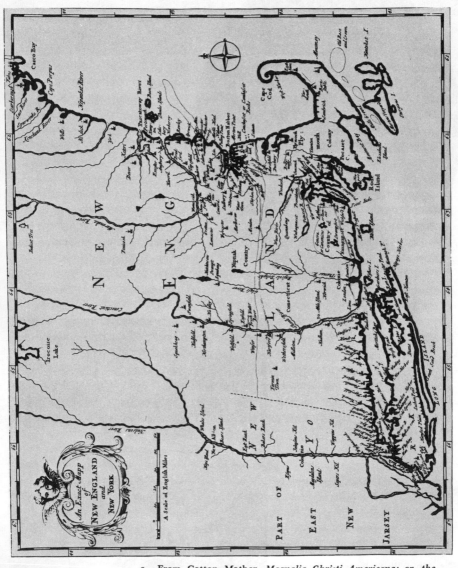

3. From Cotton Mather, *Magnalia Christi Americana: or, the Ecclesiastical History of New-England*, London, 1702

(Grenville Kane Collection, Princeton University)

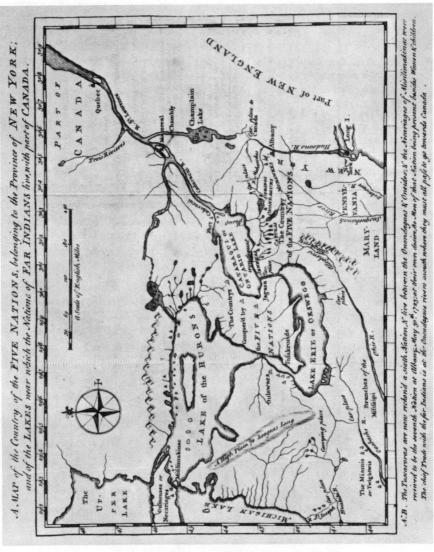

A MAP of the Country of the FIVE NATIONS, belonging to the Province of NEW YORK; and of the LAKES near which the Nations of FAR INDIANS live, with part of CANADA.

A Scale of English Miles

Part of NEW ENGLAND

PART OF CANADA

Quebec

Trois Rivieres

Montreal

Chamby

R. St. Laurence

Lake Champlain

R. Sorel

Cadaraqui

Fort Frontenac

The Country conquer'd by A CATARAQUI or ONTARIO LAKE

The FIVE NATIONS

The Country of the FIVE NATIONS

Albany

Hudson R.

NEW YORK

PENSYLVANIA

MARY LAND

Susquehanah River

LAKE ERIE or OSWEGO

LAKE of the HURONS

LAKE MICHIGAN

A High Plain 70 Leagues Long

Branches of the Missisipi

The Minnis or Twigtwies

Vrboones or Necariages

Missilimakinae

The UP-PER LAKE

Ohio R.

Carrying place

A.B. The Tuscaroras are now reckon'd a sixth Nation, & live between the Onondagoes & Oneidas; N. the Necariages of Missilimakinac were received to be the seventh Nation at Albany, May 30th 1723; at their own desire, & Men of that Nation being present hands Women & children. The chief Trade with the far Indians is at the Onondagos rivers mouth where they must all pass to go towards Canada.

4. From Cadwallader Colden, *The History of the Five Indian Nations*, 3d. ed., Vol. I, 1755

(Grenville Kane Collection, Princeton University)

5. From Richard Blome, *The Present State of His Majesties Isles and Territories in America*, London, 1687

(Grenville Kane Collection, Princeton University)

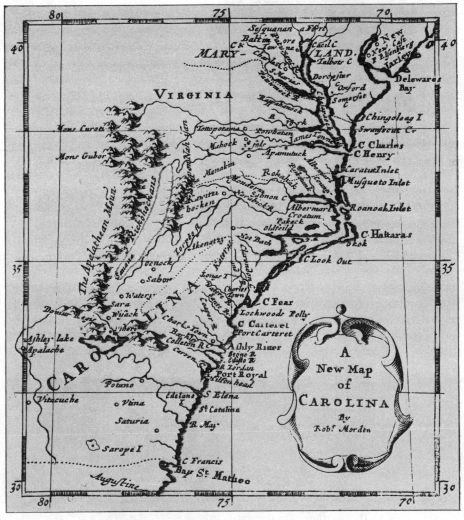

6. From *The Present State of His Majesties Isles and Territories in America*

(Grenville Kane Collection, Princeton University)

7. Charles II, engraving by
J. Smith after G. Kneller

(Princeton University Library)

8. James II, frontispiece engraved
by F. H. Van Hove, *The Present
State of His Majesties Isles and Territories in America*

(Grenville Kane Collection,
Princeton University)

JACOBUS II.ds
D. G. Angliæ: Scotiæ: Fran: et Hiber: REX.
Fidei Defensor. etc.   F. H. Van Hove Sculp.

9. William III
(Princeton University Library)

10. Queen Anne, engraving by J. Smith after G. Kneller

(Princeton University Library)

11. Indian deed of sale for land in New Jersey, 24 August 1674

(Princeton University Library)

12. John Eliot, Apostle to the Indians

(The Henry E. Huntington Library
and Art Gallery)

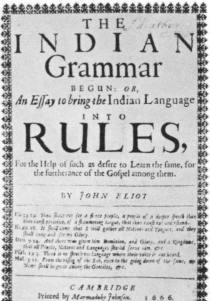

13. Title page of Eliot's *Indian Grammar*, 1666

(Library of William H. Scheide,
Princeton, N.J.)

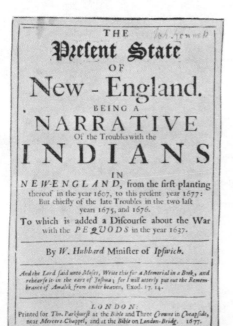

14. Title page of William Hubbard's *Narrative
of the Troubles with the Indians*, 1677

(Grenville Kane Collection,
Princeton University)

THE
CONDITIONS FOR NEW-PLANTERS
In the Territories of His ROYAL HIGHNES
THE
DUKE OF YORK

THE Purchases are to be made from the *Indian Sachims* and to be Recorded before the *Governour*.

The Purchasers are not to pay for their liberty of purchasing to the *Governour*.

The Purchasers are to set out a Town, and Inhabit together.

No Purchaser shall at any time contract for himself with any *Sachim*, without consent of his associates: or special Warrant from the *Governour* ?

The Purchasers are free from all manner of Assessments or Rates for five years after their Town-plot is set out, and when the five years are expired, they shall only be liable to the publick Rates, and Payments according to the Custome of other Inhabitants both *English* and *Dutch*.

All Lands thus Purchased, and possest shall remain to the Purchasers, and their Heires, as free Lands to dispose of as they please.

In all Territories of his ROYAL HIGHNES, Liberty of Conscience is allowed, Provided such Liberty is not converted to Licentiousnes, or the disturbance of others, in the exercise of the Protestant Religion.

The several Townships have liberty to make their peculiar Laws, and Deciding all small Causes within themselves.

The Lands which I intend shall be first Planted, are those upon the West side of *Hudson-River*, at, or adjoyning to the *Sopes*, but if any number of men sufficient for two or three, or more Towns, shall desire to plant upon any other Lands they shall have all due encouragement proportionable to their Quality, and undertakings.

Every Township is Obliged to pay their *Minister*, according to such agreement as they shall make with him, and no man to refuse his Proportion, the *Minister* being elected by the Major part of the Householders Inhabitants of the *Town*.

Every Township hath the free choice of all their officers both Civil, and Military, and all men who shall take the Oath of Allegiance to his *Majesty*, and are not Servants, or day-labourers, but are admitted to enjoy *Town-lotts* are esteemed freemen of the Jurisdiction, and cannot forfeit the same without due process in Law.

R. Nicolls.

15. Promotional broadside printed for Governor Nicolls at Cambridge, 1665

(Massachusetts Historical Society)

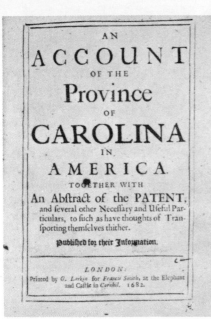

16. Title page of a Carolina promotional tract, 1682

(Rare Book Division, The New York Public Library, Astor, Lenox and Tilden Foundations)

17. Title page of a New Jersey promotional tract, 1685

(Grenville Kane Collection, Princeton University)

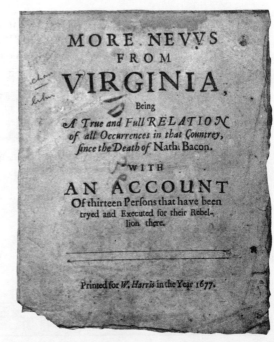

18. Title page of a report to Londoners of news from Virginia, 1677

(Tracy W. McGregor Library, University of Virginia)

19. Detail showing the fort at "New York from Brooklyn Heights, 1679," from a drawing to illustrate Jasper Danckaerts and Peter Sluyter, "Journal of a Voyage to New York in 1679-1680"

(*Memoirs*, Long Island Historical Society, Vol. I, 1867)

20. The plan for Philadelphia as it appears in *Missive van William Penn*, a Dutch translation of one of Penn's early promotional tracts published at Amsterdam in 1684

(Grenville Kane Collection, Princeton University)

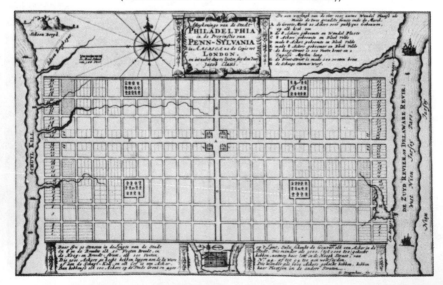

21.   Bonner's map of Boston, 1722

(I. N. Phelps Stokes Collection, The New York Public Library,
Astor, Lenox and Tilden Foundations)

22. William Penn, 1696,
by Francis Place

(The Historical Society
of Pennsylvania)

23. The Stony Brook Meeting House of the Society of Friends, Princeton, N.J.

(Photograph by Alan W. Richards)

24. Sir Edmund Andros

(From Vol. I of *The Andros Tracts*, Prince Society, 1868)

25. Increase Mather, 1688, by Van der Spriett

(Massachusetts Historical Society)

26. Henry Compton, Bishop of London

(From program for *Trinity Church Bicentennial Celebration,* 1897)

27. James Blair by Hargreaves

(The College of William and Mary)

Ten Shillings. (No. 3364)

THis Indented Bill of *Ten Shillings*, due from the Colony of New-York to the Poſſeſſor thereof, ſhall be in equal value to Money, and ſhall be accordingly accepted by the Treaſurer of this Colony, for the time being, in all publick payments, and for any Fund at any time in the Treaſury. Dated, New-York 31ſt of *May*, 1709. by order of the Lieut. Governour, Council and General Aſſembly of the ſaid Colony.

R. Walter
Jo: Cruger
Robt. Lurting

Five Shillings. (No. 3331)

THis Indented Bill of *Five Shillings*, due from the colony of New-York to the Poſſeſſor thereof, ſhall be in value equal to Money, & ſhall be accordingly accepted by the Treaſurer of this Colony, for the time being, in all publick Payments, and for any Fund at any time in the Treaſury. Dated, New-York 31ſt of *May*, 1709. by order of the Lieut. Governor, Council, and General Aſſembly of the ſaid Colony.

R. Walter
Jo: Cruger
Robt. Lurting

28. Paper money, New York issue of 1709

(Princeton University Library)

simply by noting the repeated attempts by Bacon's opponents to discredit his movement by branding it as democratic—which is to say, as nothing more than an uprising of the "rabble," the "bobtailed," and the "ragtailed."

Actually, Bacon himself had as clear a claim as any man in Virginia to gentility. To picture the rebel as a frontiersman, or even as the special spokesman for the cruder type of frontiersman, is to get the picture out of focus. Among his followers, as among those who originally pushed him forward as their leader, were other gentlemen or men who had some claim at least to being so considered. In addition to William Byrd, already mentioned, there was William Drummond, the first governor of North Carolina, as we now know it, and holder of extensive properties in Virginia. Another was Richard Lawrence, graduate of Oxford.[15] Others included Charles Scarborough, William Kendall, Giles Brent, Thomas Goodrich, and Giles Bland, who until his removal from office in 1674, after a quarrel with Berkeley, had been the king's collector of customs.[16] Among those who took Bacon's oath in August, some no doubt with little relish, were members of the Swan, Page, Lightfoot, and Ballard families.[17]

The most interesting of recent suggestions for the interpretation of Bacon's Rebellion is found in a paper by Bernard Bailyn of Harvard.[18] The paper presents a hypothesis rather than the conclusive results of intensive research, but judged by the known facts the hypothesis is persuasive. The argument is that the colonists, while borrowing heavily from the political institutions of England, were unable to transfer to the New World the social structure which in the old gave validity and stability to these institutions. In England, by long-established custom, office belonged to the well-born according to their station in a social hierarchy which was hardly distinguishable from the resulting political hierarchy. Political au-

15 Wertenbaker, *Torchbearer of the Revolution*, pp. 60–61, 130–131; Wilcomb E. Washburn, "The Humble Petition of Sarah Drummond," *William and Mary Quarterly*, 3d. ser., XIII (1956), 354–375.

16 Washburn, *Governor and the Rebel*, p. 237 n., with citation to the author's unpublished Ph.D. dissertation, "Bacon's Rebellion, 1676–1677" (Harvard, 1955), for evidence of the extensive properties held by rebels.

17 Wertenbaker, *Bacon's Rebellion*, p. 33.

18 "Politics and Social Structure in Virginia," in James M. Smith (ed.), *Seventeenth Century America*, pp. 90–115.

thority, in other words, reflected with reasonable faithfulness the location of authority in society. But in America, although Englishmen continued to be guided by the conventional assumptions, a different and as yet highly unstable social order was emerging. Not only had the great migrations from England failed to provide proportionate representation for all ranks in the English hierarchy, but energetic adventurers of humble origins often excelled their social superiors in acquiring wealth, and with wealth power. It is noticeable that the leadership of the colony after 1660 was drawn very largely from relatively recent immigrants, which is to say that the earlier settlers had not established an elite capable of extending its authority into this later period of the colony's history. Professor Bailyn suggests that we read the story of Bacon's Rebellion as testimony to the profound disorganization of a new society.

In this connection, several points need to be stated, at least briefly. Sir William Berkeley, well qualified by birth for the leadership he reassumed in 1660, associated with himself other men who had at least some pretention to full qualification for high office—such men as Sir Henry Chicheley, Colonel Henry Norwood, and Francis Moryson, all of them royalist exiles.[19] But Sir William also drew into his government still others, among them Abraham Wood, who first had arrived in the colony as a servant and who had built a fortune upon the Indian trade.[20] Among the more recent immigrants, those who founded the Byrd, Bland, Lee, Carter, Burwell, Ludwell, and other great families of eighteenth-century Virginia have a special interest. They had come in the middle of the century, many of them of royalist persuasion if without full claim to Cavalier status. Some were younger sons of well-placed merchants or tradesmen in London, or of the lesser gentry of the counties outside London.[21] Like Bacon, they brought with them a stake to start them on their New World careers. Although not in every case members of the English establishment, they were close enough to that attainment to know full well their claim to membership in a newly forming Virginia establishment. But some fared better than

[19] Moryson served as governor during Berkeley's mission to London in 1661–62, was himself agent there for the colony in 1675, and returned to Virginia in 1677 as a member of the royal commission for investigation of the rebellion. Craven, *Southern Colonies*, p. 269.

[20] See above, p. 114.

[21] For emphasis upon the London background of many settlers, see Thomas J. Wertenbaker, *Patrician and Plebeian in Virginia* (Charlottesville, 1910).

others, and notably those, like Norwood and Thomas Ludwell, who were related to Berkeley.

Those who were disappointed in their highest hopes for preferment found it easier to work their way into the short-handed magistracy of the local county courts, whence they might find an opportunity to make their voices heard in the management of provincial affairs through the newly organized House of Burgesses. At all levels of government there were too many who held office without a natural claim to it that was strong enough to free them of the suspicion with which their fellows regarded their exercise of power and their enjoyment of the emoluments of office. The point was stated most effectively by Bacon himself in his Manifesto of August 1676. Said he: "Let us trace these men in Authority and Favour to whose hands the dispensation of the Countries wealth has been commited; let us observe the sudden Rise of their Estates with the Quality in which they first entered this Country. . . . And let us see wither their extractions and Education have not bin vile, And by what pretence of learning and vertue they could [enter] soe soon into Imployments of so great Trust and consequence. . . ."[22] Bailyn would have us read Bacon's Laws as an expression of discontent with the leadership of the colony at two levels, the local and the provincial. It can hardly be said that the riddle, either of Bacon's Laws or of the Rebellion itself, has been fully solved, but Professor Bailyn's suggestions have the distinct virtue of lifting the discussion out of the context of a debate as to who was the hero and who the villain.

They also offer a clue as to why Bacon's Rebellion won no place of major importance in the colony's political tradition. No coalition of Bacon's followers emerged from the Rebellion to play thereafter a significant part in Virginia's politics. Even Berkeley's adherents, who for a number of years seem to have found some cohesion through a continuing quarrel with agents of the king, constituted no faction of enduring importance. As early as 1705, Robert Beverley, son of one of Berkeley's ardent supporters, could write in his *History of Virginia* about as judicious an explanation of the Rebellion as has since been written.[23] During the eighteenth century, Bacon was largely forgotten or remembered simply as a

---

22 Quoted by Bailyn, "Politics and Social Structure in Virginia," p. 104.
23 Louis B. Wright's edition of Robert Beverley, *History and Present State of Virginia* (Chapel Hill, N.C., 1947), pp. 74 ff.

troublemaker. Not until well past the American Revolution would he be rediscovered as a symbol of the Virginian's love of liberty and opposition to tyranny.[24]

Nor did the Rebellion have as profound an affect upon the development of political institutions in Virginia as might be expected. It marks a turning point of no small consequence, if only because it brought to an end the relatively agreeable relationship between governor, council, and burgesses that had obtained through most of Berkeley's administration. He had ruled as the king's governor, but also in his own right as a Virginian. After him would come governors who lacked this last identification, and the difference was to have great importance. But the Rebellion itself brought forth remarkably little in the way of proposals for fundamental change beyond the increased voice Bacon's Laws would have given the general populace, and these laws were promptly repealed by the assembly meeting in February, 1677. It is true that the assembly re-enacted several of the measures, but with significant modification, and those thus continued did not include the statute extending the franchise to freemen (partly no doubt because a royal instruction of October, 1676, demanded conformity with English practice), nor the one making vestries elective.[25] As a more stable social order emerged in the later years of the century, the government of Virginia bore a stronger resemblance to what Sir William Berkeley had helped to build through many years than to what Bacon's angry followers momentarily had demanded.

No part of the story has greater interest than does the king's decision to intervene. Late in 1676 he sent out from England a force of 1,130 men, all told, at a cost of better than £12,000, and joined the military commander, Colonel Herbert Jeffreys, in a commission for investigation and report with Sir John Berry, naval commander, and Francis Moryson, an influential resident of Virginia then in London as agent for the colony.[26] When placed in the context of

24 Wesley Frank Craven, *Legend of the Founding Fathers* (New York, 1956), pp. 69–71; Washburn, *Governor and the Rebel*, pp. 1–16.

25 Morton, *Colonial Virginia*, I, 285–286; for the royal instruction, Leonard W. Labaree, *Royal Instructions to British Colonial Governors, 1670–1776* (2 vols., New York, 1935), I, 93.

26 Washburn, *Governor and the Rebel*, pp. 92–95; John W. Shy, *Toward Lexington: The Role of the British Army in the Coming of the American Revolution* (Princeton, 1965), pp. 22–24; J. R. Tanner (ed.), *A Descriptive*

other recent developments, including the first dispatch of the remarkable Edward Randolph to Boston, this extraordinary show of force could have had the broadest significance for students of English colonial policy.

A promise that some tighter control over the colonies might be attempted had come three years earlier, with the enactment of a third Navigation Act. The act of 1673 enunciated no new principles of policy, but it did undertake to plug a loophole experience had revealed in the enumerated commodities clause in the Navigation Act of 1660. That law had required that enumerated commodities be shipped either to England or to one of the English plantations, and certain shippers, perhaps mainly American, had been evading the intent of the law by landing the tobacco of the Chesapeake, or the sugar of Barbados, in some other colony and then carrying it wheresoever they wished. The new legislation imposed a customs duty upon shipments of enumerated commodities from colony to colony, soon to be commonly known as the "plantations duty," and introduced additional requirements for the bonding of shipmasters to observance of the law.[27] For the enforcement of these requirements and the collection of the new duty, the act also provided for the appointment of customs officers who would function under the jurisdiction of the Commissioners of the Customs in London. Although appointed at first only in the colonies producing enumerated commodities, on an apparent assumption that the point of first shipment was the logical place for enforcement of the new controls, the customs officers represented a development of far-reaching significance. Earlier legislation had left all responsibility for its enforcement in the colonies in the hands of the governor, who consequently had enjoyed the patronage of such officers, usually known as naval officers, as he had seen fit to appoint for that purpose.[28]

What the introduction of a new establishment depending upon

Catalogue of the Naval Manuscripts in the Pepysian Library at Magdalene College, Cambridge (4 vols., Cambridge, Eng., 1903–23) , III, xxv–xxvi.

[27] Andrews, *Colonial Period*, IV, 119–24; Bailyn, *New England Merchants*, pp. 149–150; and especially Thomas C. Barrow, *Trade and Empire: The British Customs Service in Colonial America, 1660–1775* (Cambridge, Mass., 1967) , pp. 6–13.

[28] Andrews, *Colonial Period*, IV, 180–187, for the early history of the naval officers; and for the initial establishment of the new customs service, Barrow, *Trade and Empire*, pp. 14–16.

the patronage of London might mean for colonial politics is suggested by the role played in Bacon's Rebellion by Giles Bland, first of the king's customs officers in Virginia. Member of an influential merchant family in London, to whose influence he undoubtedly owed his office, Bland had quickly fallen out with Berkeley and had identified himself with Bacon's cause. Indeed, Collector Bland was one of the more important among those who were executed for their part in the Rebellion, and no less significant is the fact that his own representations to London may have been as influential as those made by Berkeley in bringing the king's decision to intervene.[29]

The beginning of what may be described as a colonial service in the colonies was quickly followed by a new and increasingly important agency of administrative supervision in Whitehall. In 1675 a standing committee of the Privy Council, commonly known as the Lords of Trade, took over responsibilities theretofore carried by a succession of special advisory councils, or committees, for trade and plantations.[30] The difference between the new and the older agencies was that the Lords of Trade, as a standing committee of the Privy Council, included more of the most powerful of the king's ministers, and so the function of advising the king became more closely linked to the power to act upon the advice given. Over the years ahead the committee's decisions were destined to bring a growing coherence and consistency into the government's actions on colonial issues, and so to give shape to new and significant lines of policy.

It must be understood, however, that this development was evolutionary in character. Precisely because their lordships were great men of the kingdom, the members of the committee had many other and heavier responsibilities. Their attention to colonial questions could be fitful. Much depended upon what was brought before them, and much that was pressed upon their attention after 1675 resulted from the troubled state of several of the more important colonies.

29 *Ibid.*, pp. 21–24; and on Bland's family, see especially Neville Williams, "The Tribulations of John Bland, Merchant: London, Seville, Jamestown, Tangier, 1643–1680," *Virginia Magazine of History and Biography*, LXXII (1964) , 19–41.

30 Andrews, *Colonial Period*, IV, 57–58; Ralph P. Bieber, *The Lords of Trade and Plantations, 1675–1696* (Allentown, Pa., 1919) .

That the king himself should have taken the lead in determining the government's response to news of rebellion in Virginia is not difficult to explain. Virginia was a royal colony, the only one in North America, and the king's right of rule was directly involved. Moreover, any prolonged disturbance there would seriously affect the royal revenues by loss in the customs collected in England upon Virginia's tobacco crop.[31] The need to restore peace to the colony was obvious, but there is no evidence that the government looked beyond that immediate need.

The arrival of over a thousand of the king's troops in a country no longer in rebellion quickly became a major source of embarrassment for all parties concerned. Planning for the return of all but a few of the soldiers was initiated in London as early as April, 1677. Perhaps most of them returned to England with Berry and Moryson in the following summer; perhaps a goodly number of them took advantage of the proffered opportunity to remain as settlers in the colony. A decision in 1678 to keep two companies on station in Virginia suggests the extent of the reduction already accomplished. Three years later, it was decided that even this small force could be kept on station only if the colony agreed to meet the cost out of its own revenues. The assembly refused, and in 1682 Virginia's brief experience with a royal garrison came to an end.[32]

Meanwhile, bitter quarrels in Virginia between the king's representatives and the once more dominant adherents of Berkeley repeatedly had forced the problems of that colony upon the attention of the Lords of Trade. The commissioners reaching Virginia early in 1677 were charged chiefly with a mission to restore the peace of the colony, as is evidenced by the royal proclamation of pardon they brought for all of the rebels, saving only Bacon, and by instructions which called for a hearing of popular grievances. A sharp dispute with Sir William Berkeley quickly developed, in which the governor's insistence upon additional exceptions to the king's pardon became an especially critical issue. Whose was the

---

31 Which, according to Washburn, *Governor and the Rebel*, p. 93, equaled the secret subsidy the king currently was receiving from Louis XIV of France. See also Washburn's "The Effect of Bacon's Rebellion on Government in England and Virginia," *United States National Museum Bulletin* 225 (Washington, 1962), pp. 137–152.

32 Shy, *Toward Lexington*, pp. 23–25; Morton, *Colonial Virginia*, I, 305; Tanner, *Naval Manuscripts*, III, 411.

original fault matters less than does the fact that the contest was protracted and unseemly. Berkeley had asked in the preceding year to be relieved of his post, and Jeffreys had come with a commission to take over as lieutenant governor upon Sir William's departure, but the governor was reluctant to yield. Not until May, 1677, did he sail for England, where he died early in July, before he had had a chance to present his case to the king.[33]

What he might have accomplished by presenting his defense is problematical. What were the influences flowing from the situation after his death are clear enough. Commissioners Berry and Moryson reached England a month after Berkeley's death. There is evidence to indicate that both were judicious men, including the account of the Rebellion they submitted in the following October.[34] But they had been involved in a struggle with Berkeley, and they had listened, as was their duty, to the grievances of the colonists. It was only natural that the Lords of Trade and the king should lean heavily upon advice from the commissioners in determining a number of issues arising from the Rebellion, and that this advice should reflect some of the doubts they entertained about the governor's conduct.[35] The judgment of the two commissioners in London was reinforced by reports from their former colleague in Virginia, where Jeffreys, until his death late in 1678, had a miserable time trying to govern the colony.

The basic source of his trouble is obvious. Berkeley's adherents, by and large, were once more in the seats of power, whether by fair means or foul, as has been suggested.[36] There is no mystery in the fact that some of the most ardent of Berkeley's friends quickly became equally ardent champions of the rights and liberties of the House of Burgesses; nor is it necessary to argue that they had changed their coats. The story has its beginning in April, 1677, when the royal commissioners demanded for use in their investigation the records of the assembly. Its clerk, Robert Beverley, father to

[33] The story of his last days in Virginia may be followed, from somewhat different points of view, in Morton, *Colonial Virginia*, I, 279–290, and Washburn, *Governor and the Rebel*, pp. 96–139.

[34] For the report, see Charles M. Andrews (ed.), *Narratives of the Insurrections, 1675–1690* (New York, 1915), pp. 101–141.

[35] The fullest account is by Washburn, *Governor and the Rebel*, pp. 139–150.

[36] Wertenbaker, *Virginia under the Stuarts*, pp. 205–206, 218–219.

the later historian, refused to yield their possession, although agreeing to their use. The commissioners, probably distrusting his good faith, seized them. The assembly was not then sitting, but when a newly elected assembly met in the following October, the burgesses registered a strong and formal protest with Governor Jeffreys. The protest was forwarded by him to London, where the king read it as a challenge to his own authority and directed the Lords of Trade to advise on appropriate steps for forcing a due submission by the house. Their lordships thought the paper "Seditious, even tending to Rebellion," and advised a formal rebuke of the assembly and punishment for the authors. The upshot was that Thomas Lord Culpeper, Berkeley's successor in the office of governor, carried with him to Virginia in 1680 instructions to administer the rebuke and punish the key offenders.[37]

Culpeper's luggage included much else besides. Extensive experience with the West Indian plantations (where attempts to govern and defend these valuable possessions at little or no cost to the king had given a distinct advantage to increasingly alert representative assemblies) had persuaded the king and his advisers that the time had come for a more vigorous assertion of the royal prerogative.[38] Nothing, it was concluded, could more effectively accomplish this purpose than the establishment of permanent revenues, independent of recurring votes by the assembly, for the administrative costs of the colony. Poyning's Law, which had forbidden the Irish Parliament to enact legislation other than that submitted to it by the king and Privy Council, suggested a precedent that might be helpful in securing the necessary appropriations, as also in establishing a desirable control over all legislative proceedings in the royal colonies. The plan was tried first in Jamaica in 1678, and none too successfully.[39] It was Virginia's turn in 1680.

The delay is probably well enough explained simply by the difficulty the king experienced in getting Lord Culpeper to his station. He had secured in 1675 a commission as governor of Virginia for life in succession to the aging Sir William Berkeley, and upon the latter's death he automatically became the governor.

37 *Ibid.*, pp. 213–215.
38 Replacing older authorities is Thornton's *West-India Policy under the Restoration*.
39 *Ibid.*, pp. 166–177, 191–210.

As one who held a share in the proprietorship of the Northern Neck under a patent first issued in 1649 and reconfirmed in 1669, and as joint beneficiary with the Earl of Arlington of another patent of 1673 which awarded the quitrents and other regalities of the entire colony to the two men for a period of thirty-one years, he might have been expected to assume the duties of office promptly.[40] But Lord Culpeper was a pleasure-loving gentleman who much preferred England to Virginia. The king finally got him off to his job by threatening to recall his commission.

Lord Culpeper's instructions were to notify the Virginians that henceforth the assembly could meet only with the consent of the king's ministers in London, and that it could consider only such legislation as had been drafted by the governor and council and approved by London. As a substantial token of what was to be expected in the future, the king had sent three bills with instruction that they be enacted: an "Act of free and generall pardon" intended to settle issues in dispute since the Rebellion, a measure defining naturalization as a prerogative of the crown, and a bill appropriating the 2s. per hogshead duty on exported tobacco, first enacted in 1658, to the crown as a permanent revenue.[41] Curiously, all three were enacted, not even excluding the act which permanently deprived the House of Burgesses of a substantial measure of its control of the purse.[42]

This acquiescence presents an unusually interesting question. The answer is partly to be found in Culpeper's diplomacy. For example, he allowed the council to talk him out of delivering the royal rebuke to the assembly the king had ordered him to give. He also disregarded that part of his instructions depriving the assembly of a right to initiate legislation, and was later upheld on the ground that considerations of distance and time made the proposal un-

[40] Andrews, *Colonial Period*, II, 234–235; [Fairfax Harrison], *Proprietors of the Northern Neck*, pp. 76–82.

[41] Wertenbaker, *Virginia under the Stuarts*, pp. 226–231.

[42] The annual revenue from the duty at this time was perhaps £3,000, which may be compared with an estimated return of £6,747 from an unusually high public levy of 1682. Flippin, *Royal Government in Virginia*, pp. 231, 244; Bruce, *Institutional History*, II, 558, 587. For the long-run effect, see Jack P. Greene, *The Quest for Power: The Lower Houses of Assembly in the Southern Royal Colonies, 1689–1776* (Chapel Hill, N.C., 1963), pp. 27–28.

workable.[43] He courted the favor of influential friends of the late Governor Berkeley by accepting Robert Beverley as clerk of assembly, despite the fact that the king had disqualified him for any public employment, and by restoring Philip Ludwell to a seat on the council from which he had been removed by order of the Privy Council after an especially offensive attack upon Lieutenant Governor Jeffreys. Further use of the governor's patronage is indicated by evidence that at least one member of the house was promised a seat on the council and got it after the session.[44]

According to recent findings, the "Act of free and generall pardon," which the assembly readily accepted, gave additional grounds for satisfaction to Sir William's friends.[45] By linking a general pardon with specific exceptions for nine of the rebels in addition to Bacon, and by authorizing legal recovery of property lost during the rebellion, the act in effect reversed the position originally taken by the government in London on the advice of the royal commissioners. If not a full vindication for Sir William and his supporters, it was a most gratifying concession on a critical issue that had been hotly debated.

The governor also had a stick at hand and did not hesitate to brandish it. Quitrents for many years in Virginia had been indifferently collected, when collected at all. They had an obvious pertinence to the question of permanent revenues for the support of the colony's government, as London would become increasingly aware. In the case of Virginia, it so happened, London had been shortsighted enough as recently as 1673 to give away this potential source of revenue to Culpeper and his associate, but the Virginians stood to gain nothing thereby. Indeed, the mere presence of Culpeper was a reminder of a fear growing over recent years that what had become little more than a formal acknowlegment of the king's right might become a costly burden. The greatest fear, it seems, was that a demand might be made for payment of accumulated arrears.[46]

---

43 Partly, no doubt, because the same conclusion was reached in the case of Jamaica.

44 The fullest account is in Wertenbaker, *Virginia under the Stuarts.* See especially pp. 214–215, 216, 229–230.

45 Washburn, *Governor and the Rebel,* pp. 146–148, especially.

46 Bond, *Quit-rent System,* pp. 221–224; Wertenbaker, *Virginia under the Stuarts,* pp. 229–231.

Perhaps the Virginians, confronted by the prospect of two heavy blows, elected to receive what promised to be the lighter in the hope of warding off the heavier one.

Perhaps it should also be suggested that the burgesses were not fully alert to the implications of what they faced. It was a very old practice in Virginia to enact laws suggested by the governor's instructions.[47] The 2s. duty had been collected for over twenty years, and its revenues devoted to the very uses, including payment of the governor's salary, that were now proposed. In one sense, the duty already had become a permanent revenue. The difference between being able to withhold it, if only temporarily for purposes of maneuver, and a permanent assignment of it to the king was great, of course, and certainly this was understood. But the Virginia burgesses, for all the complaints about high taxes at the time of the rebellion, had as yet only a limited experience with the political uses of the taxing power.[48] The understanding they later were to show owed much to what they learned from their surrender in the difficult circumstances of 1680.

Culpeper was also instrumental in depriving the assembly of one other power—its right to sit as the highest court of appeal in the colony. The conviction of Philip Ludwell in 1678, by the governor and council sitting as the General Court, for slanderous comments about the governor may or may not have been responsible for bringing the issue to the king's attention.[49] In any case, the practice ran counter to a growing assumption that the administration of justice was an inherent power of the crown. Accordingly, it was decided that the governor and council should have the final voice in the colony, and that appeals thereafter could be taken only to the king. The restriction was first included in Culpeper's instructions of 1679 and repeated more fully in his instructions of 1682.[50] On this point, as with other parts of the king's directives,

[47] Craven, *Southern Colonies*, p. 206.

[48] See above, p. 29. For evidence that it had been customary under Berkeley for representatives of the council to sit with most committees of the lower house, see Greene, *Quest for Power*, p. 27; Morton, *Colonial Virginia*, I, 250–251; Elmer I. Miller, *The Legislature of the Province of Virginia* (New York, 1907), p. 158.

[49] Clarke, *Parliamentary Privilege*, pp. 37–38, including n. 71; Joseph H. Smith, *Appeals to the Privy Council from the American Plantations* (New York, 1950), p. 80; Wertenbaker, *Virginia under the Stuarts*, pp. 219–220.

[50] Labaree, *Royal Instructions*, I, No. 442, 446.

the governor seems to have avoided unnecessarily disturbing the colonists, with the result that his successor was left to receive the brunt of Virginia's protest.[51]

Within a short time after Culpeper's arrival in the colony, he had returned to England, where he enlarged his proprietary interests by buying out other claimants under the two Virginia patents he held.[52] During his absence the peace of the colony once more was broken by the tobacco-cutting riots of 1682. The continuingly depressed prices paid for tobacco had brought popular demand for some scheme of crop reduction, an expedient Virginians had turned to occasionally in the past in the hope of stimulating the price of their staple. After the elderly Sir Henry Chicheley, serving as lieutenant governor and acting contrary to the advice of his council, called an assembly to meet in the spring for consideration of the question, he had to send the burgesses home with the announcement that he had just received instructions from the king forbidding any session of the assembly before the governor's return. Frustrated thus in their hopes, many of the colonists took the issue into their own hands as riotous mobs destroyed the tobacco already growing in the fields. Even with the government's resort to militia patrols, it took until August to suppress the last of the riots. The news brought Culpeper back to Virginia late in 1682. Placing the needs of the royal treasury ahead of every other consideration, he rejected all proposals for crop reduction and had two of the recent rioters executed as a warning against further protest. Soon, he sailed once more for England, and this time the king, in August, 1683, dismissed him from office.[53]

For Virginia, four unusually stormy years lay immediately ahead. In Lord Howard of Effingham, who reached Jamestown early in 1684 as Culpeper's successor, the king had found a far more conscientious servant of the crown. Determined to take the firm hand his instructions called for and by nature none too tactful a man, he was quickly involved in contentions as bitter as any the colony had ever known. The issues were not so much new as rather

51 Wertenbaker, *Virginia under the Stuarts*, pp. 241–242.

52 [Fairfax Harrison], *Virginia Land Grants, a Study of Conveyancing in Relation to Colonial Politics* (Richmond, privately printed, 1925) , pp. 68–69.

53 Wertenbaker, *Virginia under the Stuarts*, pp. 232–235; Morton, *Colonial Virginia*, I, 300–301, 303–308.

more clearly defined. Especially disturbing was the governor's announcement, after the king in 1684 had repossessed the colony's regalities by purchase of Culpeper's patent of 1673, that henceforth quitrents would have to be paid and that the returns from them would be used to provide another source of independent revenue for support of the king's government in the colony. While disputing with the burgesses, the governor generally was able to hold his council in line, but there was one significant exception. Philip Ludwell, now married to Berkeley's widow and living in Green Spring, won the distinction in 1686 of being kicked off the council a second time. Almost as if to foretell the future course of Virginia's political history, he subsequently ran for and won a seat in the House of Burgesses which the governor succeeded in denying to him on the ground of his suspension from the council. The end result was that Ludwell reached London in the summer of 1688 bearing a petition of grievances from the burgesses that in effect called for Lord Howard's removal from office.[54]

But to carry the history of post-Berkeley Virginia thus far is to get ahead of the main story that needs here to be told, a story of developments in all of the older areas of settlement which reached a significant turning point in 1684, or very close thereto, just on the eve of Charles II's death early in 1685. For Virginia 1684 had brought Lord Howard as successor to the inattentive Culpeper. In Carolina's Albemarle County the preceding year had seen the beginning of Seth Sothel's attempt to govern a colony recently disturbed by Culpeper's Rebellion. In Maryland, 1684 had witnessed some relaxation in the political strife which the colony had experienced since the year of Bacon's Rebellion, and Lord Baltimore sailed for England, where a number of difficulties needed to be settled with the Lords of Trade and with other officers of the crown. Most important of all, this was the year that brought the annulment of the Massachusetts charter.

Culpeper's Rebellion of December, 1677, was a petty affair by comparison with Bacon's Rebellion, to which nevertheless it may

---

[54] Morton, *Colonial Virginia*, I, 317, 326–327, 333; Wertenbaker, *Virginia under the Stuarts*, pp. 253–255, 257–258. Culpeper surrendered his patent in return for a pension of £600 for twenty-one years. [Fairfax Harrison] *Proprietors of the Northern Neck*, p. 81.

have owed some of its inspiration. At any rate, it is known that John Culpeper, from whom the rebellion took its name, mistakenly it seems, had been in Jamestown during May, 1676.

Certainly, there are parallels to be observed when one considers the underlying causes for unrest in the two colonies. Tobacco sold for no better price in Albemarle than it did in Virginia. Indeed, navigational dangers along the Carolina coast, the shallowness of the inland waterways, and the smallness of the total crop discouraged shipping of the kind which came from England each year to take away the Chesapeake crop. As a result, Albemarle had become peculiarly dependent upon enterprising New England merchants for the marketing of its tobacco. Whatever the effect of the plantation duty may have been in Virginia, it hurt in Carolina —or perhaps it should be said, rather, that it would have hurt had it been collected. Taken together, the inhabitants of Albemarle undoubtedly formed as poverty-stricken a community of Englishmen as could be found anywhere in North America. They had experienced trouble too with the Indians, whose recent uprisings, according to contemporary accounts, had been put down only with the "loss of many men."[55]

The colony had been torn by factional strife for some time. Speaking generally, the division tended to array the older inhabitants, those who had settled before the establishment of the proprietorship, against the newcomers, and more especially those who owed their influence to the patronage of the lords proprietors. The two factions are conveniently designated as proprietary and antiproprietary, but the line between the two was not so sharply defined as the use of such designations may suggest. Peter Colleton's subsequent lament that it was "a very difficult matter to gitt a man of worth and trust to go thither" suggests that the quality of Albemarle's leaders contributed significantly to the stormy character of its politics.[56] It is abundantly evident that the simplest kind of personal animosity could be as important as any other consideration.

Leader among the older settlers, and probably the largest single

[55] For these accounts, see Andrews, *Narratives of the Insurrections*, pp. 145–164.

[56] *Ibid.*, p. 160.

exporter of tobacco in the colony, was George Durant.[57] His allies included John Jenkins, who in 1673 became the acting governor. The story leading to the rebellion has its beginning two years later, when Jenkins, still in the governor's chair, undertook to destroy a personal and political enemy named Thomas Miller by having him arrested and imprisoned on a charge of "treasonable utterances." A friend of Miller who was also speaker of the assembly, Thomas Eastchurch, succeeded in persuading that body to vote Jenkins out of office, but this action by no means settled the issue. Consequently, in 1676 Eastchurch and Miller, who had broken jail, went to London for the purpose of presenting their side of the argument to the lords proprietors. Among the charges they brought against Jenkins was that for two years he had made a complete farce of the collection of the plantation duty, which probably was true enough. Sensitive to the possible effect of such a defiance of the law upon their own interest, the proprietors responded by commissioning Eastchurch to return to the colony as their governor, and by securing for Miller, through the commissioners of customs, appointment as collector for Albemarle. Thus reinforced, the two men sailed with the encouraging prospect that they might now prevail over their enemies at home. But on the way Eastchurch threw his advantage away by tarrying in the West Indies to court a lady of fortune. He sent Miller ahead with a commission of doubtful legality to act as the interim governor. This Miller attempted to do, and worse still, he undertook to collect the plantation duty. The result was Culpeper's Rebellion.

There can be little doubt that George Durant was the real leader of the rebellion. Assisting in the successful attempt to overthrow Miller's interim government was Zachariah Gillam, a Boston shipmaster whose colorful career included past service with the Hudson's Bay Company and who now undoubtedly was in Albemarle for a load of "uncustomed" tobacco.[58] Miller was seized and placed in irons. The rebels won the support of the people, and by

[57] The following account of the rebellion and its aftermath depends chiefly upon Lefler and Newsome, *North Carolina*, pp. 42–46; R. D. W. Connor, *History of North Carolina* (4 vols., Chicago and New York, 1919), I, 47–63; Andrews, *Colonial Period*, III, 252–257.

[58] For Gillam's career, see Andrews, *Colonial Period*, III, 226 n., 254 n.; and E. E. Rich, *Hudson's Bay Company, 1670–1870* (3 vols., New York, 1961), I, where the index provides the guide to a number of references.

election organized a revolutionary government. Governor East-church, having belatedly landed in Virginia with his bride, was denied even so much as admission to his province. He soon died.

Whatever may have been the extent of John Culpeper's responsibility for the rebellion, it was he who subsequently faced formal charges of treason and so gave his name to the whole affair. Perhaps he had a propensity for getting into trouble. He had migrated from Barbados to Charles Town in 1671, where he served for a time as surveyor to the new settlement. Later, and for reasons that may have included involvement in disturbances there, he moved to Albemarle.[59] His great mistake now was in accepting appointment by the revolutionary regime as collector of the customs in lieu of the ousted Miller, for the latter held that post by royal commission. When Miller, having broken jail a second time, reached England late in 1679 to charge Culpeper with having seized tobacco of a value exceeding £2,000 from the clerk's office, the rebel's position became serious.[60] The question of Culpeper's guilt, who also had come to England to defend himself, engaged the attention of the Treasury, the Commissioners of the Customs, the Lords of Trade, the Privy Council, and finally the Court of Kings Bench, where he was tried in 1680 for high treason.[61]

Culpeper was saved by the Carolina proprietors, who were anxious to discount the seriousness of the trouble in their province lest the king be invited to give its management some closer scrutiny. They abandoned Miller and, through the Earl of Shaftesbury, successfully argued that because no lawful government had existed in the colony at the time, Culpeper's guilt was more one of riot than of treason.[62] Back in Albemarle, the victory belonged to George Durant and his associates among the more substantial planters. Not

---

[59] Edward McCrady, The History of South Carolina under the Proprietary Government, 1670–1719 (New York, 1897), pp. 143, 160, 169.

[60] See Miller's petition of January, 1680, in Calendar of Treasury Books, VI, 404; Saunders, Colonial Records of North Carolina, I, 264–267.

[61] The progress of the investigations is most readily followed in Calendar of Treasury Books, VI, 412, 415, 421, 517, 569, 575, 747; see also Saunders, Colonial Records, I, 331–333.

[62] Ibid., I, 303–304. Shaftesbury also secured the release without trial of Gillam, who was in England and faced the same charge. In addition, the proprietors promised a settlement with the Commissioners of the Customs and so got them to drop proposals for charging Culpeper with embezzlement. Lefler and Newsome, North Carolina, p. 45.

until after 1683, when Seth Sothel arrived as governor, would their leadership again be seriously challenged.

Sothel had become one of the Carolina proprietors by purchase of the original rights of the Earl of Clarendon, perhaps with a view to enjoying as a prospective settler in the colony all of the advantages belonging to a resident proprietor under the Fundamental Constitutions. Whatever may be the fact, his fellow proprietors in 1678, the year after Culpeper's Rebellion, made him governor of Albemarle by a commission he managed to combine with another designating him as customs collector. The combination augured ill for the future peace of the colony, but fortunately he was captured by the "Turks" on his way to Carolina and imprisoned at Algiers. As a result, he was not able to take over the government at Albemarle until 1683. The record of his six-year rule is too blurred to permit one to speak with certainty on all points, but two points at least are clear enough. Sothel obviously was not the "sober, moderate" man his fellow proprietors described him as being when they announced his appointment to the governorship. Obviously, too, he challenged the power of the Durant faction, and for this he ultimately had to pay.[63]

There was no rebellion worthy of that designation during these years in Maryland. The Davyes-Pate uprising of September, 1676, was a relatively minor disturbance, little more than a protest meeting by inhabitants of Calvert County that hardly deserved the severe reprisal which came with the execution of its two leaders. Both the occurrence and the reprisal probably reflect the influence of Bacon's Rebellion, at that time still in progress. More persistent was the trouble given by residents of Charles County, just across the Potomac from Virginia. There "two Rank Baconists," if Lord Baltimore's description may be used, were the chief troublemakers through the course of several years.[64] One was Josias Fendall, the same man who in 1660 had been a party, though the proprietor's governor, to the assembly's attempt to make its own power paramount.[65] He was banished from the colony in 1681. The other was

[63] Ibid., pp. 45–46; Connor, North Carolina, I, 60–63; Andrews, Colonial Period, III, 223–224, 231.

[64] By all odds the best discussion of this period in Maryland's history is in Andrews, Colonial Period, II, 325–376.

[65] See above, p. 10.

John Coode, a resident of St. Mary's County, with property also in Charles, who was destined to be a leader in the overthrow of Lord Baltimore's government after the English Revolution of 1688.[66]

More important, and more revealing, than were the periodic outbursts of popular resentment was a running contest that had its main seat in the Maryland assembly. Though on occasion stormy, this contest was for the most part conducted with due regard for the proprieties. But the underlying tension is unmistakable, even in the sparse records legislative assemblies at that time kept.

After the Restoration the government of Maryland had come nearer to fulfilling the original ideal of its founder than it had at any time theretofore. The Maryland proprietorship had been intended as one in which a resident proprietor exercised a paternalistic authority, with the advice and consent of the freemen meeting in general assembly.[67] The trouble was that the first proprietor, Cecilius, second Lord Baltimore, had been denied in the beginning an opportunity to provide the personal kind of leadership in the colony that this paternalistic scheme of government so obviously demanded for its success.[68] Indeed, he died in 1675, after more than forty years as proprietor, without even once having visited his province. But when Charles Calvert succeeded his father as third Lord Baltimore in that year, he had been governor of the province since 1661, and he would keep his residence there until 1684. Hardly less important was the presence of the old proprietor's brother Philip, as chancellor and leading member of the council from 1661 to his death in 1682.[69]

In considering the causes for their failure to realize the old ideal of paternalistic leadership, one first of all should be on guard against accepting the easy answer—either that the ideal was outdated or that it was peculiarly unsuited to the American scene.

More fundamental were other considerations. For one thing, the attempt came too late in the history of the colony. As Fendall's part suggests, opposition to the proprietary claim to leadership already had some of the sanctions of a traditional resistance that was closely

---

[66] See below, pp. 231–232.
[67] Notice the provisions for the assembly in the Maryland charter in Thorpe, *Federal and State Constitutions*, III, 1679–1680.
[68] Craven, *Southern Colonies*, pp. 204–206.
[69] *Maryland Archives*, LI, xl-xliv. Charles visited England from 1676 to 1678.

identified with the lower house of assembly. The tendency all of the Calverts showed to lecture the assembly on the prerogative view of government served but to recall past, and successful, struggles to win the initiative for the lower house, and to encourage its members in a marked inclination to draw a parallel between their own house and the House of Commons in England.[70] Of still greater importance, no doubt, was the fact that the Calverts invited serious charges of abusive use of their power, especially in the use they made of their very considerable patronage. Whether one looks to those who held the more remunerative offices within the gift of the proprietor or to the membership of the provincial council which also served as the upper house of assembly, he finds that the seats of power were occupied by a small circle of men, among whom the proprietor's relatives, by blood or marriage, were especially conspicuous.[71] A very illuminating study of patronage in colonial Maryland has revealed an early tendency toward the multiplication of offices, many of them valuable for the income they provided, which both added to the costs of government and excited the envy of those not directly benefiting from their establishment.[72]

Those who experienced only the burden, or were disappointed in their own hopes for preferment, turned naturally to the lower house of assembly. They were by no means inconsequential men. For the most part they held substantial properties, and some of them were relatively recent immigrants who had contributed significantly to the impressive growth of the colony during the middle years of the century.[73] A general shortage of men fully qualified for office made it easy enough to get appointment as a justice of the local county court, and from that footing to win a seat in the assembly. The

[70] Notice the governor's sharp demand in 1669 that the house think of itself as comparable only to "the common Council of the City of London," not to the House of Commons. Craven, *Southern Colonies*, pp. 301–302.

[71] Andrews, *Colonial Period*, II, 376–378, lists the more important of them. John B. B. Nicklin, "The Calvert Family," *Maryland Historical Magazine*, XVI (1921), 50–59, 189–204; 313–318, 389–394, gives the genealogy. Especially useful is the Appendix providing a civil list for the colony in the work cited immediately below.

[72] Donnell M. Owings, *His Lordship's Patronage: Offices of Profit in Colonial Maryland* (Baltimore, 1953).

[73] Helpful here is Michael G. Kammen, "The Causes of the Maryland Revolution of 1689," *Maryland Historical Magazine* LV (1960), 293–333. For the growth, see Craven, *Southern Colonies*, p. 303.

point can be overstated, for it is evident that in Maryland, as in other colonies, some men shunned the burdens of office. But it is also evident that, as in other newly forming colonial societies, office acquired for many a peculiar importance as the badge of status.[74]

A fundamental difference of religious conviction sharpened and embittered the division. The proprietor, his family, and most of the others holding the more remunerative offices were Catholic, the large majority of the people Protestant.[75] In the council and in the upper house of the legislature the Catholics were dominant; in the lower house the Protestants held a decided majority. The potential for trouble in this kind of division hardly needs to be underscored. It will be enough merely to observe that the danger became all the greater because England at this time repeatedly experienced hysterical fear of Catholic plots to destroy its freedom. These were the years of the Test Act, of Titus Oates's fanciful plot, and of the effort by the Whigs to exclude the Duke of York as a Catholic from succession to the throne. The news of these developments at home, sometimes distorted, reinforced the suspicion with which the Protestants in Maryland viewed the leadership of their own colony.[76]

The relative calm which followed the Restoration had ended with the assembly meeting in 1669.[77] In the very next year the proprietor, after a trip to England by Governor Calvert, limited the franchise, theretofore held by all freemen, to those who had at least fifty acres of land or a personal estate of £40 sterling. Whether intended to restrict popular participation in the government or only to bring Maryland's practice into line with English usage, this limitation became a favorite grievance of the proprietor's opponents.[78] They found another in 1676, when the proprietor issued writs for the election of up to four delegates from each county, as was the custom, and then actually summoned only two of the four to serve. He may have been trying, as he claimed, to reduce the cost of the assembly, of which there also had been complaint, but he was

74 William A. Reavis, "The Maryland Gentry and Social Mobility, 1637–1676," *William and Mary Quarterly*, 3d. ser., XIV (1957) , 418–428.

75 Lord Culpeper's report in 1681 that there were thirty Protestants for every Catholic probably exaggerated the difference, but the ratio could have been 10 to 1. See Andrews, *Colonial Period*, II, 355 n.

76 *Ibid.*, II, 345–348.

77 Craven, *Southern Colonies*, pp. 301–302.

78 It was in 1670 that Virginia also restricted the franchise to freeholders.

suspected of an attempt to manipulate the membership of the house to his own advantage. This was a fundamental issue, of course, and it remained long in debate.[79] Persistent too were questions of privilege and procedure determining the influence the lower house might exert in the settlement of substantive issues affecting, among other things, taxes, fees, port duties, proprietary rents, land policies, control of the sheriff's office, and the conduct of the provincial courts.[80] The struggle one follows here for a larger measure of self-government through the assembly was hardly made for the love of a mere abstraction, as too often our histories have seemed to suggest.

By 1684 some of the more heated controversies of recent years had been settled, and the prospect for another period of calm seemed good enough to permit Lord Baltimore to sail for England in May. Several urgent considerations demanded his presence there. The Pennsylvania charter of 1681 had brought a dispute with William Penn over conflicting boundaries along the Delaware, a dispute which had been further aggravated by Penn's acquisition in 1682 of the Duke of York's title to that part of the western bank of the river lying below Pennsylvania, and attempts to reach an agreement by personal consultation had failed.[81] Complaints of favoritism toward Catholics had to be answered, as also did the much more serious charge brought by treasury and customs officials that Lord Baltimore had obstructed a Maryland customs officer in the performance of his duty. The complaint had been made in 1681, after Baltimore and his council had ruled against Nicholas Badcock, the customs officer, in a dispute between him and shipmasters regarding the payment of the plantation duty on tobacco so bonded as to permit its landing in Ireland. As a result, the proprietor had been threatened with *quo warranto* proceedings against his charter as early as 1682, and when he sailed he was under judgment for the payment of damages to the extent of £2,500.[82]

Coming just after the revealing investigations which had followed

[79] Andrews, *Colonial Period*, II, 339–342.
[80] A helpful guide is Clark, *Parliamentary Privilege in the American Colonies.*
[81] For reports of these attempts, see Clayton C. Hall, *Narratives of Early Maryland, 1633–1684* (New York, 1910), pp. 409–448.
[82] Considerations of space forbid any attempt to discuss a very technical issue that is well explained by Andrews, *Colonial Period,* II, 356–362; IV, 125–131; and by Beer, *Old Colonial System,* I, 91–100. See also Barrow, *Trade and Empire,* pp. 27–29.

Culpeper's Rebellion, the Badcock case confirmed a growing suspicion in Whitehall, as the king was advised, that his interests could be adequately protected only by bringing such "independent Governments" as Maryland into "a nearer and more immediate dependence on your Majesty."[83] Lord Baltimore's situation became the more serious when word reached England that George Talbot, a nephew to whom the government of the colony had been entrusted in May, 1684, had murdered Nicholas Rousby, customs collector, in the following October. Apparently the proprietor had left Maryland with some hope of an early return, but he was destined never to see his province again.

It was no mere chance that in Maryland, as previously in Virginia and Albemarle, there was trouble with customs collectors. Holding their office by commission from London, they were independent of the local government, and yet they might find themselves, as did Badcock, significantly dependent upon its co-operation for the effective execution of their office. The law they were expected to enforce was both new and at points vaguely phrased, with the result that its interpretation, as also the administrative procedures for its enforcement, were badly in need of clarification.[84] The collector usually was an outsider to the local establishment. If not already identified with opposition to that establishment, he was likely soon enough to find reason for making common cause with the opposition.

The point provides an easy transition into a discussion of the annulment of the Massachusetts charter. Few problems in the whole of American history are more complex, or more fascinating, than that of explaining this action, which cleared the way for an extraordinary expansion of the area in North America over which the king undertook to rule directly. Any number of factors must be kept in mind, and none more so than the record of intransigence by the Puritan leaders of the colony that reached all the way back to 1660, and that ultimately left the king little choice but acceptance of an unmistakable challenge to his claim of sovereignty. The newly established Lords of Trade played a central role, but even more

83 This recommendation by the Lords of Trade is quoted in Andrews, *Colonial Period*, II, 359.
84 Thus, in the Badcock case, Baltimore's fault seems to have been more one of ignorance than anything else.

important may have been the part assumed by Edward Randolph, the first Englishman to build an entire career in what with time can perhaps be loosely described as the colonial service. Perhaps the best way of getting at the problem is to tell the story.

Randolph came from a family having no great fortune, but one which did enjoy helpful connections.[85] Among these was Robert Mason, who claimed the proprietorship of New Hampshire and for whom the establishment of the Lords of Trade in 1675 had brought a fresh hope that his claim might be made good. Similarly, Ferdinando Gorges now renewed his appeal, presented to the government several times before, that Massachusetts be brought to account for ignoring his inherited claim to the proprietorship of Maine. The Lords of Trade, thus prompted, found other reasons for looking into the affairs of Massachusetts, including their obligation as a newly appointed committee of the Privy Council to find out what they could regarding all areas for which they were responsible, complaints from members of the English commercial community which charged that Massachusetts pursued its expanding trade in violation of the Navigation Acts, and the colony's long record of recalcitrance. Having referred the question of violation of the Navigation Acts to the Commissioners of the Customs only to receive a reply that there was no firm information on which to base a judgment as to the extent of New England's illegal trade,[86] and having dismissed the idea of sending another commission of investigation to the colony, partly because of the cost, the Lords of Trade decided to demand that Massachusetts send agents to London for response to the complaints of Mason and Gorges. It was also decided to make the demand by special courier, and Edward Randolph, no doubt at Mason's suggestion, was given the job. He landed at Boston in June, 1676, when King Philip's War still had several weeks to go, and he returned in September, thereby completing the first of many trips across the Atlantic he would make during more than a quarter of a century in the king's service.

On this, as on the later trips he made, Randolph was fully alert to the opportunity his mission provided for his own advancement. The report he submitted in October was long and full of detail, much of

[85] Michael G. Hall, *Edward Randolph and the American Colonies, 1676–1703* (Chapel Hill, N.C., 1960), is an excellent study.
[86] Beer, *Old Colonial System*, II, 258–259.

it accurate, and yet so prejudiced in its account of the Puritan government as to encourage further inquiry into its conduct. Especially notable was his suggestion that royal intervention would win substantial support from the inhabitants of New England.[87] But this was not enough to bring the action he desired. The problems of Virginia just then had a prior claim upon the government's attention, and the cost entailed in the "suppression" of Bacon's Rebellion made no one anxious to undertake another expensive colonial venture.[88] When Peter Bulkeley and William Stoughton arrived late in 1676 as agents for Massachusetts, the immediate question of Maine and New Hampshire was referred to the Lords Chief Justices. Their decision—which rejected Massachusetts' claim to jurisdiction, upheld Gorges right to the government of Maine while finding no evidence that Mason held such a right in New Hampshire, and in effect left the question of title to the soil in both areas to the colonial courts—did not come until the summer of 1677.[89]

Meanwhile, Randolph had not been content merely to cool his heels outside the offices of great men. After some research, he presented another sweeping indictment of Massachusetts which finally brought him a hearing by the Lords of Trade in June, 1677, and persuaded the committee to enlarge its investigation to include such questions as the validity of the Massachusetts charter, the enforcement of the Navigation Acts, the colony's failure to require an oath of allegiance, its denial of appeals from its courts, its religious requirement for the exercise of the franchise, and its operation of a mint. It was concluded that irregularities of trade existed and recommended that a customs officer be appointed, but this recommendation was not acted upon. What is more important, the validity of the Massachusetts charter, within its proper bounds, was accepted on the advice of the Lords Chief Justices, and, for a remedy of the faults found in the conduct of the colony's government, it was suggested that it might be provided through a supplementary and explanatory charter. Even on the question of coinage, a peculiarly sensitive area of the king's prerogative, the agents were

87 Hall, *Randolph*, pp. 24–29. As Hall observes, "If the crown could be persuaded to intervene between the Puritan government and its subjects, Edward Randolph would have a future."

88 *Ibid.*, p. 30, for a suggestion, probably by Randolph, that the fleet sent to Virginia might be used against New England.

89 *Ibid.*, pp. 36–37.

encouraged to believe that, with allowance in the new charter, the colony might continue to mint its pinetree shillings.[90] Everything considered, Massachusetts had come out of this first round remarkably well, and had good reason for celebrating the day of thanksgiving it promptly proclaimed.

For what followed the Boston government had chiefly itself to blame. Assuming perhaps that a parallel existed with the situation after Lord Clarendon's investigation of 1665, and still rigidly determined to protect the autonomy of the colony in all possible ways, the Puritans passed up opportunities to soften further the attitude of Whitehall. They might have yielded, for example, at no great cost on the oath of allegiance. Instead, they strengthened the provisions for enforcement of their own oath of fidelity to the colony. Even in the one concession they undertook to make, they so sharply challenged the superior authority of the English government as to invite an immediate showdown. Advised by the colony's agents that a "total breach" could be avoided only by submission to the Navigation Acts, the General Court in October, 1677, declared these acts in force "by the authority of this Court." Their subsequent explanation "that the lawes of England are bounded within the fower seas, and doe not reach America," probably was not seen by the king.[91] But that question matters little. The challenge was obvious, and it came at a time when the Virginia assembly faced charges of seditious conduct for nothing more than its affirmation of the privilege belonging to its clerk.[92] Here was confirmation for Randolph's previous charge that Massachusetts regarded itself as a commonwealth, an odious term for many Englishmen who still remembered Cromwell, and Randolph saw to it that this fresh evidence did not escape the attention of the Lords of Trade. In May, 1678, their lordships recommended *quo warranto* proceedings against the Massachusetts charter. In June Randolph had his appointment as collector of customs for New England.[93]

[90] *Ibid.*, pp. 32–39.

[91] *Records of the Governor and Company of Massachusetts Bay*, V, 154–155, 200; Hall, *Randolph*, pp. 40–41; Beer, *Old Colonial System*, II, 273–275; Bailyn, *New England Merchants*, pp. 158–159. The General Court based its argument on the ground that the inhabitants of the colony lacked representation in the English Parliament.

[92] See above, pp. 150–151.

[93] Hall, *Randolph*, pp. 41–47.

Titus Oates, by his fictional revelations of a "Popish plot," gave New England a brief respite, but Edward Randolph landed on these shores again in December, 1679, first at New York. Thence he went to Portsmouth, for his initial task was to inaugurate the king's government over the towns of New Hampshire. The Massachusetts agents had startled the Lords of Trade by buying Gorges' rights in Maine, and that committee had responded by advising the king to take advantage of the fault that had been found in the claims of both Mason and Massachusetts to jurisdiction in New Hampshire. Mason had agreed on the understanding that he might undertake to establish his own rights in the soil, and in January, 1680, Randolph brought into existence the second royal colony among the English settlements in North America, and this next door to Puritan Massachusetts.[94] It hardly needs to be added that the following years were very troubled years for the Puritans of New Hampshire.

From Portsmouth Randolph moved down to Boston. Because he came as collector of customs, and because he promptly made himself busy with seizures and prosecutions for violation of the trade acts, it often has been assumed that the contest between Whitehall and Boston was basically economic. But that assumption defines the issue much too narrowly.

Randolph's appointment as collector argues for less than a first glance may suggest. In the infant colonial service, if as yet it can be so described, there was no other established office to which he could have been appointed, a fact he undoubtedly had considered. As previously has been observed, the naval officers who were charged with enforcement of the shipping clauses of the Navigation Acts in the colonies constituted a service that was developing under the patronage of the several governors.[95] In Virginia and the West Indies receivers of the royal revenues were soon to be brought into some semblance of a centrally controlled service by William Blathwayt, already secretary to the Lords of Trade and, by a commission of 1680, made auditor-general for these revenues.[96] But Randolph's opportunity lay in New England, where at the time of his appoint-

---

[94] *Ibid.*, pp. 52, 53–54; Palfrey, *History of New England,* III, 312, 402–405.

[95] See again Andrews, *Colonial Period,* IV, 180–187.

[96] Gertrude Ann Jacobsen, *William Blathwayt: A Late Seventeenth Century English Administrator* (New Haven, 1932) , pp. 150–162. The only colonies

ment there were no royal revenues, and as yet no naval officers. His own office had been established under the provisions of the act of 1673, and the question whether the act extended to areas other than the staple-producing colonies had been a subject of some discussion within the home government.[97] The decision of the Customs Commissioners that it did, and their instructions to collectors calling for a general attention to the enforcement of the Navigation Acts, did not prevent Randolph himself from seeking in 1681, and securing over the protest of the Commissioners, a special commission under the broad seal intended to give him full powers for the enforcement of the Navigation Acts.[98]

This was an exceptional action for the time. Was it taken primarily for the enforcement of the trade acts? Or is it to be viewed as basically Whitehall's response to Massachusetts' open challenge to the king's sovereignty? The question is difficult, but one point is clear. Submission to the laws enacted by the king in Parliament had become, by the colony's own choice in 1677, a prime test for the settlement of even broader constitutional issues. And those issues were made no less urgent by legislation adopted by the colony in 1682 to provide for the appointment of its own naval officers, legislation obviously intended both to preserve the principle of the colony's legislative independence and to frustrate Randolph in the performance of his duties under the royal commission.[99]

It is not easy to determine how far New England may have been guilty of Randolph's repeated charge of flagrant violation of the Navigation Acts. He strove valiantly to prove his charge, but had such bad luck before the New England courts that the historian is left without the firm evidence he would like to have. Contemporary complaints by English merchants suggest that there were broadening violations of the Staple Act of 1663, but there also are indications that London's chief fear was that Boston might develop into a competing metropolis of the Atlantic trade, a prospect by no means

immediately affected were Virginia, Barbados, Jamaica, and the Leeward Islands. The revenues involved included such things as quitrents, escheats, and the 2s. per hhd. duty in Virginia after 1680, but not collections of the plantation duty.

[97] Barrow, *Trade and Empire,* pp. 14–16.

[98] Hall, *Randolph,* pp. 55–68.

[99] *Ibid.,* pp. 69–75; Andrews, *Colonial Period,* IV, 183.

wholly dependent upon illicit trade.[100] The modern student who has ·studied the economic history of the area most closely finds evidence that Boston's merchants were beginning to explore the possibilities for trades that were of doubtful legality, to say the least, but his study also supports the view that New England's trade generally remained more complementary to the interests the Navigation Acts sought to promote than in conflict with them. What is more important perhaps is that the study lends fresh emphasis to the willingness of the mercantile community to find some accommodation with the king, a point which argues strongly as to where their most important interests lay.[101]

What should be done about the king's demands had become, of course, the dominant political issue in the colony, and the debate was increasingly bitter. To a very considerable extent, the division was between the old and the new in New England's life. It was rural New England, where the farmer and the country parson shaped prevailing attitudes, which fought most relentlessly to save the autonomy of the Massachusetts government. Taught to know the shelter that autonomy had provided for their church in times past, profoundly suspicious of the Anglicans and of their power in Whitehall, peculiarly subject to persuasion by reports of a Catholic conspiracy to destroy English Protestantism, and aided by a religious qualification for the franchise which gave them great power, the people of rural Massachusetts consistently controlled the lower house of the General Court by unshakable majorities. In other words, the popular party was the conservative, the orthodox party. Actually, to speak of a party is to risk some misunderstanding. There is danger, too, that the summary given above will suggest a more sharply defined cleavage, geographical and other, than actually existed. There can be no doubt, however, that the basic division was between those who were determined to protect their wilderness Zion against the intrusions of an alien and corrupt world and those who were more willing to come to terms with that world. Traditionally, the latter have been designated as the moderates.

---

[100] English scholars especially have been inclined to emphasize this point. See Ogg's description of the New Englanders as "the Dutchmen of the empire," in *England in the Reign of Charles II*, II, 681; and Thornton, *West-India Policy*, pp. 161–167.

[101] Bailyn, *New England Merchants*, especially pp. 126–134, 143–153.

In the main, they represented an expanding commercial interest that demanded a reasonable accommodation with the outside world, and especially with London, corrupt as it might be. Many of this group were members of the church, others were not; in either case, it has been suggested, they spoke for a rising class of enterprisers who theretofore had been denied the influence and power they felt to be their due.[102] Moderation had more strength among the magistrates who conducted the day-to-day administration of the government than among the delegates who only periodically assembled to protect the colony's liberties. Simon Bradstreet, governor from his election in 1678, was a moderate; the deputy governor was not.[103] Joining with Bradstreet were three out of four of the men who had the great misfortune to serve during these years as agents for the colony in London.[104] It was a thankless task. Stoughton, the same William Stoughton who had clinched his place in history by proclaiming in the election-day sermon of 1668 that God had selected the finest grain in England to sow in the wilderness of New England, finally returned home in 1679 to advocate moderation, as he had while in London, but only to be greeted by many of his fellow countrymen as a traitor. His associate, Peter Bulkeley, also became a moderate. Joseph Dudley, who went to England on a mission of 1682, returned home to be dismissed from his seat as one of the provincial magistrates and described as an enemy to his country by vote of the Boston town meeting.[105]

Dudley may have been more open to the charge than were the others. He was to become the first royal head of government in Massachusetts, and in time quite frankly the king's man. But one can sympathize with him, as with the other moderates, for their opponents insisted upon reducing the issue to the terms virtually of an all-or-nothing proposition. They were quite prepared to accept the full loss of the charter, and its every protection, rather than to assume the guilt, as they saw it, of sacrificing by their own action a

---

[102] *Ibid.*, especially pp. 134–143, 169.

[103] Hall, *Randolph*, p. 60.

[104] Miller, *Colony to Province*, pp. 137–140; on the moderates, see also Dunn, *Puritans and Yankees*, pp. 217–219.

[105] Everett Kimball, *The Public Life of Joseph Dudley: A Study of the Colonial Policy of the Stuarts in New England, 1660–1715* (Cambridge, Mass., 1911), p. 17; Hall, *Randolph*, pp. 79–82.

single one of the colony's liberties. This was the intransigence of men persuaded by the course of history into the psychology of a peculiar people. Repeatedly confronted by the challenge of changing circumstances, they had retreated into a narrow orthodoxy, more social than religious, that was wholly defensive in its outlook. The defense of the charter had become for them the ultimate test of loyalty to New England and to the faith for which New England had been founded, and with this view a clear majority of the people of Massachusetts were in agreement. Nothing could be more misleading than has been the effort by some modern historians to picture the moderates as advocates of democracy. They were rather its victims.[106]

In the end, intransigence had its way. The Popish plot had afforded only a brief respite, and by 1681 Massachusetts faced a renewed demand for negotiation under the threat of *quo warranto* proceedings. After bitter debate, it was decided that agents would be sent to England, but the General Court stubbornly refused to empower them to negotiate revisions in the charter. Having failed to secure the return from Boston of a *quo warranto* writ in time for it to be effective in a common-law court, even though the very willing Randolph had delivered the writ, the Lords of Trade turned to the High Court of Chancery, whose writ of *scire facias* did not have to be served on the Massachusetts Bay Company in Boston. The decree of dissolution was handed down on October 23, 1684.[107]

It is a remarkable fact that in this hour of victory the government in England had no plan ready for prompt establishment of royal rule in Massachusetts.[108] Indeed, almost a year passed before full agreement was reached in Whitehall on the provisional council, headed by Joseph Dudley, which finally took office in May, 1686. Meanwhile, the old government at Boston continued to function for all of eighteen months as though the legal foundation upon which its authority depended had not been destroyed.

The delay is explained in part by the death of Charles II in

---

[106] For a detailed discussion, see Miller, *From Colony to Province;* and for a brilliant delineation of the main theme, his "Errand into the Wilderness," *William and Mary Quarterly,* 3d. ser., X (1953) , 3–19.

[107] Hall, *Randolph,* pp. 77–83.

[108] *Ibid.,* pp. 83–97, for an especially well-balanced and persuasive discussion of developments following the charter's annulment.

February, 1685, and by Monmouth's Rebellion, which followed the succession of James II. King Charles had been prompt in selecting Colonel Percy Kirke, recently returned from Tangier, for the governor's post in Massachusetts,[109] but proposals from the Lords of Trade for annexation of additional territories to the new government brought complications into the question which also help to explain the extraordinary delay in its settlement. These proposals indicate that some of the king's advisers were beginning to think of possibilities for a far-reaching reorganization of the political life of Puritan New England, but this was only a beginning. And so it was that the reign of Charles II reached its end, after twenty-five years in which the relationship of the government of Massachusetts to the government of England had repeatedly acquired critical importance, with no more than the main issue definitively settled. Henceforth, the government of the Bay Colony Puritans would depend upon an acknowledgment of their king's sovereignty.

[109] The new king found a better use for Kirke's talents in the suppression of Monmouth's Rebellion.

CHAPTER 6

The Revival of Colonization

THE later years of Charles II's reign claim close attention from students of American history for much more than the significant developments that occurred in the political life of the older settlements. These years also brought a marked revival of interest among Englishmen in colonization, and this revival, in sharp contrast with the interest shown immediately following the Restoration, depended basically upon a new opportunity for the recruitment of settlers in the British Isles. First thought goes, of course, to the Quaker settlements in the Delaware Valley, and more particularly to the founding of Pennsylvania in 1682, but the renewed transatlantic migration has an important place too in the history of Carolina. Among England's more recent territorial acquisitions in North America, only New York failed to benefit in a substantial way.

As in the earlier period of settlement, the motives for emigration to America were mixed, but one fact stands out above all others. The new settlers were so largely religious dissenters as to tempt one to say that all of them were. It was a particularly difficult time for the English dissenter, and not merely for the Quaker, who undoubtedly suffered the most. Not only had a growing fear of Catholic conspiracy strengthened the demand for conformity with a religious establishment that was hateful to the dissenter, but he himself was peculiarly subject to hysterical fear of Catholicism. After the collapse in 1680 of the Whig effort to exclude the Catholic Duke of York from the throne, it is not surprising that many of the more extreme Protestants were willing to consider removal to America.

Nor is it surprising that the Carolina proprietors, long since committed to a tolerant religious policy for their province, should have undertaken to capitalize upon the opportunity. Despite their efforts after 1669 to stimulate migration from the West Indies, and despite the much greater success they had achieved in comparison with the earlier years of their venture, the Charles Town settlement, which still claimed their chief interest, had grown but slowly. At the end of its first decade, the total population was reported to have been 1,000 to 1,200.[1] Whether considered from the point of view of the colony's exposed position above Florida or of the investment previously made, there was an obvious need to strengthen the settlement.

The proprietors may also have given thought to the possibility that an increase in the English population of the colony might offset the dominant influence the Barbadian settlers had quickly won there. Experienced colonists and fully aware of the contribution they were making to the establishment of the colony, the Barbadians easily controlled the elective part of the parliament and also held positions of influence on the council, where the governor presided over a membership that was partly elected and partly appointed. The right of each proprietor to be represented at the council by a deputy held out a strong persuasion for ambitious colonists to base their hopes for advancement upon an alliance with the proprietary interest. Among those who took advantage of this avenue to power was Stephen Bull, the founder of one of the great families of colonial South Carolina, who had migrated from England with the initial expedition of 1669.[2] Another was Joseph West, commander of that expedition, deputy for the Duke of Albemarle, and governor in succession to Sir John Yeamans from 1674 to 1682.[3] But the leadership West managed to assert during

[1] Thomas Ashe, *Carolina, or a Description of the Present State of That Country* (London, 1682), in Salley, *Narratives of Carolina*, p. 158.

[2] M. Eugene Sirmans, Jr., "Masters of Ashley Hall: A Biographical Study of the Bull Family of Colonial South Carolina" (unpublished Ph.D. dissertation, Princeton University, 1959), to which I am indebted for much that follows, as I am also to his more recent *Colonial South Carolina*.

[3] For the early history of the colony, Edward McCrady, *The History of South Carolina under the Proprietary Government, 1670–1719* (New York, 1897), the

the colony's early history owed as much to his own character and judgment, and to his readiness to seek some accommodation between the will of the proprietors and the desire of the colonists, as to the proprietary patronage he enjoyed.

By the 1680's enterprising colonists, mainly Barbadians, had virtually wrested full control of the Indian trade from the proprietors, who had hoped to develop the more distant, and therefore the more profitable, branches of the trade as a proprietary monopoly. An especially vicious feature of the trade was a traffic in Indian slaves, many of whom were exported to the West Indies. The proprietors had by no means been blameless in the beginning of this trade, but after the Westo War of 1680, first of the major Indian wars in the colony's history, the proprietors blamed the slave trade and strictly forbad its continuance.[4] Perhaps even more disturbing to the proprietors were well-founded reports that the colony was frequented by pirates, who after the Treaty of Madrid with Spain in 1670 had been denied, on the king's orders, the courtesies they formerly had received in West Indian ports.[5] The cost of such violations of Westminster's stiffening policy toward piracy could be high, for this was precisely the sort of thing which might bring embarrassing inquiries from the Lords of Trade.

That the proprietors remained alert to opportunities for a strengthening of their settlement, despite Shaftesbury's fall from power and his exile after 1679, is indicated by the lead they took in directing French Huguenot exiles to their colony. The forty or more Huguenots landing at Charles Town in 1680, the year in which the town itself was moved to its present site, constituted the first such group of significant size to reach any one of the North American colonies.[6] Although the refuge thus provided for members of a persecuted minority was wholly consistent with previously established policy, the motivation was primarily economic. None of the experi-

_____

old standard, is supplemented by David D. Wallace, *South Carolina: A Short History, 1520–1948* (Chapel Hill, N.C., 1951) .

[4] Crane, *Southern Frontier,* especially pp. 18–21, 118–120; Almon W. Lauber, *Indian Slavery in Colonial Times within the Present United States* (New York, 1913) , pp. 134–136.

[5] Shirley C. Hughson, *The Carolina Pirates and Colonial Commerce, 1670–1740* (Baltimore, 1894) ; on the general trend of English policy, Newton's *European Nations in the West Indies* provides an informed guide.

[6] Wallace, *South Carolina,* p. 37.

ments sponsored by the proprietors after 1669 as yet had brought the colony a proven staple, with the result that the colonists still depended very heavily upon a provisioning trade with the West Indies.[7] The new French settlers boasted a wide variety of skills and were charged especially with a renewed test of the old and recurrent hope of English colonizers that silk might be developed into a profitable staple. Unhappily, the silkworms died at sea, as so often had been the case before. Over the years ahead Charles Town would continue to receive Huguenot immigrants, and in numbers comparable only to those who later settled in New York and Massachusetts, but what the colony gained was neither a very great addition to its population nor an impressive diversification of its economy. Instead, this migration brought men who with time entered easily, and significantly, into the commercial life of the community.[8]

By 1682 the proprietors had agreed upon a major effort of recruitment in the British Isles. Interestingly, the leadership among the proprietors had passed from Shaftesbury the Whig to the Earl of Craven, a very stout Tory who was destined to live long enough to take his stand for King James at the time of the Glorious Revolution, and to John Archdale, a Quaker who in 1678 had purchased for his infant son the proprietary rights belonging originally to John Lord Berkeley.[9] However much political developments in England may have contributed to the opportunities the proprietors responded to, the response itself was notably lacking in political coloring.

Several promotional tracts offered encouraging advice on the prospect for new settlers in Carolina, and further advice could be had at the Carolina Coffee House in London from an agent of the proprietors.[10] The old promise of headright grants in proportion to

---

[7] Craven, *Southern Colonies*, pp. 355–359.

[8] Salley, *Narratives of Carolina*, pp. 137, 143; Wallace, *South Carolina*, pp. 60–65; Arthur H. Hirsch, *The Huguenots of Colonial South Carolina* (Durham, N.C., 1928), must be used with care.

[9] Sirmans, *Colonial South Carolina*, pp. 35–40; also his "Politics in Colonial South Carolina: The Failure of Proprietary Reform, 1682–1694," *William and Mary Quarterly*, 3d. ser., XXIII (1966), 33–55.

[10] Samuel Wilson, *An Account of the Province of Carolina* (London, 1682), as reprinted in Salley, *Narratives of Carolina*, pp. 164–176. See also the pamphlet by Ashe, *Carolina*, and for other items Crane, *Southern Frontier*, p. 27 n., and

THE REVIVAL OF COLONIZATION

the settlers' willingness at their own cost to contribute to the labor force of the colony was now renewed; but for those who might prefer an outright purchase of substantial acreages free of quitrents, the land was offered at the price of £50 for a thousand acres, subject to the nominal rent of one peppercorn per annum "when demanded." In addition, the proprietors in 1682 twice revised their Fundamental Constitutions, but more significant than the revisions made is the fact that no drastic revision of the general scheme seems to have been demanded by prospective emigrants to the colony.[11] For them perhaps the most important revision was one which guaranteed dissenters against being taxed for support of the Anglican Church. Whatever may have been the attitude of settlers already living in the colony, it seems to be evident enough that a man planning to move from England to Carolina in 1682 was unlikely to be greatly disturbed by what modern students so often have described as the archaic provisions of the Fundamental Constitutions.

Among those who responded to the proprietors' renewed promotional effort was Henry Erskine, Lord Cardross, a leader of the severely persecuted Covenanters of Lowland Scotland who now proposed to establish a Scottish colony in Carolina. Scottish colonial ventures in North America had a history going back to the reign of James I,[12] who also was James VI of Scotland, ventures which had left as their most enduring mark the name of Nova Scotia, and Lord Cardross now talked of the possibility that as many as 10,000 of his coreligionists might migrate to Carolina. Actually, the number of westland Covenanters who sailed from Scotland for Charles Town in 1684 was less than one hundred, and sickness and desertion reduced the total of those who made it to Port Royal, where the new settlement was established, to hardly more than fifty. The location of Stuart Town, as the new settlement was named, has its own significance, and one which may help to explain the propri-

Sirmans, *Colonial South Carolina*, p. 36, which declares there were at least ten promotional tracts issued by the proprietors between 1682 and 1685, two of them printed in Dublin and two in Holland for the attention of the Huguenots.

11 The first revision came in January, the second in August. For the texts, see Parker, *North Carolina Charters*, pp. 186–233. See also McCrady, *South Carolina*, pp. 191–192; Salley, *Narratives of Carolina*, pp. 173–174.

12 See especially George P. Insh, *Scottish Colonial Schemes, 1620–1686* (Glasgow, 1922).

etors' willingness to encourage its establishment. Port Royal, in addition to the southward extension it gave to the area of English settlement, lay athwart the most advantageous route from Charles Town for trade with the Yamassee and Creek Indians, and Lord Cardross intended for his settlers to share in that trade, even to win the control of it. When in 1686 the Spaniards wiped the settlement out, and it became apparent that Charles Town was not to be attacked, there probably were few regrets in that town.[13]

Much more successful had been the efforts of the proprietors to recruit English dissenters. By 1685 the number settled in the colony since 1680 may have reached a total of 500.[14] Joseph Morton, a leader in the new migration, had been made governor in 1682, when West was dismissed on the ground of his tolerance for pirates. That may have been the reason for his removal, but one has difficulty in avoiding the conclusion that the chief consideration was a desire to lend every possible encouragement to a continuing migration of dissenters. The same consideration probably also influenced the proprietors' decision in 1682 to divide the settlement into counties, each to have equal representation in the parliament, for the chief immediate effect would be to enlarge the voice of the newcomers, who settled very largely to the south of Charles Town in the area designated as Colleton County.[15] With Governor Morton came other men of ability and quality, among them Land-grave Thomas Smith, whose family was to be uniquely persistent in the use of its aristocratic title, perhaps because of the family name, Benjamin Blake, brother to Cromwell's famous naval leader, and Benjamin's son Joseph. But with this impressive accession of strength there came also many difficulties.

Unavoidably, the dissenters were identified with the proprietary interest, and this at a time when the proprietors were determined to take a firm stand on several critical questions of policy, including the question of quitrents. It was announced that these rents, due for first payment on the older grants in 1689, would have to be paid in

13 See in addition to Insh's account, Wallace, *South Carolina*, pp. 40–41, and especially Crane, *Southern Frontier*, pp. 26–32.

14 Sirmans, *Colonial South Carolina*, pp. 36–37. The oft-found suggestion that the population may have been doubled between 1680 and 1682 seems to have no foundation other than that of a claim in one of the promotional tracts of 1682.

15 McCrady, *South Carolina*, pp. 193, 198–200.

specie, and that henceforth there would be substituted, for the deeds formerly used, indentures facilitating repossession of property as the penalty for nonpayment of the rent.[16] The tendency, apparent from the earliest days of the colony, for its political divisions to turn upon a cleavage between the English and the Barbadian settlers was now accentuated and at the same time modified by circumstances which tended to unite the older settlers in opposition to the newcomers. A majority of the older settlers, and especially of the Barbadians, seems to have professed an Anglican affiliation, and the great accession of strength won now by the dissenters would lead to bitter contention in later years.[17]

Trouble came immediately. By 1684 Governor Morton had been dismissed for his failures. Once more Joseph West, himself a dissenter, assumed the responsibilities of his old office, but in 1685 he gave it up and moved to New York, where he died in 1691.[18] Back in Carolina, the advantage belonged to a loose combination of the older settlers, mostly Barbadians, that was destined to win fame through the years ahead as the Goose Creek faction.

The migration of the dissenters into Carolina had been preceded, and was accompanied, by a much larger migration of the Quakers into the Delaware Valley. Indeed, the growing interest shown by the Quakers in the opportunities offered by that inviting valley may well have been one of the considerations which prompted the Carolina proprietors to undertake their renewed efforts of 1682.

The story of the Quaker colonies has its beginning in 1674 with the sale of John Lord Berkeley's half-share in the New Jersey grant to Edward Byllynge, an acquaintance of Berkeley who happened also to be a Quaker. It is doubtful that Byllynge originally had anything more in mind than to acquire a potentially valuable property in the hope of finding a remedy for the low estate to which his personal finances had fallen. But he was a Quaker, and nothing was more natural at this time than that he should undertake to recruit settlers from among his own coreligionists. Such a development became the more likely because other Quakers, including William Penn, were quickly drawn into the management of his project. Indeed, the purchase itself had been effected through an

16 Sirmans, *Colonial South Carolina*, pp. 38–39.
17 See below, pp. 233, 278–279.
18 Wallace, *South Carolina*, p. 39.

agreement with the Quaker John Fenwick to buy in trust for the bankrupt Byllynge. When these two quarreled over the terms of their agreement, the Quakers' reluctance to air their disputes in the public courts brought Penn, Gawen Lawrie, and Nicholas Lucas into the picture, eventually as Byllnyge's trustees.[19] In that capacity, and through this chain of circumstances, William Penn acquired his first identification with a colonizing project.

It is not easy to determine the full measure of Penn's influence upon the founding of West Jersey, but one point is quite certain. The interest he found in Byllynge's project for a settlement in the Delaware Valley grew, and as it grew it profoundly shaped one of the most successful colonizing ventures in American history.

Last of the great proprietors whose interests and ideas so significantly influenced the later phase of English colonization in North America, William Penn was in most ways representative of the group. Not even the policy of religious toleration for which he has been justly celebrated can be viewed as a distinctive feature of his colonial activity.[20] And like his predecessors, he enjoyed a special influence at court. Penn was the son and heir of Admiral Sir William Penn, associate of the Duke of York, John Lord Berkeley, and others closely identified with the Navy after the Restoration. The father had won his captaincy in the parliamentary fleet during the Civil War. Thereafter, he rose to the rank of vice-admiral and general of the fleet under Cromwell, who rewarded him with an estate in Ireland and the sea command of the expedition sent in 1655 for conquest of the Spanish West Indies. The loss of Cromwell's favor resulting from the disappointment experienced in the execution of that grand design eased the transition for Penn to fresh opportunities in the service of Charles II, who knighted the admiral as a part of the ceremonies attending the king's return to England in May, 1660. As the father's fortunes advanced, the son went up to Oxford in October, 1660, visited the Continent for two years after the summer of 1662, was registered as a student of the law at Lincoln's Inn early in 1665, went to sea briefly with the admiral in the second Dutch war, and was sent by him to Ireland in 1666 to

19 Pomfret, *Province of West Jersey*, especially pp. 65–68.
20 See above, pp. 76–77, 92, 102, and my discussion of Penn's activity as the climactic phase of English colonization in the post-Restoration era in *New Jersey and the English Colonization of North America*, pp. 73–76.

look into the condition of the family estate there.[21] In the education of an English gentleman at the time, this was a normal progression. But William Penn already had set for himself a course, much to the regret of his seafaring father, that broke sharply with conventional standards. Religiously inclined from an early age, he had come under the influence of a Quaker missionary as early as 1657 and ten years later he was fully convinced. Twice before 1674 Penn experienced imprisonment for his faith. He also had made the first of three missionary tours into the Rhineland, where later his province of Pennsylvania would find many recruits.

The Society of Friends—"Friends in the Truth"—was a mystical sect whose central doctrine of the "Inner Light" inspired in its early members an extraordinary missionary zeal. Eager converts carried their testimony from England into Scotland, Wales, and Ireland and by 1660, only eight years after George Fox had founded the Society, into every area of English settlement in the New World. Not even Newfoundland or Surinam had been overlooked.[22] As is well known, four Quakers had been executed in Massachusetts by the end of 1661, and Virginia had enacted protective legislation in 1660.[23]

Modern Americans often have been puzzled to understand the resistance the Quaker so frequently met. Acquainted with him only after "Quietism" had drastically changed the spirit of the movement, they all too often have accepted the cheap answer provided by the word bigotry. Bigotry certainly had a part in this unhappy story, but it also has to be understood that the Quaker was for his time a truly disturbing radical. His belief that the "Inner Light"

21 Of the many biographies of William Penn, the latest and fullest is Catherine O. Peare, *William Penn: A Biography* (Philadelphia and New York, 1957). Other modern biographies are helpful, especially Mabel R. Brailsford, *The Making of William Penn* (London, New York, and Toronto, 1939); Arthur Pound, *The Penns of Pennsylvania and England* (New York, 1932); Bonamy Dobrée, *William Penn: Quaker and Pioneer* (London, 1932); and William I. Hull, *William Penn: A Topical Biography* (London and New York, 1937).

22 For a succinct and informed account, see Frederick B. Tolles, *Quakers and the Atlantic Culture* (New York, 1960), pp. 1–35; also Rufus Jones *et al., The Quakers in the American Colonies* (London, 1911). On the larger movement, see William C. Braithwaite, *The Beginnings of Quakerism* (2d. ed., rev. by Henry J. Cadbury, Cambridge, 1955).

23 Palfrey, *History of New England,* II, 460–485, which goes into great detail to explain the action of the Massachusetts government, and Craven, *Southern Colonies,* pp. 229–230.

might guide mankind to salvation seemed to many Christians a repudiation of scriptural Revelation, and so to strike at the very foundation of a well-ordered Christian society.[24] Perhaps the most maddening thing about the Quaker was his insistence upon carrying the logic of the Protestant position to an uncompromising extreme. For him "the priesthood of all believers" was no mere phrase; it was a principle to be literally followed. To men who had agreed to abandon most of the traditional sacraments of the Christian Church, the Quaker proposed that they all be abandoned. When Protestants were still debating the place of ritual in their worship, he insisted upon no ritual at all. Moreover, he was a pacifist; he refused to take an oath; and he rejected the conventional forms of deference for both office and social position. The "leveling" implications in his teachings became the more disturbing because of the role women were allowed to play in the movement, not to mention the readiness of the Quaker to preach his radical doctrines to servants.

If the Quaker often met with an understandable resistance, he also found a ready welcome in America. Outside Puritan New England, the colonies suffered a general shortage of ministers, and many communities lacked even an organized congregation of any faith. When in 1671 George Fox himself crossed the Atlantic for a famous missionary tour which carried him, in order, to Barbados, Jamaica, Maryland, Delaware, New Jersey, New York, Rhode Island, Virginia, and Albemarle County in Carolina, he more than once found heartening evidence of the work his predecessors had accomplished.[25] It is possible that this tour helped to stimulate an interest among Quakers in the founding of a colony of their own, but there is no evidence that such a plan existed until after Byllynge had acquired his half-interest in New Jersey.

In becoming colonizers, Byllynge and his trustees had little if any choice. When the Duke of York confirmed Carteret's half-share of the Jersey grant in 1674, he assigned to Sir George the entire settled area of the colony, thereby leaving for Byllynge the unoccupied western half of the land.[26] Fortunately for him, the Quakers,

---

[24] The statement of the case in the Virginia statute of 1660 (Hening, *Statutes*, I, 532–533) is a very full one.

[25] Fox's *Journal* (2 vols., New York, 1800) , II, 129–169.

[26] Pomfret, *East New Jersey*, p. 103; *West New Jersey*, p. 67; for the circumstances, see above, p. 106.

victims of an especially severe persecution since the Restoration, included men who were willing to consider settlement in America and, even more fortunately, men of means who were willing to invest in such an enterprise. Although Quakerism had its strongest appeal for the more humble members of society, William Penn was not the only man of substance to be drawn into the Society.[27] The trustees made their plans accordingly, and undoubtedly found help in the organization George Fox was then perfecting for the Quaker community. Its system of monthly and quarterly meetings of representatives from local meetings, and especially the yearly meeting regularly held in London after 1668, gave the Quakers a remarkably effective organization for the purpose of maintaining communication among the widely scattered members of the sect.[28] Over the years ahead, this scheme easily bridged the Atlantic to provide for the American Quakers continuingly advantageous channels of communication with Friends in Britain.[29]

The promotional plan agreed upon owed not a little to Byllynge's financial difficulties. In order to raise the funds needed to clear his debts and to launch the colony, it was decided that his half-interest in the Jersey proprietorship would be divided into 100 shares and offered for sale at £350 a share. For this sum the purchaser acquired an equity, or propriety, of one hundredth in the ungranted lands of West Jersey. The purchasers were in the main substantial Quakers from the north of England and from London, with a smaller number from Ireland. Some of the new proprietors settled in the colony, others did not; some bought more than one share, others pooled their resources to buy a single share; and with the passage of time individual proprieties were divided and subdivided again by sales to lesser purchasers.[30] Headright grants were also promised by the trustees, beginning with a grant of seventy acres for any freeman going to the colony at his own expense and

27 Frederick B. Tolles, *Meeting House and Counting House: The Quaker Merchants of Colonial Philadelphia, 1682–1763* (Chapel Hill, N.C., 1948), pp. 29–30, 38–44.

28 Arnold Lloyd, *Quaker Social History, 1669–1738* (London, 1950), pp. 1–14, 134–144. A weekly meeting for sufferings functioned in London as an executive committee of the yearly meeting during its adjournments.

29 Tolles, *Quakers and the Atlantic Culture*, pp. 29–33.

30 See especially John E. Pomfret, "The Proprietors of the Province of West Jersey, 1674–1702," *Pennsylvania Magazine of History and Biography*, LXXV (1951), 117–146; *West Jersey*, pp. 86 ff.; and *The New Jersey Proprietors and Their Lands, 1664–1776* (Princeton, 1964), pp. 21 ff.

for every able manservant taken or sent there, but above all the settlement of West Jersey depended upon a simple process of sale and resale. Competition among the proprietors for sales discouraged the reservation even of a quitrent, with the result that West Jersey quickly became a colony of freeholders in the fullest sense of the term.

First to achieve a settlement in West Jersey was John Fenwick. The trustees conceded his claim to a tenth interest in the proprietorship in the hope that he would exercise that right as a cooperative participant in a common plan for the settlement of the area, but Fenwick was determined to have his tenth in one block for the purpose of establishing a distinct and separate proprietorship of his own. By mortgaging his "tenth" and by sale of land to prospective settlers, he managed to raise the funds which enabled him to get away from England in the summer of 1675 with a group of colonists, most of them Quakers, who settled that fall at Salem.[31]

As the trustees continued with their own plans, they drafted during the summer of 1676, in agreement with the proprietors and with prospective settlers in the colony, one of the more remarkable documents in American history—"The Concessions and Agreements of the Proprietors, Freeholders, and Inhabitants of the Province of West New Jersey," which finally was dated in March, 1677.[32] The more significant of its provisions were described, in a subhead, as "The Charter or fundamentall Laws of West New Jersey agreed upon."[33] By fundamental law, it was explained in the first paragraph of the Charter, was meant "the common Law or fundamentall Rights and priviledges" agreed upon as "the foundation of the Government." This definition was further clarified by a specific prohibition of any legislative enactment in conflict with "the said fundamentalls."

"There we lay a foundation for after ages to understand their liberty as men and christians," the trustees explained in another place, "that they may not be brought in bondage, but by their own consent; for we put the power in the people."[34] The people were to exercise their power through an annually elected assembly, which

31 Pomfret, *West Jersey*, pp. 65–85; Andrews, *Colonial Period*, III, 163–166.
32 Boyd, *Fundamental Laws and Constitutions of New Jersey*, pp. 71–104.
33 *Ibid.*, pp. 83 ff.; and for discussion, Pomfret, *West Jersey*, p. 86 ff.
34 New Jersey *Archives*, I, 228.

each year would choose ten commissioners for the management of provincial affairs during its adjournment. Protected by specific guarantees of privilege, including full control over its own sessions and procedures, the assembly had no real limitation placed upon its authority except that it could not alter the fundamental law previously agreed upon.

For the seventeenth century, even for seventeenth-century America, this was an extraordinary proposal for an experiment in popular self-government, but the guarantees provided for the legal rights of the individual have even greater significance. Freedom of conscience was defined as an absolute and unqualified right belonging to all men. No inhabitant was to be deprived of "Life limb Liberty estate Property or any wayes hurt in his or their Priviledges Freedoms or Franchises upon any account whatsoever without a due tryall by the judgment of twelve jurors from his own neighborhood."[35] It was specified that the judgment belonged to the jury and not the judge. The testimony of at least two witnesses was required for the settlement of any issue, civil or criminal. Except in cases "fellonious criminall and treasonable," no person could be arrested or imprisoned until after a summons had been delivered at his place of residence by a public officer, the summons specifying the charge, the complainant, and the time and place of trial. All judicial proceedings were to be publicly conducted. No man could be imprisoned for debt.

William Penn often has been credited, quite understandably, with the authorship of these enlightened guarantees. But there is also evidence that Byllynge himself may have been principally responsible,[36] and what is more important than the unresolved question of authorship is the agreement by all parties to the enterprise that their colony would be dedicated to an extremely advanced concept of individual liberty. The Quakers were by no means the first among English settlers in North America to extend the liberties belonging by right to the king's subjects beyond the limits recognized at the time in England,[37] but to them belongs the

35 Boyd, *Fundamental Laws,* p. 85.
36 John L. Nickalls, "The Problem of Edward Byllinge," in Howard H. Brinton (ed.), *Children of Light* (New York, 1938), pp. 111–131.
37 For evidence of the Puritan contribution to a new concept of civil liberties, see Haskins, *Law and Authority in Early Massachusetts,* especially the closing

high honor of having given in the Concessions and Agreements of 1677 the fullest statement yet made in our history of the principle that the powers of government are properly checked by the rights of the governed. That the document found no perfect application in West Jersey matters less than does the record it provides of the radical political convictions the religious dissenter of this time might bring with him to America.

While drafting the Fundamental Laws of West Jersey, the trustees also reached an agreement, in the so-called Quintipartite Deed of July 1676, with Sir George Carteret for a boundary between East and West Jersey that gave the Quakers full control of the eastern bank of the Delaware River.[38] The first settlers, some 230 of them, reached New Castle in August, 1677, and they were soon settled at Burlington. By 1682 over 1,700 colonists, counting those at Salem, had migrated to West Jersey.[39] They were over-whelmingly Quaker in their religious affiliation, and as the area of settlement was extended northward and southward along the Delaware, and inland with the creeks, Quakerism remained for many years the dominant influence in the colony.[40] But the colony's development was slow after 1682, in no small part because of the magnetic attraction of the growing province of Pennsylvania, whose city of Philadelphia even today holds lower Jersey in an orbit comparable only to the pull of New York City upon what once was East Jersey.

Penn's decision to seek a proprietorship of his own on the west bank of the Delaware has been attributed in part to the difficulties experienced by the Quaker leaders in their Jersey venture, and there can be no doubt as to the trouble they faced there. Only in 1680 did the trustees get from the Duke of York a confirmation of Byllynge's title. Meanwhile, the uncertainties resulting from this delay were further complicated by the insistence of Sir Edmund Andros that the area fell under the jurisdiction of his government in New York.[41] The confirmation, which recognized Byllynge's

chapters; and for Plymouth, S. E. Morison, in *William and Mary Quarterly*, 3d. ser., XV (1958), pp. 360–362.

[38] Richard P. McCormick, *New Jersey from Colony to State* (Princeton, 1964), p. 40; Pomfret, *West Jersey*, pp. 74–75.

[39] *Ibid.*, pp. 106–107.

[40] *Ibid.*, especially pp. 216 ff.

[41] See below, pp. 203–204.

right to the government of the area, seemed to have settled that issue, but it also raised an even more troublesome one, for Byllynge proclaimed himself governor and sent Samuel Jennings to the colony as his deputy. This, of course, was in violation of the Concessions and Agreements, which had assigned executive powers to annually elected commissioners, and the colonists accepted Jennings only upon conditions which undertook to perpetuate the independence of the legislative assembly.[42] Perhaps it was only the tact and good sense of Jennings, who was destined to hold an influential position in West Jersey politics through many years, that postponed to 1683 a revolutionary attempt to overthrow Byllynge's authority. An extraordinary assembly of the freeholders meeting in that year elected Jennings to the office of deputy governor, and subsequently he was sent to England as agent in an abortive attempt to win the surrender of Byllynge's right of government to the full body of the proprietors.

Among those who attended West Jersey's extraordinary assembly of 1683 was William Penn, then briefly a resident of his newly established colony across the river. Perhaps his presence bespeaks nothing more than his consistent concern for the amicable settlement of all differences which divided Friends, but there is good reason for believing that his attendance spoke also of the broad vision he had gained of an opportunity to dedicate the entire Delaware Valley to the goals of Quaker colonization. Certainly, the record of his activity shows no inclination to abandon New Jersey because of his new interest in Pennsylvania. In 1680, the very year in which he petitioned for his own charter, he was instrumental in winning York's confirmation of Byllynge's title. After 1681 he was no longer a trustee of West Jersey, but in 1683 he bought Fenwick's tenth, thereby eliminating a troublesome problem and becoming himself for the first time a West Jersey proprietor. Already, in 1682, he had become a proprietor of East Jersey by heading a group of twelve men, mostly Quakers, who purchased the title of the recently deceased Sir George Carteret.[43] This was the year, too, in which Penn secured from the Duke of York deeds of lease and release

---

42 McCormick, *New Jersey*, pp. 46–47; Pomfret, *West Jersey*, pp. 127 ff.; Boyd, *Fundamental Laws*, pp. 106–108.

43 John E. Pomfret, "The Proprietors of the Province of East New Jersey, 1682–1702," *Pennsylvania Magazine of History*, LXXVII (1953), 251–293.

conferring upon him the Duke's title to the previously settled area (Delaware, as we know it today) extending southward from Pennsylvania to Cape Henlopen.[44] Thus, by 1683 the entrance to the great river and the lands on both of its banks, reaching eastward to the Atlantic, northward to New York, and westward above Maryland to the mountains, had been made secure for an enlarged project of Quaker colonization.

In East Jersey the initiative was taken by Scottish Quakers under the lead of Robert Barclay, but his efforts to encourage the settlement of Scottish Friends in that area met with little success. Perhaps as many as 500 Scots migrated to East Jersey between 1683 and 1685, a migration that must be attributed chiefly to Barclay's efforts to publicize the opportunities offered there, but most of the new settlers were Presbyterians.[45] Perth Amboy, a town founded at the mouth of the Raritan by Scottish adventurers which became the capital city of East Jersey, stands today as the chief monument to the interest awakened among the Scots at this time in New Jersey.

The story of Quaker colonization after 1682 is largely the story of Pennsylvania. William Penn had petitioned for the grant in June, 1680, and his charter received the final seal in March, 1681.[46] As is well known, Penn relied heavily upon Charles II's indebtedness to the now deceased Admiral Penn, for whom at the king's suggestion the province was named. The charter gave to Penn and his heirs the area lying between Maryland and New York and extending westward through five degrees of longitude. On the south side the boundary was fixed at the 40th parallel, which was the upper limit of Lord Baltimore's claim under the Maryland charter and a line coinciding approximately with the later site of Philadelphia. But the charter also stated that Penn's rights along the river extended southward to a point twelve miles above New Castle, well below the 40th parallel, and then further confused the issue by stipulating that the boundary should follow a circular line bending southward at twelve miles distance from New Castle until it intersected the 40th parallel. Little wonder that Lord Baltimore and

---

[44] Andrews, *Colonial Period*, III, 292–297.

[45] McCormick, *New Jersey*, p. 32; Pomfret, *East Jersey*, pp. 134–198.

[46] Among other places, the charter may be consulted in Samuel Hazard, *Annals of Pennsylvania, from the Discovery of the Delaware, 1609–1682* (Philadelphia, 1850), pp. 488–499.

Penn were soon involved in the opening rounds of one of the most protracted boundary disputes in American history. Not until the eve of the Revolution would it be finally settled with the running of the famous Mason-Dixon Line.

Penn's charter was the last of the great proprietary charters, and its issuance may have been resisted by the Lords of Trade. It is not at all certain that as yet they had settled upon the policy, announced in the following year, that no more such grants should be made. Nor is it certain that they openly challenged a grant known to have the backing both of the king and of the Duke of York. But there can be little doubt that the committee was responsible for the inclusion of several significant limitations upon Penn's authority as proprietor. It was stipulated that the Navigation Acts were to be strictly observed, that the proprietor would keep an agent in London to answer for all violations, that the king's customs officers would be admitted to the province, that provincial laws would be forwarded to England for royal confirmation or disallowance, that appeals from the provincial courts could be carried to the king, and that the rights of the Anglican Church would be respected.[47] It is important to observe that none of these limitations affected Penn's authority as proprietor of the soil.

William Penn's role as the founder of Pennsylvania is not an easy one to interpret.[48] Any interpretation must place first the fact that he was a Quaker. It was his Quaker faith, and his wholehearted identification with the Quaker cause, that had led him to become a colonizer. There is no room for doubt as to the sincerity with which he described the Pennsylvania venture as a "Holy Experiment." At the same time, it has to be said that this venture was intended also to serve as an extension of his own personal estate, and that in this hope Penn's motivation becomes very nearly identical with that of the original Lord Baltimore. Indeed, it may be worth noting that these two men, the first and the last of the great colonial proprietors, were the only ones to achieve the goal of them all—the establishment of a colony to be handed down from generation to generation as the property of the family. Although in other cases the king sooner or later took over, Maryland and Pennsylvania remained, except for one interval each, the properties of the Calvert

47 Andrews, *Colonial Period*, III, 278–285.
48 Andrews' discussion (*ibid.*, pp. 268–326) is especially helpful.

and Penn families until the American Revolution. But it is not enough to state the problem of Penn's role as though it is one of a simple ambivalence. The Quakers had little, if any, hope of acquiring the full control they achieved in the Delaware Valley except by depending upon William Penn's influence at court. His own substantial investment in the enterprise, an investment large enough to set him apart from other post-Restoration proprietors, goes far to explain his insistence that the interest of his personal estate be protected. On the other hand, the prospect that his estate might gain depended very heavily upon the response he found among fellow Quakers to the goals, spiritual and other, the Quaker community had set for itself in the Delaware Valley. William Penn began his career as a colonizer in the capacity of a trustee, and in a very real sense he held Pennsylvania in trust for interests larger than his own, however real that interest may have been.

Except for the great Puritan migration into Massachusetts after 1630, there is no parallel in the story of English colonization in North America for the immediate and phenomenal success attending the Pennsylvania venture. By July, 1683, fifty vessels had arrived in the Delaware bearing perhaps as many as 3,000 settlers. At the end of that year Philadelphia, which was laid out on a symmetrical plan between the Delaware and the Schuylkill, was reported to have 150 houses. The population of Pennsylvania and the previously established settlements below it on the west bank of the Delaware, where some of the first Quaker immigrants bought already developed property, may have reached a total of 12,000 by 1688.[49] By the end of the century, the population of Pennsylvania alone is authoritatively estimated at nearly 18,000.[50]

The parallel with Puritan Massachusetts is even closer than at first glance appears. Each undertaking drew its inspiration from the hopes and fears of a dissenting religious minority. Each group saw in America an opportunity to realize goals that were not attainable in the homeland. In each case, those who made the great adventure had the prayers and the assistance of many others who shared a common faith and dedication.

All too often the Quaker migration to the Delaware Valley has

[49] Greene and Harrington, *American Population*, pp. 113–114; Sutherland, *Population Distribution*, p. 144.
[50] *Historical Statistics of the U.S.*, p. 756.

been told in terms simply of an escape from persecution. It is quite true that the first years of the Pennsylvania colony coincided with a marked intensification of the persecution of Quakers in England. Subject to fine under one statute for attending their own meetings, they were also subject to fine under another law for not attending the services of the Church of England. If unable to pay the fines, the Quaker faced the further risk of having his property, including even the tools of his trade, seized in an enforced payment which might bring complete ruin to him and his family. But the Quaker's faith taught him to accept the suffering that was his lot, and there is evidence that the meeting to which he belonged, and upon which he depended for credentials that would give him standing in a New World meeting, might inquire closely when the proposed move could be viewed simply as a flight from persecution.[51] However that evidence may be weighted, there can be no doubt that the motivation was both varied and complex. Penn took pains to demonstrate, in refutation of prevailing assumptions regarding emigration from England, that the nation would be benefited by his projected settlement. Economic considerations reinforced the religious. A people whose convictions were in conflict at many points with the conventions which governed English society could be strongly drawn by the prospect of helping to build, and of living in, a society shaped by those convictions. Many of Pennsylvania's first settlers must have responded to Penn's appeal for men "that have an eye to the Good of Posterity, and that both understand and delight to promote good Discipline and just Government among a plain and well intending people"; men who might "find Room in Colonies for their good Counsel and Contrivance, who are shut out from being of much use or service to great Nations under settl'd Customs."[52]

The conditions of settlement initially offered by Penn were flexible, and so adaptable to particular needs and circumstances. Drawing upon his experience in New Jersey, he depended chiefly

[51] For an excellent brief discussion of the problem of motivation, see Tolles, *Meeting House and Counting House*, pp. 33–38; William C. Braithwaite, *The Second Period of Quakerism* (London, 1919, 2d. ed. by Henry J. Cadbury, 1961), is standard for the period after 1660.

[52] From Penn's *Some Account of the Province of Pennsilvania* (1681), in Albert C. Myers (ed.), *Narratives of Early Pennsylvania, West Jersey, and Delaware* (New York, 1912), p. 210.

upon the sale of land at the price of £100 for 5,000 acres, the land to be held subject to an annual quitrent of 1s. per 100 acres. Large blocks could be bought by groups wishing to settle as a community. By paying a higher price, it was possible to commute the proprietor's claim to a rent. For the benefit of persons not able to purchase, he offered a 200-acre estate for man and family in return for the higher rent of 1d. per acre, and this acreage could be enlarged by the fifty-acre headright allowed for any servant taken to the colony. For those who could meet the cost of their passage to the colony but lacked the means to establish themselves there, Penn promised a stake of tools, stock, seeds, and so on, on an agreement to develop an assigned acreage through a term of seven years. At the end of the term the occupant would be entitled to buy. The proprietor's willingness to assist prospective emigrants was matched by his care to protect the interest of his own estate. Anticipating a future advantage for that estate, he ordered that a tenth part of each area opened to settlement be set aside as a reserve for later disposition by the proprietor and his heirs. These proprietary reserves were to become a cause for bitter controversy in the years ahead, but at the end of 1681, when the first of Penn's settlers reached the Delaware, that difficulty still lay ahead.[53]

William Penn's extraordinary success as a colonizer is attributable to many factors. By no means least among them is his eminence as a Quaker, but hardly less important is an especially skillful promotional campaign. His promotional tracts quickly carried news of the attractive opportunities he offered for settlement in Pennsylvania into many parts of the British Isles and to the continent of Europe as well. He had made the second of his missionary tours to the Rhineland in 1677. There he had established a reputation among the Protestant inhabitants of the area that was kept alive by his writings. At least ten of his earlier works, chiefly religious, had been translated into Dutch and half that number into German. It was natural for him to think also of getting his promotional tracts translated. Beginning with the very first of these tracts, and aided especially by his friend Benjamin Furly, an English Quaker merchant of Rotterdam, Penn had a large part of his promotional

[53] Myers, *Narratives*, pp. 208–209; Hazard, *Annals*, p. 523; Harris, *Origin of the Land Tenure System in the United States*, pp. 220–222, 237–241. For later disputes over proprietary reserves, see William R. Shepherd, *History of Proprietary Government in Pennsylvania* (New York, 1896).

literature published on the continent in Dutch, German, and some even in French. Adaptations of the literature to the special interests of his foreign audience directed particular attention to his policy of religious tolerance.[54] For a long time the response to this part of Penn's promotional campaign was decidedly small, little more than is represented by the Dutch Quakers who settled at Germantown in 1683. But nothing can better suggest the extent of the promotional effort which won a quick response within the British Isles.

There Penn was notably successful in enlisting the aid of substantial Friends, and especially of Quaker merchants who had prospered and had capital to invest in the new enterprise.[55] Many of them had no thought for settlement themselves in the colony, but others, including James Claypoole of London and Robert Turner of Dublin, joined the migration. Also quickly drawn into the migration to the Delaware were other Quaker merchants—chiefly from the West Indies, Rhode Island, and New York—who previously had established themselves in America, among them Samuel Carpenter, who in ten years would be the wealthiest merchant in Philadelphia. The experience and capital brought to Philadelphia by men like Carpenter was a major factor in that city's precipitous rise to an important position in the trade of the western Atlantic.[56]

Any attempt to explain Penn's success must also include the care he took to repeat the legal guarantees for every settler in Pennsylvania which already had been made a distinguishing mark of Quaker settlement by the Concessions and Agreements of 1677. The "Laws agreed upon in England" during the spring of 1682 show the same strong devotion to the concept of a government limited in its powers by the rights properly belonging to the governed.[57] Any person professing a belief in "one Almighty and Eternal God" was

[54] William I. Hull, *William Penn and the Dutch Quaker Migration to Pennsylvania* (Swarthmore, Pa., 1935), pp. 308 ff., is especially informative on this part of Penn's promotional campaign. See also Hope Frances Kane, "Notes on Early Pennsylvania Promotion Literature," *Pennsylvania Magazine of History*, LXIII (1939), 144–168.

[55] A point well developed by Gary B. Nash in his unpublished Ph.D. dissertation entitled "Economics and Politics in Early Pennsylvania, 1682–1701" (Princeton University, 1964), and in his "The Free Society of Traders and the Early Politics of Pennsylvania," *Pennsylvania Magazine of History*, LXXXIX, (1965), 147–173. See also John E. Pomfret, "The First Purchasers of Pennsylvania, 1681–1700," *Pennsylvania Magazine of History*, LXXX (1956), 137–163.

[56] Tolles, *Meeting House and Counting House*, pp. 43–44.

[57] Hazard, *Annals*, pp. 568–574.

guaranteed a free right of worship, although only Christians could vote or hold office. All court proceedings were to be public, and trials by jury procedure. The right to bail was assured, except for cases involving a capital offense, "where the proof is evident, or the presumption is great." Court fees were to be moderate and collected according to a fixed and public schedule. Fines imposed had also to be moderate, and could not touch a man's "contenements, merchandise, or wainage"—which is to say, the means of his livelihood. Prisons were made free "as to fees, food, and lodging." It detracts nothing from the credit belonging to Penn to say that these guarantees faithfully reflect the disadvantages from which the Quakers frequently had suffered in the courts at home.

So fundamental have been these guarantees of individual right to the modern concept of democracy that William Penn has often been mistaken for a democrat. Actually, he was an aristocrat with aristocratic ideas of government.[58] Earlier he may have been momentarily committed to a more democratic view. Although there is no firm evidence that he was primarily responsible for the popular character of the initial provision for government in West Jersey, there is also no evidence that he objected to the plan. His friends included the great republican Algernon Sydney, but they also included two of the Stuart kings, and his own views of government are more accurately described as those of a whig than of a republican. His thinking on this subject, as on others, was rooted in his Quaker faith, and he remained wholly consistent only in his insistence that the liberty of the subject be protected by law. In the preface of his first Frame of Government in 1682, he declared, "any government is free to the people under it, whatever be the frame, where the laws rule, and the people are a party to those laws."[59] In this eloquent and oft-quoted statement, Penn discounts the impor-

---

[58] The fullest discussions of Penn's political ideas are found in the unpublished Ph.D. dissertation of Mary Maples, "A Cause To Plead: The Political Thought and Career of William Penn" (Bryn Mawr College, 1959), and its further development in Mary Maples Dunn, *William Penn: Politics and Conscience* (Princeton, 1967). See also her "William Penn, Classical Republican," *Pennsylvania Magazine of History and Biography*, LXXXI (1957), 138–156. Helpful is Edward C. O. Beatty, *William Penn as Social Philosopher* (New York, 1939), and the introductions by Frederick B. Tolles and E. Gordon Alderfer (eds.), in *The Witness of William Penn* (New York, 1957).

[59] For the Frame, see Hazard, *Annals*, pp. 558–568.

tance of the form, or frame, a government might take, and yet the statement can be safely interpreted only by giving attention to the frame of government which followed. Provision was made for an elected assembly of 200 representatives of the colony's freemen, but these representatives were to have no power except that of yielding or refusing their assent to laws proposed for enactment by the governor and council. The fact that the council also was to be elected can be misleading, for there is evidence that Penn counted upon social convention to assure the election of the more substantial colonists to that body.[60] He expected as a resident proprietor to serve as governor and so to preside over the council. In short, his was a paternalistic scheme of government distinguished from other such schemes chiefly by Penn's confidence that his coreligionists would readily accept the leadership he offered.

The question of local administration presented no problem. By 1680, jurisdiction over the inhabitants of the Delaware's western bank was divided among four courts, the most northerly of them sitting at Upland, within the bounds Penn's charter would establish for Pennsylvania and soon to be redesignated as Chester. Manned by magistrates holding commissions from the governor of New York, each of these courts presided over an area to which the name county had more than once been applied in recent years. All that was needed was to make that designation formal and to add two counties above Chester for the new area of settlement. By so doing, Penn gave to Pennsylvania three counties: Chester, Philadelphia, and Bucks. Below Chester came the Lower Counties, as they were destined long to be known, the three into which the state of Delaware is still divided: New Castle, Kent, and Sussex, to use the names they acquired in 1684.[61]

Penn decided to unite the six counties under a single provincial administration. An act of union adopted by an assembly meeting at Chester in December, 1682, shortly after the proprietor's first arrival in the Delaware, gave formal effect to the decision.[62] It was a decision which avoided the risk of assigning a subordinate status to

[60] See especially Nash, "Economics and Politics in Early Pennsylvania," pp. 20–29, where the evolution of the document is discussed.

[61] Especially helpful is Leon de Valinger, Jr. (ed.), *Court Records of Kent County, Delaware*, pp. i–xxii.

[62] Hazard, *Annals*, pp. 611–614.

the older Delaware settlements, but it brought into the political life of Quaker Pennsylvania an extraordinary mixture of people (all told, perhaps a thousand) who were not Quakers, who as downriver settlers were often to view Philadelphia with jealousy, and who in some instances preferred to pin their hopes upon Lord Baltimore's claim to the lower reaches of the Delaware.[63] Only a far greater degree of unity among the Quakers of Pennsylvania proper than they actually were able to achieve could have offset the advantage gained by the Lower Counties through the agreement that each of the six counties would have equal representation both on the council and in the assembly. By the revised frame of 1683 the unrealistic size of the assembly was reduced from 200 to 36, and of the council from 72 to 18.[64]

Penn's hope that he might lead the predominantly Quaker inhabitants of Pennsylvania in the paths of brotherly co-operation was by no means groundless. His standing as a Quaker, and as the honored founder of a great Quaker enterprise, gave him many advantages. Moreover, he had established in advance an effective basis for alliance with the more substantial of the First Purchasers in Pennsylvania, both by the appointments he made to office and by the privileges promised the Free Society of Traders, a corporation intended to play a large role in the establishment and supply of the colony. Aided by social conventions which prevailed, even among Quakers, in elections for high offices, and by the respect his closest associates enjoyed in the religious community, Penn usually had the support in council of a proprietary circle broad enough to include at least a few influential representatives of the Lower Counties. Even so, the council was something less than a united body of leading Friends who easily found a desirable consensus as to the action that was needed. Only a brief experience argued for the advantages of an appointed council, but Penn was trapped by a provision in his Frame that required for such a change a majority he knew to be impossible. Instead, he insisted upon a right of veto on issues critically affecting his responsibilities to the king under

[63] Robert W. Johannsen, "The Conflict between the Three Lower Counties on the Delaware and the Province of Pennsylvania, 1682–1704," *Delaware History,* V (1952), 96–132. Nash, "Economics and Politics in Early Pennsylvania," offers additional information.

[64] Hazard, *Annals,* pp. 615–619.

the royal charter, and balanced this by conceding that he would exercise his executive powers only with the consent of the council, a concession dangerously enlarging the authority that could be claimed by that body during the long periods of the proprietor's absence from the colony. As for the lower house of the General Assembly, its members immediately demanded a right of their own to initiate legislation and persisted in this demand until it was finally conceded in 1696.[65]

No one can tell what difference it might have made had William Penn remained in Pennsylvania as a resident proprietor. As it happened, he sailed for England in August, 1684, there to meet the challenge brought against his claims by Lord Baltimore, who had preceded Penn to London earlier in the year.[66] Penn would next see his province in 1699. At the end of his first visit to the colony, no hard party or factional lines had formed, but there were indications foretelling the exceedingly troublesome years that lay ahead. Jealousy of the proprietary circle had been shown not only by some of the lesser investors migrating from England but also by prosperous and increasingly influential merchants who had come from other colonies rather than from the homeland. The assembly had flatly refused enactment of the bill providing a charter for the Free Society of Traders, which through mismanagement and the competition it faced in the colony already had fallen to a very low estate. Many of the settlers were discontented with the administration of the land office, which seems to have been badly managed from the first. The Lower Counties had shown a growing restlessness in their new association with Pennsylvania. Penn could justly boast that he had "led the greatest colony into America that ever any man did upon a private credit,"[67] but the boast could hardly hide the disappointments he also had experienced.

William Penn's extraordinary achievements as a colonizer had been won at no small cost to the colony belonging to his friend and patron, the Duke of York. Since Peter Stuyvesant's day, trade with

[65] See especially studies by Nash cited in note 55, above; also Andrews, *Colonial Period*, III, 298–308.

[66] See above, p. 164, and Joseph E. Illick, *William Penn the Politician: His Relations with the English Government* (Ithaca, 1965), pp. 52–75.

[67] Quoted in Charles M. Andrews, *Colonial Self-Government, 1652–1689* (New York, 1904), p. 191.

the South River (as the Delaware was known in order to distinguish it from the North River, which was the Hudson) had been a significant item in New York's economy. The tobacco exported by the Delaware settlers, together with some peltries, was partly their own production and partly that of Marylanders living along the upper reaches of the Chesapeake who showed a preference for markets along the Delaware. New York's merchants may have exaggerated when in 1685 they complained that the proprietor's recent surrender of his claims to jurisdiction on the Delaware and in the Jerseys had cost the city a third of its trade.[68] But there can be no doubt that the loss, which included the migration of several New York merchants to the Delaware, was substantial, and all the more so because New York could ill afford the loss of any part of its trade.

By comparison with the commercial activity of Boston, and all too soon with that of Philadelphia, New York's trade was small.[69] Lacking the established contacts with London that Boston enjoyed, and denied the right it more than once had sought to trade with Holland, New York traded mainly with the other colonies, including the West Indian. After the loss of the Delaware trade, its chief exports were beaver skins, flour, and the oil drawn from the whale fishery of eastern Long Island.[70] New York-owned bottoms were small in number and generally of a small tonnage. For its supply of European goods the colony depended chiefly upon Boston, and struggled to prevent a complete dominance of the economy by that commercial center.[71] A cause for special concern was the natural tendency for a direct trade between New England and the Puritan towns of Long Island to flourish at the expense both of New York merchants and of provincial revenues.

All questions affecting the colony's trade had a peculiarly important bearing upon the ever difficult problem of provincial finance. The government of New Netherland had depended almost exclu-

---

[68] Brodhead, *History of New York*, II, 426.

[69] Curtis P. Nettels, "The Economic Relations of Boston, Philadelphia, and New York, 1680–1715," *Journal of Economic and Business History*, III (1930–31), 185–215.

[70] On the whale fishery, see Alexander Starbuck, *History of the American Whale Fishery* (1878; new ed., New York, 1964) I, 9–15.

[71] See *Colonial Laws of New York*, I, 165–167 for legislation of 1684 imposing a 10 per cent duty upon all European goods brought in from another colony.

sively upon customs duties and excise taxes. Although the English had added a property tax, the exceedingly slow growth of the colony was reflected in a continuingly heavy dependence upon the returns from customs and excises.[72] Quitrents provided no more than a negligible supplement; indeed, a commission of 1674 to the receiver-general failed even to list the rents among proprietary revenues.[73] Any stagnancy in the colony's trade might critically reduce the income of the provincial government.

The resulting combination of economic and fiscal considerations invited policies favoring a monopolistic organization of the trade. Thus, the special privileges belonging to New York City as the staple port of the province found much of its justification in the guarantee they presumably gave for the largest possible return from the customs. The city's claim to a monopoly of port privileges, which had a deep rootage in Dutch policy, bred not a little discontent in other communities, and notably in the towns of eastern Long Island and in Albany, which incidentally had its own monopoly of the Indian trade. Governors Lovelace and Andros experimented with certain concessions to the Long Island towns, but the general trend after 1674 was toward a tightening of the city's control over trade both internal and external. For this trend the favored explanation has been the influence enjoyed by the city's merchants through the large representation they had on the governor's council.[74] That this advantage counted heavily is not to be questioned, but it also has to be remembered that public policy is often shaped by the peculiar needs of government itself.

Helping to maintain, and probably to strengthen, the city's claim to a widening list of monopolies was the insistence by Governor Andros that its monopoly of port privileges included the neighboring part of New Jersey, a policy determined very largely, if not wholly, by fiscal considerations. Although there is remarkably little

[72] Van Rensselaer, *History of the City of New York*, II, 29–30; Osgood, *American Colonies in the Seventeenth Century*, II, 356–360; N.Y. *Colonial Documents*, III, 317–318.

[73] Bond, *Quit-rent System*, p. 112; such as were collected seem to have come largely from the Delaware. N.Y. *Colonial Documents*, III, 400–401.

[74] On the privileges of the city, see especially Bernard Mason, "Aspects of the New York Revolt of 1689," *New York History*, XXX (1949), 165–180; Beverly McAnear, "Politics in Provincial New York, 1689–1761" (unpublished Ph.D. dissertation, Stanford University, 1935).

evidence to support the frequently popular view that the Duke of York hoped to profit by his proprietorship, he undoubtedly did hope not to be out of pocket for the cost of its administration. And out of pocket he was in 1674, perhaps as much as £2,000 merely for the cost of repossessing the territory from the Dutch.[75] Much of that cost was for the company of regulars sent with Andros to re-establish the English garrison, a garrison unhappily destined to become a permanent charge against the English administration of the New York colony.[76] One can wonder why the Duke did not seize the opportunity he seemingly had in 1674 to correct the earlier mistake he had made by deeding away New Jersey, as more than one of his advisers had urged him to do. Perhaps he felt morally bound by the previous grant, at any rate, to Carteret. Perhaps Sir George's influence with the king was too great. Whatever the fact, Carteret's grant was renewed in 1674, but once again by a device that conferred no more than title to the soil.[77] The legal foundation upon which Andros' actions depended was made complete by a commission giving him authority as governor over the entire area embraced by the Duke's extraordinary charter. Whether by deliberate design or with some help from chance, the way had been prepared for the governor's insistence that he represented a higher jurisdictional right that entitled him to command the trade of the whole area.

Andros was a soldier. Scion of the leading family of Guernsey, he had grown up as a royalist exile in Holland, where he gained his first military experience under Prince Henry of Nassau. The second Anglo-Dutch War had carried him with a military command to Barbados, as also had the third and final conflict with Holland. Having been a member of the household of the Queen of Bohemia, he had a close acquaintance with the Earl of Craven, whose niece he married, and at one time he may have considered a venture to Carolina. At any rate, he had been made a landgrave of that province. Instead, and soon after his return from his second tour in Barbados, he received the New York post, in part perhaps because

[75] Brodhead, *History of New York,* II, 279; Van Rensselaer, *History of the City of New York,* II, 169–170.

[76] See especially Stanley M. Pargellis, "The Four Independent Companies of New York," *Essays . . . Presented to Charles McLean Andrews,* pp. 96–123.

[77] On this point see again Andrews, *Colonial Period,* III, 138 n.

of his previous experience in Holland.[78] He is not an easy person to interpret, but one point seems clear. As a soldier, he was inclined to follow his orders, and his commission had made him governor throughout the Duke's territories.

For so long as Governor Philip Carteret accepted New York's monopoly of port privileges, there was no interference with the government he headed. There was indication enough, however, of what could be expected from a challenge to that monopoly in Andros' dealings with the early settlers of West Jersey. John Fenwick was promptly warned that his rights there must be established to the satisfaction of the government in New York, and that no shipping whatsoever could enter his settlement without having paid the customs at New Castle. When Fenwick proved stubborn, he was twice haled before the Court of Assizes in New York, and eventually Andros undertook to subordinate the government of Salem to New Castle by the appointment of magistrates made answerable to the court across the river.[79] Significantly, the Quakers sent out by Byllynge's trustees called at New York on their way to the Delaware. In the absence of specific instructions, Andros solved the problem by giving his own commissions to the commissioners designated by the trustees for the administration of the colony, but they too were considered subordinate to New Castle's court and Andros continued to demand payment there by the Burlington settlers of a 5 per cent customs.[80] No doubt because he had been warned to avoid stirring up the "choller" of Sir George Carteret,[81] Andros seems to have made no early demand in the case of East Jersey for a formal acknowledgment of the superior authority he represented. But after Governor Carteret in 1679 declared the ports of East Jersey free to shipping without payment of customs in New York, Andros charged Carteret with an unwarranted exercise of jurisdiction and in the spring of 1680 had him carried to New York for trial. Although the jury failed to convict him, Carteret was forbidden to exercise any authority whatsoever in East Jersey, and

[78] The fullest account of his career is Jeanne G. Bloom, "Sir Edmund Andros: A Study in Seventeenth Century Colonial Administration" (unpublished Ph.D. dissertation, Yale University, 1962).

[79] Pomfret, *West Jersey*, pp. 80–84.

[80] *Ibid.*, pp. 103–104, 107–108.

[81] Pomfret, *East Jersey*, pp. 117–118.

subsequently Andros himself virtually assumed the office of governor there.[82]

There is no reason for believing that Andros' actions with regard to East Jersey had anything to do with his recall to England late in 1680. Indeed, the evidence argues that he could have been charged in this affair with nothing more than an overzealous adherence to his instructions. The charges he faced upon his return to London were for maladministration of the colony's finances, and of these charges he was cleared.[83] He retained the Duke's favor and was destined to be called by him within a few years to undertake an even more important assignment in America.

Less certain is the record of the Duke's own conduct, for by the summer of 1680, and possibly before, he had decided to abandon all claim to jurisdiction in New Jersey. It was a difficult time for him. The Whig movement to exclude him from the throne was at its height, and at more than one critical point in the story he was living outside the kingdom in virtual exile. Urgent pleas from the West Jersey Quakers had enlisted the aid of influential men, among them William Penn. The fact that the king had agreed in 1679 that the New York garrison would become a charge, to the extent of £1,000 annually, upon the royal purse may have had some influence.[84] When in the next year the question of the Duke's right to a 5 per cent duty in New Jersey was referred to Sir William Jones, a Whig and known opponent of York, his negative answer must have been both expected and desired. In August, 1680, Byllynge finally had his deed of confirmation, together with assurance as to his right to the government of West Jersey and his freedom from the payment of "any customs or other duties" to the Duke of York. A few weeks later the same assurance was given Sir George Carteret's heir.[85] Unhappily for New Jersey, the legitimacy of its two governments remained in question, in part because the Duke had given what legally he had no power to give. The right to govern was a preroga-

[82] *Ibid.*, pp. 110–120.

[83] Andrews, *Colonial Period*, III, 100. Pomfret implies and Bloom, "Andros," pp. 41–42, asserts that following the death of Sir George Carteret in January, 1680, Andros was instructed to proceed against the governor of East Jersey. It should not be forgotten that Andros had visited England as recently as 1678, where he consulted with his superior and when he was knighted.

[84] Bloom, "Andros," p. 28.

[85] Pomfret, *West Jersey*, pp. 110–112.

tive of the king, and only by his grant could a clear title have been secured.

The New York government, of course, remained unreconciled to the prospect that free ports in New Jersey, by the encouragement they gave to smuggling, might undermine its entire fiscal system. For New York's merchants the fear was that business increasingly would migrate across the river or to the Delaware. There were fears, too, for Albany's monopoly of the Indian trade, that it might be diverted to New Jersey, and this fear was soon linked with the further fear that it might be diverted to Philadelphia. Penn's charter had given him possession of the main stretch of the Susquehannah River, a stream offering ready access to the more westerly of the Iroquois nations, and he had been quick to see the importance of pushing his possession as far up the river as was possible. When Thomas Dongan reached New York in 1683, as successor to Andros, he hurried on to Albany in order to counter the effort of agents sent there by Penn to purchase the upper Susquehannah Valley from the Iroquois. By 1684 the land in question had been deeded to Dongan himself.[86]

This was merely one of several steps he took toward the establishment of an alliance between the New York government and the Five Nations. Contrary to a common assumption, neither the Dutch nor the English theretofore had been formally allied with the Iroquois. The relationship had been basically a business one, with responsibility for the regulation of the Anglo-Indian trade belonging to the local court at Albany, whose clerk after 1675 was Robert Livingston.[87] But some greater involvement by the provincial government had become inevitable under the circumstances prevailing by 1684. Such now was the critical importance of the Iroquois to other colonies that New York had either to assume a new responsibility or else stand by while agents from Virginia, Maryland, Pennsylvania, or one of the New England colonies negotiated directly on questions unavoidably affecting New York's vital inter-

---

[86] Trelease, *Indian Affairs in Colonial New York*, pp. 254–257, 264; Brodhead, *History of New York*, II, 375–376, 393, 397, 465; and Gary B. Nash, "The Quest for the Susquehanna Valley: New York, Pennsylvania, and the Seventeenth-Century Fur Trade," *New York History*, XLVIII (1967), 3–27.

[87] Trelease, *Indian Affairs*, pp. 207–209; Lawrence H. Leder, *Robert Livingston, 1654–1728, and the Politics of Colonial New York* (Chapel Hill, N.C., 1961), pp. 15–16.

ests.[88] For the simultaneous intensification of the international contest with the French in Canada, Dongan himself seems to have been as responsible as was any other person.

An energetic and ambitious Irishman, whose Catholic faith (whatever the doubts it raised in the minds of New York's overwhelmingly Protestant population) did not deter him, Dongan made a bid to win for Albany the dominance of the western fur trade that Montreal also hoped to have. The alliance then existing between the English and French governments imposed some restraint upon their governors in America, but already the Iroquois had responded to French adventures into the country of the Illinois by going to war with the Illinois in 1680. Emboldened by Dongan's policies but by no means completely submissive to his will, the Iroquois, not without provocation by the French, invaded Canada itself in 1687. Among the results was a further intensification of the financial difficulties of an overcommitted New York government.[89] Reliable evidence as to the size of the Albany fur trade is surprisingly incomplete, but there is reason for believing that annual shipments that had been as high as 46,000 pelts in the later years of Dutch rule had fallen by 1687 as low as 14,000, chiefly perhaps because of the Indian wars.[90] Each beaver skin exported in Andros' term had paid ls.3d. duty, and under Dongan 9d.[91] Dongan, who reported to London that in 1687 his total revenue was only £3,000, was reduced by 1688 to appeals for help from Virginia, Maryland, Pennsylvania, and the Jerseys.[92]

However much Dongan's ambitious policy may have been respon-

88 By 1684 both Maryland and Virginia had each sent two separate missions to Albany to negotiate for the peace of their own frontiers.

89 Trelease, *Indian Affairs*, pp. 254–290; Leder, *Livingston*, pp. 46–50; Clarence W. Alvord, *The Illinois Country, 1673–1818* (Springfield, Ill., 1920), pp. 83–87, 91. For the French side of the story, see W. J. Eccles, *Canada under Louis XIV, 1663–1701* (Toronto, 1964), pp. 113–162, and his *Frontenac, the Courtier Governor* (Toronto, 1959), which calls for major revision of traditional views, especially of Frontenac's role.

90 Trelease, *Indian Affairs*, pp. 216–217, which also notes the declining popularity of beaver hats in Europe; Curtis P. Nettels, *The Money Supply of the American Colonies before 1720* (Madison, Wis., 1934), p. 75.

91 N.Y. *Colonial Documents*, III, 262; N.Y. *Colonial Laws*, I, 116–122.

92 Trelease, *Indian Affairs*, pp. 287–288. The £500 Effingham drew from the quitrents of Virginia, after the burgesses had refused an appropriation, seems to be all that came by way of response.

sible for his difficulties, he was by no means wholly responsible. The plain fact is that the New York jurisdiction, especially after 1680, made no sense at all—whether the test be geographical, economic, or political. Long Island, main center of the population as late as the end of the century,[93] belonged historically, culturally, and geographically with New England. The Duke's territories in Maine served only to impose upon New York additional costs for administration and defense in an area where conflict with Massachusetts was almost as sure as was conflict with the French. As Dongan pointed out, he had three separate forts to man and maintain: at Albany, at New York, and at Pemaquid.[94] The total population remained small and scattered, except for the concentrations on Manhattan and Long Island. The Duke had instructed Andros to give every encouragement to new settlers, especially by offering conditions of settlement comparable to what could be had in neighboring provinces.[95] Andros in 1681 claimed for his administration a considerable migration into the colony, but the claim is of doubtful validity, and thereafter one hears more of emigration from New York than of immigration into it.[96] There are indications that New York enjoyed a relative prosperity during Andros' term, but there can be no doubt as to the depression which followed. By 1685 property valuations in New York City, for example, had fallen to a figure 25 per cent below that given for 1676.[97]

Not only were New York's inhabitants few in number; they were also sharply divided and remarkably lacking in social cohesion. Partly Dutch, partly English, and partly a wide variety of other peoples, they gave their first loyalty to the lesser communities to which they belonged. The City of New York strove to protect its long-enjoyed dominance. Albany fought back, or yielded only what it had to yield in order to maintain its own special privileges. Much of Long Island resented its very identification with New York. A

[93] See the census of 1698 in Greene and Harrington, *American Population*, p. 92.
[94] N.Y. *Colonial Documents*, III, 406.
[95] *Ibid.*, III, 216–217, 218; Brodhead, *History of New York*, II, 286.
[96] *Ibid.*, II, 346. As late as 1698, a census showed a total population of 18,000 persons, and this after more than thirty years of English rule. Although this figure may reflect some of New York's more recent difficulties, the total was no more than Pennsylvania probably had achieved in less than half the time. Greene and Harrington, *American Population*, p. 92.
[97] Mason, "New York Revolt of 1689," pp. 172–173.

dramatic demonstration of the political weakness of the colony, if that it may be called, had immediately preceded Governor Dongan's arrival there. The customs and excise duties had been collected under a law having life for a three-year term. The law was due for renewal late in 1680, but for some reason Andros departed for England without its having been renewed. Subsequent attempts to collect the duties met a general and continuing resistance which threatened to reduce the government to a state of anarchy.[98] Perhaps only the steady habits of local self-government, for which Richard Nicolls had laid a secure foundation, preserved the peace of the province.

It is not intended to suggest, however, that the inhabitants of New York had nothing in common, for they did and that was a growing distrust of the great powers that were concentrated in the hands of the governor and his council. Perhaps simple jealousy of the special privileges that seemed to have been fostered by this concentration of power was primarily responsible for the demand for a representative assembly that had been heard before but that first became insistent, and general, in the protests of 1681.[99] Certainly, the example of the other English colonies, all of whose governments included an assembly, had its influence; but significantly, the standard to which the protesters most frequently appealed was that of the English government itself, no doubt because of the position held by the proprietor as a member of the royal family and heir to the throne. As is well known, the Duke considered assemblies to be more troublesome than useful, but in the financial and political crisis that had overtaken the colony, he yielded to the demand on the condition that the assembly provide revenues adequate to the needs of the government and of the garrison.[100] On his arrival at New York in August, 1683, Governor Dongan bore instructions for summoning the first assembly.

The assembly met on the following October 17, with eighteen representatives in attendance, the majority of them apparently

[98] Van Rensselaer, *History of the City of New York*, II, 232–240, provides the fullest account.

[99] The Long Island Puritans had been the earliest and most persistent in making the demand.

[100] See especially David S. Lovejoy's excellent discussion, "Equality and Empire: The New York Charter of Libertyes, 1683," *William and Mary Quarterly*, 3d. ser., XXI (1964), 493–515.

Dutch. It proved to be an extraordinarily fruitful first session. The revenue measure enacted left the colony's finances more than ever dependent upon customs and excise duties, and probably was less than the proprietor had hoped for. Another measure divided the jurisdiction into twelve counties, thereby rounding out the work begun by Richard Nicolls with the establishment of York County in 1665. But the assembly's greatest accomplishment was the drafting of its justly famous Charter of Libertyes.[101] This charter undertook to establish the government of the colony on a secure constitutional basis in order "that Justice and Right may be Equally done to all persons." The powers and the privileges of the assembly were carefully stated, as also were guarantees for the protection of individual liberties. Liberty of conscience was guaranteed for all Christians in a provision specifically assuring the Puritan towns on Long Island of a right to continue the public maintenance of their churches. Those who drafted the Charter, among whom Matthias Nicolls, relative of the first English governor and speaker of the assembly, was probably chief, showed a remarkable acquaintance with English constitutional and legal history, and in effect they demanded for the inhabitants of New York rights fully equal to those enjoyed by Englishmen.[102]

It was a very brave effort, but it was destined for ultimate defeat. The assembly continued, meeting again in 1684, until it was dissolved in 1685 on Governor Dongan's assumption that the death of Charles II had terminated its existence. A second and newly elected assembly met briefly in the fall of that year. Early in October, 1684, the Duke gave his approval to the Charter of Libertyes, but it was never delivered back to New York. Perhaps the explanation turns primarily upon the revocation of the Massachusetts charter that came a little later in the same month. To suggest this, however, is not to suggest anything more than that the final victory over Massachusetts raised a number of questions regarding future policy which could have argued for further consideration of so broad a grant of power and right as had been proposed in the New York charter. The death of Charles II and the succession of New York's proprietor as King James II in the follow-

---

101 For the Charter, see N.Y. *Colonial Laws*, I, 111–116, and 116–123 for the other two measures.
102 In addition to Lovejoy, see Andrews, *Colonial Period*, III, 112–119.

ing February made such a reconsideration almost compulsory. New York now automatically became a royal colony; the grant would be from the king, and whatever he gave to New York would establish a precedent unavoidably affecting what he would be expected to give other royal colonies, including Massachusetts. Although the question of what should be done about the government of Massachusetts, and related problems of New England in general, was yet to be decided, it is not surprising that the Lords of Trade promptly subjected the Charter of Libertyes to a very close scrutiny. Nor is it surprising that they discovered that the document would confirm for New York greater privileges than were enjoyed by any other of the royal colonies. The decision, made early in March and with the king present, was not to confirm, but to leave the privileges of New York dependent upon "the Constitution that shall be agreed on for New England."[103] The delay in the final settlement of that question easily explains the postponement of a formal disallowance of the New York charter until May, 1686.

The promptness of the king's advisers in seeing the connection between the New York and New England problems was matched by the promptness with which Governor Dongan seized the opportunity to reopen the question of New York's boundaries. There can be little doubt that his primary concern was with East Jersey, with the effect its continuing independence might have upon the trade of New York City and upon the revenues of the New York government, for as recently as February, 1684, he had persuaded the city's council to submit to the proprietor a formal complaint of the "unhappy separation" of New Jersey from the Duke's jurisdiction that asked especially for the reannexation of East Jersey "by purchase or other ways."[104] But when in May, 1685, the city once more, and again on the governor's prompting, complained to James of the hardships it had suffered from the loss of "Delaware and the two Jersies," it asked for much more—that the king would "reunite those parts and enlarge this government Eastward, and confirm and grant to this his City such privileges and immunities as may again make it flourish, and increase his Majesty's revenue."[105]

103 Lovejoy, "Equality and Empire," gives the specific objections.
104 Brodhead, *History of New York*, II, 392. The address stressed the natural advantages of the city as a commercial center and "the great inconveniences of having two distinct Governments upon one River."
105 *Ibid.*, II, 426; N.Y. *Colonial Documents*, III, 361.

Just what Dongan had in mind in making this proposal for an eastward extension of his government's jurisdiction is uncertain. One thinks at once of the claim, under the Duke of York's charter, to a jurisdiction reaching all the way to the Connecticut River. That claim had been dormant for a decade after Governor Andros briefly had asserted it against the Hartford government in 1675. Dongan recently had revived it, but possibly only for bargaining purposes in a dispute over the boundary with Connecticut that chiefly involved possession of the town of Rye, and that had been settled in New York's favor in February, 1685. There is some evidence to suggest that he may have had in mind primarily the unsettled boundary between New York and Massachusetts.[106] We can be certain only that the ambitious Governor Dongan was alert to any and all opportunities recent developments in England might bring, and that his continuing efforts to keep his superiors advised on the situation in New York would be an important factor in the final settlement of issues still pending.

[106] Brodhead, *History of New York*, II, 387–389, 412–413.

CHAPTER 7

The Glorious Revolution

IT would be difficult to exaggerate the importance of the very brief reign of James II for students of American history. The reign began in February 1685; it ended less than four years later in what Englishmen, on both sides of the Atlantic, would long remember as the Glorious Revolution. Just when it became Glorious is hard to say, for no student, on either side of the Atlantic, as yet seems to have asked the question. We can be certain only that for those who lived through this climactic development in a long constitutional struggle, the issues it settled were hardly more impressive than were those it left unsettled. Such, at any rate, is the conclusion that must be drawn from attention to the American side of the story.

In America the years immediately preceding the Revolution had brought evidence of a new determination on the part of Whitehall to have the upper hand in the government of those colonies for which the king was directly responsible. At the same time, it repeatedly had been threatened that the king might take direct responsibility for the government of other colonies, and in the case of Massachusetts the threat finally had been made good when King Charles had only a few weeks to live. The charter of the Bermuda Company also had been recalled in 1684, but more it seems by chance, and through a comedy of errors, than through any action that can be viewed as significantly indicative of a settled course of policy.[1] The critical question of what to do about Massachusetts

[1] Richard S. Dunn, "The Downfall of the Bermuda Company: A Restoration Farce," *William and Mary Quarterly,* 3d. ser., XX (1963), 487–512.

had been left to the new king, the former proprietor of New York who more than once had been apprised of the intimate connections linking the interests of that jurisdiction with New England and New Jersey. The end result was the Dominion of New England, a daring administrative experiment launched in the spring of 1686 that might have changed the course of American history. By late in the summer of 1688 the Dominion extended, by proclamation at least, all the way from the Delaware to the St. Croix, and in half a dozen colonies its proclamation had resulted in the suspension of formerly established representative assemblies. In this sequence, contemporaries, and later scholars, were invited to see a close parallel between the issues at stake in America and those upon which the Revolution in England itself turned.

For a long time American historians were content to take their cue from the Whig historians of England, and so to view the Dominion of New England, or Lord Howard of Effingham's stormy career in Virginia, as a simple extension of Stuart tyranny into the New World. More recently, the Imperial School of historians has advanced a more sophisticated view, one holding that the actions of the government in Whitehall were guided by a growing conviction that the problems presented by the colonies could be resolved only by a drastic reorganization of the empire.[2] Use of the term empire for this period of time would be debatable were it not for the fact that the interpretation itself depends upon an assumption that a new concept of empire now guided Whitehall in the more important of its decisions. The argument leans heavily upon the fact that some threat of *quo warranto* proceedings had been made against every one of the colonial charters by 1686.[3] In the fullest development of this interpretation, the Dominion of New England becomes the probable forerunner of other and similar dominions into which it may have been intended to regroup all of the colonies.

It has to be agreed that such a result might have followed, had the Dominion of New England been successful. It also has to be agreed that by 1685 the government at Westminster was both more

[2] The most influential study has been Viola F. Barnes, *The Dominion of New England: A Study in British Colonial Policy* (New Haven, 1923).

[3] Philip S. Haffenden, "The Crown and the Colonial Charters, 1675–1688," *William and Mary Quarterly*, 3d. ser., XV (1958), 297–311, 452–466, is the most comprehensive of recent summaries.

willing and better equipped to impose its will upon the colonies than it had been at any time theretofore. Not to be overlooked are the recent proceedings against the borough charters of England which toward the close of his reign had helped Charles II to enjoy greater power than had been held by any other member of his family. Nor can the role played by the Lords of Trade after 1675 be ignored. Their lordships had been prompt to recognize that the only secure foundation for policy is knowledge of the problem faced. They had been energetic, and for that time systematic, in their efforts to collect information regarding the colonies. The office of the committee's clerk in Scotland Yard was on the way to becoming the Plantations Office of later fame, an office possessed of expanding files and staffed by men whose knowledge of the files made them increasingly expert on the questions confronted by their superiors. Its head was William Blathwayt, secretary to the Lords of Trade since 1679 and auditor-general of the royal revenues in America after 1680, the first among Whitehall's bureaucrats to find a way to power by becoming a specialist on colonial questions.[4] But there are indications that the influence of the Lords of Trade was by this time a declining one; that the king himself and the more influential of his advisers actually were in charge.[5] Perhaps James had a clear notion of where he was headed, of the course he wanted to take, but it would be hard for any close student of the New York proprietorship to believe it.

Whatever may be the fact on that score, it is certain that the Dominion of New England took its shape as much from a peculiar combination of circumstances as from conscious design. Suggestions that a governor-general for the whole of New England might be appointed had been repeatedly heard from the earliest years of the Restoration era. New England's own confederation, though for most purposes defunct since 1665, offered a suggestive precedent, as did also the repeated occasions on which Massachusetts had moved to expand its own jurisdiction. The most recent of these had brought the purchase by the Bay Colony of the Gorges claim to Maine, while the king picked up the right of government in New

4 For an account of this significant career, see again Miss Jacobsen's *William Blathwayt.*

5 This is indicated both by Haffenden and by Thornton, *West-India Policy,* pp. 210–213. See also Andrews, *Colonial Period,* III, 120, 120 n.

Hampshire, and now once more New Hampshire presented a problem. Edward Cranfield, the first royal governor, had shown himself to be so narrow an Anglican and so willing to support Mason's efforts to establish his proprietorship of the soil there as to bring the colonists to a rebellious mood. By 1685, when Cranfield left the colony, London was almost as disenchanted with the man as was New Hampshire.[6] What Massachusetts could not claim in Maine, the king could in that part of the area attached to New York. Lord Clarendon's commissioners in 1665 had sought a solution of the dispute between Rhode Island and speculators depending upon the Connecticut charter for their claims in the Narragansett country by designating the region as the King's Province. Through fifteen years that designation had had little meaning beyond the continuing life it helped to give to speculative land claims, but when Lord Culpeper called at Boston on the way home from his first visit to Virginia in 1680, his aid had been enlisted by the New England speculators with a suggestion that he might be cut in on the deal, a promise that seems later to have been made also to William Blathwayt.[7] Influential men on both sides of the water would be happy to see the King's Province brought under the king's government.

The provisional council which took office at Boston in May, 1686, with Joseph Dudley at its head and Edward Randolph as its secretary, held jurisdiction over Massachusetts, New Hampshire, the King's Province, and that part of Maine not belonging to New York.[8] When Sir Edmund Andros reached Boston in the following December, his commission as governor and captain-general of the Dominion included in addition Plymouth, which never had enjoyed the protection of a royal charter and so was defenseless. The governor's instructions called too for the annexation of Rhode Island, which had elected not to contest the writ previously issued against its charter but to depend instead upon a petition for its continuance. Andros bore the answer to that petition in his instructions, and Rhode Island, its territorial claims under the royal charter already having been ignored in the decision on the King's

6 For a summary of developments there, Frank B. Sanborn, *New Hampshire: An Epitome of Popular Government* (Boston and New York, 1904), pp. 83–114.

7 Dunn, *Puritans and Yankees*, pp. 159–160, 222–224.

8 Barnes, *Dominion of New England*, pp. 47–50.

Province, soon surrendered to Andros' demand for submission. This left out of the Dominion of New England only Connecticut, if Cornwall County, as the New York assembly had designated the Duke's part of Maine in 1683, be ignored. Not that it should be, for in the spring of 1687 it was decided to add both of them to the new Dominion.[9]

That decision, when given full effect in the fall of 1687 by Connecticut's submission to Andros, put an end to Thomas Dongan's hope that New York might regain the boundaries originally established in the Duke's charter of 1664. Dongan had persisted in warning Whitehall of New York's weakness at a time when hostilities with the French in Canada were to be feared and, encouraged by reports and rumors of the king's intentions, he repeatedly had urged that the Jerseys and Connecticut be united with New York. Finally, on the very eve of Connecticut's incorporation into the Dominion, he advised that in that event New York also should be included. This advice was given in October, and a decision to include both New York and New Jersey came in the spring of 1688, when on April 7 a new commission for Andros gave him authority reaching westward to the Delaware, eastward to the St. Croix, and northward to the St. Lawrence. The annexations were proclaimed by Andros at New York early in August, and later in the month at Elizabeth and Burlington.[10]

Grand as were the final dimensions thus given the Dominion, it is hard to view it as the product of a grand design for a thoroughgoing reorganization of the English colonies. Especially difficult to accept is the view, based essentially upon the evidence provided by Governor Dongan's ambitious proposals, that consideration was given at

[9] *Ibid.*, pp. 69–70; Hall, *Randolph*, p. 108; Langdon, *Pilgrim Colony*, pp. 211–214.

[10] Barnes, *Dominion of New England*, pp. 38–39; Brodhead, *History of New York*, II, 512; Pomfret, *East Jersey*, p. 267; Dunn, *Puritans and Yankees*, pp. 235–243. Dongan's appeals in behalf of New York are found in N.Y. *Colonial Documents*, Vol. III, and in the *Calendar of State Papers, Colonial, 1685–1688*, where the letter advising the annexation of New York is located on pp. 457–458. The fact that Dongan's attempts to capitalize upon the apparent opportunities of a new situation at times ignored the limits fixed by the New York charter, even included direct negotiation with Connecticut for a union of the two jurisdictions, should not obscure the basic fact that he was pressing an old cause, in which the recovery of the Jerseys and the Delaware had been the chief hope. See above, pp. 201–207, 210–211.

this time to the establishment of two separate dominions. What Dongan had proposed, and what he must have been understood in Whitehall as proposing, was nothing more than the re-establishment of viable boundaries for New York. An enlarged New York jurisdiction undoubtedly would have been very similar to the newly created Dominion of New England, for New York's representative assembly had been suspended since 1685 and the Dominion was to be governed with the aid only of an appointed council. But to say more than this is to go beyond what seems to be warranted by the evidence so far advanced.[11] The Dominion of New England was in the first instance just what its designation implies. It was an effort to resolve on a comprehensive basis the peculiar problems of an area in which its formerly existing governments, as Massachusetts had made abundantly clear, were altogether too independent of the king's authority. That it became something more is attributable chiefly to Dongan's success in alerting Whitehall to the strategic significance, and the special problems, of New York.[12] No doubt, the decision was influenced by the firsthand acquaintance Sir Edmund Andros had with the problems he would face there. And not to be overlooked is the fact that his appointment created (in the hands of an experienced soldier and on the eve of a great contest with France) a single military command embracing almost the entire northern frontier of the English colonies.

In the establishment of the Dominion nothing is more remarkable than the peaceful submission of the people. Andros had landed at Boston with a company of Grenadiers commanded by Captain

11 Miss Barnes' second chapter, entitled "An Experiment in Consolidation," seems to have been primarily responsible for the popularity of this view, but surely she stretches the evidence provided by Dongan's appeals to London, and by his effort to strengthen his hand through negotiation with the Hartford government, beyond a supportable point. The inclusion of gossipy evidence from London, or elsewhere, as to what the king had in mind does not greatly alter this conclusion. A basic difficulty experienced by more than one historian, American and English, has been a failure to understand that the issuance of a writ of *quo warranto* argues less as to the settled conclusions of the government than it does for a decision to employ a ready legal weapon for the purposes of negotiation. Witness the long struggle with Massachusetts. It must be agreed, however, that the writs sworn out in the name of King James do testify to a purpose to bring the situation in the colonies under some general review at this time. This criticism is not intended to deny the very great value of Miss Barnes' study.

12 The king's own experience as proprietor of New York has also to be considered.

Francis Nicholson, another soldier now beginning an especially long career in the colonial service,[13] but this was hardly more than a bodyguard. A hundred Grenadiers could never have made an effective stand against an armed and aroused populace. Quite evidently, Whitehall had acted upon Randolph's long-standing assurance that there were in New England men of substance and influence who would welcome the king's rule, which proved to be true enough.[14] Those who in Massachusetts accepted service on the council, first with Dudley and later with Andros, were mainly representative of the so-called moderate faction, and especially of the ambitious merchant group.[15] As each new area was added to the Dominion, responsible men, most of them already in office, accepted appointment as its representatives on the council, except for New Jersey, which for some reason had no seat at all.[16] Among those who welcomed their appointments were both of the sons of former Governor John Winthrop of Connecticut.[17]

Even so, Sir Edmund had a difficult time. His responsibilities, military and other, were stretched out over a vast area, one exceeding the capacity of any colonial administration yet devised by Englishmen to govern. The people he had to rule were divided by old jealousies and disturbed by new uncertainties as to what the future might hold. Boston found cause, even before the annexation of New York, to fear that the governor's old acquaintances there might be favored;[18] New Yorkers, long fearful of Boston's threatened dominance of their economy, viewed a government seated in that city with apprehension; and everywhere the presence on the Dominion's council of the greedy and grasping Edward Randolph and Robert Mason, not to mention Captain Nicholson, invited

[13] See Bruce T. McCully, "From the North Riding to Morocco: The Early Years of Governor Francis Nicholson, 1655–1686," William and Mary Quarterly, 3d. ser., XIX (1962), 534–556, and Stephen S. Webb, "The Strange Career of Francis Nicholson," ibid, XXIII (1966), 513–548.

[14] See again Hall, Randolph, pp. 88–89, for a more recent expression of fear that there might be resistance, and Barnes, Dominion of New England, p. 49, for the king's ship which took up a continuing station there in 1686.

[15] Barnes, Dominion of New England, pp. 49, 73–76; Bailyn, New England Merchants, pp. 169–170, 175–176, 180–182.

[16] Barnes, Dominion of New England, p. 73.

[17] Dunn, Puritans and Yankees, pp. 229–251.

[18] Hall, Randolph, p. 108, for Boston's later complaint of "a Crew of abject Persons fetched from New York," and p. 109 for Randolph's lease of the secretary's office to John West of New York in the spring of 1687.

sober reflection on what might be the ultimate cost for the colonists of Westminster's fresh assertion of its power.[19] The attempt to lend the council a broadly representative character was frustrated by uncertain attendance, except by members who lived in or close to Boston. Some of those who had greeted the viceroy with enthusiasm quickly proved themselves to be self-seeking men who easily became disgruntled. Nor did it take long for the moderates (and historians as yet have found no better term to describe the New Englanders who most readily co-operated with Andros) to demonstrate that they constituted no cohesive party or faction upon which the governor could unfailingly depend. Indeed, the most prominent of them, former Governor Simon Bradstreet, had declined even to serve in the new government. Finally, mention belongs to Sir Edmund himself. As the son of the leading family on the Isle of Guernsey, as a courtier who while winning no high place at the king's court moved easily in the company of men who had, as a soldier accustomed to command, and as a colonial administrator whose experience heretofore had been limited to New York prior to the drafting of its Charter of Libertyes, he seems to have expected an implicit submission to authority that New Englanders long since had forgotten they owed to any authority except one securely grounded in the will of God according to their own interpretation of God's will.

The first serious challenge to the authority of the Dominion came, as would be expected, in Massachusetts and on an issue of taxation. Provincial taxes had been imposed by action of the General Court, a representative body for which there was no parallel in the arbitrary structure of the Dominion's government, probably by the king's own decision to reject advice that an assembly be included.[20] Dudley, who headed a caretaker's government, had avoided raising the issue of taxation, but for Andros there was no escape from putting it to a test. This he did in 1687 by adopting a necessary revenue measure. It met resistance in several places, but especially in Essex County, where at Ipswich the Reverend John Wise provided vigorous leadership. The governor showed equal vigor in his response. Among others, Wise was ar-

---

[19] Ibid., pp. 95–97, for an impressive list of the offices Randolph had acquired before he left England as the harbinger of the new regime in New England.
[20] Ibid., pp. 83–84, 93–94.

rested, imprisoned, and after trial heavily fined, and so the resistance was broken.[21] Thereafter the taxes were paid, a fact modern historians at times have tended to slight, though not without some justification. For undoubtedly the fact that the taxes were collected is of less importance than that they were paid under protest, and that the protest revealed a sophisticated understanding of the constitutional principles of representative government. Wise laid claim to the full rights of Englishmen "according to Magna Charta" and the statutes protecting the subject in his property. No longer able to depend upon the colony's charter as the palladium of their liberties, the people of Massachusetts had discovered a new line of defense in their rights as Englishmen.[22] That the inhabitants of New York recently had defined their rights in the same terms makes the development all the more significant.

Other grievances accumulated. The protest on taxes had found its natural center in the town meeting, now the chief agency of self-government left to the people, with the result that the governor subsequently restricted each town to a single annual meeting for the purpose of electing its officers.[23] The towns eventually were also denied the right to collect the church rate levied for the support of their ministers, by a decision that few New Englanders outside Rhode Island could view as anything other than an attempt to undermine the church to which most of them still gave their loyalty.[24] It is impossible to say how many persons may have welcomed the proclamation by Dudley, as his instructions required, of a new policy of religious tolerance, but the frequently popular view that lack of membership in the church is bona fide evidence of hostility to it is no longer tenable. Certainly, the most important immediate effect was the widespread fear the policy stirred for the safety of the old religious establishment. As Governor Andros, members of the garrison, and a few Anglicans paraded their use of Cranmer's Prayer Book in a Boston meetinghouse perforce made available for the purpose, no one could be certain how far this assertion of royal power in behalf of William Laud's church might be carried. When

[21] George Allan Cook, *John Wise: Early American Democrat* (New York, 1952) , pp. 44–58; Barnes, *Dominion of New England*, pp. 87–90.
[22] Miller, *Colony to Province*, pp. 156–157.
[23] Barnes, *Dominion of New England*, pp. 95–96.
[24] *Ibid.*, pp. 124–126.

King James's Declaration of Indulgence, which relieved both dissenter and Catholic alike from the statutory penalties for nonconformity, was published at Boston in August, 1687, the Puritan ministers saw in it the hope "of deliverance from an approaching Persecution," and called their congregations to observance of a special day of thanksgiving. The governor, knowing full well the danger in such a demonstration, forbade the rites.[25] What lends the incident importance is the evidence it bears of a fear deep enough to cause the Puritans to take a step at least toward embracing, for the defense of their own church, a broad policy of toleration.

To arbitrary taxation, to restriction of the town meeting, and to his sponsorship of the Anglican Church, Andros added a highly disturbing land policy. Indeed, this last, more than any other single factor, may account for the virtual unanimity with which New England cast off the Dominion in 1689. The welcome many of the more substantial inhabitants had given the king's governor depended upon the assurance they had that existing titles would be respected and speculative hopes for title confirmed. Instructions to Andros left much to his discretion. All new grants of undeveloped land were to be made subject to a quitrent of 2s.6d per 100 acres, and all existing titles were to be reviewed for confirmation subject to such payment as the governor might decide upon. This last instruction is suggestive of the ambivalence which for so long had characterized James' attitude on rents in New York, but quite evidently, as the story in Virginia makes clear, Whitehall was becoming alert to the possibility that quitrents might provide an independent source of revenue for the costs of colonial administration, one that might remove the need for quarreling with petty assemblymen while maintaining the cardinal principle of policy laid down for Sir William Berkeley in 1662—that a colony properly paid its own way.[26] Quite evidently, too, Whitehall was still impressed by the extent to which disputed land claims divided the New England colonists. Sir Edmund was to settle all such disputes. The details of the story are far too many for inclusion here, but from them emerge two extraordinarily significant points.[27] He

25 *Ibid.*, pp. 126–127.
26 See above, p. 40.
27 Barnes, *Dominion of New England,* pp. 174–211. In Maine and New Hampshire, where a long history of conflicting jurisdictional claims clouded

managed in very short order to persuade most, if not all, of New England's landholders, heretofore very largely free of quitrents, that they faced the prospect of assuming a new and hateful burden. At the same time, he disappointed some of the more enthusiastic and greedy of his supporters.

Especially instructive is the example of Richard Wharton, member of council, lawyer, merchant, landholder, relative of the Winthrops and participant with them in the King's Province speculation, and leading adventurer in the so-called Million Purchase of land on the Merrimac River, as also in an ambitious joint-stock venture for the promotion of a variety of industrial enterprises.[28] Sir Edmund, with a rectitude that would have brought him great credit in the service of any other cause than the one he served, failed to back Wharton's ambitions. Even in the case of the King's Province, where so many of his influential supporters were involved, Andros ruled against them on the ground that their speculation had retarded the development of the area.[29] It was a soundly based ruling, but it left Sir Edmund with few friends in Boston in the spring of 1689.

Significantly, Wharton had sailed for London before 1687 was ended in the hope of winning there the influence he had been denied in Boston. He was followed in the next year by Increase Mather, leading Puritan clergyman, acting president of Harvard, and spokesman for the traditional authority in New England.[30] The two agents were on somewhat different missions, but they had one thing in common. They understood that an obvious response to any projection of London's power into the New World was an appeal to London, where there was authority to overrule even the

---

many titles, not a few men welcomed the opportunity to have their titles confirmed by the new government, even with the quitrent Sir Edmund decided to impose upon all confirmed titles and with the fees he charged for the confirmation. But elsewhere the resistance was such that the governor in 1688 resorted to a test in the courts against five of the larger landholders, among them Samuel Sewall.

28 Viola F. Barnes, "Richard Wharton, A Seventeenth Century New England Colonial," *Publications of the Colonial Society of Massachusetts*, XXVI (1927), 238–270; Bailyn, *New England Merchants*, pp. 174–176.

29 Dunn, *Puritans and Yankees*, pp. 244–245.

30 Kenneth B. Murdock, *Increase Mather: The Foremost American Puritan* (Cambridge, Mass., 1925), pp. 153 ff.

most pretentious of governors. That course, rather than revolution, was New England's first choice.

But soon old England gave New England another choice, a resort to revolution in circumstances which on their face denied that the act was revolutionary. For this opportunity James II himself was mainly responsible.

Whatever else he may have been, James II was not a wise man. A Catholic, he insisted upon introducing members of that faith into office, civil and military, with a disregard for the Test Act of 1673 that raised the most fundamental of constitutional issues regarding the right of the king to dispense with parliamentary statutes. Tests in the courts raised the specter of judges wholly subservient to the royal will. The Declaration of Indulgence of 1687, though welcomed by William Penn and other dissenters, was too patently designed to win support for the king's pro-Catholic policy. When to allay the growing suspicion of the nonconformists he issued a second Declaration in the spring of 1688, he found himself in a direct clash with the Anglican establishment. The birth of a son in June, 1688, by a second marriage altered the succession to the throne. Theretofore, the king's oldest daughter Mary, Protestant granddaughter of the old Earl of Clarendon who was married to the Protestant William of Orange, had been the prospective successor, but the son, who obviously would be reared as a Catholic, now took precedence. The end result was an invitation to William, in which Whigs and Tories alike joined, to assist in restoring the liberties of the kingdom. William, who badly needed an alliance with England against Louis XIV, accepted the invitation and landed in England with a Dutch army on Guy Fawkes Day, November 5, 1688. James, deserted by all but a few of his people, fled the kingdom in December, a convention parliament in January offered the throne to William and Mary, the conditions for its acceptance were agreed upon in February, and the joint coronation of William and Mary took place on April 11, 1689.[31] Such were the main steps by which the Glorious Revolution was accomplished, and most happily without bloodshed.

News of these momentous developments came piecemeal to New

[31] See David Ogg, *England in the Reigns of James II and William III* (Oxford, 1955).

England, as to other colonial communities. Not until May 26 did official confirmation of the accession of William and Mary, together with instructions to proclaim the new sovereigns, reach Boston. But report of William's intended invasion had come in February, of his successful landing early in April, and the town buzzed with rumors of a great triumph for Protestantism and the liberties of Englishmen. It is no easier to reconstruct from contemporary accounts what happened at Boston on April 18, when the people of that city brought the Dominion of New England to its end for all practical purposes, than it is on other such occasions. Andros, who seems to have been better informed than were the colonists, had hurried down from Maine, where he was leading a campaign against the Indians and where the militiamen he had impressed for that service subsequently mutinied and headed also for Boston. There is evidence of spontaneous mob action, and evidence too of prearranged direction. What matters is that by the end of day Andros, Randolph, the captain of the king's ship on station there, and other key figures had been arrested, and that on the next day both the fort and the vessel were in the rebels' hands. Joseph Dudley, being out of town, was apprehended later and imprisoned with his fellows. A "Council for Safety of the People and Conservation of the Peace," headed by former Governor Bradstreet, took charge and called a convention of representatives from each of the Massachusetts towns.[32] Happily, again, there had been no bloodshed.

The Council of Safety included a heavy representation for the former moderates, among them Boston's merchants. The convention brought into the deliberation more of the country party, if that designation may be used for those who represented the more rural constituencies. There was not always full agreement, and yet on the essentials there was agreement: that the Dominion government had depended upon a usurpation of power and that the last elected government under the old charter properly could hold office until the new king's will was known. On May 29, the proclamation of

---

[32] Barnes, *Dominion of New England*, pp. 231–261; Hall, *Edward Randolph*, pp. 121–125; Palfrey, *History of New England*, pp. 570–598, is still useful; for contemporary accounts, Andrews, *Narratives of the Insurrections*, pp. 167 ff.; and for a judicious selection from the record, together with judicious comment, Michael G. Hall, Lawrence H. Leder, and Michael G. Kammen, *The Glorious Revolution in America* (Chapel Hill, N.C., 1964), pp. 9–79.

William and Mary was joyfully celebrated. Already, Plymouth had re-established its former government on April 22, Rhode Island on May 1, and Connecticut on May 9, all on the assumption that a usurpation of power might find a proper correction from the new king.

News of the Boston uprising reached New York on April 25, where word of William's landing in England had been received and suppressed at the beginning of March.[33] The position of Francis Nicholson, who had been left in New York as Andros' lieutenant after the proclamation of the Dominion's westward extension, was a difficult one. It must be understood that the Dominion was not a federal structure in which the several provinces survived under a superior jurisdiction. Instead, Andros had been at pains in New York, as elsewhere, to deface and break the seal of the former government in evidence of its total obliteration. It can be said that Nicholson and the three Dominion councilors residing in New York City constituted a *de facto* government, but the only *de jure* authority was that of the Dominion, whose head was in no position after April 18 to offer instructions, and no instructions came from England. A more daring man might have gambled on a proclamation of William and Mary, though at the risk of seeming to repudiate his superior. But Nicholson was not a daring man, and what he did was to wait, and while he waited the situation became explosive.[34]

The Dominion of New England had no strong claim upon the loyalty of any part of New York's population, and least of all the Puritan part. By early May the inhabitants of Suffolk County on Long Island were demanding that the example set by their neighbors in New England and by their fellow countrymen in England, "for securing our English nations liberties and propertyes from

[33] *Ibid.*, p. 102; Brodhead, *History of New York*, II, 549, for evidence that it was Nicholson who alerted Andros in Maine that William had invaded England.

[34] Of the general accounts of Leisler's Rebellion, the most judicious is that of Andrews, *Colonial Period*, III, 124 ff. Especially helpful is Lawrence Leder's section of Hall *et al.*, *Glorious Revolution in America*, pp. 81–140. Brodhead's *History of New York*, II, 548 ff., though vigorously anti-Leisler, and Osgood, *American Colonies in the Seventeenth Century*, III, 444 ff., continue to be helpful. Jerome R. Reich, *Leisler's Rebellion: A Study of Democracy in New York, 1664–1720* (Chicago, 1953), though the fullest study, is disappointing.

Popery and Slavery, and from the Intented invasion of a foraign French design," be followed.[35] However much Nicholson may have hoped to keep the lid fastened until he received instructions from Whitehall, the news spread, and nowhere in America did men more quickly read the implications of a diplomatic alliance between England and Holland. In May, Nicholson himself warned Albany to expect and prepare for an early war with France.[36] No attempt to assess the state of mind in New York during the summer of 1689 can safely ignore the simple fact that the defense of Protestantism, and of the English liberties to which so many Dutch settlers had recently subscribed as their own, had been entrusted to a Dutch prince and one, moreover, whose very name called up magic memories for every Dutchman who loved his freedom. The Dominion of New England had an inescapable identification with James II's disallowance of New York's Charter of Libertyes. Inescapable too was the Dominion's identification with the old fear of dominance by Boston. It was no time for Nicholson to wait upon instructions from England.

Not only did he wait. He abdicated, as James II was said to have done when in December, 1688, he fled the kingdom, much to the comfort of English Tories who found themselves involved in a revolution. On June 11, 1689, Nicholson sailed for England to bring charges against those who had dared to seize the initiative he himself had refused to take. The crisis had come at the end of May, when the militia, a large part of it at any rate, took possession of Fort James at the lower end of Manhattan. This seizure was also attended by some mob action on the part of the general populace, but it would be difficult to demonstrate that the mob played any larger role in the New York rebellion than it had in the Boston uprising. Certainly, the main difference is that in Boston accepted leaders of the people effectively employed the mob for the achievement of a common purpose, whereas in New York the rebellion revealed a fundamental division in the community. Nicholson and his councilors refused to accept the challenge to their leadership by ordering the militia out of the fort. Instead, they decided to leave the militia, of which Captain Jacob Leisler had become leader, in

---

[35] Hall *et al.*, *Glorious Revolution in America,* p. 103.
[36] *Ibid.*, p. 104.

possession of that critical symbol of power, and that Nicholson should report in person to England.[37]

Perhaps this was only a blunder, betraying chiefly a lack of judgment, but there are reasons for believing that the *de facto* government of New York dared not put its authority to the test, and at the same time was unwilling to yield to the pressure it faced. Andros had appointed as members of the Dominion council Stephen Van Cortlandt, Nicholas Bayard, and Frederick Phillipse, three men who for several years had been influential members of council in the provincial government. Van Cortlandt was also mayor of the city and brother-in-law to Peter Schuyler, the mayor of Albany.[38] In other words, Nicholson's advisers represented a long-dominant group in a government too long identified with a narrow circle of men who enjoyed special opportunities for access to, and influence with, the governor.

In New England the Dominion had introduced arbitrary government; in New York it merely continued it. Maria Van Rensselaer had summed up the story of New York's government in a single sentence, when she wrote her sister in 1684 regarding a dispute over the family property: "Livingstone will have his way, for he has the governor on his side."[39] This, of course, was Robert Livingston, youngest son of an eminent Scottish divine who had grown up during his father's exile in Holland, and who migrated to New York in 1675 with little more in the way of assets than a name favorably known in Calvinist circles, native shrewdness, a winning personality, and the ability to speak both English and Dutch. He quickly won the hand of Alida Schuyler, the widow of a Van Rensselaer who brought him connections also with the rising tribe of Van Cortlandts. With these helpful connections, he was soon on the way to building a fortune held in his own right. Having acquired the clerkship at Albany and a firsthand knowledge of Indian affairs, he enjoyed a special influence with Governor Dongan, as is testified by the collectorships carrying fee or salary Livingston held, and by the grant to him in 1686 of Livingston Manor, an estate ultimately embracing 160,000 acres.[40] The objection to arbitrary

---

[37] *Ibid.,* pp. 108–111.

[38] Osgood, *American Colonies in the Seventeenth Century,* III, 450.

[39] Nissenson, *Patroon's Domain,* p. 296.

[40] Leder, *Robert Livingston,* provides a full account of this significant career.

government in New York was based upon no abstract love of liberty. It was based rather upon the advantages a few enjoyed at the apparent expense of others in a community where few men as yet had earned an acknowledged right to special advantage, and where for some time the economy had been depressed. By 1689 there were many who were ready to defy the existing political regime, given the peculiar circumstances which helped to crystallize the more general of the people's grievances.

This is not to say that New York's so-called rebellion of 1689 was a democratic protest, as on occasion has been unpersuasively argued.[41] Nor should it be suggested that the jealousies dividing the several regions had been overcome. They continued to view one another with suspicion: Albany and New York City, a still predominantly Dutch New York and the predominantly English Long Island, the City and all those outside of it who paid tribute to its several monopolies.[42] The complexity of New York's politics continued, and became in fact all the more complex as a result of what happened in 1689. There is no neat solution to the problem of Leisler's Rebellion.

Jacob Leisler himself was responsible for much that happened, and it is important that we understand what he himself represented. A native of Frankfurt, he had migrated to New Amsterdam in 1660 at the age of twenty as a penniless soldier enlisted in the service of the Dutch West India Company. Three years afterward he married a widow with some means, who also brought him a connection with the influential Van Cortlandt and Bayard families. Leisler thus found himself on the road upward Robert Livingston later would take, but Leisler never quite made it. Although he prospered well enough in the mercantile adventures he undertook, he quarreled not only with his wife's relatives but with other persons of influence, who in turn held him in scorn.[43] Narrowminded, obstinate, and impetuous, he found himself, very largely through his own personal faults, in the company of the near-great

---

[41] See especially Reich, *Leisler's Rebellion.*

[42] See again Mason, "Aspects of the New York Revolt of 1689," *New York History,* XXX (1949), 165–180.

[43] Stanley M. Pargellis has a discriminating short biography in the *D.A.B.* See also Lawrence H. Leder, "The Unorthodox Domine: Nicholas Van Rensselaer," *New York History,* XXXV (1954), 166–176, and Reich, *Leisler's Rebellion,* pp. 58–61.

rather than those who enjoyed full access to the center of power and the rewards in its gift. His own frustrations undoubtedly contributed to the decision he took in June, 1689, that gave him leadership of the "rebellion" in New York which ended so ingloriously for him two years later with the hangman's noose about his neck. When he was executed, only his son-in-law, Jacob Milborne, met the same fate, but there were others who had been associated with him who were also attainted with treason, and who fortunately had the means to carry the issue to England, where eventually they won acquittal.

After June, 1689, when Nicholson sailed for England, Captain Leisler became for all practical purposes the head of government in New York. Seeking sanction for the power he held, he proclaimed the accession of William and Mary on June 22, forwarded a loyal address to them, and called for an election of delegates from the several counties to a representative convention. That convention, meeting from late June to mid-August, though unhappily without full representation for all constituencies, entrusted executive authority to a Committee of Safety, which in turn designated Leisler as the commander in chief. In this progress toward the establishment of what might be recognized as a lawful government, Albany refused to co-operate. Distrusting Leisler, and probably fearful of a loss of its monopoly of the Indian trade, Albany formed its own convention and separately proclaimed the accession of William and Mary in October. Not until March, 1690, after the sack of Schenectady by a joint French and Indian force, was Albany brought under the government Leisler headed at New York.[44]

Meantime, Leisler's position had been strengthened by the arrival in December, 1689, of instructions from the new king addressed to Nicholson, or "in his absence to such as for the time being take care for Preserving the Peace and administering the Lawes of our said Province in New York in America." Leisler, taking full advantage of this phrasing and of the powerless situation of his opponents, thereafter claimed to govern by the king's authority.[45] For himself he assumed the title of lieutenant governor, and to the Committee of Safety he assigned the dignity of a provincial council. The latter's

44 On the situation in Albany, see especially Leder, *Robert Livingston*, pp. 60–70.

45 Andrews, *Colonial Period*, III, 126–129.

membership included men of substance, among them Peter de la Noy and Gerard Beekman, but the former grandees of the province, except for Frederick Phillipse, remained in bitter opposition and the more important of them, Bayard and Van Cortlandt, in jail. Leisler's call for an elected assembly early in 1690 was only partially successful. Although it sat in two separate sessions that year, it was a partisan body and by no means representative of all parts of the province. A continuingly dangerous political situation dragged on into 1691, largely because the English government took a year and a half to get Governor Henry Sloughter, chosen in September, 1689, to his post.[46]

Third among the colonies to experience a major upheaval in 1689 was Maryland. Lord Baltimore had been absent from the colony since 1684. The government had remained in the hands of the council—which is to say, in the hands of his relatives and special friends.[47] William Joseph, sent from England in 1688 to serve as president of the council, was inept, so much so as to read the assembly, at its first meeting with him in November of that year, an unnecessary lecture on the divine-right doctrine of government.[48] It was no fault of his that he also bore instructions, at the insistence of crown officers, to secure a prohibition of the export of bulk tobacco, which generally speaking was the lower-grade leaf not packed in hogsheads that broadened the market for the colony's staple through the willingness of sailors to smuggle it and the willingness of merchants other than those from London to load it.[49] Joseph sought agreement too that quitrents, ever a touchy subject, henceforth were to be paid in specie, usually a scarce commodity in the American colonies. Indian trouble on the frontier, caused chiefly by roving bands of the Iroquois as recently as 1687,[50] contributed to the colony's uneasy state of mind as the year 1689 approached, when the colony was disturbed by rumors of an Indian-French-Catholic conspiracy.[51]

Lord Baltimore, acting upon instructions from the Privy Council,

[46] Ibid., III, 128 n.

[47] See above, pp. 161–165.

[48] Kammen includes this, with other very useful selections from the record, in Part III of Hall et al., Glorious Revolution in America, pp. 143–214.

[49] Gray, History of Agriculture in Southern U.S., I, 219–220.

[50] Trelease, Indians Affairs in Colonial New York, pp. 257–260.

[51] Morton, Colonial Virginia, I, 332–333.

drafted an order for the proclamation of William and Mary in February, 1689, but that order never seems to have been delivered, apparently because of the death of his messenger en route.[52] In any case, Joseph and the council took no action to proclaim the new sovereigns. Nor did they call into consultation the assembly, prorogued in December, 1688, after a quarrelsome session until the spring. Instead, when the assembly was supposed to meet in April, 1689, the prorogation was continued until the following October. Some of the councilors bothered little to conceal their sympathy for James II. Others perhaps were primarily motivated by loyalty to the proprietor and by fear that the occasion might invite an attempt to overthrow the proprietorship.

While the authorities in Maryland waited, other colonies proclaimed William and Mary, including nearby Virginia on April 26.[53] By July, 1689, Lord Baltimore's government was in serious trouble. John Coode, a strange, somewhat disreputable, and longtime opponent of the proprietor, was raising volunteers. He was soon joined by more reputable men: Henry Jowles, colonel of the militia and assemblyman for Charles County; Nehemiah Blakiston, collector of the king's customs for the Potomac; and Kenelm Cheseldyne, speaker of the lower house of assembly. As with the rebels in New York, these were men of substance, but men also who were outside the proprietary circle. The rebellion they led was largely confined to the western side of the Chesapeake, and more especially to St. Mary's, Calvert, and Charles Counties.[54] These counties constituted the main center of the colony's population, however, and contained the seat of government at St. Mary's, which the rebels experienced no difficulty in seizing.

Joining together in a Protestant Association, the insurgents drew up a statement of their grievances against the proprietor's govern-

---

[52] Andrews, *Colonial Period,* II, 372 n. and 371–376, for general discussion of the rebellion. Kammen, in Hall *et al., Glorious Revolution,* has the latest discussion and the fullest, except for Bernard C. Steiner, "The Protestant Revolution in Maryland," A.H.A. *Annual Report for 1897,* pp. 279–353. See also Kammen, "The Causes of the Maryland Revolution of 1689," *Maryland Historical Magazine,* LV (1960), 293–333; Craven, *Southern Colonies,* pp. 413–415; Beverly McAnear (ed.), "Mariland's Grevances Wiy The Have Taken Op Arms," *Journal of Southern History,* VIII (1942), 392–409.

[53] Morton, *Colonial Virginia,* I, 333.

[54] Hall *et al., Glorious Revolution,* pp. 168–169.

ment,[55] and issued a call for election of delegates to a special
assembly which met in August. By no means did the response to this
call reveal that the Protestant inhabitants of the province were
united in their support of the rebellion. Many of them remained
loyal to the proprietor, or at any rate refused to collaborate with the
insurgents, and in several of the more remote counties the number
of those voting in the election was small.[56] Nevertheless, when the
assembly met on August 22, representatives were on hand from all
but one of the counties. The assembly affirmed its loyalty to
William and Mary, agreed that communication should be established with the loyal leaders of other colonies for protection against
the Catholic-French-Indian menace, and entrusted administrative
responsibility during its adjournment to a committee headed by
Blakiston. The insurgents proclaimed William and Mary early in
September. Through the following months Maryland continued in
a state of uncertainty, and of occasional turbulence, while its in-
surgent government vainly waited for instruction and endorsement
by the new sovereigns. In August, 1690, Coode and Cheseldyne
sailed for London on a mission to persuade the king to take over the
colony's government.

The uprising in Carolina's Albemarle County may have had no
more than a coincidental relationship to the Revolution in England. Little is known of what actually occurred. There is even some
uncertainty as to the date, but the best evidence argues for a time
falling after May, 1689, rather than in the preceding year, the date
customarily given.[57] Governor Seth Sothel, who had been in office
since 1683 and was himself one of the Carolina proprietors, may
well have been as great a rascal as the familiar charges of tyranny,
usurpation, and disregard for the people's liberties brought against
him by his enemies undertook to prove. We can be certain only
that he suffered from some personal shortcomings, and that he ran
afoul of some of the more substantial of Albemarle's planters,

---

[55] *Ibid.*, pp. 171–175; Andrews, *Narratives of the Insurrections*, pp. 301–314.
The paper, first printed by William Nuthead for distribution in Maryland, was
also printed at London in November, 1689.

[56] Kammen, "Causes of the Maryland Revolution," and David W. Jordan,
"The Royal Period of Colonial Maryland, 1689–1715" (unpublished Ph.D. dissertation, Princeton University, 1966) .

[57] Andrews, *Colonial Period*, III, 257, 257 n. See also Lefler and Newsome,
North Carolina, pp. 45–46; Connor, *History of North Carolina*, I, 60–63.

possibly as collector of the king's customs.[58] Surprised at his residence by an armed band under the leadership of Thomas Pollack,
one of the wealthier planters, Sothel was forced to renounce his
office as governor.

From Albemarle, Sothel made his way in 1690 to Charles Town,
and so into another troubled situation. James Colleton, brother to
Sir Peter, one of the proprietors, had become the governor there
when he migrated from Barbados in 1686 as a newly designated
landgrave of Carolina. His attempt to carry out the proprietors'
intents, in line with the reorientation of policy adopted in 1682,
soon brought him the unyielding hostility of the powerful Goose
Creek faction.[59] Some of the dissenters, who in the circumstances
constituted the governor's natural support, were won away from
him, among them Joseph Morton, former governor. So far were
Colleton's enemies in control of the parliament that he made no
effort to use it after 1687, and when Sothel arrived the colony was
under martial law. Colleton's opponents immediately rallied in
support of Sothel's claim to the governorship as a resident proprietor. A parliament dominated by Colleton's enemies banished
him from the colony, and permanently disbarred his key supporters
from public office. Disenchantment with Governor Sothel soon
followed, but for the moment the Goose Creek faction was back in
the saddle, or so it thought. One of its chief men, Maurice Mathews,
was promptly sent as agent to England.[60]

Thus by the end of 1690, uprisings had occurred in no less than
five of the North American colonies since the accession of William
and Mary. Only in the cases of Massachusetts, New York, and
Maryland can it be said that the explosions were unmistakably
triggered by the news of developments in England. But even if it be
conceded that local conflicts provided the dominant influence in
the two Carolinas, the end results were much the same, for there
too unauthorized governments waited on decisions to be taken
in England. Waiting also on word from London were five additional colonies in which there had been no resort to force, but
in which, as a result of recent developments, government now

58 See above, p. 160.
59 See above, pp. 178–181.
60 Sirmans, *Colonial South Carolina*, pp. 44–49; Andrews, *Colonial Period*, III,
231–233; Crane, *Southern Frontier*, pp. 31–32; Wallace, *South Carolina*, pp. 47–48.

rested upon an uncertain and irregular basis. The revolutionary government of Massachusetts had re-established the jurisdiction of that province over New Hampshire, on petition from its inhabitants, in February, 1690.[61] In Plymouth, Rhode Island, and Connecticut the former governments had reasserted their authority on grounds that were defensible enough in the circumstances, but that nevertheless had to be defended in London.[62] Although the incorporation of New Jersey into the Dominion had been more nominal than actual, it had been preceded by the proprietors' surrender of the rights of government to the king on an understanding that their title in the soil would be confirmed. Such was the case in East Jersey at least, and such seems to have been the case with West Jersey. Whatever the fact in the latter instance, the governments in both provinces faced after the spring of 1689 an awkward question as to the authority by which they ruled. In each province an agent was chosen for dispatch to London.[63]

Virginia had an agent on hand in London when the Revolution occurred. In fact, Philip Ludwell had presented the burgesses' petition against Lord Howard of Effingham to the king in September, 1688, too late for action by King James, and well ahead of time for the attention of King William.[64]

The new king, of course, faced many other and more pressing issues than those presented by the colonies. Through the earlier weeks of 1689 he was busy negotiating with the political leaders of the country the conditions upon which he and his wife would hold the throne, conditions formally stated on February 12 in a parliamentary Declaration of Rights that was embodied the following December in England's famous Bill of Rights.[65] The Parliament elected in January remained in session until August and reassembled in October. Its legislation included the Toleration Act of May, 1689, which relieved dissenters of penalties for separate worship

---

[61] Sanborn, *New Hampshire*, pp. 113–114.

[62] Barnes, *New England Dominion*, pp. 248–249.

[63] Whitehead, *East Jersey*, pp. 159–163; Pomfret, *West Jersey*, pp. 159–162; Pomfret, *East Jersey*, pp. 261–262, 267–268, 274. East Jersey sent Governor Andrew Hamilton. James Budd, West Jersey's designated agent, died before he could sail.

[64] See above, pp. 155–156.

[65] For an informative brief discussion of the Revolution, Ogg, *England in the Reigns of James II and William III*, pp. 222–245.

while retaining the special privileges of the established Church of England. In this same month William and Mary were crowned as the sovereigns of Scotland, where a revolution had run a course closely parallel to that of England.[66] In that month too came England's declaration of war against France and the beginning of a conflict that would continue until the peace of Ryswick in 1697. James and his family had found a refuge in France, but he himself sailed in February, 1689, for Ireland, whose Catholic population quickly rallied to his support. Not until July, 1690, would William win there the decisive Battle of the Boyne.[67]

The king, busy with many pressing matters and actually not very much interested in colonial questions, was inclined to leave these questions to the Lords of Trade, a body which had lost much of its former energy and efficiency. Under James the Lords of Trade had been transformed from a special committee of the Privy Council into a committee of the whole, which is to say that it was now, for William perpetuated the arrangement, the whole body of the council sitting in committee. As a result, and in the absence of the interest James had shown, what had become "anybody's business," as Professor Andrews has observed, tended to be "nobody's business."[68] William Blathwayt, still serving as secretary, provided an important element of continuity, but his influence for the time being was in decline.[69] Moreover, the political considerations which had forced William to seek a balance in his government between men and factions had the effect of lowering the standard of public administration throughout the government. In this situation, the colonists with claims to press found both advantages and disadvantages. There could be interminable delay, but there was also the prospect that in the end at least a compromise settlement might be won.

It is not intended to suggest that William took no part in the settlement of colonial questions, for he frequently did, if only because he had a jealous regard for the prerogatives of the crown. It may be helpful at this point to substitute something more exact for the standard textbook generalization on the English Revolution. It

66 On the Revolution in Scotland, *ibid.*, pp. 263–280.
67 *Ibid.*, pp. 246–263.
68 Andrews, *Colonial Period*, IV, 274.
69 Jacobsen, *William Blathwayt*, pp. 140–143.

is true that William and Mary ruled at the invitation of Parliament, and on conditions laid down by Parliament in the Bill of Rights. But while the Bill of Rights established beyond dispute, as the most significant achievement of the Revolution, that the king ruled subject to the law, the document made no attempt to strip the crown of all its powers.[70] It deliberately avoided any reference to the social contract upon which John Locke depended while justifying the Revolution in the *Treatises of Government* he published in 1690. The framers of the Bill of Rights preferred the fiction that James, in fleeing the country, had abdicated, with the result that his daughter and her husband ruled by right of succession. This was a fiction upon which the co-operation of Whig and Tory depended— upon which, in other words, the very success of the Revolution depended. There was nothing in the Revolutionary settlement to challenge the king's traditional control over administration, and nothing in William's attitude to encourage a challenge from the colonists to the royal prerogative.

After hearings on the charges brought against Lord Howard of Effingham, he was confirmed in his office as governor of Virginia under an arrangement that sent Francis Nicholson to the colony in 1690 as lieutenant governor.[71] When late in the following year Lord Howard decided against a return to Virginia, Sir Edmund Andros took his place.[72] As this expression of confidence in Sir Edmund suggests, the attempt by Increase Mather to convict Andros of misrule in New England had failed totally.[73] Edward Randolph, though also exonerated of the charges brought against him, momentarily lost his footing. For a time he faced the discouraging prospect of going to Barbados in a subordinate position, but he quickly recovered and in October, 1690, won a commission as surveyor-general of the customs for all of North America at a salary of £200.[74] Andros, Nicholson, and Randolph, each of them promi-

---

[70] The document is conveniently consulted in George B. Adams and H. M. Stephens (eds.), *Select Documents of English Constitutional History* (New York, 1924), pp. 462–469.

[71] Morton, *Colonial Virginia*, I, 334; Osgood, *American Colonies in the Seventeenth Century*, III, 307–308.

[72] Morton, *Colonial Virginia*, I, 340–341; Jacobsen, *William Blathwayt*, p. 142.

[73] Murdock, *Increase Mather*, pp. 230–231.

[74] Hall, *Randolph*, pp. 129–135.

nent in the recent Dominion of New England, had all been rewarded with fresh appointments in America, and in no instance could the new position be viewed as a demotion. Even Joseph Dudley was taken care of by appointment as president of council in New York. However much these rewards may have been determined by the influence friends and relatives were able to exert in an uncertain political situation, it is obvious that a reputation for upholding the royal prerogative in America constituted no disadvantage for those who sought preferment from the new government.

Nor did it hurt to be a soldier. There was nothing startlingly new in the preference William showed in his choice of colonial governors for men who had at least some pretence to military experience,[75] but wartime conditions naturally lent to that consideration a fresh emphasis. This was especially true in the case of appointments for the more northerly situated colonies, those whose frontiers faced toward Canada or Nova Scotia. Neither the king nor his government entertained ambitious thoughts of carrying the war against France into North America, but the colonists themselves had been quick to develop an extraordinary plan for military operations aimed at nothing less than the total expulsion of the French from the continent. The resulting effort, and more particularly its dismal failure, lent additional urgency to considerations of colonial defense.

The story, in its beginning, takes us back to Jacob Leisler. After the French and Indians had sacked Schenectady in February, 1690, Governor Leisler, as he then described himself, appealed for assistance from other colonies, as far south as Virginia and even from Bermuda and Barbados, in the defense of Albany. The correspondence thus initiated was for Leisler generally disappointing, but it did lead to a conference at New York in April between him and the governors of Massachusetts, Plymouth, and Connecticut that prepared the way for ultimate agreement on a plan to co-ordinate an amphibious assault upon Quebec with an overland march from Albany against Montreal.[76] Thus early, and with no evident

---

[75] See again Webb's article on Nicholson, and Leonard W. Labaree, "The Early Careers of the Royal Governors," in *Essays . . . Presented to Charles McLean Andrews*, pp. 144–168.

[76] Andrews, *Colonial Period*, III, 130–131.

prompting from England, did the grand strategy that was destined to shape so much of the later contest for the possession of North America take form.

Lest it be assumed that Leisler was a greater strategist than he actually was, it should be noted that the plan owed much to the success of an expedition sent in May by Massachusetts against Port Royal in French Acadia. Its leader was Sir William Phips, a native of Maine and a man of no fortune who had won a great fortune by recovery of sunken treasure in the Caribbean. As a nineteenth-century historian observed, he had succeeded "in enterprises so hopeless at first sight that men of sober judgment would never have engaged in them."[77] For dividends enriching his influential backers in London, Phips had been knighted by King James. His victory at Port Royal, where a weak French garrison surrendered without resistance, made Sir William a great man in Boston, rewarded participants with a gratifying quantity of plunder, and for a short time eliminated an annoying base for French corsairs.[78] What is more important, it emboldened men to believe that even Quebec might be seized by an amphibious force carried up the St. Lawrence, provided the French had to divide their own forces in order to meet a simultaneous assault upon Montreal. The cost obviously would be high, but the booty taken at Port Royal argued that a successful campaign might even be profitable.

Unhappily, the actual campaign, which was launched late in the summer of 1690, had only one element of grandeur, and that was the plan.[79] Fitz Winthrop, son of Connecticut's Governor John, former captain in Cromwell's army, and more recently major general of militia by commission from Governor Andros, led the march from Albany by a combined force of Connecticut and New York

[77] Francis Bowen, *Life of Sir William Phips* (New York, 1856), p. 100. For a readable account of Phips's career, see Alice Lounsberry, *Sir William Phips: Treasure Fisherman and Governor of the Massachusetts Bay Colony* (New York, 1941). All modern biographers lean heavily upon Cotton Mather's life, originally published in the *Magnalia* and reprinted with a preface by Mark Van Doren (New York, 1929).

[78] For the French side, Eccles, *Canada under Louis XIV*, pp. 174–175.

[79] The best over-all account is in Gerald S. Graham, *Empire of the North Atlantic: The Maritime Struggle for North America* (Toronto, 1950), pp. 67–76. See also Howard H. Peckham, *The Colonial Wars, 1689–1762* (Chicago, 1964), pp. 32–38; Eccles, *Frontenac*, pp. 233–243, and *Canada under Louis XIV*, pp. 175–184; and for John Wise as chaplain, Cook, *John Wise*, pp. 61–69.

troops who had been joined by a disappointingly small Indian contingent.[80] The march dragged to a halt in the face of logistical and other problems, including an epidemic of smallpox which seems to have spread from the Indians to the English, below Lake Champlain, except for one detachment sent ahead for an indecisive raid upon the Canadians that also fell short of reaching Montreal. Meanwhile, Sir William had sailed from Massachusetts with a fleet of thirty-two vessels and some 1,300 soldiers—a most impressive achievement for an interim government relying chiefly upon the threat of impressment, the promise of booty, and the first issue of paper currency in the history of the colonies. Phips, depending, it seems, upon sheer luck for pilotage, made a great show in getting up the river to Quebec. In fact, he proved himself to be hardly more than a pompous ass, but, fortunately for his subsequent career, the blame for the failure at Quebec could be assigned very largely to John Walley, who commanded the ground forces.

The entire venture could be set aside simply as a military fiasco were it not for several considerations. First of all, it reminds us of how early the American showed his inclination in time of war to reach for the total, the final solution. Perhaps it was because the French menace had for him so close an identification with the Indian foe against whom he previously had fought wars of annihilation. After 1676 the Indians surviving within the older areas of settlement possessed a very limited capacity to harm the English, but those living along or beyond the imperfectly defined borders of settlement could still be dangerous, and especially so wherever the prospect of assistance from another European community gave them encouragement. For the English colonist the long contest with France was from the first a French and Indian war. Perhaps it was only that long, exposed, and difficult-to-defend frontiers, on the coast as well as inland, left the colonists little choice within their limited means other than an attempt to "cut off the fountain of trouble at the head," to quote the explanation given by the Massachusetts government in 1690.[81]

There is also room for speculation on the effect the capture of Quebec and Montreal might have had upon the fate of Jacob

80 Dunn, *Puritans and Yankees*, pp. 241, 243, 289–294; Trelease, *Indian Affairs in New York*, pp. 302–305.
81 Quoted in Graham, *Empire of the North Atlantic*, p. 71.

Leisler. By no means could he have claimed full credit. Even in his own province a large share of credit would have belonged to one of his chief enemies, Robert Livingston, who did much to bring about the co-operation of New England with New York.[82] Nevertheless, it would have been difficult to deny Leisler a prominent place among those who had rendered a signal service to king and empire, and in this fact may be found an important clue to his conduct in the tragic spring of 1691.

Never a man to undervalue his own services and self-righteously certain that the blame for the failure in New York belonged to Winthrop, Leisler knew the recognition to which he was entitled. Unfortunately, Governor Sloughter was not only unbelievably late in reaching his post but he was preceded at the end of January by a subordinate, Richard Ingoldesby, in command of a company of royal troops for reinforcement of the New York garrison. Ingoldesby sought to take over, and when Leisler refused to surrender command to any other than a lawfully commissioned successor in the governor's office, the captain was successful in calling up some reinforcement from the Long Island towns. When the governor finally arrived on March 19, the king's troops had been fired upon, two of the soldiers had been killed, and seven others wounded. Even then Leisler stood on his dignity in refusing to surrender the fort at night, and after his surrender of it on the following morning he was charged with treason. The governor listened to Leisler's enemies, who demanded his blood, and following trial and conviction by a court headed by Joseph Dudley, the exile from Massachusetts for whom William Blathwayt had found a place as head of council to Sloughter,[83] Leisler and Jacob Milborne, Leisler's son-in-law, were hanged on May 16, 1691. Six other men among Leisler's supporters were condemned but reprieved by the governor. In 1694 they were to win royal pardons, and in the next year both Leisler and Milborne were cleared of their convictions for treason by an act of the English Parliament.[84] Such was to be the final end of Leisler's so-called rebellion, except for the bitter memories that would poison the colony's politics for many years thereafter.

Finally, the expedition against Canada, and especially the risk of

[82] Leder, *Robert Livingston*, pp. 64–75.
[83] Kimball, *Public Life of Joseph Dudley*, pp. 57–64.
[84] Andrews, *Colonial Period*, III, 132–134; Reich, *Leisler's Rebellion*, pp. 108–125; White, *The Beekmans of New York*, pp. 131–142.

French retaliation its failure seemed to entail, helps to explain Whitehall's persistent concern for the security of Albany. This, of course, was by no means a new concern, and the sack of Schenectady in itself was enough to lend it fresh emphasis, but the unhappy sequel to that attack can hardly be ignored in explaining demands for assistance to Albany that complicated the king's relations with his North American colonies from Virginia northward.

When one turns from this military problem to consider the action taken on other questions presented to the government by recent developments in the continental colonies, it is difficult to define any broad lines of policy that are not best stated in negative terms. It can be said that the king showed no interest in perpetuating the Dominion of New England or in undertaking any other ambitious reorganization of colonial administration, that he had no inclination to surrender any right of government previously belonging to the crown, but that at the same time he displayed no marked desire to extend his responsibilities by annexing other governments to the crown. There were two instances in which powers of government under existing charters were suspended, but not a single colonial charter was actually sacrificed to the demands of the new government. Instead, two charters previously brought into question were confirmed and, as is well known, Massachusetts succeeded in winning for itself in 1691 a second charter. The decisions taken by the king's government turned more largely upon the circumstances peculiar to each case than upon a comprehensive view of policy capable of lending positive direction to the course of events.

There is room only for a brief review, and it is as convenient as perhaps it is proper to begin with the king's assumption of responsibility for the government of Maryland. The Catholic Lord Baltimore, of course, had nothing to gain from a Protestant revolution, and he faced moreover a continuing distrust in official circles as to his management of the colony. It is not easy to determine the influence agents of the revolutionary regime may have exerted, but certainly their presence helped to persuade the government that a potentially dangerous situation existed in the colony. On that assumption it was decided that the proprietor's right of government could be suspended, and accordingly Sir Lionel Copley received a royal commission as governor in June, 1691.[85] That commission

<hr />

[85] Andrews, *Colonial Period*, II, 375–376; Mereness, *Maryland as a Proprietary Province*, pp. 41–42.

marked the beginning of what would become twenty-five years of royal rule in Maryland, but throughout those years the lords Baltimore retained their charter, possession of the soil, and the revenues derived from the proprietorship of the soil. In 1715, after the conversion of the then Lord Baltimore to the Anglican Church, the full rights of government would be restored.

William Penn, the Quaker, fared no better in 1692 than had the Catholic Lord Baltimore. A long-standing friend of the Stuarts who had supported the religious policy of King James, and who did not support the Revolution, Penn remained suspect. Indeed, it had been widely rumored, even before the Revolution, that he actually was a Jesuit in disguise, and for a time in 1689 the Privy Council had a warrant out for his arrest on a suspicion of high treason.[86]

Developments in his colony gave Penn neither help nor comfort. During his absence from Pennsylvania, now eight years long, factional divisions among the settlers had been sharpened and resistance to proprietary claims had hardened. An assembly persistently demanding a larger voice in the government had been held in check by a council dominated by Thomas Lloyd, who enjoyed a comparable success in resisting the proprietor's authority. Penn's attempt in 1688 to assert his authority by appointing John Blackwell, a relative and old-line Puritan then living in Connecticut, to the governor's post had ended in the virtual paralysis of government and Blackwell's relief from office in the next year. The continuing power of Lloyd and a circle of the great men of Philadelphia and its environs strengthened the discontent of the Lower Counties, and that discontent was further strengthened by the apprehensions awakened by the war with France.[87] A victory by an Anglo-Dutch fleet over the French at the Battle of La Hogue in May, 1692, relieved England's fear of an immediate invasion in behalf of James II, but it did nothing to remove the threat of roving French corsairs whose depredations upon English shipping were subsequently in-

[86] Illick, *William Penn*, pp. 77–128; Peare, *William Penn*, pp. 306, 310–311, 313.

[87] Nash, "Economics and Politics in Early Pennsylvania," Chaps. 4–6; Andrews, *Colonial Period*, III, 306–312; Shepherd, *Proprietary Government in Pennsylvania*, pp. 252–273; Roy N. Lokken, *David Lloyd, Colonial Lawmaker* (Seattle, 1959), pp. 21–51; and Robert L. D. Davidson's discussion in *War Comes to Quaker Pennsylvania, 1682–1756* (New York, 1957).

tensified.[88] The more exposed inhabitants of the lower Delaware Valley showed as much concern for problems of defense as did the Philadelphia Quakers to avoid compromising their pacifist principles. Calls for help to Albany also went unheeded, but not unnoticed in London. Among those giving warning that Pennsylvania was a particularly weak link in the defenses of the English settlements was Francis Nicholson, who in 1692 had been given a lien on the lieutenant governorship of Maryland.

There could have been little surprise for William Penn when his right of government was suspended and in October, 1692, Colonel Benjamin Fletcher, who had assumed the governorship of New York in the preceding August, was commissioned as governor also of Pennsylvania. The surprising thing is that his rights were so quickly restored to Penn, in 1694 upon his assurance that Pennsylvania would co-operate in the defense of Albany.[89]

The Carolina proprietors were more fortunate than either Baltimore or Penn. There had never been anything more than a threat of *quo warranto* proceedings against their charter, and so no real action was pending to demand attention from the new government. Moreover, the proprietors moved with reasonable promptness to quiet the disturbances in their province by recruiting Philip Ludwell, Virginia's agent, to serve as governor over both parts of the province, with a right to designate a deputy governor for the upper part. His efforts to restore peace and quiet were destined for failure. As a result, his commission of 1691 has been chiefly remembered for the beginning of a formal distinction between North Carolina and South Carolina.[90]

Even the New Jersey proprietors, for all the repeated attacks that had been made upon their rights of government, and notwithstanding the continuing importance of that area for any sensible solution of New York's peculiar problems, eventually emerged victorious. As late as the spring of 1692 the Lords of Trade, who had been urged by Governor Fletcher of New York to effect the annexation of the Jerseys to that province, decided that a writ of *scire facias* should be issued against the proprietors. But in the end the committee

[88] Graham, *Empire of the North Atlantic*, pp. 58–64; Ogg, *England in the Reigns of James II and William III*, pp. 366–371.
[89] Andrews, *Colonial Period*, III, 315–316.
[90] *Ibid.*, III, 232, 258.

dropped the plan. Dr. Daniel Coxe, who had purchased Byllynge's title to West Jersey in 1687 and in March, 1692, had sold out to forty-eight men, mainly London merchants, seems to have been chiefly instrumental in winning a decision that returned Andrew Hamilton, agent for East Jersey, to America as the governor of both Jerseys on the assurance that he would secure New Jersey's assistance in the defense of Albany.[91] In time of war, it seems, governments are likely to reject proposals for a difficult and time-consuming reorganization of existing arrangements in favor of some simpler solution to their problem.

Perhaps it was this same consideration that explains the good fortune of the New England colonies. Both Connecticut and Rhode Island won opinions from the crown's law officers in 1690 that their charters never had been legally invalidated, and so constituted sufficient warrant for the governments re-established in the preceding year.[92] These opinions in no sense foreclosed the possibility of later proceedings against the two charters, but for the moment all was well except for such disturbing demands as might be made for contributions to the defense of Albany. Significantly, New Hampshire once more was separated from Massachusetts by a decision which excluded it from the territorial provisions of the latter's second charter, and so it continued as a royal colony under the governorship of Samuel Allen, a London merchant who had purchased the Mason claim to the soil and was represented in the colony by his son-in-law, John Usher, in the capacity of a deputy governor.[93] Even so, Massachusetts had little cause for real complaint over the territory it could claim under the new charter. Included was the older colony of Plymouth, which now reached its end as a distinct province in a transition that seems to have been easily made.[94] Nantucket and Martha's Vineyard were repossessed from New York. New York's claim to a part of Maine was terminated by the grant to Massachusetts of the whole of Maine and even Nova Scotia, this last because London had not heard in October,

91 Pomfret, *West Jersey*, pp. 171–172; *East Jersey*, pp. 276–278; *New Jersey Proprietors*, p. 55.

92 Andrews, *Colonial Period*, IV, 373; Bates, *Charter of Connecticut*, pp. 58–59.

93 Palfrey, *History of New England*, IV, 207–208. Allen's commission was granted early in 1692.

94 Apparently without resistance. See discussion in Langdon's *Pilgrim Colony*.

1691, the date of the charter, that Frontenac had repossessed Sir William Phips' conquest.

Sir William had joined Increase Mather in London during the later stages of the negotiations. Also associated with Mather were Elisha Cooke and Thomas Oakes, agents sent from the colony early in 1690. Sir Henry Ashurst, son of a London merchant and lifelong friend of New England, and especially of its Indian missions, was repeatedly helpful. But the credit, or the blame, for the new charter belongs chiefly to Mather. It had been for him a long embassy, and one filled with many disappointments, for his hope had been to re-establish the old charter. His first audience with the king had come as early as January, 1689. Twice more that year Mather pled his cause with William, but the king was busy and Massachusetts had many enemies. By the spring of 1691 some of the more vigorous of these were back in America, assigned by William to new posts of responsibility, the queen's interest had been enlisted, and the king, momentarily returned from the wars, had listened to Mather again. By fall Mather had assurance that he would get his charter, not the charter he originally had hoped for but one confirming a compromise settlement that returned to Massachusetts many of her cherished liberties.[95]

The king had insisted upon a royal governor, who held the power also to designate the lieutenant-governor and secretary of the province. A council of twenty-eight members was to be annually elected by the general court according to the old custom, but the king's governor would have a right of veto in the election. A house of representatives embodying two delegates from every town, and four from Boston, to be annually elected by 40s. freeholders and others possessed of £40 worth of property, rounded out the general court, which included the governor and council sitting as the upper house. An annual meeting of the general court, in keeping with long established usage, was fixed by the provisions of the charter, but that document also gave to the governor a new power to adjourn, prorogue, and dissolve the court. The governor possessed a veto over such legislation as it might propose, and all of its legisla-

95 Murdock, *Increase Mather*, pp. 211–261; and Michael G. Hall (ed.), "The Autobiography of Increase Mather," *Proceedings of the American Antiquarian Society*, LXXI (1962), 322–343.

tion was to be submitted to England for royal approval or disallowance. Appointments of judges, sheriffs, and local magistrates belonged to the governor and council. Mather had yielded much, but he also secured inclusion at a late hour of a vital passage confirming existing titles in the land. There would be no fees to pay for new grants of long-held property and no quitrents.[96] On the question of who should be the first royal governor, the king had insisted only that he be a military man. And so, on Mather's motion, the choice was Sir William Phips.

When we look back on the experience of the North American colonies at the time of England's Glorious Revolution, one point stands out. Again, as in the Restoration era, the New England colonies came out best. Perhaps God was with them, a hope that had been recently expressed by many prayerful supplications, but a more likely explanation is that the government of William and Mary had at first no consistent colonial policy. Its fixed aim had been to recruit the strength of Protestant England for reinforcement of the resistance to the ambitions of Louis XIV, a Catholic monarch who backed James II after failing to support him when in 1688 it might have counted. After three wars with Protestant Holland, England once more, as in the days of Elizabeth and Philip of Spain, was allied with the forces of Protestantism on the continent. In this fact there perhaps were advantages for New England, and Increase Mather knew how to turn them to advantage. Perhaps too a small credit belongs to Sir William Phips. For all his faults and failures, his presence in London in 1691 bespoke the willingness of New England to fight the French, even in the remote corners of the American wilderness.

---

[96] For the charter, see Thorpe, *Federal and State Constitutions*, III, 1877–1883.

CHAPTER 8

The Revolutionary Settlement

I N America, as in England, the full meaning of the great revolution which had occurred, whether for the development of imperial policy or for the institutional life of the colonies, waited on time for clarification. There is no single explanation for the delay, but undoubtedly a heavy emphasis belongs to the simple fact that for most of the twenty-five years immediately following the Revolution, England was at war. After King William's War reached its indecisive end in 1697, there followed a brief interval of peace before the renewal of hostilities in 1702, the year of William's death. Queen Mary had died in 1694. The new war, the War of the Spanish Succession, was to take its customary designation among the colonists from Queen Anne, Mary's younger sister and William's successor. Queen Anne's War ended with the Peace of Utrecht in 1713.

Only with the coming of the second of these wars were any of the colonists, after 1690, again seriously involved in hostilities with European foes on the North American continent. Because Spain adhered to William's Grand Alliance against Louis XIV, the southern frontier remained quiet until a new Franco-Spanish alliance dangerously altered the situation in1702. On the northern frontier, Massachusetts and New Hampshire fought a continuing, and occasionally costly, war with the border Indians, and New York experienced renewed alarms and some skirmishing, but there was no revival of grand designs for the dislodgment of the French, not even in Acadia and not even when in 1693 Admiral Wheeler called briefly at Boston to offer his assistance in such an effort. Had this offer represented a serious purpose on Whitehall's part to assume the military initiative in North America, the story might have been different. But from the beginning to the end of the war the king's attention to military problems in that area had a very sharp focus upon the need to strengthen the defenses of Albany, whether by the financial contributions demanded for that purpose from most of the colonies or by a variety of experiments with command arrangements that were undertaken in the hope of facilitating the reinforcement of Albany by the militia of neighboring provinces. Fortunately, the sluggish response which met the king's appeals for assistance was offset by the weakness of the enemy in North America. Canada too had to be content with a defensive posture, except for limited assistance to its Indian allies, a sally now and again against the Iroquois, and the help it could render to privateers and other raiding forces moving by sea against the foe.[1]

The sea quickly became the main theater of operations seriously affecting the fortunes of the English colonies. In addition to the privateers who became active in the North Atlantic, the Caribbean, and along the seaways converging on England, the French sent out special raiding forces whose hit-and-run tactics were especially damaging to English positions on Hudson's Bay and in Newfoundland. Among those who sustained thereby significant loss were the New England merchants whose trade with Newfoundland had become an important item in the area's economy.[2] But there is reason for believing that the planters of Virginia and Maryland suffered the most grievous of the losses sustained at sea, if only because so much of their tobacco was captured by French privateers during the course of the war that the product won its way to new favor in France and so to a postwar market destined to have major

[1] See especially Herbert L. Osgood, *The American Colonies in the Eighteenth Century* (4 vols., New York, 1924), I, 106–115, 232–236; Eccles, *Canada under Louis XIV*, pp. 185–206; Samuel A. Drake, *The Border Wars of New England* (New York, 1897), pp. 66–128; and Douglas E. Leach, *The Northern Colonial Frontier* (New York, 1966), pp. 109–118. On the command of the militia, see below, pp. 256–257.
[2] Graham, *Empire of the North Atlantic*, pp. 76–82; Curtis P. Nettels, *The Money Supply of the American Colonies before 1720* (Madison, Wis., 1934), pp. 76–78.

importance for the economy of the Chesapeake settlements.[3] Colonial shipping, of course, was subjected to hazards comparable to those visited upon the English vessels which each year carried the bulk of the tobacco crop to England. Other items of ultimate cost to the colonists include the loss or disruption of markets on the European continent for colonial produce; a reduction in the shipping that could be sent from England, whether occasioned by wartime demands from the Navy upon the merchant fleet or by the depredations of the enemy; and increased charges for freightage and insurance. It is not at all certain, however, that the balance sheet, were the evidence available for a reasonably exact one, would add up with an emphasis on the debit side for the colonies lying outside the Chesapeake.

Whatever may have been the disruptive effect of the war upon emigration to the newer settlements on the Delaware, and it does seem to have had its effect, the war seems also to have boosted the trade of Philadelphia by broadening the market for foodstuffs in the West Indies. New York too apparently drew some benefit from this development, which depended partly upon the opening of Spanish possessions to North American traders.[1] In the latter province, as is well known, letters of marque against the French served to cover a lucrative trade with Red Sea pirates in which Frederick Philipse and Stephen DeLancey were heavily involved. The war too brought relaxation of restrictions upon the traditional welcome accorded pirates in colonial seaports from Charles Town northward, enough at any rate to bring at its end a renewed and newly successful effort by government to accomplish the suppression of piracy, with Captain William Kidd, whether rightly or wrongly, cast in a stellar role.[5] Not to be overlooked is the stimulation war

[3] Jacob Price, "The Economic Growth of the Chesapeake and the European Market, 1697–1775," *Journal of Economic History*, XXIV (1964), p. 504.

[4] Edwin B. Bronner, *William Penn's "Holy Experiment": The Founding of Pennsylvania, 1681–1701* (New York, 1962), p. 85; and James Logan to Penn, August 22, 1705, in Edward Armstrong (ed.), *The Correspondence between William Penn and James Logan* (2 vols., Philadelphia, 1870–72), II, 53, where Logan commented that in the last war, "when we had a free trade with Spain, and provision was at the same time high in England, this place and York enriched themselves much by supplying all the English islands, and selling the Spaniards besides." For this citation I am indebted to Gary B. Nash.

[5] Osgood, *American Colonies in the Eighteenth Century*, I, 525–546, provides a convenient summary.

brought to New England's mast trade, or the evidence indicating that wartime conditions enabled her merchants to strengthen their leadership in intercolonial trade along the coast as far south as Carolina. Such losses as the New England fleet sustained at sea were significantly offset by the capture of enemy vessels, and Boston reached the end of the war with enough shipping to give her a probable third rank, after London and Bristol, among the empire's seaports.[6]

It is impossible to say just what the balance would be in an over-all accounting of the economic effect of the war upon the colonies. Some communities obviously fared better than others, as no doubt did some individuals. It is possible that the special opportunities provided by the war did nothing more than to alleviate the effect of its disturbance of the normal channels of trade. Whatever the fact, certainly the advantage could be gained at times only through adjustments that were difficult to make.

Certainly, too, the war years were in other respects a difficult time. The sources of division and contention which had lent turbulence to the colonial scene for many years past had been by no means suddenly eliminated. Even in New England, where recent events had moved with more of the appearance of unanimity among the people than in other areas, there was trouble, serious trouble.

One might hesitate to introduce the subject of the Salem witch-craft trials in a context that is largely political except for the fact that there is good authority for so doing. Although a belief in witches was so widely held in the seventeenth century that the delusion might manifest itself anywhere and under a variety of circumstances, the late Professor Kittredge has demonstrated that the manifestation tended to occur in irregular outbreaks which were "likely to accompany, or to follow, crises in politics or religion."[7] Certainly, the Salem trials occurred at a time of disturbing dislocations in the old Puritan order, and of many uncertainties as to what finally would take its place. If the Revolution of 1689 had

[6] Curtis P. Nettels, "The Economic Relations of Boston, Philadelphia, and New York, 1680–1715," *Journal of Ecomomic and Business History*, III, 185–215; Bernard and Lotte Bailyn, *Massachusetts Shipping, 1697–1714* (Cambridge, Mass., 1959), pp. 20, 24.

[7] George L. Kittredge, *Witchcraft in Old and New England* (Cambridge, Mass., 1929), p. 372.

saved the people from the "despotism" of Sir Edmund Andros, it also had raised in many hearts a false hope that the old Zion might be re-established. This was the hope that Elisha Cooke had carried with him as he journeyed across the Atlantic after the Revolution to join Increase Mather in the suit for confirmation of the colony's liberties. Mather faced the facts and, like so many men identified with the English Revolution, accepted a compromise. Cooke refused to accept it, as apparently did also his colleague Thomas Oakes.[8] Though both Cooke and Oakes, in addition to serving as agents for the colony, had been members of council in the provisional government, their names were omitted from the list of twenty-eight first councilors incorporated in the new charter on nominations by Mather, a list including many men who had collaborated with Andros. The list speaks well for Mather's judgment, for it represents a cross section of the leaders who had co-operated in the overthrow of the Dominion, but it left Mather exposed to bitter attack by the unreconciled faction among the old Puritans which now took shape around the leadership of Elisha Cooke. Mather weathered the storm well enough, better perhaps than he had expected, but at the cost of having Phips exercise his right of veto in the election of 1693, first under the new charter, in order to keep Cooke from a seat on the council.[9]

The witch trials at Salem were conducted under the authority of the new government. When Phips and Mather reached Boston with the charter in the middle of May, 1692, preliminary investigations of witchcraft charges in Essex County, which five years earlier had been the center of abortive efforts to obstruct arbitrary taxation by Andros, had filled the Salem jail with suspects. One of Phips's first acts as governor was to establish a special commission of oyer and terminer headed by Lieutenant Governor William Stoughton. The trials, in which the court depended upon spectral evidence and so denied common-law protections, proceeded intermittently through the summer. By the end of day on September 22 a total of twenty persons had been hanged since the first execution in June. One other, the elderly Giles Gory, taking advantage of the ancient rule

---

8 The authorities differ. See Murdock, *Increase Mather*, p. 247; Palfrey, *History of New England*, III, p. 82.

9 Murdock, *Increase Mather*, pp. 331–334.

of *peine forte et dure* to avoid a hopeless plea, had been crushed to death by stones. Thereafter the panic subsided, and never again would a person be tried for witchcraft in New England. As the hysteria gave way to a tormenting memory, there were recriminations, in which much of the blame was laid at the door of the two Mathers, Increase and his son Cotton. Certainly, they were partly to blame, but in the case of Increase it should be noted also that he assisted substantially in the restoration of sanity, and at the cost of further differences with his natural allies.[10]

It would be unfair to require that so limited a man as Sir William Phips shoulder a major share of the responsibility. Pathetically anxious to please and understandably inclined to follow better-qualified judges than he could claim to be, he rode simply with the current, and afterward had no better plea to make than that provided by his own escape at the height of the panic to look into the Indian problem on the frontier. More at home in the forecastle than in the governor's chair, he was called back to England after two years and died there before he could clear himself of charges which, in part, had been brought by Joseph Dudley. It was Dudley's ambition to succeed Phips, a hope that had for a while yet to be postponed.[11]

The spectrum of political opinion in New England ranged all the way from the intransigence of Elisha Cooke to the wholehearted imperialism of Joseph Dudley—even beyond that. In Connecticut, Gershom Bulkeley's *Will and Doom* of 1692 affirmed the right of the king to rule in terms as absolute as any contemporary English Tory could have desired. By its surrender to Andros in 1687, Bulkeley argued, the colony had lost every legitimate claim to its charter. The argument reflected more than the irreversible commit-

[10] In the long bibliography of this tortured subject, Charles W. Upham, *Salem Witchcraft, with an Account of Salem Village, and a History of Opinions on Witchcraft and Kindred Subjects* (2 vols., Boston, 1867), remains fundamental. Of modern accounts, Marion L. Starkey, *The Devil in Massachusetts* (New York, 1949), is readable, judicious, and informed by the findings of modern psychology. Palfrey, *History of New England, IV*, 96–133, is conveniently useful. For interpretation, and in addition to Kittredge, *Witchcraft*, the following are important: Murdock, *Increase Mather*, pp. 287–316; Miller, *From Colony to Province*, pp. 191–208; Morison, *The Puritan Pronaos*, pp. 248–257. George Lincoln Burr (ed.), *Narratives of the Witchcraft Cases, 1648–1706* (New York, 1914), provides a convenient reference to original sources for all of the colonies.

[11] Kimball, *Joseph Dudley*, pp. 66–69.

ment he himself had made at the time of the Dominion. It showed too the disgust with which this son of one of New England's most eminent divines viewed his own provincial society.[12]

That others shared this contemptuous attitude, though not without some chance of recovery, is indicated by the career of Fitz Winthrop, head in the third generation of New England's first family. He had known London in his youth, and for many years thereafter he viewed life on the paternal estate in America as an unrewarding exile. After being exceedingly slow to assume any of the responsibilities to which he was called by birth, he had been quick to cast his lot with Andros, energetic in his efforts to persuade Connecticut to surrender to the Dominion,. and unresponsive to proposals that he take the governorship of the colony after the Revolution. Though disappointed enough in Andros to avoid the trap into which Bulkeley fell, only the chance for military glory as leader of the expedition against Montreal had brought him again into active public service before 1693, when he sailed for England as Connecticut's agent on a mission to defend the charter his father had won. Bulkeley had precipitated the crisis by moving through Governor Fletcher of New York to secure a return of royal government in Connecticut.[13] Perhaps it was because Winthrop had a strong distaste for some of those associated with Bulkeley's effort; perhaps it was the chance to visit London again that persuaded him. In any case, after a successful mission of four years' duration, he ended an otherwise undistinguished career where he belonged, in the governor's chair of a still-autonomous Connecticut.

Lest it be assumed that only New Englanders shared Fitz Winthrop's difficulty, let it be noted that William Fitzhugh, who as an emigrant to Virginia had accumulated an impressive estate, kept the property on the market for a number of these years in the hope that he might comfortably live out his life at home in England. His explanation, in a letter of 1687, was that in Virginia "society that is good and ingenious is very scarce and seldom to be come at except in Books."[14] It may be worth adding that the younger William

12 Miller, *From Colony to Province*, pp. 151–155.

13 Dunn, *Puritans and Yankees*, pp. 191–355, provides a very helpful study of the careers of Fitz Winthrop and his younger brother Wait, who sat as one of the judges in the Salem witchcraft trials.

14 Quoted in Craven, *Southern Colonies*, p. 404.

Byrd, of the same province, would spend more than thirty of his seventy years of life in Europe, chiefly as a resident of London, a city he always left for return to his vast properties in Virginia with deeply felt regret.[15] All too many of the colonists of this generation, and especially of those whose property called them to positions of leadership, seem to have had no other strong tie to America than the property they held there. In this fact King William had a decided advantage, or rather he would have whenever he found the time for attention to his somewhat imperfectly structured empire.

The time finally was found in 1696, when William's uncertain and drifting colonial policy gave way to more purposeful action. For this development the war was largely responsible, because it had hurt in a variety of ways commercial interests to which the Whig majority in Parliament was sensitively responsive. Also partly responsible were the king's Scottish subjects, who in 1695 had organized the Company of Scotland for a final attempt to challenge England's leadership in overseas enterprise.[16] Influential too were William Blathwayt, Edward Randolph, Francis Nicholson, and others who had found careers in the field of colonial administration, men who had never left off in their efforts to call attention to the shortcomings of the existing system.

Randolph, again back in London, played an especially important role in the drafting of the Navigation Act of 1696, last in a series reaching back to the act of 1660.[17] The new bill added nothing in principle to previous legislation. Its purpose is accurately indicated by its title: "An Act for preventing Frauds and regulating Abuses in the Plantation Trade." A catchall measure that was loosely drawn and at times difficult to interpret, it strengthened and regularized the customs service in America as a part of England's own establishment; tightened the obligations resting upon the colonial governor, however appointed, for enforcement of the trade acts; prepared the way for a system of colonial vice-admiralty courts established in

---

[15] See especially the brief life by Louis B. Wright in *William Byrd of Virginia; The London Diary (1717–1721) and other Writings* (New York, 1958).

[16] See George P. Insh, *The Company of Scotland Trading to Africa and the Indies* (London and New York, 1932).

[17] Hall, *Edward Randolph*, pp. 154–165; Harper, *English Navigation Laws*, pp. 60–62; Michael G. Hall, "The House of Lords, Edward Randolph, and the Navigation Act of 1696," *William and Mary Quarterly*, 3d. ser., XIV (1957), 494–515.

1697 with special responsibilities for enforcement of trade regulations; and, of course, undertook to prevent interloping by Scotsmen.[18] Insofar as legislation could accomplish the job, the old colonial system was now complete, except for laws, beginning with the Wool Act of 1699, designed to prohibit or to encourage specific kinds of manufacture in the colonies.

The year 1696 saw also the replacement of the Lords of Trade by the Board of Trade. The Lords Commissioners of Trade and Plantations, as the new board was officially designated, took its authority from a royal commission of May 15, after Parliament had threatened to move by way of legislative enactment. Though naturally subordinate to the will of the Privy Council, the Board of Trade was in no sense a committee of the Council. Instead, its working membership comprised eight men who were paid each an annual salary of £1,000, three to five of whom constituted a quorum, according to the business at hand, and one of whom served as president. In addition, eight high officers of state held *ex officio* membership, and for a time some of these took an active part in the work of the board. This participation, however, was occasional rather than regular and disappeared after a few years. Of the original members the Earl of Bridgewater was president, John Locke the most famous, and William Blathwayt the best informed on the business in hand. Blathwayt, promptly became, and remained until his dismissal in 1707, the most influential member of the Board. Strictly speaking, the Board of Trade had no power of its own, not even control over an expanding colonial patronage. Its function was advisory. The authority to act on its recommendations lay in other agencies of the government.[19]

The expertise the Board of Trade acquired in the discharge of its special responsibilities, and from the accumulated knowledge of the Plantation Office over which it now had control, gave great influence to the Board's opinion, but in no real sense had colonial administration been departmentalized. Instead, and partly because colonial issues acquired their primary importance from a general concern for the welfare of England's trade, the handling of these

18 Andrews, *Colonial Period,* IV, 157–174.

19 *Ibid.,* IV, 272–315, provides the most authoritative discussion of the board's history, but does not supplant the long-standard reference, Oliver M. Dickerson, *American Colonial Government, 1696–1765* (Cleveland, 1912).

issues remained broadly dependent upon the governmental machinery serving the kingdom itself. The king, still the unquestioned head of administration, might choose to act in council. Parliament, tentatively exploring the implications of the Revolutionary settlement, might take the initiative, as it did in 1696. The Secretary of State, and after 1704 the Secretary of State for the Southern Department, had a critically important voice. Others whose influence could be determinant, according to the character of the issue, included the admiralty, the war office, the treasury, the customs commissioners, the law officers, the high courts, and the bishop of London, formerly a member of the Lords of Trade and now one of the *ex officio* members of the Board of Trade.[20] In such a system, or lack of system, in which delay and inefficiency were natural concomitants, and in which colonial questions stood usually on the periphery of the government's attention, there were both advantages and disadvantages for the colonists.

Ad hoc decisions taken by the king since 1689 discouraged any thought by the Board of Trade for a return to the concept embodied in the Dominion of New England. The provincial distinctions many of the colonists were learning to cherish would be accepted, as would also their claim to some form of representation in the administration of provincial affairs. But nothing had occurred to forbid experimentation with a modified form of governor-general who at the executive level might serve to win some of the advantages of a closer union among colonies, especially for the purposes of military co-operation. Indeed, there was precedent for such an experiment in Sir William Phips's commission, which had given him command of all the New England militia, and in the subsequent transfer in 1693 of the Connecticut militia from Phips to Fletcher in New York. There was also the precedent of Fletcher's term as governor both of New York and Pennsylvania.

Faced early in its career by the need to replace Phips and by complaints of Fletcher's conduct in New York, the Board of Trade proposed the appointment of a single governor for New York and all New England, he to have command as well over the New Jersey militia. Naturally, there were objections. New York feared a return

20 A. B. Keith, *Constitutional History of the First British Empire* (Oxford, 1930) , pp. 266 ff., is helpful here.

to government from Boston. Connecticut, especially resentful of Fletcher's command, protested through Fitz Winthrop, its agent in London. As a result, the best that the Board of Trade could secure was a commission in 1697 for Richard Coote, Earl of Bellomont, to serve as governor of Massachusetts, New Hampshire, and New York, with residence in the last named and with command over the militia of Rhode Island, Connecticut, and New Jersey. Actually, Lord Bellomont received much less than at first glance he appears to have, for a schedule of interdependent quotas, accepted at the insistence of Winthrop and other agents, greatly reduced the broad powers conferred upon him.[21] The experiment had no lasting consequence, except that for forty years thereafter the governor of Massachusetts doubled, on a separate commission, as the governor of New Hampshire. In commissioning Joseph Dudley to succeed Lord Bellomont as governor of Massachusetts in 1702, Whitehall returned to the pattern of Phips' commission. Dudley would hold command in time of war or threat of war over the militia of the other New England colonies.[22]

These were fumbling efforts to resolve a problem that William Penn probably saw more clearly than did any other person involved. The Board of Trade was seeking to employ the inherent powers of a commander in chief without actually giving him the full authority of a governor in chief. In 1696, Penn proposed that the governor of New York be made a high commissioner for the king, that he preside over a regularly assembled congress of delegates representing all of the North American colonies for the purpose of fixing quotas of men and money to be contributed to the common defense, and that he then have command over all forces thus assigned to the common service, but presumably no other. It was an ingenious proposal and farsighted, given the later course of American history, but the advice was not followed.[23]

21 Andrews, *Colonial Period,* IV, 377–378; Osgood, *American Colonies in the Eighteenth Century,* I, 98–103; Dunn, *Puritans and Yankees,* pp. 308–310.

22 Kimball, *Public Life of Joseph Dudley,* pp. 79–80.

23 See Tolles and Aldefer, *Witness of William Penn,* pp. 135–137. The plan did, however, provoke some discussion. Published in 1698 by Charles Davenant in his *Discourses on the Publick Revenues,* it provoked an interesting counter proposal by a Virginian (probably Robert Beverley). See Louis B. Wright (ed.), *An Essay upon the Government of the English Plantations on the Continent of America (1701)* (San Marino, Calif., 1945).

Perhaps it was the hope of facilitating a desirable unity for purposes of military co-operation that explains, as much as any other consideration, the Board of Trade's attempt after 1696 to bring all of the colonies directly under the king's rule. In any case, this became the main aim of the newly established Board, which quickly found that the chief hope it had of achieving that aim lay in the new interest Parliament had taken in questions of trade. Following closely after enactment of the Navigation Act of 1696, a committee of the House of Lords in February, 1697 entered upon an extensive investigation in which William Penn, with Edward Randolph acting virtually as a prosecuting attorney, was given an especially rough time.[24] The end result was that the so-called private colonies were put on notice, by royal letters of April, 1697, that they must either show a better record of co-operation in the enforcement of the trade acts, the suppression of piracy, and the defense of the colonies or expect to sacrifice their charters. Even so, when the Board of Trade undertook in 1701 to secure enactment of a bill "reuniting" all proprietary and chartered colonies to the crown, the effort failed, as did a second attempt in 1702 and a third, with a much less drastic bill, in 1706.[25] Parliament, it appeared, though responsive enough to the interests of trade, was reluctant to endorse so sweeping an assault upon the rights of property, and its Tory members saw in the proposed legislation an encroachment upon the royal prerogative. By lumping all of the "private" colonies together, moreover, the bill multiplied the special interests that could be enlisted against it. The Board's effort seems to have suffered, too, from the very substantial progress that had been made by the end of the century toward the development of a uniform administration of the trade laws.

At that time, in Virginia, Maryland, New York, Massachusetts, and New Hampshire, not to mention the West Indian plantations, the governor was appointed by the crown. In Carolina, Pennsylvania, and New Jersey the right of appointment lay with proprietors, but all such appointments after 1696 were subject to royal approval and the appointees were bound by the same obligations

[24] Hall, *Edward Randolph*, pp. 171–175; Illick, *William Penn the Politician*, pp. 139–155.

[25] Andrews, *Colonial Period*, IV, 378–386; Jacobsen, *William Blathwayt*, pp. 335–337; Alison G. Olson, "William Penn, Parliament, and Proprietary Government," *William and Mary Quarterly*, 3d. ser., XVIII (1961), 176–195.

for enforcement of the trade acts as were royal governors. In law, at least, this was also true of the elected governors of Connecticut and Rhode Island, though obviously the obligations were more difficult to enforce in these instances. The Board's desire to complete the job is readily understandable, if only because consistency always has appeal for the mind schooled by administrative responsibility. But it could be argued, as did William Penn in 1701, that the Board's proposal was superfluous to any real need.[26] By then a system of customs officers, directly responsible to the Customs Commissioners in London and strengthened by provisions of the Navigation Act of 1696, was being shaken down and rounded out. Naval officers, appointed by the governors in accordance with the legislation of 1696, functioned under bond to these same commissioners.[27] Since 1697 vice-admiralty courts had been erected in eleven jurisdictions, not always adhering to provincial boundaries, with a grant of power depending upon commission from the High Court of Admiralty and disturbingly large for many of the king's colonial subjects, especially in the courts' substitution of civil- for common-law procedures.[28] What more was needed? The Board of Trade had evidence enough to support its case, but the evidence itself was not without a flaw. The shrill charges of Edward Randolph, accumulating over the years, had not always drawn as sharp a distinction between the record in royal and other colonies as might have been helpful in 1701, when incidentally he had fallen from grace. Penn, at least, had a case to argue and he argued it vigorously.

Only the surrender by the New Jersey proprietors in 1702 of a long-contested right of government saved the Board of Trade from complete defeat. The Jersey proprietors were peculiarly vulnerable. Repeated challenges to their political authority had kept the issue to the fore and linked it with critical questions of imperial administration and defense. By comparison with any rational standard of colonial administration, the proprietorship itself had become a patent absurdity. Daniel Coxe in 1692 had sold the Berkeley-Byllynge claim in West Jersey to no less than forty-eight men (for

---

[26] Hall, *Edward Randolph*, pp. 210–213.

[27] Andrews, *Colonial Period*, IV, 178–221. For a more recent discussion of the customs service, see Barrow, *Trade and Empire*, pp. 48–83.

[28] See especially Charles M. Andrews, *Vice-Admiralty Courts in the Colonies*, a reprint of the introduction to *Records of the Vice-Admiralty Court of Rhode Island, 1716–1752* (Washington, 1936).

the most part not Quakers), who were interested primarily in a return upon the investment made, and the East Jersey proprietors, mostly Quakers, had numbered twenty-four since shortly after the purchase of the Carteret share in 1682. Moreover, the collective judgment of these unwieldy bodies had not been free of serious error. Their choice of Andrew Hamilton in 1692 for the deputy governorship of both provinces had been wise, but Hamilton was a Scotsman whose right to office was called into question by the Navigation Act of 1696. The apprehensive proprietors, on notice by 1697 as were all other proprietors to clean house, replaced Hamilton by Jeremiah Basse, a man of more ambition than of substance and character. Already *persona non grata* in West Jersey as a former agent of the proprietors, his difficulties were further complicated by his failure to win approval of the appointment from the Board of Trade, by the proprietors' decision in the case of East Jersey to revive the old challenge to land titles depending upon grants made by Governor Nicolls of New York, and by revival of the old question of New Jersey's right to have ports free of New York's demand for the payment of customs at New York City.[29] Not even the return of Hamilton to office in 1699, after a favorable ruling on his eligibility by the crown's law officers, could fully repair the damage.

The decision finally was to negotiate for a surrender of what the opposing side described as "pretended" rights of government in return for a renewed assurance as to the proprietorship of the soil. While the settlement was pending, the most interesting suggestion came from Edward Randolph, who proposed that West Jersey be annexed to a royal colony embracing Pennsylvania and the Lower Counties of the Delaware, and that East Jersey be added to New York.[30] The suggestion made a good deal of sense, but Randolph's star was on the wane and the Board of Trade was willing to settle for what it could most readily get. As a result, New Jersey became a royal colony in April, 1702, but without prejudice to the proprietors' title in the land. In the following November, Queen Anne, not surprisingly, designated Lord Cornbury, recently commissioned

---

[29] Andrews, *Colonial Period*, III, 173–181; Pomfret, *West Jersey*, pp. 172–215; *East Jersey*, pp. 308–335; *New Jersey Proprietors and Their Lands*, pp. 58–86; McCormick, *New Jersey from Colony to State*, pp. 34–36.

[30] Pomfret, *West Jersey*, pp. 209–210.

governor of New York, as first of the royal governors.[31] Until 1738 the governor of New York would continue to double as the governor of New Jersey. East Jersey and West Jersey were now united under a single government. Henceforth the distinction between the two would be perpetuated chiefly by cultural and geographical considerations which tended to draw them into the orbits, respectively, of New York and Pennsylvania.

With the surrender of New Jersey's proprietors, only Pennsylvania, Carolina, Connecticut, and Rhode Island, among the North American colonies, remained free of the king's own government. The list of royal colonies might soon have been lengthened, for William Penn, after many disappointments in Pennsylvania, negotiated off and on through several years following 1703 for a possible sale of his rights of government, but with no agreement.[32] When the Calvert family repossessed the government of Maryland in 1715, the list was for a brief time reduced, but this was offset a few years later by the king's purchase of the Carolina proprietorship. Speaking generally, it is not too much to suggest that the English empire in North America would experience, prior to the era of the American Revolution, very little in the way of fundamental change from the character into which it had settled by 1702.

It was an empire of which it ever would have to be said that it lacked consistency in its over-all organization. Two policies only were pursued with anything approaching complete consistency: the trade of the colonies was to be directed into channels intended to strengthen the metropolis of a would-be self-sufficient empire, and each unit in that empire was to meet its own administrative costs. For a considerable period of time after 1660 the unsettled state of England's political life had given comparable importance to the question of whether all Englishmen, wherever they might live, acknowledged the right of the king to rule, and this had been hardly less true of William III than of Charles II. But as the Revolutionary settlement of 1689 stood the test of time, and Queen Anne succeeded William, purely political considerations gave way to those that were basically economic or military. The result was an empire as much characterized by compromise as was any part of England's own Revolutionary settlement.

[31] Boyd, *Fundamental Laws and Constitutions of New Jersey,* pp. 127–154; McCormick, *New Jersey from Colony to State,* pp. 58–63.
[32] Andrews, *Colonial Period,* IV, 395–396.

The most impressive single development of recent years had been the extension of royal authority into the colonies, whether through the customs service, the admiralty courts, or the governors who now presided over most of the provinces by royal commission, but this had been balanced by a new security for the principle of representation in the government of the colonies. Indeed, it was now for the first time that the representative assembly can be said to have become a fixed feature of English colonial administration. Some form of representation, it is true, had been a normal part of government in the colonies for many years past, so much so that the more recent promoters of settlement had adopted the principle almost as a matter of course. But there had been the important exception of New York, and the even more significant experiment with an executive type of administration under the Dominion of New England. The establishment of New York's assembly in 1691, according to the provisions of Governor Sloughter's commission, and the re-establishment of assemblies in the other colonies formerly subordinated to the Dominion, marked a highly significant turn in policy. At no time thereafter did England undertake to govern a colony of Englishmen without provision for a representative assembly.[33]

Moreover, the circumstances shaping this turn in policy provided the firmest kind of foundation for the development of a vigorous tradition of legislative self-government in the colonies. The new policy found expression in no single all-embracing decree of the king. Rather, by his action in individual cases, and in other instances by a virtual failure to act at all, he gave fresh and enduring sanction to a right of representation that the colonists were inclined to view as a long-enjoyed right—a right their recent experience encouraged them to believe stood above the power of a king either to give or to withhold. This was an idea that would grow upon the colonists, and as it grew, it would feed upon the growing tradition of England's own Glorious Revolution.[34]

[33] Leonard W. Labaree, *Royal Government in America: A Study of the British Colonial System before 1783* (New Haven, 1930) , pp. 175–177.

[34] Nor was this connection made only by Americans. Labaree (*ibid.*, p. 176) quotes the Board of Trade's advice in 1756 to Governor Charles Lawrence of Nova Scotia that while there were early precedents for an exercise of legislative power by governor and council, "it was a power of very short duration and in

In still other ways that Revolution was destined to mark a significant turning point in the history of the American legislative assembly. It is not to be assumed, as too many historians seem to have done, that this history is all of one piece. The seventeenth-century assembly had been basically a consultative body, in which the elected delegates were expected to give their consent to what was proposed by the established leadership of the colony, and in normal circumstances usually did. A right to take the initiative had been won by the representatives in most places before the Revolution, but only with Penn's surrender on this issue in 1696 could it be said that the practice was universal. Several of the assemblies had kept the unicameral organization all had had at first, and only in the 1690's did the bicameral become the unmistakable standard, perhaps as much as for any other reason because of a new desire to follow the pattern set by the English Parliament.[35] All of the older assemblies, those having their origins in the first half of the seventeenth century, had exercised broad judicial powers, and especially those belonging to the highest court of appeal. Partly through royal instructions which insisted that appellate jurisdiction inherently belonged to the king, partly through the development of a bicameral organization of the assembly which served to sharpen the distinction between the functions of governor and council when sitting in their judicial and legislative capacities, and partly through the natural tendency toward a sharper differentiation of function by governments presiding over larger and more complex societies, the eighteenth-century assembly was to become one much more accurately described as a *legislative* assembly.[36] For so long, of course, as it held its right of impeachment, or its right to conduct investigations of its own, it would never entirely lose the character of a judicial body.

The parallel between the American assembly and the English

---

later times, since the constitution of this country has been restored to its true principles [that is, since the Revolution of 1689], has never been thought advisable to be executed."

[35] As previously noted (p. 27), the change occurred in Rhode Island in 1696, in Connecticut in 1698. The Commons House of Assembly in South Carolina dates from 1692, but it could be argued that constitutional sanction for this development came only in 1698.

[36] A useful summary discussion is found in Clarke, *Parliamentary Privilege in the American Colonies*, pp. 14–60.

Parliament had been drawn more than once before 1689, and especially in Maryland, where the contest with the proprietor encouraged appeals to the English standard.[37] There and elsewhere the title of speaker had been borrowed for the chief officer of the lower house, but only on the eve of the great Revolution does one notice a new care to observe the familiar parliamentary ritual of presenting the speaker to the governor together with a petition for acknowledgment of the privileges belonging to the house.[38] This is not to say that the elected representatives theretofore had been indifferent to privilege. On the contrary, two privileges especially, freedom from arrest and freedom of speech, seem to have been generally recognized, if only as conditions essential to the conduct of the public business. But there can be no doubt that the well-known inclination of the American representative assembly (whose roots were much more deeply imbedded in the corporate structure of the London business community than in the usages of Westminster) to draw an increasingly close parallel between itself and Parliament belongs much more to the eighteenth century than to the seventeenth.

Why this should be so will be better understood if we pause to consider the full composition of the assembly as it shaped up in the later years of the seventeenth century.[39] So critical was the presence of the elected members to any concept of a *general* assembly, and so important is the power later acquired by the lower house, that the modern student has to be on guard against equating the assembly with what was merely its elective element. Its membership at this time included, first of all, the governor, who everywhere outside Connecticut and Rhode Island, whether the colony be royal or proprietary, represented a superior authority resident in England. His powers included the right to summon, prorogue, and dissolve the assembly, and so to limit severely its control over its own sessions. Quite literally, the governor had a seat in the assembly, for

[37] Andrews, *Colonial Period*, II, 301, 337.

[38] Clarke, *Parliamentary Privilege*, pp. 62–70, finds the first instance in 1677 in Jamaica. The date for Maryland is 1682, for Virginia 1684.

[39] Two general works have great importance for the history of the assembly from this point forward: Labaree, *Royal Government in America*, and Greene, *Quest for Power*. Suggestive are the earlier chapters of J. R. Pole, *Political Representation in England and the Origins of the American Republic* (New York, 1966).

he normally presided over the council when it sat as the upper house of the legislature, just as he did when it was acting in its executive or judicial capacity. He had, of course, a continuing right to propose legislation, and since no bill had the force of law without the governor's approval, he also possessed a veto power, but the usual practice was to bargain from his place in the upper house for laws that were acceptable. The elected representatives, burgesses, or deputies (their designation varied from colony to colony, as did some details of organization and procedure) sat for the towns in New England, and elsewhere for the counties, except that in New York certain manors and boroughs also enjoyed representation, as did an occasional "borough" in other colonies.

To some of these observations Pennsylvania, under the provisions of its famous Charter of Privileges of 1701, became a notable exception. William Penn had returned to his province in 1699, after an absence of fifteen years and with the hope that he might live out his life there. He found his people prosperous, but with their politics still subject to turbulence. Since the death of Thomas Lloyd in 1694, David Lloyd had become the dominant personality in Pennsylvania politics. A shrewd and skillful man, who also possessed a helpful knowledge of the law, his slogan might be stated in a paraphrase of an argument advanced by Penn himself to the Board of Trade, that no man had come to the American wilderness for fewer privileges than he would have enjoyed by staying at home in England.[40] Lloyd, actually a Welshman rather than an Englishman, had made the assembly the chief arena of an opposition to proprietary authority that enlisted for him the support of the more substantial of the colonists. When the presence of Penn, who still enjoyed great prestige among Quakers, and whose re-established influence in England was properly considered to be the colony's chief protection against royal government, tended to upset previously existing alliances, Lloyd further displayed his political gifts by rallying behind him many of the less substantial settlers. Through long years of controversy the main objectives had been well defined.

[40] Penn's actual statement in a letter of December, 1700, as quoted by Nash, "Economics and Politics in Colonial Pennsylvania," p. 314, was as follows: "What is the right of the English subject at home should be allowed here, since more and not less seems the Reasons . . . to Plant this Wilderness." For Lloyd's career, see David Lokken, *David Lloyd, Colonial Lawmaker* (Seattle, 1959) .

What was needed for their achievement was some special opportunity, and that was provided by the Board of Trade's renewed campaign of 1701 to bring all colonies under the direct authority of the king.[41] Penn knew that he would have to return to England, but before he did he settled, none too happily, upon a Charter of Privileges intended partly to protect the colonists against the possibility that the crown might take over, and destined to be regarded thereafter as the palladium of their liberties. In fact, the Liberty Bell, which later rang out the determination of Americans to be fully free of Whitehall's control, originally was cast for celebration of the fiftieth anniversary of Pennsylvania's charter of 1701.

What Penn conceded, above all, was that the council, which, beginning in 1700, had been appointed by the proprietor, would be excluded from the legislative process. Actually, there is some room for debate on this point, for the governor's approval continued to be required for all legislation, and should he consult with the members of his council on the question, the process could be not too greatly different from that followed in other colonies. But in law intent is no small part of the law, and there can be no doubt that the intent was to place the legislative power in the hands of the elected deputies of the people. So far had Pennsylvania moved from the original concept of a people who yielded their consent to laws proposed by their governors. The charter also contained a provision which allowed the Lower Counties to have their own separate legislature, an option they elected to exercise in 1704. Thereafter, although the governor of Pennsylvania continued to act as the governor in the three counties, they were for practical purposes a separate province.[42]

In Pennsylvania, as in all of the colonies now, the franchise in provincial elections depended upon the possession of property. Beginning with 1670 in Virginia and Maryland, the trend had been toward adoption, though with many modifications in detail, of the English freehold qualification, a trend greatly strengthened by developments immediately preceding and following the English

[41] Nash, Chaps. VI and VII; Bronner, William Penn's "Holy Experiment," pp. 207–249; Peare, William Penn, pp. 365–382.

[42] For its anomalous position (it had in fact not even a name), see especially Andrews, Colonial Period, III, 321–326. For the charter of 1701, see Thorpe, Federal and State Constitutions, V, 3076–3081.

Revolution. Special religious qualifications, with all their democratic implications, had given way, except for such as might exclude Catholics and Jews, to property qualifications which generally seem not to have reduced participation by the democratic element of the populace in the political life of the colonies, simply because property, like Godliness, could be widely distributed and was especially so in New England.[43] But this point, seemingly well enough established now, can be seriously misleading with regard to the character of contemporary politics.

Not only did undemocratic conventions continue to govern the electorate's choice of representatives, but power was still very largely centered in the governor's council. Even in the general assembly, the increasing demand by the lower house for a larger voice in the government has been authoritatively interpreted as basically a bid for equality with its opposite number.[44] The members of the council, normally about twelve men, were all appointed, either by royal or proprietary authority, except in Massachusetts, Connecticut, and Rhode Island. Whether elected or appointed, they were consistently representative of the wealthier families in their province, except for the occasional placeman whose appointment spoke more of his influence in London than of any position as yet attained in colonial society.[45] That influence, however, could provide a powerful boost to quick attainment of both wealth and standing for the new immigrant whose helpful connections in London brought an early appointment to the council, as with Caleb Heathcote of New York.[46] The youngest son of an unusually successful ironmonger, and brother to a man who would be among the founders of the Bank of England and lord mayor of London, Heathcote reached New York in 1692 as a disappointed

[43] In addition to McKinley's long-standard work, see Robert E. Brown, *Middle Class Democracy and the Revolution in America, 1691–1780* (Ithaca, 1955); Richard P. McCormick, *The History of Voting in New Jersey: A Study of the Development of Election Machinery, 1664–1911* (New Brunswick, 1953); Chilton Williamson, *American Suffrage: From Property to Democracy, 1760–1860* (Princeton, 1960), pp. 3–19.
[44] Jack P. Greene, "The Role of the Lower House of Assembly in Eighteenth Century Politics," *Journal of Southern History*, XXVII (1961), 451–474.
[45] See especially Leonard W. Labaree, *Conservatism in Early American History* (New York, 1948), pp. 1–31.
[46] See again Dixon Ryan Fox, *Caleb Heathcote.*

suitor and as factor for a number of prosperous London merchants. In 1692, also, he went on the council by appointment of Governor Fletcher, who apparently knew who Heathcote was, and this in about the time it had taken Nathaniel Bacon, Virginia's great rebel, to win the same recognition. When he died in 1721, Heathcote had served on the council for more than twenty-five of his twenty-nine years as a resident of the colony, had accumulated vast properties, and by every test belonged to the circle of New York's ruling families. Conversely, there were men of position in the colonies who managed so to cultivate connections in England as to win for themselves a power that could be extremely embarrassing for the king's own governor, even destructive of his authority. Perhaps it is ever this way in an empire, where authority resides partly in the colony and partly in the dominant metropolis. Certainly, this is true of the old English empire, run as it was on a principle of cheap administrative costs that left to each separate community a large right of self-government by those in the community who could assert, by whatever tactic, their right to govern.

The story in Virginia has a special interest, if only because it is Virginia's story. In contemporary discussion of the government of the colonies, of which there was more than a little and much of which naturally focused attention upon the government of the oldest and largest of the English colonies, one of the chief criticisms was of a dangerous concentration of power in the governor and council.[47] On the first reading, the modern student is inclined to jump at once into a discussion of the historic conflict between governor and burgesses, and there can be little doubt that this criticism has importance in that connection. But such observations on the constitution of government can be safely interpreted only in the light of current political contests, and the historic conflicts of this era in Virginia were between the governor and certain members

47 See especially Hunter D. Farish (ed.), *The Present State of Virginia, and the College,* by Henry Hartwell, James Blair, and Edward Chilton (Williamsburg, 1940). Written in 1697, this work was first published in 1727. Both Hartwell and Blair had been members of the Virginia council. Chilton had been attorney general. Blair was in London at the time for the purpose of securing the removal of Sir Edmund Andros. The same argument is made in *An Essay upon the Government of the English Plantations,* of which Robert Beverley was the probable author. See also Beverley's *History* of 1705.

of his council. Indeed, in the most famous of them all the burgesses sided with the governor.

One man dominates the story. He was James Blair, an Anglican clergyman of Scottish birth who settled in Virginia in 1685 and subsequently displayed an extraordinary talent for getting rid of governors he could not control. Blair's very great power came originally from the backing he received from Henry Compton, Bishop of London, one of the Lords of Trade, and later one of the *ex officio* members of the Board of Trade. Compton was the first Bishop of London to take seriously a responsibility for the church in the colonies that tradition seems to have assigned to his diocese, and it was at his urging that Blair had settled in Virginia. Four years afterward, in 1689, Blair was made the bishop's commissary by the first appointment in the colonies to an office carrying a general supervisory authority over church and clergy, though considerably less than full episcopal powers.[48] That appointment made Blair a man to be reckoned with by any governor of Virginia, for the commissary had a direct line of communication with the bishop, for whom many avenues to the seats of power lay open. More than that, the Blair-Compton alliance, if it may be so baldly described, represented the first stirring of a new missionary impulse within the Church of England that would lead to the organization in 1701 of the Society for the Propagation of the Gospel in Foreign Parts. Freed at last from its long contest with nonconformity in England, and having conceded to Protestant dissent through the Act of Toleration nothing more than toleration, the church was turning its attention after a long delay to the colonies. No political leader in America, whatever his ambition, could ignore the potent implication of this simple fact for his own fortunes.

Among those who read the signs rightly, at least on his first attempt, was Francis Nicholson, who scored a brilliant triumph during his administration as the lieutenant governor of Virginia from 1690 to 1692 by helping to found the College of William and Mary, which promised to become a seminary that would greatly strengthen the church throughout the Chesapeake settlements.

48 On the office, see Cross, *Anglican Episcopate*, pp. 3–4. This study provides much information on the activities of Compton, whose full career can be followed in Edward F. Carpenter's *The Protestant Bishop, Being the Life of Henry Compton, 1632–1713, Bishop of London* (London, 1956).

Blair, who was a leader in the project, was sent to England on a successful mission to win support from the king and queen, and became the first president of the college.[49] After Sir Edmund Andros succeeded to the governorship of Virginia in 1692, Nicholson was transferred to Maryland, where he had an opportunity further to strengthen his reputation as a patron of religion and learning while helping to keep the authorities in Westminster alert to the shortcomings of Quaker Pennsylvania, an old and generally successful rival of Maryland. In 1698, Blair and Compton picked Nicholson to succeed Andros as the governor of Virginia.[50] There had been a bitter quarrel between Sir Edmund and Commissary Blair, partly because the new authority of the Bishop of London's representative clashed with the quasi-episcopal powers the governor of Virginia had acquired in the absence of a resident bishop, and as a result Blair had been suspended from his seat on the council and restored to it on orders from London.[51] By the end of 1697 Blair had gone himself to London, where he forced Sir Edmund's removal despite the support given the governor by William Byrd II, then also in London.[52]

Blair had first taken his seat as a member of council in 1694. His appointment came directly from the king, on an assumption that the church should have representation there, an assumption that may also have helped to terminate a second suspension resulting from a question as to whether he had been disqualified as a Scotsman by the Navigation Act of 1696.[53] Although Blair clearly owed his place on the council to London's persistence in keeping him there, he was by no means lacking in qualifications of his own as a Virginian. In 1687 he had married the daughter of Benjamin Harrison II, a rising merchant-planter who later became a member

[49] Morton, *Colonial Virginia*, I, 336–341; the basic documents are in Edgar W. Knight, *A Documentary History of Education in the South before 1860* (5 vols., Chapel Hill, N.C., 1949–53), I, 368–441.

[50] Morton, *Colonial Virginia*, I, 356–357.

[51] *Ibid.*, I, 350.

[52] *Ibid.*, I, 351; Cross, *Anglican Episcopate*, p. 43; Louis B. Wright, "William Byrd's Defense of Sir Edmund Andros," *William and Mary Quarterly*, 3d. ser., II (1945), 47–62; Knight, *Documentary History of Education*, I, 442–470.

[53] Farish, *Present State of Virginia*, pp. xxiv, 37, 39; Andrews, *Colonial Period*, IV, 168 n. The action of governor and council was reversed by the Board of Trade and its decision was upheld by the attorney general in 1699.

of council, who married another of his daughters to the younger Philip Ludwell, future member of council, and whose own son Benjamin Harrison III married the daughter of Colonel Lewis Burwell, member of council. In other words, Blair had gained entry into a newly forming circle of great families, increasingly interlocked by marriage, that was destined to dominate Virginia's political life through many years thereafter. By 1703, when Blair was bitterly quarreling with Nicholson, the commissary sat in council with his father-in-law and a brother-in-law, and two other brothers-in-law were influential members of the lower house.[54] It is not intended to suggest that Blair controlled the council, which seems consistently to have supported Andros against the commissary and was perhaps evenly divided in the dispute with Nicholson. The point is that when Blair went to London, and he happened to be there on the occasion of every change of administration in the colony for fifteen years after the English Revolution, he increasingly could speak for some of the more powerfully situated men in Virginia.

Nicholson began his second term as head of administration in Virginia late in 1698. For a time, although the quarrel began quite early, he and the commissary worked toward certain common ends, chiefly in reaching a decision of 1699 fulfilling Blair's desire to have the seat of government transferred from the recently burned out Jamestown to Middle Plantation, where the College was already located and where the city of Williamsburg was subsequently raised.[55] Nicholson, who seems to have had a quick temper, no doubt contributed by his own indiscretions to the extraordinary indictment brought against him in the spring of 1703 by Blair and five other members of the council, including Benjamin Harrison and Philip Ludwell, but it is difficult to believe that any man could have been guilty of all the sins charged here against the governor.[56]

54 Morton, *Colonial Virginia*, I, 380; and for an account of the Harrison family, Clifford Dowdey, *The Great Plantation: A Profile of Berkeley Hundred and Plantation Virginia, from Jamestown to Appomattox* (New York, 1957). On the more general subect of Virginia's ruling aristocracy, see Labaree, *Conservatism in Colonial America*, Chap. I; and Louis B. Wright, *The First Gentlemen of Virginia: Intellectual Qualities of the Early Colonial Ruling Class* (San Marino, Calif., 1940; Charlottesville, 1964), pp. 38–62.

55 Morton, *Colonial Virginia*, I, 357–361.

56 "A Memorial Concerning the Maladministration of His Excellency Francis Nicholson" is conveniently consulted in Merrill Jensen (ed.), *English Historical*

So comprehensive and unqualified was this bill of particulars that it can be trusted only as evidence of a bitter struggle between Nicholson and a part of his council for control of the government.

Obviously, a principal source of the difficulty was a constitutional question arising from the fact that historically the governor and council had been joined together in a common commission, originally because the early adventurers dared not leave their enterprise entirely dependent upon the judgment of a single man. So far did Virginia's experience as the first of the royal colonies give shape to the commissions issued to other royal governors that this problem was in no sense peculiar to Virginia.[57] The trouble now was that increasingly long and specific instructions from the Board of Trade to the royal governor seemed to give him a new independence of his council.[58] It is significant that Nicholson's enemies charged him with a refusal to show his instructions, even in council, that they condemned him for attempts to represent his own side of the quarrel in London without the concurrence of the council, and that they complained that he had used the friendly agencies of men outside Virginia to build up his credit with the home government. Of very great historical interest is the further complaint that the governor sought to overawe the council when sitting with it as the upper house of the legislature, and the demand made that he be excluded from all such sessions.[59] And of even greater historical interest is the fact that Nicholson won and held in this bitter contest a clear majority in the House of Burgesses.

Perhaps it was because, as charged, the governor took care in the appointment of sheriffs, justices of the peace, and clerks of court to cause men at the county level of administration to look to him for patronage. Perhaps it was because the burgesses were jealous of the profitable offices and other privileges members of council had long

---

Documents: American Colonial Documents to 1776 (New York, 1955), pp. 254–260. For the original date, see Morton, Colonial Virginia, I, 381. The memorial was signed in addition by Robert Carter, John Lightfoot, and Mathew Page.

[57] A useful discussion of this general problem is found in Evarts B. Greene, The Provincial Governor of the English Colonies of North America (New York, 1898), pp. 80 ff.

[58] Labaree, Royal Government, pp. 31–33, 95–97, which shows that Nicholson was within his rights and the problem general.

[59] A demand ultimately to be successful in most of the colonies.

enjoyed.[60] Perhaps it was because so many of the burgesses were vestrymen in their own parishes, and so suspicious that Commissary Blair intended to upset a control by the vestry over the clergy that made the Virginia church virtually congregational in its basic organization. Certainly, Blair had proposed change for the benefit of the church that challenged the accustomed usages of virtually every local authority which consistently found representation in the lower house.[61] It is also significant that the majority of the clergy, unaccustomed to episcopal interference, also supported the governor.[62] Perhaps Nicholson owed his success to the skill and tact he had shown in courting the support of the burgesses. The mace and gown he presented to the newly elected speaker in December, 1700, are small details, but they are not to be overlooked by anyone who would understand the growing sense the lower house had of its own dignity and authority.[63] In any contest between governor and council the elected element of the general assembly could be invited, and by either party to the dispute, to arbitrate the difference.

Blair, who in 1703 evidently had full support from only half the councillors, and who may have anticipated Nicholson's success with the burgesses, soon sailed a third time for England, there to press for Nicholson's recall. Interestingly, it took him until 1705 to accomplish his purpose. The queen referred the charges back to the governor for reply, and he laid the question before the House of Burgesses, which in the spring of 1705 by a vote of 27 to 18 registered its confidence in Nicholson, and afterward adopted by a vote of 27 to 17 the following resolution: "That whoever pretends to take upon himself to represent the country in general under any grievance or pressure without the consent and authority of this house so to do is thereby guilty of an unwarrantable act tending to the prejudice of the country."[64] It is an extraordinarily significant resolution, but it came too late. Nicholson already had been

---

[60] For contemporary evidence of how extensive these were, see Farish, *Present State of Virginia*, pp. 34–37.

[61] Especially, Samuel C. McCulloch, "James Blair's Plan of 1699 to Reform the Clergy of Virginia," *William and Mary Quarterly*, 3d. ser., IV (1947), 70–86.

[62] Morton, *Colonial Virginia*, I, 385–387.

[63] *Ibid.*, I, 371.

[64] *Ibid.*, I, 383–384.

replaced, for the ultimate power lay in London and Councillor Blair had been able finally to swing the weight he needed there.

Virginia was by no means the only colony to find its political life newly agitated by questions turning on the claims of the Church of England. In nearby Maryland, for one, the issue of an Anglican establishment was under debate, often heated, for a full decade after 1692, when Lionel Copley took office as the first royal governor. Although the Revolution in Maryland had been a distinct triumph for Protestants, the Protestant majority was far from united, even in its attitude toward the revolution that had occurred. It is impossible to speak in any but the most general terms regarding the religious affiliations of the people. Many doubtless were nominal Anglicans in the sense that they had no fixed allegiance to one of the dissenting sects or to the Roman Catholic Church, but an Anglican minister had reported to Canterbury in 1676 that there were only three Anglican priests in the entire province. Baltimore himself had replied to a subsequent request for information by declaring that three-fourths of his people were Presbyterian, Independents, Anabaptists, and Quakers, which at this time in English history was to say little more than that they were a varied assortment of dissenters.[65] The Quakers, who so often found a ready response to their missionary efforts in colonial communities deprived of adequate provision for organized religious life, had made great progress in Maryland, so much as probably to make of the Friends not only the largest dissenting sect in Maryland by the 1690's but also one of the largest Quaker communities in North America outside the Delaware Valley.[66] The Quakers were to be the most persistent opponents of an Anglican establishment.

Governor Copley, of course, was an Anglican, and his instructions, modeled after those previously issued to other royal governors, called upon him to advance the interests of the church. The members of his council may have been all Anglican, or at least nominally Anglican. In their selection, care had been observed to avoid the extremes. The members had been picked from suggestions

[65] George Petrie, *Church and State in Early Maryland* (Baltimore, 1892), pp. 37–45; Mereness, *Maryland as a Proprietary Province*, pp. 436–437.

[66] In addition to Jones, *Quakers in the American Colonies*, see Kenneth L. Carroll, "Maryland Quakers in the Seventeenth Century," *Maryland Historical Magazine*, XLVII (1952), 297–313, and his discussion of Quakerism in Talbot County, *ibid.*, LIII (1958), 326–370.

made by Copley himself, by Lord Baltimore (it must be remembered that only his rights of government were in suspension), by London merchants trading with the Chesapeake, and by Marylanders who happened at the time to be in London, of whom Captain John Hammond, a Maryland merchant, seems to have been the most influential. Only one of the new council could have been suspected of a Catholic identification, and he actually was an Anglican convert. Neither Coode nor Cheseldyne, agents for the provisional government in Maryland, made the list, but their colleague, Nehemiah Blackiston, did, perhaps because as a collector of customs in Maryland he was known to the English authorities. Those authorities seem to have been anxious above all to choose men of substance who were loyal to William and Mary, and who by their geographical location would give the new government a broad representation of all sections of the province. The result was a council made up for the most part of men who had migrated to Maryland since midcentury, or the sons of such immigrants, men relatively free of identification with the bitter disputes which previously had divided the province, men not so much marked by the offices they formerly had held as by the economic success they had achieved in what undoubtedly has been, down through the generations, the first objective of any emigrant to America.[67] In short, they were men who had prospered in a new society and were ready to identify themselves with a new order.

That members of the council should have supported an act of establishment is not surprising. The question is why the lower house, which was gaining new stature and influence now through the advantages it could claim from the general practices of the king's government in America,[68] went along three times, first in 1692. One thinks immediately of the inclination many men must have felt in 1692 to co-operate with a political regime which promised a quick restoration of stability to the colony. It has to be remembered also that the Anglican Church was Protestant, whatever else it might be, and that its establishment could be viewed as

[67] In this paragraph I am especially indebted to David W. Jordan, "The Royal Period of Colonial Maryland, 1689–1715" (unpublished Ph.D. dissertation, Princeton University, 1966).

[68] See especially the second chapter of Mereness, *Maryland as a Proprietary Province*.

a safeguard against a return to power by Catholics.[69] Even more important, and not merely for Maryland, may have been the response men felt to the promise that an establishment would help to provide more adequately for the religious life of the people. It too often is forgotten that the dissenters settling in America during the seventeenth century very largely represented sects having little ability to provide over time for the spiritual leadership of their widely scattered flocks. The New England Congregationalists and the Quakers were the exceptions, not the rule. In colony after colony there is evidence that many communities lived without a minister to baptize the child, marry the couple, or provide at the graveside the comfort of religious ritual.[70] In such communities, as the history of the American frontier repeatedly testifies, men either become indifferent to religious concerns or come to assume that any church is better than no church at all.

Certainly, the final act of establishment in Maryland was preceded by concrete evidence that the church might greatly enrich the spiritual resources of the province. This was the work of Thomas Bray, founder of the Society for the Propagation of the Gospel, as also of the earlier Society for the Promotion of Christian Knowledge which had as its main aim the provision of parish libraries for the assistance of local priests, whether in England or the colonies. Indeed, the origin of each of these influential societies could be traced, if one wished to narrow the considerations which gave them shape, to the enlistment of Bray by Bishop Compton in 1695 as commissary in Maryland.[71] That colony's initial act of establishment, after vigorous protest from the Catholics and the Quakers, had been disallowed by the king on technical grounds. Francis Nicholson, who had succeeded the deceased Copley in 1694, and who as a founder of the college in Virginia had helped to

[69] Catholics were promptly disqualified for office by a test act, but they held the franchise until well into the eighteenth century. Osgood, *American Colonies in the Eighteenth Century*, II, 12. The Quakers were denied seats in the first royal assembly because of their refusal of the oath. *Ibid.*, I, 360.

[70] Much of the evidence has an Anglican bias, as with John Miller's *New York Considered and Improved* of 1695 (edited by Victor H. Paltsits, Cleveland, 1903), but it is nonetheless impressive. Nor did the Revolution improve the capacity of dissenting sects in England to offer assistance. See Carl Bridenbaugh, *Mitre and Sceptre: Transatlantic Faiths, Ideas, Personalities, and Politics, 1689–1775* (New York, 1962), pp. 32–36.

[71] H. P. Thompson, *Thomas Bray* (London, 1954) is particularly helpful.

provide impressive evidence of what the church might accomplish, managed to push through a second act of establishment in 1696. Once more the Quakers, who never seemed to lack connections in London that could help make their wishes known to the government, protested and after three years were again successful in winning a disallowance on technical grounds. It was policy, however, to assume that an act not yet disallowed had force, and so the work of building up the new establishment went forward, aided chiefly by the inspired enthusiasm of Commissary Bray. Although Bray himself did not come to Maryland until 1700, he met there in the spring of that year with seventeen Anglican clergymen, most of them undoubtedly recent recruits to his own missionary zeal.[72] He had sent his first parish library, of better than a thousand volumes, to Maryland in 1696 for the new capital town of Annapolis, and others followed.[73] He remained in Maryland only a short time, and returned to England. He helped to shape the final act of establishment adopted in 1702, several years after Nathaniel Blakiston had succeeded the departed Nicholson. In this act Bray got considerably less than he desired, and its final enactment depended upon significant concessions to opponents of the establishment. Among other provisions, the act assured to every dissenter the benefit of the English Act of Toleration and freed the Quakers from a former political disability by allowing them to substitute an affirmation for the standard oath.[74] Bray never returned to Maryland, or even to America, but his influence continued to be felt there, if only because of the role he played in the organization of the S.P.G. in 1701.

Among those in England who followed this development with interest were the Carolina proprietors. They had escaped the close scrutiny to which William Penn's record had been subjected in 1696 and 1697, partly because of the circumstances which had made of

[72] For evidence of his recruiting activity between 1695 and 1701, the year of the S.P.G.'s founding, see John Clement's data in *The Historical Magazine of the Protestant Episcopal Church*, XVI (1947) , 318–349.

[73] For the not inconsiderable bibliography on Bray's famous libraries, in the distribution of which Maryland was especially favored, see Louis B. Wright, *Cultural Life of the American Colonies*, pp. 263–264.

[74] Mereness, *Maryland as a Proprietary Province*, pp. 437–440; Osgood, *American Colonies in the Eighteenth Century*, II, 11–14. Reference can be made also to Nelson W. Rightmyer, *Maryland's Established Church* (Baltimore, 1956) .

Penn the chief target, and partly because they had taken steps to heal the factional divisions which for a decade past had troubled the Charles Town settlement. In 1694 John Archdale, in effect one of the proprietors, for he still sat with the board in behalf of his son, had been commissioned as governor. Taking office in 1695, he won the assembly's agreement in the next year to a compromise settlement of long-standing differences between the colonists and the proprietors, in which questions of land policy were of critical importance, through what came to be known as Archdale's Laws.[75] That the proprietors only eight years later should have invited a return of factional strife by raising the religious issue, and this at a time when the new war had subjected the colony to peculiar pressures, may be attributable to their sensitive regard for every interest which might affect the attitude of the English government toward the "private" colonies. Perhaps it was merely that the palatine court was headed at the turn of the century by Lord Granville, a zealous Anglican.

The elevation to the governor's post in 1703 of Sir Nathaniel Johnson, a former governor of the Leeward Islands who had migrated to Carolina in 1689, gave warning of what was to come. In 1704 the assembly enacted a statute excluding dissenters from its membership and another providing for an Anglican establishment. The dissenters, who may have been outnumbered by those who were at least nominally Anglican but had more houses of worship than did the Anglicans, bitterly protested and rightly charged grave irregularities in the enactment of the legislation. John Ash, sent to London as agent, failed to persuade the proprietors, but after his death Joseph Boone, who replaced him, won the ear of the House of Lords and stirred up such a fuss that the Board of Trade was encouraged to believe that an opportunity to secure annulment of the proprietary charter was at hand.[76] The details are too many and too complicated for narration here. In the end the proprietors did not lose their charter, the objections to the statutes of 1704 were sustained by them on order from the queen, and revised legislation of 1706, which among other changes eliminated membership in the Church of England as a test for office, permanently established the

75 Sirmans, *Colonial South Carolina*, pp. 61–64.
76 *Ibid.*, pp. 75–89; Andrews, *Colonial Period*, III, 241–245.

church in colonial South Carolina. It was a church whose preeminence was not only sanctioned by statute but which drew upon provincial revenues for its support. Increasingly, the great families —those who enjoyed wealth, social position, and political power— would be identified with it, including more than a few of the Huguenots. Its parishes, provided for in the act of 1706, would be the only local units of government to experience significant development at any time before the very eve of the American Revolution.[77]

As would be expected, the story in North Carolina is somewhat different. The Albemarle and Charles Town settlements had never had much in common except for such influences as flowed from their subordination to the same proprietors. Settled very largely by Virginians, North Carolina remained in most essentials a projection of the Chesapeake community. Not only did its economy depend upon the tobacco grown on widely scattered farms, but it had not a single town that so much as promised to provide the leadership and control Charles Town already had asserted in the life of South Carolina. There the counties established by the proprietors in the 1680's had experienced no real development as agencies of local government, and they were soon even to surrender their function as electoral units to the newly established parishes, but in North Carolina precinct courts of resident magistrates were on the way to becoming county courts essentially very similar to those serving Virginia and Maryland.[78] In its religious life, North Carolina had much more in common with Maryland than with Virginia, for Virginia's church had lacked the resources to follow its people into Carolina, and Quaker missionaries had found there a ready response to their preaching. As a result the proprietors' proposal for a church establishment precipitated, as in Maryland, a bitter contest with the Quakers, one that postponed a final settlement in favor of the church to 1711.[79] The defeat sustained by the dissenters at that

77 Wallace, *South Carolina*, pp. 68–74; Davidson, *Establishment of the English Church*, pp. 58–66; and McCrady, *History*, pp. 402–449, which, though somewhat dated, contains additional detail. The parish became in 1716 the electoral unit in elections for the Commons House of Assembly.

78 See especially Paul M. McCain, *The County Court in North Carolina before 1750* (Durham, N.C., 1954).

79 Davidson, *Establishment of the English Church*, pp. 47–57; Lefler and Newsom, *North Carolina*, pp. 52–55.

time was anything but complete. Their resistance continued, and North Carolina's establishment was never to acquire the strength of South Carolina's.

Much earlier, the sorely divided province of New York had found yet another subject of bitter contention in Governor Fletcher's proposals for an Anglican establishment. The tragic sequel to New York's "rebellion" of 1689 had restored to power the enemies of Jacob Leisler, for the most part great merchants and landholders who after 1691 were firmly entrenched in the governor's council and who, by one device or another, managed to control four of the five assemblies meeting between 1691 and 1698. Except for Peter Schuyler, who from 1692 sat for the Albany region, the members of council resided in the southern part of the province.[80] Fletcher perhaps had no choice but to enter into an alliance with the anti-Leislerian faction, which upriver included also Robert Livingston, but the governor cemented the alliance by carrying his full share in its conversion into what is accurately enough described as a corrupt bargain. To mention only one area of collaboration, this was the time when New York had fastened upon it the manorial system of land grants which so largely shaped its economic, social, and political history in the eighteenth century. All told, the English governors of New York made a total of nineteen manor grants within the present bounds of the state, the last by Governor Cornbury in 1704 to Rensselaerswyck, the sole survivor of the Dutch experiment with the patroonship. Of these nineteen grants, seven were made by Benjamin Fletcher, and five of the seven went to members of his original council.[81] If the governor needed in this and other ways to court the support of the anti-Leislerians, they in turn needed whatever support might be had from Whitehall. Their enemies in the colony were by no means inconsequential men. They were men who had the means and the connections needed to get a hearing in London. Perhaps Fletcher's cronies were anxious to

[80] McAnear, "Politics in Provincial New York," remains an indispensable overall account, but see also Osgood, *American Colonies in the Eighteenth Century*, I, 237–265; and Leder, *Robert Livingston*, pp. 77–128.

[81] For a convenient listing, see Harry C. W. Melick, *The Manor of Fordham and Its Founder* (New York, 1950), pp. ix–x. Only five such grants had been made before Dongan, who added five more, the first in 1686. No less than twelve of the nineteen grants were made by Dongan and Fletcher over the period extending from March, 1686, to September, 1697.

build up their own credit there when in 1693 they helped to put through the governor's proposal for an Anglican establishment in New York.

The population of the colony outside Long Island was still predominantly Dutch, and the majority of its English inhabitants had a Puritan heritage. Little wonder that the proposed establishment was restricted to four counties, all situated within the immediate environs of New York City. Even in that limited area the law's provisions for the creation of parishes, election of vestries, and collection of church rates for the support of "good and sufficient Protestant ministers" became bones of contention when vestries with dissenting majorities undertook to give the advantage to nonconforming clergymen. In New York City, Governor Fletcher's insistence won appointment for his own chaplain as rector, and subsequently, in 1697, a special charter of incorporation gave to the Anglicans of the city a vestry of their own. A lease of land in lower Manhattan, later confirmed as an outright grant by Queen Anne, guaranteed Trinity Parish a fabulous future.[82] Very largely through the enterprise of Caleb Heathcote, manor lord of Scarsdale after 1702, the church, with the aid of the S.P.G., of which Heathcote became a member, made progress in the towns of Westchester County.[83] But the Anglican Church in colonial New York remained a very small denomination, drawing its main strength from the sponsorship of the royal governor and the inclination ambitious men repeatedly showed to make the king's church their own.

In its earlier years not even the governor could be counted upon for unfailing support. Fletcher's sponsorship of the church had tied it to the fortunes of a regime ultimately brought under serious indictment before the home government for its corruption. When Lord Bellomont replaced Fletcher in 1698, the Leislerians, who had identified themselves with the dissenting resistance to an establishment, were the new governor's natural allies. Moreover, he himself had played a part in the action of the English parliament which won for Jacob Leisler and some of the more important of his

82 Osgood, *American Colonies in the Eighteenth Century*, II, 14–17; Davidson, *Establishment of the English Church*, pp. 39–46; John A. Dix, *A History of the Parish of Trinity Church in the City of New York* (5 vols., New York, 1898–1950), of which Vol. I covers the colonial period.
83 Fox, *Caleb Heathcote*, pp. 195–233.

supporters a belated escape from the taint of treason. Lord Bellomont showed no inclination to push the interest of the Church,
thereby undoubtedly identifying his administration with the great
majority of the colonists.[84]

But this was not an age in which majorities held control. The
governor was soon in conflict with a council still dominated by
Leisler's enemies, who also won the election for Bellomont's first
assembly, apparently because he forgot the central role of the sheriff
in an English election and so neglected to replace Fletcher's sheriffs.
An early dissolution of the assembly, the appointment of new
sheriffs, and a fresh election brought a resounding victory for the
Leislerians. It was not too difficult to get rid of some of the more
violent of the anti-Leislerians on the council, because of their
obvious identification with Fletcher's sins. Others, including
Stephen Van Cortlandt, were becoming moderates in the sense that
time, or the desire for continuing preferment, was softening an old
bitterness. Cortlandt's brother-in-law, Robert Livingston, one of
Leisler's most bitter enemies, who had quarreled also with Fletcher,
was now brought onto the council. Perhaps he too should be viewed
as a moderate, a man willing to forget. Perhaps it was only the
desire he had to protect the profitable contracts he held for supply
of the Albany garrison.[85]

Several more years would pass before it could be said that New
York had escaped the consequences of its tragic experience at the
time of the Revolution. The death of Lord Bellomont in 1701
brought to the colony as his successor Edward Hyde, Lord Cornbury, who courted the support of the anti-Leislerians and backed
the Anglicans in a continuing quarrel with the dissenters.[86] Probably the most unscrupulous governor New York has had, Cornbury
helped to prolong the bitterness which had disturbed the colony's
political life for more than a decade. Even so, there had come with
Lord Bellomont a promise that the division need not remain hard
and fast for all time, and time was soon to make the promise good.

It may be that the foregoing pages have placed too much stress
upon the religious issue, but it would be hard to overemphasize its

---

[84] In addition to McAnear, see Osgood, *American Colonies in the Eighteenth
Century,* II, 19.
[85] *Ibid.,* I, 272–286; Leder, *Robert Livingston,* pp. 102–140.
[86] Bridenbaugh, *Mitre and Sceptre,* pp. 119–124.

importance for the political history of the period, or to find a more
ready way of illustrating the interaction between distantly separated centers of political power in the post-Revolution empire.
Moreover, the religious issue was as much political as it was
religious. For a people very largely identified with a tradition of
religious dissent, or else grown accustomed to freedom from traditional ecclesiastical controls, the new activity of the church stirred
fear of an old alliance of civil and ecclesiastical power, a fear made
the greater because of early proposals for an Anglican bishop to be
resident in the colonies.[87] Even in Anglican Virginia there was
strong and effective resistance to the intrusion of episcopal authority,[88] and elsewhere an act of establishment might become
acceptable only through inclusion of fresh guarantees for the right
of religious dissent. As a result the English Act of Toleration
acquired an importance for the colonists it otherwise might not
have had, among other places even in New England. There was no
attempt to establish the Church of England there, but the great
influence it held in Whitehall, the obvious connection between that
fact and the power that might be asserted by the royal governor in
Massachusetts, plus early indications that the newly awakened
evangelical zeal of the church might be directed chiefly against
colonial dissenters, caused many of the Puritan leaders, for the
protection of their own peculiar establishment, to profess their
acceptance of the Act of Toleration [89] It would be some time yet
before Puritan New England became truly tolerant of dissent from
its own religious order, and the same point can be made in the case
of Virginia, where in 1699 the Assembly gave the Act of Toleration
a place in the laws of that province.[90] Each of them, nevertheless,
had taken a significant step toward abandonment of an old and
cardinal principle of public policy.

One more comment belongs to the efforts made at this time to
establish the Anglican Church, and that is for the testimony they
bear to an extraordinary range of legislative competence conceded
by imperial authority to the colonial assembly. It was fully in

---

87 *Ibid.*, pp. 25–27, 57–59; Cross, *Anglican Episcopate,* pp. 88–101.

88 See especially Blair's report of limitations imposed upon the commissary in
Cross, *Anglican Episcopate,* pp. 43–44.

89 See especially Miller, *Colony to Province,* pp. 164–168.

90 Morton, *Colonial Virginia,* I, 388.

keeping with English precedent, of course, that religious policy should be determined by parliamentary action, but that precisely is the point. Despite the great power held by the church in England, the pressure exerted upon the colonists in its behalf fell short of an attempt to dictate, except for the demand that its presence in all colonies be tolerated.

An equally impressive illustration of how far such concessions of legislative competence might be carried is found in a substantial body of legislation affecting the judiciary, which historically had in England a special identification with the royal prerogative. That the king might insist upon his prerogative in the administration of colonial justice had been indicated more than once before the Revolution. As early as 1661, instructions to the governor of Jamaica had restricted the establishment of courts to ordinances issued by governor and council. Very early in the long contest with Massachusetts, acknowledgment of a right of appeal to the king had become a critical test of that colony's loyalty. Also to be recalled is the denial of a right in the general assembly to interpose its authority as an appellate court between the king and his colonial subjects, a restriction which carried past the Revolution to become a permanent feature of policy.[91] These developments suggest the possibility that King William might have insisted upon direct control by the crown of all questions affecting the administration of justice. Instead he conceded, in the Massachusetts charter of 1691, the authority of the General Court to establish courts of law, both superior and inferior. Laws enacted for that purpose seem to have been subjected to closer scrutiny in England than were others, but mainly to make sure that the right of final appeal to the king was duly protected. Perhaps their ultimate approval owed something to the care New England's legislators took to bring their courts, even in such minor details as the employment of justice of the peace for the designation of a local magistrate, into closer conformity with English models.[92]

91 See again Clarke, *Parliamentary Privilege in the American Colonies*, Chap. I.
92 Joseph H. Smith (ed.), *Colonial Justice in Western Massachusetts (1639–1702): The Pynchon Court Record* (Cambridge, Mass., 1961), especially pp. 82–88; and the introductions by Neal W. Allen, Jr., to *The Court Records of York County, Maine, Province of Massachusetts Bay, November, 1692–January, 1710–11* (Portland, 1958), and by John T. Farrell to *The Superior Court Diary of William Samuel Johnson, 1772–1773* . . . (Washington, 1942).

The instruction of 1661 found new life in the case of New Jersey, where after 1702 the governor and council insisted upon an exclusive power to establish courts of law. But more representative is the fate of a Virginia statute of 1705 for the regulation of the courts which was at first disallowed and then allowed on nothing more than the assembly's assurance that no invasion of the royal prerogative had been intended.[93]

That action points perhaps as clearly as could any other incident to the final and essential character of the Revolutionary settlement in America. The government of England, though guided as much by considerations of expediency as by any well-conceived plan of imperial control, had conceded no part of its claim to ultimate authority that might deny it a right to some more vigorous assertion of the claim at a later time. Nor had the colonists, for their part, bothered to challenge directly the principle that ultimate authority belonged to Whitehall. What had been won (possibly the word should be preserved) was the practical right of the colonists to determine very largely for themselves questions of public policy fundamentally affecting their domestic life. In this large measure of self-government the colonists were to find with time good cause for remembering the Revolution as a glorious one and, by remembering it, fresh and potent defenses for their rights of self-government.

---

[93] Labaree, *Royal Government in America*, pp. 373–404; Greene, *Quest of Power*, pp. 332–335.

CHAPTER 9

Toward the Eighteenth Century

B Y the strict accounting of chronology, the eighteenth century
had its beginning very close to the time at which King William
died and Queen Anne succeeded him on the English throne. But
neither the reigns of kings nor the rounded numbers that have become so congenial to the modern mind serve quite so well for the
periodization of history as do other considerations, including those
arising from the fact that wars frequently have marked especially
significant turning points in the history of a people. Certainly, the
Treaty of Utrecht, in 1713, which for the first time since 1688
brought the English colonists in North America to an extended
period of freedom from the uncertainties imposed by European warfare, provides a more logical terminal point for the present discussion than does any intervening development that might be
selected. Even so, there may be some advantage in pausing, just on
the eve of Queen Anne's War, for a brief survey of the colonial
scene, if only for the purpose of giving the war its rightful place as
the climactic event in our story.

During nearly a century of pioneering effort, the English colonists
had established for themselves an unbroken possession of the coast-
line extending from Maine to South Carolina. There was no
unbroken line of settlement, of course, and the gap of several
hundred miles separating the Albemarle community in North
Carolina from Charles Town was especially impressive. Nor did the
settled area extend far inland, except along the rivers, which above

the Chesapeake generally had led the colonists northward and which below the Susquehannah invited him to move westward across the Piedmont toward the mountains. But as yet hardly more than the first steps had been taken into the Piedmont, where after the war the Virginians would take great strides westward.[1] As in Virginia, so in Maryland settlement along the Potomac had been extended little if any distance beyond the fall line.[2] In Pennsylvania the colonists still lived close to the Delaware, and in New York, where the Mohawk Valley offered as easy a natural route westward as was to be found anywhere in the colonies, Schenectady marked for all practical purposes the westward limit of settlement, just as it had in 1664.[3] Albany continued to guard the northern perimeter along the Hudson, as did the stockaded town of Deerfield on the Connecticut. Even after the conquest of Nova Scotia in 1710 had brought a new security for thinly manned outposts in lower Maine, that part of the coast was extremely slow to fill up.[4] Similarly, on the far southern frontier an expanding cattle industry carried now the chief hope that the area actually occupied by the English could be extended to Port Royal, where the Carolina proprietors at first had hoped to build Charles Town.[5]

To a remarkable extent the boundaries thus roughly delineated had been staked out by the original settlers, or at the latest by their sons. What has been said above for the year 1701 could be easily adapted to meet the need for such a description at any time

[1] See Herman R. Fries, "A Series of Population Maps of the Colonies and the United States, 1625–1790," *Geographical Review*, XXX (1940), 463–470. The first distinctly Piedmont counties, in the sense that they lay largely beyond the fall line, to be organized in Virginia were Spotsylvania and Hanover, both created in 1720, and much of the latter actually lay east of the fall line. See Morgan P. Robinson, *Virginia Counties* (Bulletin of Virginia State Library, 1916); also, Gray, *History of Agriculture*, I, 115–117.

[2] The recently created Prince George's County (1695), though open-ended as border counties continued to be, seems at this time to have embraced no settlers living beyond the general vicinity of the present District of Columbia. Edward B. Mathews, *The Counties of Maryland* (Spec. Pub., Maryland Geological Survey, 1907), p. 526.

[3] Ruth L. Higgins, *Expansion of New York, with Especial Reference to the Eighteenth Century* (Columbus, Ohio, 1931), p. 21. By the end of Queen Anne's War, the line of settlement had advanced only a few miles westward to the Schoharie Valley.

[4] Mathews, *Expansion of New England*, continues to be helpful.

[5] Crane, *Southern Frontier*, pp. 162–163.

theretofore after 1670. There had been, it is true, an impressive expansion since that year, but it had been less an extension of the general area occupied than a filling up of that to which a claim already had been established, and so it would be until virtually the end of the second war with France. It is not merely the war that has to be considered, for it can be suggested that the colonists also had some reluctance to break away from the navigable waters which provided an unbroken link with the seaboard and with Europe.[6]

Although the population of the colonies remained quite small in proportion to the area that had been occupied, or by comparison with the totals reached in later years, there had been nevertheless an extraordinary growth since the middle of the century. The conventional estimate, as recently and authoritatively confirmed, places the total in 1700 at the round figure of 250,000, distributed as follows: New England, 92,000; the Chesapeake settlements of Virginia and Maryland, 88,000; the Middle Colonies, 53,000; and Carolina, 16,000, with the larger part of this total in North Carolina.[7] There is room enough for debate as to the accuracy of these or any other estimates that might be made, but even if one allows for so gross an error as 20 per cent, the result would show that the population of the colonies had doubled since 1660 by comparison with the most exaggerated estimates which have been given for that year. If the more conservative estimates suggested on an earlier page be accepted, the increase would be something like threefold.[8]

In considering possible explanations, first thought goes to the question of how far immigration may have determined the totals. Even an approximate answer is difficult to establish, but there is reason to believe that only in the Delaware Valley and possibly in South Carolina can the size of the population be attributed mainly to immigration from outside the North American continent. Perhaps an exception should be made in the case of the Chesapeake colonies, where the tobacco fleet continued for a number of years after the Restoration to bring in an annual increment of 1,500 or

<hr>

[6] For example, V. J. Wyckoff, "The Sizes of Plantations in Seventeenth Century Maryland," *Maryland Historical Magazine*, XXXII (1937), 331–339, suggests that this may have been partly responsible for the tendency of the average size of landholdings to turn downward during the later years of the century as men divided larger properties by sale or will to meet the demand for desirable locations within the settled area.

[7] Stella H. Sutherland in *Historical Statistics of the United States*, p. 756.

[8] See above, pp. 15–16.

more new settlers, most of them indentured servants, but evidence as to the size of this migration after 1670 is surprisingly incomplete. It is generally assumed that there had been a marked decline by the end of the century, when the Chesapeake planters turned more and more to the use of Negro labor.[9] Except for the original Dutch, Swedish, and Finnish settlers, and for the more recently arriving French Huguenots, there had been as yet no numerically significant immigration from the continent of Europe. The size of the Huguenot migration is difficult to estimate, for practically all of the colonies received some of these refugees, but it is agreed that the largest number settled in South Carolina and the total there in 1700 probably fell short of 500.[10] The Palatine settlement of 1710 at Newburgh in New York and the founding in that same year of New Bern in North Carolina mark the beginning of another significant migration from the European continent, but not until later in the century would it reach large proportions.[11] Although all of the colonies had benefited in some measure by a continuing migration from the British Isles, there is good reason for believing that the over-all growth in their population owed much more to a natural increase than to any other factor, and that this is especially true of New England.[12]

9 See Wertenbaker, *Planters of Colonial Virginia,* pp. 41, 134; Smith, *Colonists in Bondage,* pp. 307–337, for a convenient tabulation of remarkably incomplete data; and Richard B. Morris, *Government and Labor in Early America* (New York, 1946), p. 36, for an estimate that early in the new century Maryland imported a minimum of 500 servants annually.

10 Wallace, *South Carolina,* p. 62.

11 See especially Walter A. Knittle, *The Early Eighteenth Century Palatine Emigration* (Philadelphia, 1936).

12 Very little has been attempted in the way of demographic analysis for this period of our history, and for the obvious reason that the data is most inadequate. But a recent and adventuresome effort restricted to a single New England town offers interesting, though tentative, conclusions that may have general application. See Kenneth A. Lockridge, "The Population of Dedham, Massachusetts, 1636–1736," *Economic History Review,* XIX (1966), 318–344. This study finds that the population leveled off after the years immediately following the first settlement, and that a gradual increase beginning at midcentury continued until near the end of the century, when there occurred a precipitous upturn. Immigration is dismissed as a factor, and with it the long-popular assumption that an early age of marriage or unusually high birth rate was critical. Actually, the average age of marriage was considerably higher than in modern times, a point confirmed by John Demos, "Notes on Life in Plymouth Colony," *William and Mary Quarterly,* 3d ser., XXII (1965), 264–286. Demos finds a higher productive rate per marital unit than does Lockridge, but both studies suggest that

The most significant change that had occurred in the composition of the population during the later years of the seventeenth century is represented by the presence, for the first time in impressive numbers, of the Negro. As is well known, Negroes had been brought to Virginia as early as 1619, but at midcentury there seem to have been no more than 300 of them in the colony. The number may have been approaching 1,000 at the time of the Restoration. According to Sir William Berkeley, in 1670 there were 2,000 Negroes and 6,000 white servants in a population standing over all at 40,000; and after the passage of another decade, Lord Culpeper estimated the number of Negroes as 3,000.[13] Modern estimates have run as high as 9,000 for 1690, 16,000 for 1700, and 23,000 for 1710.[14] But these figures seem to be much too high. The Royal African Company, which until 1698 held a monopoly of the English African trade, is known to have favored consistently the West Indian plantations, and especially Barbados.[15] The more conservative estimate of 6,000 for 1700 advanced by Philip Alexander Bruce,[16] an unusually well-informed student of seventeenth-century Virginia, appears to be nearer the truth, and this conclusion is supported by contemporary testimony. Edmund Jenings, acting governor, reported to the Board of Trade in 1708 that the colony had then 12,000 Negroes, and that nearly 6,000 had been brought in during the preceding decade by "Separate Traders," those outside the company who had gained rights in the trade by the act of Parliament which in 1698 terminated the monopoly of the Royal African Company.[17] It thus is possible that the number of Negroes in Virginia was doubled within the decade following 1698.

---

favorable conditions of life (with regard to food, fuel, housing, etc.) affecting life expectancy could have been the critical factor. See also Philip J. Greven, Jr., "Family Structure in Seventeenth-Century Andover, Massachusetts," *William and Mary Quarterly*, 3d. ser., XXIII (1966), 234–256.

[13] Wertenbaker, *Planters of Colonial Virginia*, pp. 124–125; Greene and Harrington, *American Population*, pp. 136, 137.

[14] *Historical Statistics of the U.S.*, p. 756.

[15] Davies, *Royal African Company*, pp. 299, 363, concludes that the company delivered to the English colonies between 1672 and 1713 a total of 100,000, of which 90,000 were sent to the West Indies.

[16] In his *Economic History of Virginia*, II, 108.

[17] Elizabeth Donnan, *Documents Illustrative of the History of the Slave Trade to America* (4 vols., Washington, 1930–35), IV, 89. The company is credited here with an additional 679.

Although Virginia held a decided lead in converting her economy to a heavy dependence upon Negro labor, she was by no means alone. Maryland had perhaps three to four thousand Negroes in 1700, and the following decade may have seen the total more than doubled.[18] In South Carolina there could have been 2,400 at the end of the century. Certainly, the number was large enough in proportion to a total population of probably less than 6,000 as already to have brought fear that the white inhabitants might soon be outnumbered, as is shown by a statute of 1698 intended to encourage the importation of white servants which cited in its preamble "the great number of negroes which of late have been imported into this Collony."[19] In New York, the only northern colony leaning heavily upon Negro labor, a census of 1698 showed 2,170 Negroes in a total population of just over 18,000.[20] No other colony at the end of the century had more than a few hundred Negroes, but every one of them had at least a few.[21]

The data so far given, however uncertain, points our attention to several general considerations that were fundamental in determining one of the more significant developments in American history. In New York the critical factor seems clearly to have been the shortage of manpower from which the colony long had suffered. The Dutch colonists, enjoying an advantage from the interest of the West India Company in the African trade, had turned to Negro labor as a supplement to an insufficient number of European workmen, and the commitment thus made to the use of the Negro in a wide variety of employments was increased by the English after 1664.[22] New York's problem was in some ways special, but everywhere in colonial America the high ratio of undeveloped natural resources to the available labor force had placed a premium upon

---

[18] *Historical Statistics of the U.S.*, p. 756; Greene and Harrington, p. 124, quote a contemporary estimate for 1710 of 7,945 out of a total population of 42, 741, figures which have been accepted by Miss Sutherland.

[19] Donnan, *Documents*, IV, 250.

[20] Greene and Harrington, p. 92.

[21] According to Miss Sutherland's estimates, New Jersey had 840, Massachusetts 800, and Connecticut, Pennsylvania, and North Carolina something over 400 each.

[22] See especially Edgar J. McManus, *A History of Negro Slavery in New York* (Syracuse, 1966). The heaviest concentration was in New York City and on Long Island. See also Van Rensselaer, *History of New York*, I, 191–193, 465.

labor, so much so that it has been calculated that colonial workmen commanded real wages in excess of those paid English laborers by 30 to even 100 per cent.[23] The Negro migration, destined to become the greatest single migration into the colonies during the eighteenth century, was but one of many which have rested basically upon the demand for labor in an expanding American economy.

In South Carolina, where the Negro came originally with the migration from Barbados that so largely shaped the colony's early history, the story calls attention first of all to the important fact that the English colonies in the West Indies had been converting to Negro labor on an increasingly large scale for sixty years before 1700.[24] Although this development had had the effect of diverting from the mainland colonies most of the Negroes shipped by English traders from Africa, it seems also to be true that until late in the century many of the Negroes reaching the North American colonies, including Virginia and Maryland, had come by way of the West Indies, where Barbados served as an emporium for the English trade as did Curaçao for the Dutch trade.[25] More important for an understanding of later developments is the fact that South Carolina's especially heavy commitment to the use of Negro labor coincided closely with the development of rice as a new and profitable staple. Although experiments with rice date from very early in the colony's history, success apparently came only in the last decade of the century, when new channels for the supply of Negro labor to the North American colonies also were opened.[26] It is possible that by 1708 there were as many Africans as there were

[23] Morris, *Government and Labor*, p. 45.

[24] It has been estimated that there may have been 40,000 in Barbados alone by 1670, and that Jamaica may have reached this total soon after 1700. Davies, *Royal African Company*, pp. 300–302.

[25] See again McManus, *Negro Slavery in New York*, and Jenings, as cited in note 17, above, who reported that he had been informed by the older inhabitants that before 1680 "what negroes were brought to Virginia were imported generally from Barbados for it was very rare to have a Negro ship come to this Country directly from Africa." A practice of the African Company was to supply Negroes for shipment to the Chesapeake on contract with London merchants trading to that area, but the company's records make it impossible to say how many were thus shipped. Davies, *Royal African Company*, p. 295.

[26] The evidence on experimentation with rice is summarized by Gray, *History of Agriculture*, I, 277–279; see also *ibid.*, p. 287, for evidence that rice exports may have risen by tenfold between 1699 and 1711.

Europeans in South Carolina, even perhaps a few more.[27] Be that as it may, it was the staple-producing colonies, and they alone, which now converted their economies to a primary dependence upon Negro labor.

The situation in the tobacco colonies has a special interest. In contrast to South Carolina, where the commitment to Negro labor depended, certainly in part, upon the inviting opportunity offered by a new staple, the conversion on the Chesapeake came in an effort to recover from the long-depressed fortunes of an old and established staple. Partly through its very cheapness Chesapeake tobacco had been winning its way into new markets, and so participating importantly in the general transformation of what originally had been a luxury commodity into the "poor man's luxury." Although an expanding re-export trade from England had not kept pace with production in the colonies, the gap had been narrowed in recent years, enough to help explain an improvement in prices which came with the later years of the century.[28] Even before the first of the French wars, an increasing number of planters had elected to gamble on quantity production at a small margin of profit that depended partly upon the relative cheapness of Negro labor.[29] When the peace of 1697 brought a new prospect that continental markets, always important for the re-export trade, would become fully open to English tobacco,[30] the colonists were soon riding the upward trend of what was to become a "boom and bust" cycle.[31]

[27] A report of 1708 from the colonial council (cited in Sirmans, "Masters of Ashley Hall," p. 89) gives the Negro population as 4,100, the white 4,000.

[28] For statistics on the re-export trade, see Price, *Tobacco Adventure to Russia*, p. 5; see also the statistical data Price has compiled on the tobacco trade for *Historical Statistics of the U.S.*, pp. 765–766.

[29] Thus, William Fitzhugh in a letter of 1686 declared his possession of twenty-nine Negroes and made no mention of an apparently much smaller number of European servants. At his death in 1701, he owned fifty-one Negroes and had six indentured servants. Richard Beale Davis (ed.), *William Fitzhugh and His Chesapeake World, 1676–1701* (Chapel Hill, N.C., 1963), pp. 14–15, 54, 175–176, 382. On the marked increase in headright grants for Negroes during the 1690's, see Bruce, *Economic History of Virginia*, II, 85.

[30] Again, Price's discussion in his *Tobacco Adventure to Russia* is especially helpful, as also is his "The Ecomomic Growth of the Chesapeake and the European Market, 1697–1775," *Journal of Economic History*, XXIV (1964), 496–511.

[31] I follow here the argument by John M. Hemphill in "Virginia and the English Commercial System, 1689–1733" (unpublished Ph.D. dissertation, Princeton University, 1964).

English ships now reached the Chesapeake in large numbers, and freighted with such plentiful supplies of European goods as to lift the price of tobacco. The initial cost of investment in Negro labor remained high, for the very great increase in the supply was not accompanied by a reduction in price,[32] but such was the optimism in London that liberal extensions of credit could be had. The temptation to shoulder debts for the purchase of Negroes became perhaps the greater because Virginia in 1699 eased its land policy so as to permit the purchase of new land at costs below those obtaining under the headright system of land grants, a system which had been abandoned in Maryland as early as 1683 for sales also made at generally lower costs.[33] The boom lasted for hardly more than the five years of peace which ended with the opening of the War of the Spanish Succession in 1702, when many planters found themselves seriously overextended. What had persuaded them to assume the risk, and more particularly the risk of an early downturn in the market for their tobacco, was the long-run advantage that could be anticipated from the Negro's enslavement under a condition of lifetime servitude that was transmitted to his offspring.

The point brings us to the troubled question of the Negro's status in early America, and it may be helpful to begin the discussion with a contemporary definition of Negro slavery. "Their servants," reported Robert Beverley in his *History and Present State of Virginia* in 1705, "they distinguish by the Names of Slaves for Life, and Servants for a time. . . . Slaves are the Negroes, and their Posterity, following the condition of the Mother. . . . They are call'd Slaves, in respect of the time of their Servitude, because it is for Life."[34] The definition of slavery at that time in Virginia is thus made clear enough. But how early Beverley's distinction between servant and slave existed, and how early the latter designation acquired a peculiar identification with the Negro, and why, have become very controversial questions.[35]

[32] Davies, *Royal African Company*, p. 364; Gray, *Agriculture*, I, 368–371, where attention is also given relative prices for Negroes and European servants.

[33] Manning C. Voorhis, "Crown Versus Council in the Virginia Land Policy," *William and Mary Quarterly*, 3d ser., III (1946), 499–514; Harris, *Land Tenure System*, pp. 219, 248.

[34] Wright edition, p. 271.

[35] See especially Oscar and Mary F. Handlin, "Origins of the Southern Labor System," *William and Mary Quarterly*, 3d. ser., VII (1950), 199–222; Carl N.

They are also difficult questions. Since contemporary English law did not know slavery and because the English government showed little interest beyond its concern for the prosperity of the African trade, the colonial legislators were left remarkably free to settle as they saw fit all questions arising from the presence of the Negro. Indeed, the development of the institution of Negro slavery in the North American colonies has to be viewed as an especially impressive example of the extent to which these communities were self-governing. But the colonial assemblies were very slow to define the Negro's status in any way at all, and through many years they dealt only piecemeal or incidentally with the question. That this should have been true is not surprising. The Negro first of all found himself placed as a servant in a society accustomed to servitude in more than one form—to the idea, as it has been helpfully expressed, that varying degrees of freedom and unfreedom normally exist in society.[36] Everywhere, moreover, the number of Negroes remained for some time small, so small as to pose no urgent problem for the legislature. The more elementary questions that might be raised by the presence of Negro servants readily found an answer in the long-established custom and law which viewed any servant as a member of some family unit, and which conceded to the head of the family prerogatives appropriately balancing the responsibilities he had assumed. And wherever, as in Virginia, the community had come to depend heavily upon an unfree labor force, statutes already carried relatively elaborate specifications both as to the rights belonging to the servant and the limitations imposed upon the rights he could claim. To mention but one example, no legislature needed to be hasty in enacting legislation regarding the fugitive Negro servant where laws already were on the books defining the obligation of every public officer and every inhabitant for assistance in the return to his master of any fugitive servant.[37]

Degler, *Out of Our Past: The Forces That Shaped Modern America* (New York, 1959), pp. 26–39; Stanley Elkins, *Slavery: A Problem in American Institutional and Intellectual Life* (Chicago, 1959); and Winthrop D. Jordan, "Modern Tensions and the Origins of American Slavery," *Journal of Southern History,* XXVII (1962), 18–30. John Hope Franklin, *From Slavery to Freedom: A History of American Negroes* (New York, 1950), is standard.

[36] Handlin and Handlin, "Southern Labor System."

[37] Craven, *Southern Colonies,* pp. 215–218; Morris, *Government and Labor,* especially the chapter on "The Legal Status of Servitude."

To suggest that the colonists originally depended upon the law and custom governing servitude generally is to raise immediately the question of how far Negro servants may have benefited from the fact that the most familiar form of servitude was for a fixed period of time. The answer is that some of them did, either by action of the courts or by the act of manumission on the part of a master who felt that he had had his due. The free Negro—a man free enough to own his own land, and perhaps to exercise the franchise—may be as old a feature of American society as is the enslaved Negro.[38]

The difficulty in the legislative record is readily suggested by no more than a glance at the earliest legislation in Virginia which unmistakably identifies the Negro with a condition of lifetime servitude. The first such law, enacted in 1661, covered the problem of runaway "negroes who are incapable of makeing satisfaction by addition of time," which was to say, of paying the normal penalty by serving an additional year.[39] A second law, of 1662, indicates the existence of lifetime servitude that could be transmitted to the Negro's child. The question was whether a child "got by any Englishman upon a negro woman should be slave or free," and the law assigned to the child the status of the mother.[40] A statute of 1670, revealing incidentally the basic assumption that was used to justify the Negro's enslavement, declared "that all servants not being christians imported into this colony by shipping shall be slaves for their lives."[41] Additional statutes could be mentioned,

[38] Bruce, *Economic History of Virginia*, II, 121–128; James H. Brewer, "Negro Property Owners in Seventeenth-Century Virginia," *William and Mary Quarterly*, 3d ser., XII (1955), 575–580; John H. Russell, *The Free Negro in Virginia, 1619–1865* (Baltimore, 1913). Russell and James C. Ballagh, *A History of Slavery in Virginia* (Baltimore, 1902), seem to have been originally responsible for the assumption that some other form of servitude preceded the Negro's enslavement, a conclusion accepted by Ulrich B. Phillips, *American Negro Slavery* (New York, 1918), pp. 75–76. Susan M. Ames, *Studies of the Virginia Eastern Shore,* has questioned this conclusion and the Handlins have replied.

[39] Hening, *Statutes*, II, 26. The act dealt specifically with the English servant who ran away with such a Negro servant, and required the Englishman to pay the penalty for both.

[40] *Ibid.*, II, 170.

[41] *Ibid.*, II, 283. The basic question was whether an Indian enslaved by other Indians and sold to an Englishman could be held for life, and the law imposed terms upon the servitude in all such cases. Maryland in 1664 had preceded Virginia in the enactment of a statute declaring "That all Negroes or other slaves already within the Province And all Negroes and other slaves to be hereafter

but to do so would serve little purpose here. The seventeenth-century assemblies, and not merely in Virginia, continued to act only as specific questions regarding the Negro were thrust upon their attention. Toward the end of the century the increasing number of Negroes, and perhaps the increasing number of them who had come to the colonies direct from Africa, finds reflection in laws pointing ahead to the special police regulations that were to become all too familiar in the eighteenth century.[42] But as yet there were no slave codes, properly speaking, nothing comparable to the detailed and comprehensive statutes of later date which ultimately placed the Negro under laws that were distinctly different from those governing all other members of the community. At this time, many questions were left unanswered by statute law. Even so fundamental an issue as whether the Negro slave should be viewed as chattel or real property could still be debated.[43] The modern historian is thus invited to assume that Negro slavery predated any legislation recognizing its existence, and simultaneously he is prompted to observe that the institution was not fully developed until the eighteenth century.

On the first point, there can be little doubt that well before 1660 the normal lot of the Negro in the English plantations had become that of a lifetime servant, that this condition of servitude was transmitted to his children, and that it was this transmissible condition which the colonists had in mind when they described him

---

imported into the Province shall serve Durante Vita." *Maryland Archives*, I, 526, 533–534. This act is often assigned to the year 1663, apparently through the error of a nineteenth-century compiler. I am indebted to David W. Jordan for assistance in clarifying the question. Jeffrey R. Brackett, *The Negro in Maryland: A Study of the Institution of Slavery* (Baltimore, 1889), pp. 28–29, gives the right date.

[42] Bruce, *Economic History of Virginia*, II, 117–121, for example.

[43] In the Chesapeake he seems consistently to have been treated as personal property, but Virginia's revision of the laws in 1705 defined him under some circumstances as real property. *Ibid.*, II, 98–99. Not until 1740 did a statute in South Carolina make the slave a chattel, though the courts adopted that view much earlier. See M. Eugene Sirmans, "The Legal Status of the Slave in South Carolina, 1670–1740," *Journal of Southern History*, XXVIII (1962), 462–473. In this connection, see also David B. Davis, *The Problem of Slavery in Western Culture* (Ithaca, 1966), pp. 248–251, for the influence of the fact that chattel property was more easily subject to seizure for the satisfaction of debt than was real property.

as a slave.[44] Whether because of the Negro's distinctly different physical appearance, or because he came originally from outside the European and Christian community, or because of a long established custom among Europeans in America to hold him in some such form of servitude, the institution of slavery, as defined immediately above, was quickly established in the English West Indian plantations.[45] That this development influenced the usages of the mainland colonies can hardly be disputed, and not only because in the case of South Carolina there is unmistakable evidence in the proprietors' guarantee of 1669 to every planter migrating from the West Indies with his "Negro slaves" that he need fear no loss of the "Power and Authority" he held over them.[46] It is difficult, for example, to explain the early development of Negro slavery in New England except in terms of the many commercial ties linking the Puritan community with the sugar plantations. It is also difficult to escape the assumption that many of the Negroes who reached other mainland colonies by way of the West Indies carried the condition of lifetime servitude with them. There is no intention here of suggesting that the institution of slavery in the North American colonies depended originally upon a simple act of borrowing. Rather, the purpose is to direct attention to a basic similarity of usage throughout the community of Englishmen living then in America. The point is made succinctly in the preamble to Rhode Island's statute of 1652, which comments upon the "common course practised among English men to buy negers, to that end that they may have them for service or slaves forever."[47]

---

[44] It is significant that before midcentury, Negro servants in the Chesapeake carried higher evaluations than did others in inventories of probated estates. Russell, *Free Negro in Virginia*, pp. 35–36; Winthrop D. Jordan, "White over Black: The Attitudes of the American Colonists toward the Negro, to 1784" (unpublished Ph.D. dissertation, Brown University, 1960), pp. 62–63. Jordan's important study offers much additional support for the view stated above.

[45] The evidence is summarized by Winthrop D. Jordan in "The Influence of the West Indies on the Origins of New England Slavery," *William and Mary Quarterly*, 3d. ser., XVIII (1961), 243–250. The standard authority on the development of the institution in New England is Lorenzo J. Greene, *The Negro in Colonial New England* (New York, 1942). On the prevalence of enslavement for the Negro in European communities of the New World, see especially the recent and admirable *The Problem of Slavery in Western Culture* by Davis.

[46] See above, p. 101.

[47] Quoted by Jordan in "The Influence of the West Indies," p. 245. The statute then prohibited servitude without a term. There is some question

To be a lifetime servant, even to have that condition of servitude transmitted to one's children, was not, of course, to suffer the same full degree of enslavement that later would be imposed upon the Negro. Nor was the Negro the only slave known to the colonists, for there were also Indian slaves.[48] The problem is to explain the progressive development of an institution which with time acquired a peculiar identification with the Negro and such refinement of his legal status as to make of American Negro slavery one of the more absolute forms of enslavement known to history.

The question of popular attitudes toward the Negro has acquired critical importance, if only because of its bearing upon the modern issue of how far present-day prejudices are attributable to the Negro's previous condition of servitude. On this question it has to be said, first of all, that the earlier records betray some ambivalence. As early as 1640 the Virginia assembly, at a time of impending trouble with the Indians, required that all men be armed except Negroes, but seventy-five years later South Carolina would arm several hundred Negroes for employment in the Yamassee War.[49] A Virginian in 1630 was severely punished "for abusing himself to the dishonor of God and shame of Christians, by defiling his body in lying with a negro," but ten years later the same offense seems to have been treated as merely another case of fornication.[50] It is clear enough that the justification for enslaving the Negro depended at first upon the fact that he was not a Christian, that like the Indian he was "heathen." And yet, testimony to an impulse to bring the Negro within the fold of the Christian church is found in statutes, beginning with those of Maryland and Virginia in the 1660's stipulating that conversion could not affect the master's right to his slave.[51]

---

whether the statute was lawfully enacted, but that matters no more in this connection than does the fact that its intent thereafter was more honored in the breach than in the observance.

[48] Notably in the case of South Carolina, where at the beginning of the eighteenth century there seem to have been several hundred.

[49] Crane, *Southern Frontier*, pp. 91, 171, 173, 178, 181, 187 n.; John W. Shy, "A New Look at Colonial Militia," *William and Mary Quarterly*, 3d ser., XX (1963), 181; Benjamin Quarles, "The Colonial Militia and Negro Manpower," *Mississippi Valley Historical Review*, XLV (1958–59), 643–652.

[50] Craven, *Southern Colonies*, p. 218 n.

[51] Russell, *Free Negro in Virginia*, p. 21. Jordan, "Black over White," p. 82 n., credits Maryland with the first such statute, one of 1664 which had that intent

There can be no mistake, however, as to the trend of sentiment after 1660. In Virginia's previously cited statute of 1662 there was imposed a double penalty for all cases of fornication involving a Christian and a Negro. The Maryland assembly, on being advised in 1664 that there were free Englishwomen who "to the disgrace of our Nation" entered into marriage with Negro slaves, ordered that the children born of "such Shamefull Matches" should "be slaves as their fathers were." The substitution in 1692 of servitude to the age of twenty-one could be viewed as testimony chiefly to the confusion Maryland's lawmakers had brought upon themselves by providing that the condition of enslavement could descend through the father as well as the mother, except that the revision can as easily be viewed as evidence that the assembly simply disliked enslaving the child of a white woman, however culpable she may have been.[52] There is multiplying evidence by this time of an increasing tendency for slavery to acquire a peculiar identification with the Negro, and for his color to become, in the absence of concrete evidence to the contrary, the special mark of a slave. Already, statutes dealing with the Negro slave were likely to deal simultaneously with the mulatto and the free Negro, as in Virginia's statute of 1691 restricting the right of a master to manumit Negroes and mulattoes to those masters who were willing to pay the cost of transporting the new freeman beyond the limits of the colony.[53] The term mulatto had been in use for a number of years, and it was used, then as now, not so much for the purpose of distinguishing the mulatto from the Negro as rather to identify the mulatto with the Negro.[54]

Because of the fundamental importance of slavery for the devel-

without specifically saying so. Frank Tannenbaum, *Slave and Citizen: The Negro in the Americas* (New York, 1947), a comparative study, has suggested the importance of the failure of the church, or churches, in the English colonies to provide the shepherding care they might have. Frank J. Klingberg, *Anglican Humanitarianism in Colonial New York* (Philadelphia, 1940), and his *An Appraisal of the Negro in Colonial South Carolina* (Washington, 1941), record some efforts by the S.P.G. to meet this need in the eighteenth century. See also Robert C. Twombly and Robert H. Moore, "Black Puritan: The Negro in Seventeenth-Century Massachusetts," *William and Mary Quarterly*, 3d ser., XXIV (1967), 224–242.

52 *Maryland Archives*, I, 533–534; XIII, 546–549.

53 Russell, *Free Negro in Virginia*, p. 51.

54 Winthrop D. Jordan, "American Chiaroscuro: The Status and Definition of Mulattoes in the British Colonies," *William and Mary Quarterly*, 3d ser., XIX (1962), 183–200.

opment in the staple-producing colonies of a type of plantation that was destined to lend a new and more restricted meaning to the term itself, which originally had been virtually synonymous with colony or settlement,[55] there is risk that it may be mistakenly assumed that the commitment to Negro labor was made by only a few of the colonists. No one should slight the importance of the emergence at this time of the great planter, nor overlook the opportunity to get a glimpse of life on the early plantation that is afforded by the revealing diary of William Byrd of Westover, whose inherited Virginia fortune, very largely built upon trade, had been increasingly invested in land and Negroes.[56] But it is no less important to notice evidence suggesting that the small slaveholder was more representative. Thus, it appears that in 1716 two-thirds of the taxpayers in Virginia's Lancaster County were slaveholders, that three fourths of these had four slaves or less, and that the number of planters holding above twenty was limited to four.[57] Although by that year Virginia was launched upon another postwar boom that brought its own fresh investments in Negro labor, there is no reason for doubting that slaveholding at the beginning of Queen Anne's War was comparably widespread.

The effect of the war upon the Chesapeake colonies was peculiarly disastrous. Already overextended and for a time slow to cut back either on new commitments or on production, the planters, large and small, faced once more a critical shortage of shipping, freight rates that rose to more than double the peacetime norm, drastically reduced prices for such of their crop as they were able to get to the market, and in addition bills of exchange protested by hard-pressed tobacco merchants in London.[58] Even when provision

[55] As in the official designation of the Rhode Island and Providence Plantations.

[56] See Louis B. Wright and Marion Tinling (eds.), *The Secret Diary of William Byrd of Westover, 1709–1712* (Richmond, 1941); also Wright, *First Gentlemen of Virginia*, pp. 312–347. At Westover, though not yet in the great house he would raise as late as the 1730's, Byrd supervised the slave quarter located at his home seat and received overseers called in to report upon conditions in outlying quarters situated on newly opened frontiers of settlement.

[57] Including Robert Carter, who may have owned 126 slaves. See Wertenbaker, *Planters of Colonial Virginia*, p. 153.

[58] Again the authority is Hemphill, "Virginia and the English Commercial System"; also his "Freight Rates in the Maryland Tobacco Trade, 1705–1762," *Maryland Historical Magazine*, LIV (1959), 36–58, 154–187; and Price, "Growth of the Chesapeake and the European Market."

for improved protection by naval convoy got the tobacco fleet through its voyage, the result might be nothing more helpful than to glut a market that had been seriously restricted by wartime interruptions of the re-export trade to the European continent.[59] Maryland as early as 1705 was described as almost bankrupt;[60] for Virginia 1706, 1709 (when a crop failure gave variance to the pattern), and 1711 were particularly difficult years. That the planters understood the contribution their own folly had made to their troubles is indicated by Virginia's enactment in 1710 of a prohibitive duty of £5 per head on all slaves imported into the colony,[61] and by its adoption of a tobacco inspection act in 1713 intended both to reduce the quantity and to improve the quality of the leaf shipped to market. Unfortunately, the lessons taught the colonists by wartime experience were soon to be forgotten, and after the war efforts to restrict the importation of slaves would be prohibited by Whitehall as an unwarranted interference with trade.[62]

It is more difficult to estimate the war's effect upon the economy of the colonies lying below the Chesapeake. Although North Carolina long had depended upon tobacco for its money crop, and probably doubled the number of its slaves during the decade following 1700,[63] there can be no doubt that the more serious of its difficulties at this time are attributable to internal rather than external developments. The divisive issue of a church establishment helped to reduce the political life of the colony to a virtual state of

---

[59] On the provisions for convoy, see Middleton, *Tobacco Coast*, pp. 293–297, 318–325; also the works cited in note 84, below.

[60] By James Logan of Pennsylvania. See Armstrong, *The Correspondence between William Penn and James Logan*, II, 53.

[61] A tax of 20s. per head had been imposed as early as 1699, but for the professed purpose of securing revenue to meet the cost of the new capitol at Williamsburg. Maryland imposed the same duty in 1704. Massachusetts had been the first to adopt a prohibitive duty of £4 in an act of 1705, "for the Better Preventing of a Spurious and Mixt Issue," that provided for a drawback of the duty paid should the Negro be transported from the colony. After the slave rebellion of 1712 in New York, Pennsylvania and New Jersey adopted prohibitive duties of £20 and £10 respectively. All such legislation is conveniently summarized in W. E. B. DuBois, *The Suppression of the African Slave-Trade to the United States of America, 1638–1870* (New York, 1896), App. A. See also Herbert Aptheker, *American Negro Slave Revolts* (New York, 1943), pp. 172–173.

[62] See again DuBois, *Suppression of the African Slave-Trade*.

[63] *Historical Statistics of the U.S.*, p. 756, but the total seems still to have been less than 1,000.

chaos that culminated in the "Cary Rebellion" of 1711. This was suppressed, but almost immediately came the Tuscarora War, which began with a massacre that fell with especially disastrous effect upon the newer settlements in the neighborhood of New Bern. Twice South Carolina sent military expeditions to the aid of its neighbor, but not until March, 1713, was a conclusive victory won.[64]

The Tuscarora War was only one in a succession of emergencies which had imposed a heavy burden upon the limited resources of South Carolina since the beginning of Queen Anne's War. Louis XIV's decision to place his grandson upon Spain's throne as Philip V had brought into existence a Franco-Spanish alliance that carried more ominous implications for South Carolina than for any other of the English settlements in North America. La Salle's exploration of the lower Mississippi had been followed, though somewhat belatedly, by d'Iberville's establishment of a French base in 1699 on the Gulf of Mexico at Biloxi. As a result, there had been added to the old Anglo-Spanish contest a new Anglo-French rivalry, and the prospect that Biloxi and a recently established French base at Mobile would be teamed with St. Augustine and Pensacola, previously occupied by the Spanish as a check to the French advance into the Gulf, against Charles Town. The Spaniards struck first, early in 1702, as if hoping to settle the issue before their new allies could claim any part of the benefit. The overland attack was beaten off by the Carolinians, who responded with an assault upon St. Augustine late in the same year. They were successful in seizing the town, which they ultimately burned, but the fort still stood when the invaders were forced to withdraw, very largely because of their own weakness. South Carolina was unable to mount another such offensive, and after successfully resisting in 1706 a second attack upon Charles Town, this time by a combined Spanish and French amphibious force dispatched from Havana, the government had to be content with diplomatic and military maneuvers, depending chiefly upon the employment of Indian forces, that were directed in the main against the newer threat from Louisiana.[65]

64 Lefler and Newsome, *North Carolina*, pp. 54–61.
65 See especially Crane, *Southern Frontier*, pp. 47–107; also Charles W. Arnade, *The Siege of St. Augustine in 1702* (Gainesville, Fla., 1959); and John J. Tepaske, *The Governorship of Spanish Florida, 1700–1763* (Durham, N.C., 1964), pp. 108–122.

When the war ended, South Carolina was heavily indebted and her people much inclined to reflect upon what might have been accomplished had the proprietors given the assistance it was assumed they could have given.[66] No doubt, the unusual balance in the colony's economy provided a cushion against the type of disaster repeatedly visited upon Virginia and Maryland.[67] But the war had disrupted the Indian trade, apparently with no offsetting advantage except the help that might be expected from a decision of the assembly in 1707 to subject the trade to public regulation, and from a virtually final elimination of competition from Virginia's traders.[68] Parliament in 1704 had added rice to the list of enumerated commodities, thereby reducing the opportunity to find a better market for it in Portugal.[69] The only economic gain that unmistakably could be attributed to the war was the stimulation it had given to the production of naval stores. Disturbed by the extent of England's dependence in this regard upon Scandinavia, and by the unfriendly attitude of Sweden, Parliament in 1705 offered substantial bounties for naval stores produced in the colonies. It was expected that the supply would come chiefly from New England and New York, where the English government invested substantially for this purpose in the Palatine settlement at Newburgh. But the advantage was actually destined to go to the Carolinas, for their tar and pitch, and first to South Carolina.[70]

When one turns from the southern frontier to the northern, he finds a story as different in its main outline as in its detail. Except for the early renewal of an all too familiar type of harassment by French and Indian forces along the New England frontier, hostilities were very slow to develop. And when finally the English colonists undertook to confront the French in a decisive action, they enjoyed substantial assistance from England.

[66] For a discussion of wartime finance, see below, p. 324. Although the rebellion against the proprietors did not come until 1719, it is generally agreed that discontent with proprietary rule had some of its roots in this earlier experience.

[67] See Gray, *History of Agriculture*, I, 57–58.

[68] Crane, *Southern Frontier*, pp. 89, 137–161.

[69] Gray, *History of Agriculture*, I, 284–285.

[70] *Ibid.*, I, 153–155; also Eleanor L. Lord, *Industrial Experiments in the British Colonies of North America* (Baltimore, 1898), especially App. B; Joseph J. Malone, *Pine Trees and Politics: The Naval Stores and Forest Policy in Colonial New England, 1691–1775* (Seattle, 1964).

Along the frontiers separating French Canada from New England and New York, both parties to the contest assumed at first a defensive posture. The support Louis XIV had given to d'Iberville's ambitious ventures in Louisiana had so dispersed the resources made available to the French in North America as to deprive Canada of the strength she might have enjoyed through concentration upon an effort to strengthen the main bastion of the French position in North America.[71] Even the offensive assumed by the French on the New England frontier, which included the famed sack of Deerfield in 1704, was basically a defensive maneuver intended to cover the extreme vulnerability of Acadia, which guarded all too weakly the approach to the St. Lawrence Valley.[72] On the English side, New York was content initially to depend upon Quebec's ready acceptance of the idea that a policy of neutrality would be mutually advantageous. A principal consideration for both parties was the neutral policy recently adopted by the Iroquois. After years of intermittent strife with the French in Canada, the Iroquois had made peace in 1701, just on the eve of the European war.[73] Consequently, no French invasion of New York could have been tried without the risk of throwing the Indians back into the arms of the English; and conversely, New York no longer could count upon the Iroquois for assistance in an aggressive move against Canada. The observation is not intended to suggest that otherwise New York might have taken the offensive, for its mood in 1702 was far from aggressive. Lord Bellomont had proposed action in the west that was reminiscent of the policy formerly pursued by Thomas Dongan, but only to find the assembly indifferent. Albany's merchants were reluctant to allow the war to interfere with a profitable trade they had opened with Montreal, and they could view with equanimity the insistence of the Iroquois upon a right to

71 See especially the concluding chapters of Eccles, *Canada under Louis XIV*.

72 Graham, *Empire of the North Atlantic*, p. 84; J. Bartlet Brebner, *New England's Outpost: Acadia before the Conquest of Canada* (New York, 1927), pp. 42–51. Although Francis Parkman's judgment of men and developments has been subject to some revision, his narrative of the war in *A Half-Century of Conflict* remains the classic account. Samuel A. Drake, *The Border Wars of New England*, provides a still useful summary.

73 Trelease, *Indian Affairs in Colonial New York*, pp. 332–363; A. F. C. Wallace, "Origins of Iroquois Neutrality: The Grand Settlement of 1701," *Pennsylvania History*, XXIV (1957), 223–235.

trade with both towns. Consistently, the English trading goods Albany had to offer were superior in quality to those of the French traders and could be sold at a lower price.[74] The corrupt Lord Cornbury, who succeeded Bellomont in 1702, was hardly the leader to substitute empire building for business as usual.

As a result, the war in the north came very close to being, until it was halfway through, Massachusetts' war and its alone, except for the limited assistance New Hampshire could give. The other New England colonies on occasion sent aid, sometimes grudgingly, to their beleaguered neighbor, but Joseph Dudley, governor of Massachusetts and New Hampshire in succession to Bellomont, bore by far the heaviest responsibility. New York undertook to strengthen the defenses of New York City and some improvement of the fortifications at Albany, but this last was financed in substantial part through grants allowed by King William in response to Lord Bellomont's late appeals. The king's concurrent and now usual instructions calling for assistance from neighboring colonies met the usual response.[75]

More general in its immediate effect upon the northern colonies was the war at sea, where again French strategy favored what Admiral Mahan later would describe as "commerce-destroying warfare."[76] New York, which during the earlier years of the war spent more money on the defenses of New York City than it did for the defense of its frontiers, complained in 1704 of the loss of nearly thirty vessels.[77] For Philadelphia the war brought a sudden end to a period of renewed prosperity. Cut off by Spanish decree from a

[74] Trelease, Indian Affairs, and Arthur H. Buffinton, "The Policy of Albany and English Westward Expansion," Mississippi Valley Historical Review, VIII (1922), 327–366.

[75] Pennsylvania, on Penn's advice, reluctantly voted the £350 demanded. Davidson, War Comes to Quaker Pennsylvania, p. 15. The details can be followed in Kimball's Joseph Dudley, pp. 100–123, 143–144, 148–149, and Osgood, American Colonies in the Eighteenth Century, I, 401–423. See also Dunn, Puritans and Yankees, pp. 335–344, and Trelease, Indian Affairs, pp. 353–355. Buffinton (in Flick's History of the State of New York, II, 217) has estimated that New York spent for "frontier defense" in the period 1702–6 approximately £3,500 as against an annual expenditure of £30,000 by Massachusetts.

[76] A. T. Mahan, The Influence of Sea Power upon History, 1660–1783 (Boston, 1906), p. 209.

[77] Buffinton in Flick's History of the State of New York, II, 218–219; Herbert A. Johnson, The Law Merchant and Negotiable Instruments in Colonial New York, 1664 to 1730 (Chicago, 1963), pp. 11–12.

trade with the Spanish Indies that had been a principal source of specie, confronted by the continuing efforts of Maryland to exclude it from the trade of that colony, and finding that the tobacco shipped from the lower Delaware fared no better in the market than did that shipped direct from the Chesapeake, Philadelphia was seriously embarrassed in its efforts to make needed payments in London. Depression in the port city spread out to embrace the countryside.[78] Boston, still enjoying a decided lead over all other colonial ports, had more to lose than did either New York or Philadelphia, but for that very reason it was better able to withstand the shock of war.

Indeed, there is evidence which strongly suggests that the war actually had a stimulating effect upon Boston's economy. Certainly, the shipping and shipbuilding activities upon which its prosperity significantly depended sustained a high level of performance throughout the war. Indices for the measurement of economic activity at this time are very inadequate, but we are especially fortunate in having an unusually revealing record for the Boston port. A provision in the Navigation Act of 1696 required that all shipping engaged in trade with the colonies, including ships trading from one colony to another, be licensed. Among the surviving fragments of the resultant registry is one covering Massachusetts from 1697 to 1714, and we are doubly fortunate in the sophisticated analysis it recently has been given.[79] This reveals that Massachusetts in 1698 had a fleet of 171 seagoing vessels, not including the fishing fleet or ships engaged only in a local coastal trade; that 124 of the 171 belonged to Boston; and that Boston, judged by the tonnage of its fleet, probably was outranked among the empire's ports at the beginning of Queen Anne's War only by London and Bristol. The Massachusetts fleet was overwhelmingly home-owned and very largely home-built. What is more important for the immediate discussion is the astonishingly large number of vessels added to the list after 1698: a total of over 1,100 ships, of which 678 were added during the ten years (1702–11) in which England was

[78] Frederick B. Tolles, *James Logan and the Culture of Provincial America* (Boston, 1957), p. 24; Gary B. Nash, "Maryland's Economic War with Pennsylvania," *Maryland Historical Magazine*, LX (1965), 231–244.

[79] Bernard and Lotte Bailyn, *Massachusetts Shipping 1697–1714: A Statistical Study* (Cambridge, Mass., 1959).

actively involved in hostilities. Except for the first two war years, and for 1710 and 1711, captured vessels at no time figured prominently in the new listings, and privateering, over all, counted for much less in determining the size of the colony's fleet during this period than it had during King William's War. There is no way of drawing from the list an estimate of what may have been the net increase in the size of the fleet, but obviously such vessels as were lost, sold, or retired from service were being quickly replaced. The figures also indicate replacement by shipping of a larger average tonnage, especially in the case of that part employed in Boston's trade. While meeting the demands of its own fleet, Massachusetts supplied from its shipyards between 1697 and 1714 over 19,000 tons of shipping to the British Isles, and sold an additional tonnage in the West Indies, Newfoundland, and other English possessions in the Atlantic area.[80] The lead Boston held over lesser centers of trade in New England became now more pronounced, and this trend may have brought to more than one community unsettling dislocations. But the total view speaks of vitality, not stagnancy.

Any one attempting to explain this vitality should begin perhaps by observing that the shipping interest ranked high among the economic activities which at this time in history were most likely to be stimulated by war.[81] It should be observed, too, that England's overseas trade, though depressed in the earlier stages of the war, took a favorable turn after 1705, so much so that a modern authority has described its state five years later in terms of a boom.[82] By no means did every branch of the trade prosper, the tobacco trade being an especially notable exception, but there is evidence to suggest that colonial seaports, among which Boston continued to enjoy the greater advantages, shared in this general upturn of trade.[83] Especially helpful was the marked improvement

[80] For the material used here, see especially *ibid.*, pp. 15, 20, 28, 42–43, 45–46, 53, and Tables I, II, VI, XIII, and XIV.

[81] Notice in this connection Lawrence Harper's observation (*Navigation Acts,* p. 369) that wars "tended to cause a shipping inflation, and England seldom fought a war in which she did not have more ships after it ended than before it began."

[82] G. N. Clark, "War Trade and Trade War, 1701–1713," *Economic History Review,* I (1927–28) , 262–280; also his *Later Stuarts,* pp. 225–241.

[83] In 1710, for example, Isaac Norris reported optimistically on the prospect in Philadelphia, mentioning especially a new trade with Portugal. Armstrong, *Correspondence between Penn and Logan,* II, 435.

in the protection provided by naval convoys after 1708 for all shipping approaching and departing from the British Isles. Of further help in cutting down the depredations of French privateers were the one or two men-of-war more or less regularly stationed at Boston, New York, Virginia, Barbados, and the Leeward Islands, plus the squadron based on Jamaica.[84] In the West Indies, always critical for Boston's trade balance, an ambitious French challenge had spent itself before the end of 1706 and was not to be renewed, although privateers and pirates continued to be troublesome.[85] In Newfoundland, where New England also had important trading interests, the year 1708 brought almost complete disaster to the English settlements there;[86] but whatever the loss for New England's merchants, it undoubtedly was more than offset by the subsequent decision of Whitehall to take an active part in New England's war with the French. The result was an ultimate commitment by the imperial government of military forces to the North American theater on an unprecedented scale and for operations based chiefly on Boston.

Apparently, no full accounting of the expenditures made there in behalf of these forces exists, but there is evidence enough to suggest the scale. During the Walker expedition of 1711, bills of exchange for more than £23,000 sterling seem to have been drawn in Boston for the army forces alone.[87] A dependable estimate further indicates that bills of exchange drawn on various departments of the British government forwarded from Boston during the three years beginning with 1711 amounted at least to £57,100 sterling. During the same period more than £44,000 sterling in bills were drawn in New York on Whitehall agencies, largely for military purposes, and many

---

84 J. H. Owen, *War at Sea under Queen Anne, 1702–1708* (Cambridge, 1938), especially pp. 55–70; R. D. Merriman, *Queen Anne's Navy: Documents Concerning the Administration of the Navy of Queen Anne, 1702–1714* (Navy Records Society, London, 1961), pp. 337–353.

85 Nellis M. Crouse, *The French Struggle for the West Indies* (New York, 1943), pp. 246–306; also his *Lemoyne d'Iberville, Soldier of New France* (Ithaca, 1954); and Ruth Bourne, *Queen Anne's Navy in the West Indies* (New Haven, 1939).

86 For a summary of war operations there, Graham, *Empire of the North Atlantic,* pp. 87–90.

87 See Gerald S. Graham's discussion in *The Walker Expedition to Quebec, 1711* (Navy Records Society, London, 1953), pp. 46–50. It is possible that no account of costs for the navy was ever prepared.

of these bills found their way to London by way of Boston.[88] Massachusetts' own expenditures for the war, according to a report of Governor Dudley, were maintained at an approximate annual average of £30,000 for several years preceding 1711, when they rose to almost £50,000.[89]

The chief cost had been for the establishment and maintenance of a frontier line of defense running some 200 miles from Deerfield in western Massachusetts to Wells in Maine. This line was held by stockaded towns, each of whose inhabitants were reinforced by forty to fifty militiamen. In addition to serving as a garrison, the militiamen conducted regular patrols between the towns, in the winter on snowshoes, and periodically they were joined by reinforcements brought up for deep forays into the Indian country beyond the line, or for sweeps up the coast above the eastern extension of the line. The purpose was to deny the Indian who was or might be an ally of the French an opportunity to attack by keeping him off balance—through the burning of his village, the destruction of his crops in the field, and the denial of an opportunity to fish for food. It was a brutal war fought with the savagery of a people who saw themselves engaged in a struggle with savagery itself, and one fought on the whole quite successfully. Governor Dudley could later boast that not a single town had been abandoned to the foe. His chief dependence was upon drafts from the militia which served much as does the draft today to stimulate volunteer enlistments that were further encouraged by liberal promises of a share in whatever plunder might be taken, by comparably liberal bounties for Indian scalps brought back, and by the benefit to be derived from selling captive Indians too young to count militarily into slavery, somewhere outside Massachusetts.[90]

---

88 Nettels, "England's Trade with New England and New York," *Publications of the Colonial Society of Massachusetts,* XXVIII, (1935) , pp. 346–347; also his *Money Supply of the American Colonies,* Chap. VII, which indicates that only two-thirds of this total may have been paid by the government, the loss possibly sustained by English rather than Boston merchants. Included in the total were payments for ships on regular station at Boston and for the newly established garrison in Nova Scotia, which depended upon Boston for its supplies.

89 *Calendar of State Papers, Colonial, 1711–1712,* pp. 257–260.

90 *Ibid.,* especially, but also earlier reports in the calendars of *State Papers, Col.,* for 1704–5, 1706–8, pp., respectively, 66, 99; 29, 120, 128. For the legislation implementing this defensive program, see *Acts and Resolves, Public and Private, of the Province of the Massachusetts Bay,* I (Boston, 1869) , *passim,* beginning p. 530.

Perhaps it was the success attained through these tactics which explains the slowness of the Bay Colony to mount an offensive against either Nova Scotia or Canada.

Perhaps it was more because the memory of her experience in King William's War was all too fresh. That experience argued that while Acadia might be easily seized, it could be retaken by the French so long as they continued to hold Quebec, and that even with New York's collaboration an assault upon Canada depending wholly upon colonial resources was an exceedingly doubtful venture. Perhaps the emphasis belongs to Boston's awareness that only on the initiative of the home government could the co-operation of other colonies, and especially New York, be expected. There was no debate as to the grand strategy needed for the elimination of the French menace. The enemy's forces would have to be divided by co-ordinated attacks upon Montreal from New York and upon Quebec from Boston. When finally in 1707 the Bay government, prompted chiefly perhaps by privateers based on Port Royal, undertook on its own to seize the place and twice ingloriously failed, mainly through the ineptitude of the command, the need for assistance from England was doubly reinforced.

The man who more than any other was responsible for persuading Whitehall to give the needed assistance was Samuel Vetch, a Scotsman relatively recently settled in New York. Like Robert Livingston, he was the son of a convenanting minister who had gone into exile in Holland during the reign of Charles II. The younger Vetch had returned to the British Isles in 1688 as a volunteer in King William's invading army. Subsequently, he had served with a Scottish regiment on the Continent, and after the war he had entered into the service of the Company of Scotland Trading to Africa and the Indies, a corporation recently organized for what was destined to be Scotland's final effort to win for itself a separate overseas empire.[91] Vetch was a member of the original expedition sent by the company to Darien, and as one of the survivors of the ill-fated colony on the Isthmus of Panama he landed in New York in 1699. There he quickly won the advantage, so familiar in American history, of belonging to an ethnic group already estab-

91 See especially G. M. Waller, *Samuel Vetch, Colonial Enterpriser* (Chapel Hill, N.C., 1960); also George P. Insh, *The Company of Scotland Trading to Africa and the Indies* (London, 1932).

lished despite the prejudice its establishment had formerly met. His early marriage to Livingston's daughter gave him influential connections that were helpful in launching him upon ventures which included an illicit trade with Canada and Acadia, some of it under flags of truce for the exchange of prisoners. That activity ultimately got him into trouble in Massachusetts, where his friends included Governor Dudley, and where in 1706 at the insistence of the lower house he was convicted by the General Court of trade with the enemy.[92] Having gone to England in 1707, among other reasons for the purpose of clearing himself of this conviction, he laid before the Board of Trade in July, 1708, a remarkable paper entitled "Canada Survey'd."[93]

There was nothing original with Vetch in what he here proposed—the immediate elimination of France from the competition for empire in North America by a combined Anglo-colonial attack upon Canada. Nor was he alone in urging the government in Whitehall to assume the lead. Dudley had been advocating such an undertaking for some time; Francis Nicholson, out of a colonial post since 1705, enthusiastically joined in pressing for favorable action; Jeremiah Dummer, who reached London in the fall of 1708 and would become agent for Massachusetts in 1710, lent assistance; and even Lord Cornbury, soon to be relieved of his job, joined in the chorus.[94] Vetch's special contribution was detailed intelligence, much of it apparently based upon his own firsthand observations, regarding the vulnerability of the French position in North America. He described the French colonists as a "handfull" of men who were "vastly dispersed to possess a country of above 4,000 miles extent," reaching from the Atlantic to the Mississippi and southward to the Gulf of Mexico, thereby "quite encompassing and hemming in betwixt them and the sea, all the British Empire upon the . . . Continent of America." They now could be easily expelled by the proposed attack upon the as yet imperfectly defended

[92] On this complex affair, see in addition to Waller's *Vetch*, Kimball's *Joseph Dudley*, pp. 114–119.

[93] *Calendar of State Papers, Colonial, June, 1708–1709*, pp. 41–51; Waller's discussion in *Vetch*, pp. 94–120.

[94] Graham, *Walker Expedition to Quebec*, pp. 6–9; Kimball, *Joseph Dudley*, pp. 119–120; Clifford K. Shipton, *Sibley's Harvard Graduates*, IV, 456–457; *Calendar of State Papers, Colonial, June, 1708–1709*, pp. 71–72, 177.

citadels of Quebec and Montreal, but to wait until the French became "more numerous" would be to endanger "the British interest over all America, as well as upon the Continent." Vetch thus made possession of the continent the key to holding all of Britain's possessions in the western Atlantic, including those in Newfoundland, menaced by French possession of the nearby mainland, and the West Indian plantations, fed and otherwise supported by the trade the continental colonies carried to them. It was a cogently argued paper leading finally to the suggestion that nothing more would be required of the queen than two battalions of regular troops and six men-of-war.

A number of circumstances combined to bring a favorable response from the queen. On the Continent, Marlborough had won all save one of the great victories that would fix his fame in the annals of warfare. At sea, as previously noted, the war was increasingly favorable to England. News of the fall of St. John's in Newfoundland stirred concern. Perhaps Vetch also was indebted to the acts of union by the English and Scottish parliaments which in 1707 had created the United Kingdom of Great Britain, thereby admitting the Scots to partnership in overseas enterprises from which English policy theretofore had sought to exclude them. Certainly, the union had cleared the way for Vetch to take the lead he now took, and his consistent use throughout the paper of the terms Britain and British Empire suggests an effort to win over some of the Scots enjoying a new influence in Whitehall, as also an appeal to the Whigs, who had brought about the union of the two kingdoms and who were currently dominant both in the Parliament and the ministry. By the end of February, 1709, the queen had agreed, and before spring Vetch was on his way back to America in the company of Nicholson, who had volunteered his services. The two landed at Boston late in April.[95]

Vetch had been commissioned as a colonel, and was charged with raising the colonial forces he had promised would be provided by the northern colonies. Everywhere, except for Pennsylvania and New Jersey, where the Quaker influence counted heavily, the response was enthusiastic. Even New York set aside much, though by no means all, of its accustomed prejudice against a Boston-based

95 Waller, *Vetch*, pp. 108–119.

operation. When death claimed Lord John Lovelace, newly appointed governor of New York who had been expected to lead the march on Montreal, the command was given to Nicholson. By summer he had a force of perhaps 1,500 men deployed along the Hudson River–Lake Champlain corridor, and in New England the enthusiasm promised that the troops assembling at Boston would greatly exceed the assigned quota of 1,200. But these were hopeful preparations for the arrival of the expedition from England, which, for reasons that are none too clear, had been canceled as early as May. After an extraordinary delay, even for that day, official notice of the cancellation reached Boston in mid-October. Already the expectation there that the plan could be fully implemented that year had been abandoned, but it was hoped that Acadia might be seized before winter and that Nicholson's troops could be held in place for an attack on Canada in 1710. When the vessel bringing the unwelcome news from England brought the total of the queen's ships on hand to six, it was proposed that the assembled New England forces be employed immediately against Port Royal, but the ships' captains had other orders, including those for patrol in the waters of New York and Virginia, and so the proposed operation was canceled. The disappointment was made complete at the end of October, when Nicholson's army, beset by logistical and other difficulties, disintegrated.[96]

The remarkable display of colonial co-operation that had been given, plus the suggestion from Whitehall that its decision could be viewed as a postponement rather than abandonment of the project, served to keep hope alive. On the recommendation of the New England governors, Nicholson hurried to London to press for renewal of the queen's commitment. He was followed after several weeks by Colonel Peter Schuyler, who shepherded a delegation of four Indian chieftains from New York (three Mohawks and one River Indian) who were intended to be impressed by England's might and to suggest that the attack on Montreal might have substantial assistance from the Iroquois.[97]

[96] *Ibid.*, pp. 121–157, is the fullest account, but see also Bruce T. McCully, "Catastrophe in the Wilderness: New Light on the Canada Expedition of 1709," *William and Mary Quarterly*, 3d. ser., XI (1954), 441–456.

[97] For a full account, see Richmond P. Bond, *Queen Anne's American Kings* (Oxford, 1952). The original proposal was to send a chieftain from each of the Five Nations.

Although the Indians scored a huge social success in London, Nicholson returned in July, 1710, with less than he had hoped for—no more than 400 marines and two men-of-war to be employed under his command for the conquest of Acadia. The experience of 1709 had taught its obvious lesson, and so the colonists had made no previous preparations. Two months were required to make ready the New England regiments and to bring in the two warships then on station in New York, which with the one stationed at Boston brought the naval complement up to five vessels. When these and over thirty transports carrying something like 2,000 troops appeared at Port Royal on September 24, the invaders held an overwhelming superiority over their foe. Subercase, the French governor, had not more than 300 men at his command; for a few days he put up a brave front and then yielded to the inevitable.[98] Appropriately, Vetch was left in charge of the newly renamed province of Nova Scotia while the victorious Nicholson returned by way of Boston to London. He left behind half the marines and a comparable number of colonials for a garrison.

At Whitehall the Tories had won control of the government during the latter half of 1710 in a succession of developments which included an election in October bringing them a majority in Parliament. Ever less responsive than were their rivals to the demands of trade and empire, and responding now to evidences of war-weariness among the people, the triumphant Tories were inclined toward negotiations for peace. But they also were not indifferent to the advantage the conquest of Canada might give them as an offset to Marlborough's victories, or as an additional card to play at the peace table. The ships required were easily spared, for France "no longer maintained even a pretence of an active fleet."[99] The Board of Trade had been committed to the venture since 1708, and the government itself had come close to a firm commitment in a decision of July, 1710, for appointment of Henry Boyle, Viscount Shannon, as the commander of land forces to be employed in the reduction of Canada. Five regiments actually had embarked from Portsmouth in October, though only to be recalled because of

98 Waller's *Vetch* provides the most informative account, but see also the previously cited works by Graham and Brebner.
99 Graham, *Empire of the North Atlantic*, p. 92.

the lateness of the season.[100] Nicholson's easy victory in Nova Scotia added persuasiveness to renewed appeals from Dudley, Vetch, Dummer, and others. Before the winter had passed, the decision was made.

At the beginning of May, 1711, an expedition of sixty-four ships, eleven of them men-of-war, set sail from England for Boston with over 5,000 troops and some 6,000 seamen aboard. Nicholson had been sent ahead with two men-of-war to alert the colonists, and with arms and ammunition for the equipment of 2,000 men once more to be commanded by him in an overland march from Albany against Montreal.[101] Nothing comparable to this expedition had been seen in the history of the North American colonies. Nor would anything comparable to it be seen again until the days of William Pitt.

Unhappily, the expedition was ill-fated from its very beginning. The command had been given by Henry St. John (later Viscount Bolingbroke) to Admiral Sir Hovenden Walker, of whom a judicious student has observed "that nothing we know about Walker's career would seem to justify his appointment to high command."[102] The troops, most of them veterans of Marlborough's campaigns, were entrusted to the command of Brigadier General John Hill, whose chief claim to the assignment seems to have been the fact that he was brother to Mrs. Masham, the current favorite of the queen in succession to Marlborough's wife. Nicholson's arrival in Boston was delayed by unfavorable weather until June 8, and so his efforts to effect necessary arrangements with the colonial governments was behind schedule when the main fleet, after an unusually rapid passage, came in on June 25. The delay complicated a logistical problem that had been underestimated in England. It had been expected that the ships and the troops could be provisioned in New England, not only for their stay there but for the voyage to Quebec and the ensuing winter. The military forces arriving in Boston at the beginning of summer were considerably larger than the total population of the town.[103] The resulting strain upon available

---

[100] Graham, *Walker Expedition*, pp. 10–11.

[101] Unless otherwise indicated, the authority is Professor Graham's helpful introduction and the documents he provides in his *Walker Expedition*.

[102] *Ibid.*, p. 16.

[103] Bridenbaugh, *Cities in the Wilderness*, p. 143, estimates Boston's population in 1710 at 9,000.

resources put a strain also upon the tempers of every person who struggled to meet the demand or to control the upward trend of prices. Everything considered, the job was handled well, for Walker sailed out with a three-month supply in addition to what remained of his British rations. His forces had been augmented by better than 1,000 New England recruits, most of them from Massachusetts, and by their transports. Meanwhile, in New York Robert Hunter, the new and able governor of that province, had assembled a force of more than 2,000 men, including a contingency from Connecticut, volunteers from New Jersey, and some 800 Indians, most of them Iroquois.[104] When Walker sailed, Nicholson hurried to New York to take command.

The inglorious end to the entire enterprise followed all too soon. It had been assumed that pilots competent for the navigation of the St. Lawrence would be readily available in New England, but this proved not to be the case. Walker had sailed without a pilot in whom he had confidence, and with no dependable charts.[105] On the night of August 23, fog, gale winds, and miscalculations as to position brought eight transports and one sloop to destruction in the lower St. Lawrence with the loss of almost 800 lives, mainly among the British soldiers. The fainthearted Walker abandoned the expedition and returned to England, while the disappointed colonial contingency sailed back to Boston. Nicholson, who had gotten up to Lake George, on hearing the news withdrew in disgust to Albany.

Again there were appeals for revival of the plan, but it is difficult to say how seriously they were intended. Certainly, they stood no chance of success. A government which momentarily had seized an apparent opportunity to bolster its prestige quickly reverted to its preference for peace. The truce agreed upon in 1712 led to the final peace sealed at Utrecht in March, 1713. Although Walker and Hill had compounded their fault by failing to seize an opportunity on

104 McIlwain, *Wraxall's Abridgement*, p. 91, lists a total of over 600 Indians as having been recruited from the Iroquois. See also Osgood, *American Colonies in the Eighteenth Century*, I, 441–443. The force included the independent companies of regulars, beefed up by some of the recently arrived Palatines.

105 On this critical question, Graham's discussion is the fullest, but see also Waller's *Vetch*, pp. 218–225. For a time Vetch, who commanded the New England contingent, was allowed to lead the way, but he was not leading at the time of the disaster. As Graham observes, Sir William Phips' successful negotiation of the passage in 1690 argues nothing, except for his good luck.

the way home for an attack upon the French in Newfoundland, neither of them seems even to have received a reprimand and both men won new assignments. The withdrawal of Walker's half pay by a Whig government after the accession of George I may have been, as much as anything else, punishment for his Tory convictions and affiliations. As Gerald Graham has observed, the Walker expedition "fitted into no carefully wrought scheme of imperial expansion."[106] Even the colonists, with whom the idea of expelling the French from North America had its origin, were thinking defensively rather than acquisitively. It was not new empires they desired but rather security in what they already possessed.

Nowhere does the point receive more emphasis than in their long-continuing neglect to exploit, except for the purposes of fishing and some small trade, the conquest of Nova Scotia. That province has been aptly described as *New England's Outpost*, but outpost precisely is what it remained for many years after its acquisition.[107] English possession of the place was confirmed in the treaty of 1713, very largely perhaps because the French had made no effort to repossess it and in the bargaining had to be content with confirmation of their own title to Cape Breton Island, where Fort Louisburg would soon be raised to guard the entrance to the St. Lawrence. The addition of Hudson's Bay to Britain's possessions might be viewed as representing some broad plan to encroach wherever possible upon the French position in North America, except for evidence that this marks chiefly the victory of "a persistent pressure group."[108] In its long contest with French agents for the fur trade of that area, the Hudson's Bay Company had been disappointed in the Treaty of Ryswick, and thereafter kept all ministries, of whatever party, fully posted as to an interest shared by more than one influential person.

The acquisition of full sovereignty in Newfoundland represented a radical departure from long-established policy, but only for the purpose of providing better protection for the fisheries, England's great "nursery of seamen," by denying France an opportunity to

---

[106] In *Empire of the North Atlantic*, p. 101.

[107] See Brebner's work of that title, especially Chaps. III and IV.

[108] Rich, *Hudson's Bay Company*, I, 424, and the excellent chapter of which the quotation is a part.

occupy any onshore position.[109] A long and troubled history, which had had its beginning almost a century before in the establishment of both French and English colonies upon the Isle of St. Kitts in the West Indies, now reached its end in a provision of the treaty confirming an English military victory early in the war. Other provisions, including especially those giving England possession of Gibraltar and Minorca, and the Assiento, a contract for supply of slaves to Spanish America, assured for Utrecht a significant place in the history of the British Empire. But for the English colonists in North America the war had been an extremely disappointing experience, one that brought them nothing more than an incomplete easterly extension of the northern frontier and a better understanding of the threats that might still be posed for them by Cape Breton, Canada, Louisiana, and Florida.

Even so, the war holds a place of great importance for students of American history. It invites comment once more upon the inclination of the colonists in time of war to reach for the total solution, for some definitive answer to the problem of their security. It presents a significant contrast between the brutality with which warfare against the Indian could be prosecuted and the general observance of the rules of "civilized" warfare among the contending Europeans.[110] In South Carolina, as in New England, a specified part of the plunder promised for enlistment in offensive expeditions was Indian captives to be sold into slavery.[111] Simultaneously, the previously enslaved Negro found himself the victim of new fears for the advantage he might take of wartime emergencies. A South Carolina statute of 1704 provided for special mounted patrols to keep the slaves under strict surveillance in time of alarm, and a system of coastal "watch" stations, which became a main feature of the defensive measures taken by that province, was made to serve the additional purpose of apprehending slaves who might attempt

[109] The best brief discussion of Newfoundland's history I have seen is Gerald S. Graham, "Newfoundland in British Strategy from Cabot to Napoleon," in R. A. MacKay (ed.), *Newfoundland: Economic, Diplomatic, and Strategic Studies* (Toronto, 1946), pp. 245–264.

[110] Subercase was allowed to surrender at Port Royal with full military honors, and the exchange of prisoners through familiar procedures seems to have been common.

[111] Thomas Cooper and D. J. McCord (eds.), *The Statutes at Large of South Carolina* (10 vols., Columbia, 1836–41), II, 212, 321, 324, 325.

an escape to St. Augustine. Rewards for the capture of runaway slaves were among the inducements offered for enlistment in the "watch" garrisons.[112] The dependence, both on the northern and the southern frontiers, upon relatively long-term enlistments for garrison or ranger duty and for distant campaigns probably carries the fundamental explanation for evidence strongly suggesting that warfare was becoming the business primarily of the less fortunately placed of the European colonists—those who were likely to be most responsive to special inducements for enlistment, including wages that might be four times the rate then paid European regulars.[113] Of general interest also are Admiral Walker's bitter complaints over his inability to impress colonial seamen for the purpose of replacing the many English seamen who deserted at Boston. The issue had risen in the preceding war and became critical with the increased number of vessels assigned by the Navy to American stations in the second war. Unfortunately for Walker and fortunately for New Englanders who knew the ropes, the government in Westminster had been remarkably responsive to the protests of English merchants trading to America and of colonial governments which consistently resisted impressment by the Navy in American waters.[114] The right of impressment by the colonial governments remained untouched, but their preference seems to have been for some form of "voluntary" response to the public need with compensation.

If not everywhere, then certainly in the colonies engaged in military operations, the war years also brought a significant increase in power for the lower houses of assembly. Accustomed by repeatedly confirmed precedent to a right of consultation on all major questions of public policy, the assemblymen had to be consulted on any venture calling for the co-operation of the community in giving effect to a dangerous and expensive enterprise. No man who knew the colonists, be he Joseph Dudley, Samuel Vetch, or Francis Nicholson, acted upon any other assumption. Not even the prospect

---

112 *Ibid.*, II, 254–255, 300–302, 319–320, 354–357; IX, 623.

113 See especially Shy, "New Look at Colonial Militia." The statement regarding wages depends upon Vetch's observation in 1709 that the eighteen pence per day, plus an allowance for subsistence, paid the troops advancing toward Montreal represented four times the normal pay in Europe. Waller, *Vetch*, p. 135.

114 See Dora Mae Clark, "The Impressment of Seamen in the American Colonies," in *Essays . . . Presented to Charles McLean Andrews*, pp. 198–224.

of military assistance from the imperial government reduced this dependence, for in every instance the promise of such support had been made in response to prior assurances of full co-operation from the colonists. Nor had the governor been able to gain from the colonists' hope for imperial aid quite the advantage it might be assumed he could have. At one point early in the war the Board of Trade pointedly suggested that the queen might be more willing to help Massachusetts out of her difficulties if the General Court made some more appropriate provision for the governor's salary.[115] Dudley's proposals for a permanent establishment of salaries, both for himself and for the judges in the courts, had been a subject of dispute since the beginning of his administration. And so it remained to the end, with the governor and the judges continuing to receive what the General Court each year elected to grant or give.

Dudley had begun his administration under many disadvantages. None too well remembered by most of the colonists for his past identification with their history, he had to work with an elected council over which he had little control beyond that provided by the veto power in elections to the council he repeatedly exercised, the patronage at his command, and the not inconsiderable talent he displayed as a wartime leader. He had also to win the co-operation of a House of Representatives led by two old enemies, Elisha Cooke and Thomas Oakes. In addition, the governor's enemies included Sir Henry Ashurst, long-time influential friend of New England in England, and in Massachusetts both of the Mathers, Increase and Cotton. Dudley stoutly defended the prerogatives of the governor's office as they were defined in his instructions, but the demands of war could be imperative, as is illustrated by a fight over the speakership in 1705. The House elected Oakes, to whom Dudley persistently had denied a place in council; the governor rejected the choice; the House refused to elect another; the council failed to back the governor; and he finally yielded because of his "just Sence of the pressing Affairs of the War that demand a very Sudden dispatch of this Session"—"Saving to Her Most Sacred Majesty her just Rights . . . at all times."[116] In other words, the governor's concession to expediency was not to be understood as a sacrifice of

115 Kimball, *Joseph Dudley,* pp. 96–97.
116 *Ibid.,* p. 93.

constitutional principle, but an important precedent nevertheless had been established.

It would be easy, however, to exaggerate the extent to which the war years were marked by conflict between the executive and the legislature. If Dudley had a war on his hands, so too did the House of Representatives. In any over-all view, the emphasis undoubtedly belongs to the generally effective collaboration of the governor and the lower house in the prosecution of the war.[117] At the same time, it has to be said that this collaboration was maintained at not a little cost to the authority of the governor's office, not so much in the settlement of (or the failure to settle) clean-cut constitutional issues as rather in what may be described as the silent concessions that were made for the sake of agreement on urgent war measures. The point has general significance, for this was true of other colonies involved in the war as well as of Massachusetts.

The authority belonging to the colonial governor as chief executive and commander in chief long since had been whittled down by the need he invariably faced in time of emergency, if only because he had no military force at his command except such as might be drawn from the general population of the colony, to win the support of the general assembly or court. But the governor's repeated consultations during Queen Anne's War with assemblymen on a wide variety of urgent questions—the forces to be raised, the strategy to be followed in their employment, even the commanders to be appointed, and of course the best way to apportion the burden, financial and other—lends to that war a place of no small importance in the development of the characteristic American assumption that the power to make war belongs to the representatives of the people who must fight it and pay for it.

Nowhere does this become clearer than in the provisions that were made for financing the war, a subject as important for the economic history of the colonies as for their political history. The extraordinary demands the war made upon colonial treasuries were met very largely by issues of paper currency which launched the colonies upon a pioneering and unusually significant venture in monetary history. There is no obligation here to undertake an

---

[117] Osgood, *American Colonies in the Eighteenth Century*, II, 142–143, especially.

evaluation of the long, and occasionally stormy, history of paper money in colonial America, but it may be well to note by way of introduction that modern historians have studied the subject much more sympathetically than did an earlier generation of scholars, who often were guided by their own predilections for "sound" money, as the term was understood in the day of William Jennings Bryan. It is now suggested that the colonial experiments with paper money deserve to be remembered more for their success than for their failings, and that without the new medium of exchange the economic growth of eighteenth-century America might have been retarded.[118]

Certainly, the paper issued during these war years served not only to finance expensive military ventures but to meet also a long existing need for an adequate medium of exchange. Faced with a trade balance which tended to draw coin toward London, and denied a right either to mint their own coins or to prohibit the export of such coins as found their way into the colonies (most commonly the Spanish piece of eight), the colonial governments had been able to provide little in the way of remedy beyond the tolerance they often showed for pirates and the progressive efforts they made to attract foreign coins by inflating their monetary value.[119] After 1700 the first of these expedients could provide only limited help, for by that time the attempts of the English government to suppress piracy were more successful than formerly they had been. As for the second resort, it never had served to solve the basic problem. Moreover, it had precipitated a running contest among several of the colonies to outbid one another for coin, with the result that the queen, by proclamation in 1704, and Parliament, by a statute of 1708, undertook to limit and make uniform the inflation that would be allowed for foreign coins circulating in the colonies. The colonists found ways of evading the new restriction, but whatever the advantage so gained, a need for some additional medium of exchange continued. That need probably would have led, sooner or later, to experimentation with some form of the "land

118 For a survey of the literature on this subject and a judicious re-evaluation of the topic, see E. James Ferguson, "Currency Finance: An Interpretation of Colonial Monetary Practices," *William and Mary Quarterly*, 3d ser., X (1953), 153–180.

119 Nettels, *Money Supply*, especially Chap. IX.

bank" which acquired popularity in the postwar years, for there had been discussion of such a possibility even before the English Revolution.[120] Instead, the first experiments with a paper currency came as a result of the imperative demands of wartime finance.

Massachusetts had pointed the way in 1690 with paper issued in support of Sir William Phips' expedition to Quebec. Among the other colonies, South Carolina was the first to follow this lead, with an issue in 1703 to cover the debt incurred in the abortive attack of the preceding year upon St. Augustine. Additional emissions, amounting in all to £20,000, were made between 1707 and 1712, when new bills for £52,000 were issued, partly for the retirement of older bills and partly to create a fund for loans to private individuals on security given, usually in the form of a land mortgage. One follows here a significant transition from the original use of paper money for the payment of public charges to its emission in a more general service to the community through the first "land bank" actually to be established in colonial America. Massachusetts, which had kept a limited amount of paper in circulation since 1690 and had started the new war with perhaps £5,000 of it outstanding, may have raised the total of its outstanding bills to £160,000 by the end of the war. New York first turned to this resort in 1709 with an emission of £13,000, and followed with an issue of £10,000 in 1711. In 1709 or 1710, New Jersey, Connecticut, Rhode Island, and New Hampshire were added to the list of provinces depending upon paper money for the purpose of meeting their military obligations. North Carolina in 1712, as a result of the Tuscarora War, became the eighth and final province to do so before the end of Queen Anne's War.[121]

The first paper money took the form of a bill of credit through which future revenues were anticipated for the payment of immediate charges. This use of the device was by no means entirely novel. Colonial governments, presiding over predominantly agricultural communities and necessarily receiving the "produce of the country"

[120] *Ibid.*, pp. 251–254; Andrew M. Davis, *Tracts Relating to the Currency of the Massachusetts Bay, 1682–1720* (Cambridge, Mass., 1902), pp. 1–12; Bailyn, *New England Merchants*, pp. 183–185.

[121] The information used here and in the following paragraph depends almost entirely upon Nettels, *Money Supply*, Chap. X, where the footnotes carry a great deal of helpful detail.

in payment of taxes, through most of any tax year had to meet their own costs for supplies purchased or services rendered by the promise of a deferred payment when the taxes were collected. The bill of credit in its simplest form was a written promise of such a payment that normally was expected to be redeemed within a year of its issuance. By endorsement from person to person it often had served as currency, and so to familiarize the colonists, as did such other circulating evidences of credit as the bill of exchange, with the possibilities of a paper form of currency. What was new in the early paper-money legislation was its extension of the period of time over which the revenues of the government were anticipated for immediate use and the scale on which these drafts upon the future were made. Some of the issues were to be redeemed in no more than two years, but there were instances of revenues mortgaged for as much as twelve or more years ahead. In most cases, the statutes stipulated the taxes to be imposed for redemption of the bills, at times by an increase of the taxes regularly imposed, at times by the addition of special taxes, and in other instances by some combination of the two. A few of the provinces undertook to make their bills legal tender and some of them carried interest, apparently on the theory that the province was a borrower. Usually, the bills were not defined as legal tender, but in all cases they became lawful money receivable in the payment of taxes. In short, the new money was backed by taxes, and in theory at least its issuance was a self-liquidating operation that would reach its end when the paper money returned to the treasury in payment of the taxes which backed it. The record on the collection of the taxes imposed for redemption of the bills, as on the faithfulness with which bills returning to the government were retired, is an uneven one. But there was no serious problem of depreciation during the war years, and on the whole this first experiment with paper money has to be viewed as a remarkably successful one. Joseph Dudley probably spoke a plain truth when he insisted after the war that he "could never have subsisted nor clothed the forces, that have defended . . . these colonies . . . but must have left all to ruin and mischief" without paper money.[122]

Legally and constitutionally, the legislation upon which these

122 *Ibid.*, p. 255.

monetary issues everywhere depended represents an extension of the power to tax, a fact well understood by the lower houses of assembly. They had shown since 1689 a growing awareness that control of the purse was critical for the influence they could exert on public policy. The explanation lies partly in their conscious attempt to follow the model provided by the English House of Commons, partly in the fact that wartime conditions lent greater importance to fiscal questions, partly in a natural inclination to counter assertions of authority from outside the colony by strengthening the defenses upon which a desire for local self-determination could depend, and occasionally, with New York as the chief example, by a need to correct abuses in the administration of finance. Over the years the questions in debate had included the right of the lower house to initiate all money bills, which proved not too difficult to win; the more difficult question of a right in the upper house to amend such bills; the right of the elected branch to be consulted on, or even to control, the selection of officers administering the funds it appropriated; and the right of the house to demand an accounting of the expenditures actually made. These issues arose at different times in different provinces, according to circumstance, and with differing degrees of success for the assemblymen. It is difficult to make any summary statement and impossible in the space allowable here to follow in detail the story in each colony.[123] But several general observations can be offered.

Debates of constitutional issues usually were precipitated by practical and substantive questions of public policy. The constitutional arguments employed by assemblymen spoke more for their desire to prevail on the substantive issue in debate than of any broadly conceived view of what the constitution ought to be. Demands made by the house were frequently in more or less obvious conflict with the governor's instructions, whether royal or proprietary, and no really conclusive settlement of the larger question was possible for so long as the superior authority in England

---

[123] General studies of major importance are Labaree, *Royal Government in America*, and Greene, *The Quest of Power*. See also chapters on the several colonies in Osgood, *American Colonies in the Eighteenth Century*, I–II; Henry R. Spencer, *Constitutional Conflict in Provincial Massachusetts* (Columbus, Ohio, 1905) ; Charles W. Spencer, *Phases of Royal Government in New York 1691–1719* (Columbus, Ohio, 1925) .

continued to be recognized as a part of generally accepted constitutional arrangements. Consequently, constitutional issues disputed in this period survived to be disputed again as substantive issues of a later date might dictate. But in the history of parliamentary schemes of government, precedent has a way of gaining new power as with time men find new occasions to call it into play, and so it was to be in the history of the colonial legislative assembly. One traces here no more than the beginning of a contest continuing, off and on, to the time of the American Revolution, and in this beginning the house probably won more through its collaboration with the governor in a common search for the answer to wartime problems than it did from concessions won in open dispute with him.

The special opportunity the house faced through these years was to establish a degree of control over extraordinary revenues that may have been denied it in the control of ordinary revenues, those which over time had become the standard dependence of government for meeting its recurring charges. The ordinary revenues were derived from taxes levied and managed according to long-established custom, and so precedent might be against the house in whatever desire it displayed for a fuller control than theretofore it had bothered to demand. But members of the house now called together in extraordinary circumstances, if not actually in an extraordinary session having the character essentially of a supreme war council, were likely to find themselves easily admitted to full partnership in the drafting of paper-money legislation which specified the military purpose for which the issue was made, prohibited its use for any other purposes, designated the officers charged with its administration, and made them responsible to the general assembly or court for the faithful performance of their duties.[124] That body, let it be noted again, included the governor and council. The insistence upon an ultimate accounting to the general assembly is not to be viewed as a claim to exclusive control by the lower house. What the house had won was a highly significant concession of the right to a share in the exercise of powers historically identified with executive authority.

[124] A number of the acts which I have consulted could be cited here by way of example, but at the cost of unduly burdening these notes.

There are a number of subjects that might be picked up at this point for the sake of a more complete account of developments in the years which preceded the Treaty of Utrecht. An example would be the failure of Whitehall through much of the war to fill the governor's post in Maryland, as though to foretell the ease with which the proprietor soon thereafter recovered his full rights there. Another would be the beginning in 1710 of Alexander Spotswood's long and significant administration in Virginia, but in the space available one could only emphasize the postponement of the governor's later contest with the assembly while he sought its cooperation in efforts to resolve the colony's economic difficulties. And so once more the focus would fall upon the war and the influence of wartime conditions upon the fortunes of the colonists.

It had been a war, as had King William's War, in which the colonists showed great daring and more than a little skill in the organization of extraordinarily ambitious ventures, even on occasion a remarkable capacity for interprovincial collaboration. But it is also notable that such occasions had come to depend, for all the initiative taken by the colonists in proposing grand schemes of conquest, upon the initiative England herself might take for their implementation. While the English colonists of North America were beginning to think in terms their descendants would describe as continental, they were forced anew to learn the extent of their continuing dependence upon England.

That lesson repeatedly had been forced upon them during the half-century that had passed since 1660. If now they were more reconciled to its acceptance than at times before they had seemed to be, it was not merely because they had committed their hopes for security to plans far exceeding their own ability to execute them. Equally important were other lessons they had been taught by a lengthening experience. They had learned that the frequently disturbing intrusion of imperial authority into the management of their affairs had come to be fixed upon objectives more limited than earlier they were feared to be, that the primary purpose of Whitehall's policy was to control the external trade of the colonies, and that questions of public policy fundamentally affecting the domestic life of the colonists were still very largely subject to the persuasions of local interest. Moreover, they had learned that the governing agencies of Whitehall in their exercise of an ultimate power to settle disputed issues were both subject to manipulation in behalf of an American interest and encouragingly responsive to the colonist's claim that he enjoyed the rights of an Englishman, according to the interpretation given those rights by the Revolution of 1689. That those rights were not quite so full as some of the colonists earlier had dared to think they ought to be matters less than does the fact that in all of the colonies, and nowhere more so than in the proprietary colonies, men had found it helpful to identify their political aims with principles of government more enlightened than those generally prevailing theretofore, either in England or America.

Bibliographical Essay

For the sake of space, a number of works cited only incidentally in the text have been omitted from the following listing, which may be helpfully supplemented by reference to the bibliography in Louis B. Wright, *The Cultural Life of the American Colonies, 1607–1763* (New York, 1957), an earlier volume in this series.

From time to time I have had occasion to consult original sources in search of an answer to some question that seemed to be left unanswered by the secondary literature. In each such instance the citation in the foregoing text is specific, in every instance the reference is to one of the more obvious and familiar printed collections or calendars, and in some instances reference to particular sources will be made below. I have thought there would be little point in giving here the incomplete list of published sources I actually have consulted, and even less point in a full listing of what I have not found occasion to consult. Helpful collections of source materials are Francis N. Thorpe, *Federal and State Constitutions, Colonial Charters, and Other Organic Laws of the States, Territories, and Colonies Now or Heretofore Forming the United States of America* (7 vols., Washington, 1909), the most convenient place to consult any of the colonial charters; Merrill Jensen, *American Colonial Documents to 1776* (New York, 1955); the many volumes of "Original Narratives" published early in this century under the general editorship of J. Franklin Jameson, several of which will be mentioned below and of which the most generally useful volume for this period is Charles M. Andrews, *Narratives of the Insurrections* (New York, 1915); and Michael G. Hall, Lawrence H. Leder, and Michael G. Kammen, *The Glorious Revolution in America* (Chapel Hill, 1964).

General

Comprehensive histories to which students of the period must turn repeatedly are Herbert L. Osgood, *The American Colonies in the Seventeenth Century* (3 vols., New York, 1904–7) ; its less successful continuation, *The American Colonies in the Eighteenth Century* (4 vols., New York, 1924) ; and Charles M. Andrews, *The Colonial Period of American History* (4 vols., New Haven, 1934–38), of which the third volume provides the most authoritative single history of the post-Restoration settlements and the fourth an especially authoritative study of colonial policy and administration. Andrews was nowhere more at home than when discussing the English background of the American story, but the student needing guidance on the fuller context of contemporary English history will find David Ogg's *England in the Reign of Charles II* (2d. ed., 2 vols., Oxford, 1955) and his *England in the Reigns of James II and William III* (Oxford, 1955) conveniently and dependably helpful. G. N. Clark, *The Later Stuarts, 1660–1714* (Oxford, 1934), is more compact.

The Imperial Context

Nothing stands out more prominently in any review of the bibliography for this period in American history than the concern it shows for an understanding of colonial policy and administration. This is not surprising, for it was the period, almost precisely, in which the "Old Colonial System" took shape—a shape that was not to be drastically altered until the eve of the American Revolution.

Especially important has been the influence of George Louis Beer and Charles M. Andrews, two superbly equipped scholars who early in the century insisted upon the need for a fuller and more sympathetic study of British policy by American historians. Beer's *The Origins of the British Colonial System, 1578–1660* (New York, 1908), though ending where this present volume begins, was essentially an informed commentary upon the basic legislation of the Restoration era. Its sequel, *The Old Colonial System, 1660–1754: Part I, the Establishment of the System, 1660–1688* (New York, 1912), still carries an abundance of useful information. The fourth volume of Andrews' *magnum opus* was preceded by his study of *British Committees, Commissions, and Councils of Trade and Plantations, 1622–1675* (Baltimore, 1908) ; his lengthy and separately published introduction to the *Records of the Vice-Admiralty Court of Rhode Island, 1716–1752* (Washington, 1936) ; and his suggestive essays on *The Colonial Background of the American Revolution* (New Haven, 1924) . His *Colonial*

Self-Government, 1652–1689 (New York and London, 1904) was one of the more distinguished volumes in the original *American Nation* series. Unusually influential works by students of Andrews include Viola Barnes, *The Dominion of New England: A Study in British Colonial Policy* (New Haven, 1923) ; Leonard W. Labaree, *Royal Government in America: A Study of the British Colonial System before 1783* (New Haven, 1930), and his repeatedly helpful collection of *Royal Instructions to British Colonial Governors, 1670–1776* (2 vols., New York, 1935) ; and Gertrude A. Jacobsen, *William Blathwayt: A Late Seventeenth Century English Administrator* (New Haven, 1932). *Essays in Colonial History Presented to Charles McLean Andrews by His Students* (New Haven, 1931) is an unusually rewarding *festschrift*.

Lawrence A. Harper, *The English Navigation Laws* (New York, 1939), is a work of major importance, as also is Robert G. Albion's study of the related subject of *Forests and Seapower: The Timber Problems of the Royal Navy, 1652–1862* (Cambridge, 1926). Joseph H. Smith, *Appeals to the Privy Council from the American Plantations* (New York, 1950), is definitive. Michael G. Hall's *Edward Randolph and the American Colonies, 1676–1703* (Chapel Hill, N.C., 1960) has a value out of proportion to its length, and especially for the light it sheds upon the frequently uncertain course of policy at critical points in its development. That the special concerns of current scholarship promise to lend a continuing emphasis to the imperial context is suggested by Thomas C. Barrow's very recent *Trade and Empire: The British Customs Service in Colonial America, 1660–1775* (Cambridge, Mass., 1967).

Among other recent studies, special mention belongs to a number of articles appearing in the third series of the *William and Mary Quarterly*, as follows: Michael G. Hall, "The House of Lords, Edward Randolph, and the Navigation Act of 1696," XIV (1957), 494–515; Philip S. Haffenden, "The Crown and the Colonial Charters, 1675–1688," XV (1958), 297–311, 452–466; Alison G. Olson, "William Penn, Parliament, and Proprietary Government," XVIII (1961), 176–195; Bruce T. McCully, "From the North Riding to Morocco: The Early Years of Governor Francis Nicholson, 1655–1686," XIX (1962), 534–556; Richard S. Dunn, "The Downfall of the Bermuda Company: A Restoration Farce," XX (1963), 487–512; and Stephen S. Webb, "The Strange Career of Francis Nicholson," XXIII (1966), 513-548. Special mention also belongs to a paper by Mildred Campbell, "The Conflict of Opinion on Population in Its Relation to Emigration," in William A. Aiken and B. D. Hening, *Conflict in Stuart England: Essays in Honour of Wallace Notestein* (London, 1960), pp. 169–201.

The frequently overlapping interests of economic and imperial historians is well illustrated in Curtis P. Nettels, "The Economic Relations of Boston, Philadelphia, and New York, 1680–1715," *Journal of Economic and Business History*, III (1930–31), 185–215; his study of "England's Trade with New England and New York," *Publications of the Colonial Society of Massachusetts*, XXVIII (1935), 322–350; and especially his *The Money Supply of the American Colonies before 1720* (Madison, Wis., 1934). Jacob M. Price, *The Tobacco Adventure to Russia: Enterprise, Politics, and Diplomacy in the Quest for a Northern Market for English Colonial Tobacco, 1676–1722*, in *Transactions of the American Philosophical Society*, new ser., LI, Pt. 1 (1961), and his article on "The Economic Growth of the Chesapeake and the European Market, 1697–1775," *Journal of Economic History*, XXIV (1964), 496–511, emphasize the importance of markets for that part of the tobacco crop that was surplus to any need of England herself, a factor too often discounted by some of the earlier apologists for colonial policy. In this connection, Ralph Davis, "English Foreign Trade, 1660–1700," *Economic History Review*, 2d. ser., VII (1954), 150–166, is helpful. Mention belongs also to John M. Hemphill's unpublished Ph.D. dissertation, "Virginia and the English Commercial System, 1689–1733" (Princeton University, 1964), and his "Freight Rates in the Maryland Tobacco Trade, 1705–1762," *Maryland Historical Magazine*, LIV (1959), 36–58, 154–187; E. Lipson, *The Economic History of England* (3 vols., London, 1920–31); and Richard Pares, *Yankees and Creoles: The Trade between North America and the West Indies before the American Revolution* (Cambridge, Mass., 1955).

Studies of British expansion in areas outside the later limits of the United States have greatly enriched the bibliography. In addition to such older works as Vincent T. Harlow, *A History of Barbados, 1625–1685* (Oxford, 1926); George P. Insh, *The Company of Scotland Trading to Africa and the Indies* (London and New York, 1932), and his earlier *Scottish Colonial Schemes, 1620–1686* (Glascow, 1922); or J. Bartlet Brebner, *New England's Outpost: Acadia before the Conquest of Canada* (New York, 1927); particular mention belongs to A. P. Thornton, *West-India Policy under the Restoration* (Oxford, 1956); Kenneth G. Davies, *The Royal African Company* (London, 1957), a most welcome addition to George F. Zook, *The Company of Royal Adventurers Trading to Africa* (Lancaster, Pa., 1919); and E. E. Rich, *Hudson's Bay Company, 1670–1870* (3 vols., New York, 1961), which was originally published by the Hudson's Bay Record Society as *The History of the Hudson's Bay Company, 1670–1870* (2 vols., London, 1958–59).

No historians have better understood the role of warfare in the history of the Old Empire than have two of the United States' most eminent historians, Francis Parkman and Admiral Mahan, but more recently British and Canadian scholars have held the lead in further pursuit of the subject. Parkman's account of the first phase of the Anglo-French contest for the possession of North America remains the classic account, but it should be read with a view to the corrections made by W. J. Eccles in his *Frontenac: The Courtier Governor* (Toronto, 1959), and his *Canada under Louis XIV, 1663–1701* (Toronto, 1964). Mahan's themes are best explored today in Gerald S. Graham, *Empire of the North Atlantic: The Maritime Struggle for North America* (Toronto, 1950), and his introduction to the documents published in *The Walker Expedition to Quebec, 1711* (Navy Records Society, 1953). Also helpful are John Ehrman, *The Navy in the War of William III, 1689–1697* (Cambridge, Eng., 1953); J. H. Owen, *War at Sea under Queen Anne, 1702–1708* (Cambridge, Eng., 1938); R. D. Harriman, *Queen Anne's Navy: Documents Concerning the Administration of the Navy of Queen Anne, 1702–1714* (Navy Records Society, 1961); and G. N. Clark, "War Trade and Trade War, 1701–1713," *Economic History Review*, I (1927–28), 262–280.

Among modern works by American scholars, the most helpful is G. M. Waller, *Samuel Vetch: Colonial Enterpriser* (Chapel Hill, N.C., 1960), which is more exact on some of the details of military operations in North America during Queen Anne's War than is any other study I have used. Dora Mae Clark's essay, "The Impressment of Seaman in the American Colonies," in *Essays . . . Presented to Charles McLean Andrews*, pp. 198–224, calls attention to a significant and all too often overlooked chapter in our history. John Shy's "A New Look at Colonial Militia," *William and Mary Quarterly*, 3d. ser., XX (1963), 175–185, as also the introductory chapter of his *Toward Lexington: The Role of the British Army in the Coming of the Revolution* (Princeton, 1965), invite attention to changing military practices and policies as the colonists became more largely involved in conflict with other European forces rather than with merely the Indians. Ruth Bourne, *Queen Anne's Navy in the West Indies* (New Haven, 1939), supplements the more general works listed above. Nellis M. Crouse, *The French Struggle for the West Indies* (New York, 1943), and *Lemoyne d'Iberville, Soldier of New France* (Ithaca, 1954); John J. Tepaske, *The Governorship of Spanish Florida, 1700–1763* (Durham, N.C, 1964); and Charles W. Arnade, *The Siege of St. Augustine in 1702* (Gainesville, 1959), are all useful for students of this period. An old interest in wartime efforts to stimulate the production of naval stores in the colonies, represented by Eleanor L. Lord, *Industrial Experiments in the British Colonies of North America* (Baltimore, 1898), finds renewed expression in Joseph J. Malone, *Pine Trees and Politics: The Naval Stores and Forest Policy in Colonial New England, 1691–1775* (Seattle, 1964). No modern author has bothered, nor is it likely that one will, to spell out the helpful details of warfare that are to be found in Samuel

A. Drake, *The Border Wars of New England* (New York, 1897). Howard H. Peckham, *The Colonial Wars, 1689–1762* (Chicago, 1964), provides a brief and authoritative summary.

New England

Second only to the interest in imperial policy and administration has been the American's continuing concern with his Puritan ancestry, a subject on which some of the older histories continue to be useful, and especially John G. Palfrey, *History of New England* (5 vols., Boston, 1858–90), which too often is dismissed from consideration because of its filiopiety. It still contains much information that is helpful to the modern historian. James Truslow Adams, *The Founding of New England* (Boston, 1921), was an exceptionally influential work at the time of its publication, but it is remembered today chiefly for the many corrections it has received from an extraordinary array of talented historians.

Among these Kenneth B. Murdock held the lead with a learned and detailed biography of *Increase Mather: The Foremost American Puritan* (Cambridge, Mass., 1925). S. E. Morison provided a powerful stimulant for more sympathetic study of the Puritan in his *Builders of the Bay Colony* (Boston and New York, 1930), which helped to destroy a stereotype that had become all too popular. He followed up, to mention only the works pertinent to study of the later period, with *The Puritan Pronaos: Studies in the Intellectual Life of New England in the Seventeenth Century* (New York, 1936; 2d. ed. under the title *The Intellectual Life of Colonial New England*, 1956); and *Harvard College in the Seventeenth Century* (2 vols., Cambridge, 1936). Perry Miller's penetrating study of the region's intellectual history fortunately includes *The New England Mind: From Colony to Province* (Cambridge, Mass., 1953), which is fundamental for an understanding of much more than the intellectual life of New England during the later years of the century. Perhaps Miller will be best remembered for an essay, "Errand into the Wilderness," first published in the *William and Mary Quarterly*, 3d. ser., X (1953), 3–19, and subsequently (at Cambridge, 1956) in a collection of his essays which took its title from this piece. Hardly less important was his paper, "The Half-Way Covenant," *New England Quarterly*, VI (1933), 676–715, which made clear an often misunderstood chapter in New England's ecclesiastical history. Edmund S. Morgan, *Visible Saints: The History of a Puritan Idea* (New York, 1963), has added further to our knowledge of this subject and to its place in New England's history.

Bernard Bailyn's illuminating study of *The New England Merchants in the Seventeenth Century* (Cambridge, Mass., 1955) carried us far toward an understanding not only of the region's economic and social history but also of the peculiar tensions reflected in its political history. Bernard and Lotte Bailyn, *Massachusetts Shipping 1697–1714: A Statistical Study* (Cambridge, Mass., 1959), lends an unusual and welcome exactness to our knowledge of the area's mercantile activity. Richard S. Dunn, *Puritans and Yankees: The Winthrop Dynasty of New England, 1630–1717* (Princeton, 1962), revealingly concentrated upon the second and third generations of New England's "first family," and in its second section provided the fullest study we had of John Winthrop, Jr., before the publication of Robert C. Black, III, *The Younger John Winthrop* (New York, 1966). Dunn had previously published "John Winthrop, Jr. and the Narragansett Country," *William and Mary Quarterly*, 3d. ser., XIII (1956), 68–86; and "John Winthrop, Jr., Connecticut Expansionist: The Failure of His Designs on Long Island, 1663–1675," *New England Quarterly*, XXIX (1956), 3–26.

For Mather's account of his later mission to England, see Michael G. Hall, "The Autobiography of Increase Mather," *Proceedings of the American Antiquarian Society*, LXXI (1961), 920–344. George Allen Cook, *John Wise: Early American Democrat* (New York, 1952), is the fullest study of that important figure. Alice Lounsberry, *Sir William Phips: Treasure Fisherman and Governor of the Massachusetts Bay Colony* (New York, 1941), is readable. George D. Langdon, Jr., *Pilgrim Colony: A History of New Plymouth, 1620–1691* (New Haven, 1966), is a welcome addition to the bibliography for the coverage it provides of a long and strangely neglected subject. See also John Demos, "Notes on Life in Plymouth Colony," *William and Mary Quarterly*, 3d. ser. XXII (1965), 264–286. On the witchcraft hysteria at Salem, Charles W. Upham, *Salem Witchcraft, with an Account of Salem Village, and a History of Opinions on Witchcraft and Kindred Subjects* (2 vols., Boston, 1867), is supplemented among modern studies especially by George L. Kittredge, *Witchcraft in Old and New England* (Cambridge, Mass., 1929), and by Marion L. Starkey, *The Devil in Massachusetts* (New York, 1949). Lois K. Mathews, *The Expansion of New England* (Boston and New York, 1909) remains a repeatedly useful compendium. Isabel M. Calder, *The New Haven Colony* (New Haven, 1934), contributes significantly to our understanding of some of the more important chapters of New England's history and of New Jersey's beginnings as well.

Until recently the New England town, for all the talk about it, has been the subject of little close study. John F. Sly, *Town Government in Massachusetts, 1620–1930* (Cambridge, Mass., 1930), remains the standard study, though one to be checked against the findings of Sumner Chilton Powell, *Puritan Village: The Formation of a New England Town* (Middletown, Conn., 1963); Kenneth A. Lockridge and Alan Kreider, "The Evolution of Massachusetts Town Government, 1640–1740," *William and Mary*

Quarterly, 3d. ser., XXIII (1966), 549–574; and Lockridge's unpublished Ph.D. dissertation, "Dedham, 1636–1736: The Anatomy of a Puritan Utopia" (Princeton University, 1965). Leonard W. Labaree, *Milford, Connecticut: The Early Development of a Town as Shown in Its Land Records* (New Haven, 1938), is an especially helpful guide, but one the historian must keep in mind because librarians have not always catalogued it apart from the entry they have made for the Connecticut Tercentenary Series, in which it is one of the more significant titles. Philip J. Greven, Jr., "Old Patterns in the New World: The Distribution of Land in 17th Century Andover," *Essex Institute Historical Collections*, CI (1965), 133–148, is a helpful supplement.

On the county, see especially Zechariah Chafee, Jr. (ed.), *Records of the Suffolk County Court, 1671–1680*, in *Publications of the Colonial Society of Massachusetts*, XXIX (Boston, 1933); Joseph H. Smith (ed.), *Colonial Justice in Western Massachusetts (1639–1702): The Pynchon Court Record* (Cambridge, Mass., 1961); Neal W. Allen, Jr. (ed.), *The Court Records of York County, Maine, Province of Massachusetts Bay, November, 1692–January, 1710–11*, in *Province and Court Records of Maine*, IV (Portland, 1958); and the introduction by John T. Farrell to *The Superior Court Diary of William Samuel Johnson, 1772–1773, with Appropriate Records and File Papers of the Superior Court of the Colony of Connecticut for the Terms, December 1772, through March 1773* (Washington, 1942).

Harry M. Ward, *The United Colonies of New England, 1643–1690* (New York, 1961), is the most recent study of the New England Confederation. Chilton L. Powell has contributed a useful article on "Marriage in Early New England," *New England Quarterly*, I (1928), 323–334. Paul R. Lucas, "Colony or Commonwealth: Massachusets Bay, 1661–1666," *William and Mary Quarterly*, 3d. ser., XXIV (1967), 88–107, emphasizes the divisions of opinion in that province on issues raised by the Restoration.

Although the more important studies in this general category have been written in the larger context provided by the dominant influence of Puritanism, one finds occasion to consult such more narrowly focused studies as Samuel G. Arnold, *History of the State of Rhode Island and Providence Plantations* (2 vols., Providence, 1894); Frank B. Sanborn, *New Hampshire: An Epitome of Popular Government* (Boston and New York, 1904); or Albert C. Bates, *The Charter of Connecticut* (Hartford, 1932).

Other Regional Studies

Only the New England colonies can be viewed as constituting in the seventeenth century a distinct region whose common history transcends in importance the history of any one part of the community. But the interest historians have found in the background of later regional groupings of great importance in our national history has resulted in some of the more informative studies of colonial America. One has only to mention Lewis C. Gray, *History of Agriculture in the Southern United States to 1860* (2 vols., Washington, 1933) ; or Edgar W. Knight (ed.) , *A Documentary History of Education in the South before 1860* (5 vols., Chapel Hill, N.C., 1949–53) ; or Verner Crane's unusually valuable *The Southern Frontier, 1670–1732* (Durham, N.C., 1928) . My own study of *The Southern Colonies in the Seventeenth Century, 1607–1689* (Baton Rouge, 1949) , probably would not have been written except for an invitation to contribute to the multivolume *A History of the South* sponsored on the Littlefield Fund by the University of Texas and published by the Louisiana State University Press.

Other studies to be mentioned in this connection include Avery O. Craven, *Soil Exhaustion as a Factor in the Agricultural History of Virginia and Maryland, 1606–1860* (Urbana, Ill., 1926) ; William P. Cumming, *The Southeast in Early Maps, with an Annotated Check List of Printed and Manuscript Regional and Local Maps of Southeastern North America during the Colonial Period* (Princeton, 1958) ; and Arthur P. Middleton, *Tobacco Coast: A Maritime History of Chesapeake Bay in the Colonial Era* (Newport News, Va., 1953) . No doubt, Clarence W. Alvord and Lee Bidgood, *The First Explorations of the Trans-Allegheny Region by the Virginians, 1650–1674* (Cleveland, 1912) , speaks more for the modern interest in the history of the West than of the South. William P. Cumming (ed.) , *The Discoveries of John Lederer* (Charlottesville and WinstonSalem, 1958) , restores Lederer's reputation as an explorer.

The so-called Middle Colonies have yet to claim a historian of their own, and Thomas J. Wertenbaker's *The Founding of American Civilization: The Middle Colonies* (New York, 1938) is one of the few major works even to get the designation into a title.

Provincial Histories

Except for the New England settlements, the historian of colonial America is heavily dependent upon a bibliography falling generally into the category of provincial or state history. Some of the studies are quite old and so representative of dated scholarly interests, but others demonstrate that the modern scholar still finds within the limits of a single colony profitable opportunities for the pursuit of his own special interests.

The Carolinas

Edward McCrady, *The History of South Carolina under the Proprietary Government, 1670–1719* (New York, 1897) , and David D. Wallace, *South*

Carolina: A Short History, 1520–1948 (Chapel Hill, N.C., 1951), have been most helpfully supplemented by M. Eugene Sirmans, *Colonial South Carolina: A Political History, 1663–1763* (Chapel Hill, 1966). R. D. W. Connor, *History of North Carolina* (4 vols., Chicago and New York, 1919), of which Vol. I covers the colonial and Revolutionary periods, has been replaced as the standard by Hugh T. Lefler and Albert R. Newsome, *The History of a Southern State: North Carolina* (Chapel Hill, N.C., 1954; rev. ed., 1963). Paul M. McCain, *The County Court in North Carolina before 1750,* Historical Papers of the Trinity College Historical Society (Durham, N.C., 1954), is helpful. Because of the peculiar importance of Shaftesbury's leadership, Louise F. Brown, *The First Earl of Shaftesbury* (New York, 1933), should be added. Shaftesbury's own papers published in the *Collections of the South Carolina Historical Society,* V (1897), and Alexander S. Salley, Jr., *Narratives of Early Carolina, 1650–1708* (New York, 1911), are especially useful. Erma Edwards Parker (ed.), *North Carolina Charters and Constitutions, 1578–1698* (Raleigh, 1963), has helpfully established the texts for the successive issues and revisions of the Fundamental Constitutions of Carolina.

Delaware

The State of Delaware has yet to find the historian who will write comprehensively and fully of its experience as an English colonial community. Although close attention has been given the earlier Swedish-Dutch period of its history, much of the information for the years after 1664 must be sought in widely scattered writings that are primarily concerned with the histories of New York, Pennsylvania, or New Jersey. Recently, several helpful papers have appeared in *Delaware History,* especially H. Clay Reed, "The Early New Castle Court," IV (1951), 227–245; and Robert W. Johannsen, "The Conflict between the Three Lower Counties on the Delaware and the Province of Pennsylvania," V (1952), 96–132. On institutional development, the introduction by Leon de Valinger, Jr., to the *Court Records of Kent County, 1680–1705* (Washington, 1959) is especially useful, as is also his *Colonial Military Organization in Delaware, 1638–1776* (Wilmington, 1938).

Maryland

Maryland, too, has been strangely neglected by recent historians, despite the fullness with which the state's provincial records have been made readily available in the *Maryland Archives.* Except for Donnell M. Owings' revealing study of *His Lordship's Patronage: Offices of Profit in Colonial Maryland* (Baltimore, 1953); David W. Jordan's unpublished Ph.D.

dissertation, "The Royal Period of Colonial Maryland, 1689–1715" (Princeton University, 1966); Nelson W. Rightmyer, *Maryland's Established Church* (Baltimore, 1956); and such helpful papers as Michael G. Kammen, "The Causes of the Maryland Revolution of 1689," *Maryland Historical Magazine*, LV (1960), 293–333; Beverly McAnear (ed.), "Mariland's Grevances Wiy The Have Taken op Arms," *Journal of Southern History*, VIII (1942), 392–409; William A. Reavis, "The Maryland Gentry and Social Mobility, 1637–1676," *William and Mary Quarterly*, 3d. ser., XIV (1957), 418–428; Vertrees J. Wyckoff, "The Sizes of Plantations in Seventeenth-Century Maryland," *Maryland Historical Magazine*, XXXII (1937), 331–339; or the two informative articles by Kenneth L. Carroll on Maryland Quakers, *ibid.*, XLVII (1952), 297–313, and LIII (1958), 326–370, the student of this period is likely to find himself dependent upon Charles M. Andrews' chapters in the second volume of his *Colonial Period* and Newton D. Mereness, *Maryland as a Proprietary Province* (New York, 1901), which fortunately continues to be helpfully dependable. Joseph H. Smith and Philip A. Crowl (eds.), *Court Records of Prince Georges County, Maryland, 1696–1699* (Washington, 1964), has a lengthy and informative introduction.

New York

For this period New York has a bibliography that is surprisingly full of modern studies of significant topics, but one which over all leaves much to be desired. Henry H. Kessler and Eugene Rachlis, *Peter Stuyvesant and His New York* (New York, 1959), is refreshingly free of the reverence with which older historians treated the Dutch period; S. G. Nissenson, *The Patroon's Domain* (New York, 1937), is very informative on a subject of fundamental importance; Dixon R. Fox, *Caleb Heathcote: Gentleman Colonist, the Story of a Career in the Province of New York, 1692–1721* (New York, 1926), and his *Yankees and Yorkers* (New York, 1940), are as illuminating as they are readable; Lawrence H. Leder, *Robert Livingston, 1654–1728, and the Politics of Colonial New York* (Chapel Hill, N.C., 1961), and Philip L. White, *The Beekmans of New York, 1647–1877* (New York, 1956), offer detailed guidance on the founding of two of the state's great families; Harry C. W. Melick, *The Manor of Fordham and Its Founder* (New York, 1950), is helpful on a related subject; Julius Goebel, Jr., and T. Raymond Naughton, *Law Enforcement in Colonial New York: A Study in Criminal Procedure* (New York, 1944), offers assistance on much more than the title may suggest. The value of Beverly McAnear's unpublished Ph.D. dissertation on "Politics in Provincial New York, 1689–1761" (Stanford University, 1935) finds its best testimony in the extent to which it has been mined by practically all who since have written on the period of its coverage. Walter A. Knittle, *The Early Eighteenth Century Palatine Emigration* (Philadelphia, 1936), is full on the Newburgh settlement. Allen W. Trelease, *Indian Affairs in Colonial New York: The Seventeenth Century* (Ithaca, 1960), offers sure guidance on an especially critical part of the story. Richard B. Morris (ed.), *Select Cases of the Mayor's Court of New York City, 1674–1784* (Washington, 1935) has a full and informative introduction which, among other topics discussed, is especially helpful on the transition from Dutch to English rule.

In addition, several articles deserve special mention, and particularly Stanley M. Pargellis, "The Four Independent Companies of New York," in *Essays . . . Presented to Charles McLean Andrews,* pp. 96–123; Isabel M. Calder, "The Earl of Stirling and the Colonization of Long Island," *ibid.,* pp. 74–95; Bernard Mason, "Aspects of the New York Revolt of 1689," *New York History,* XXX (1949), 165–180; and David S. Lovejoy, "Equality and Empire: The New York Charter of Libertyes, 1683," *William and Mary Quarterly,* 3d. ser., XXI (1964), 493–515.

Also, a number of older studies have continuing utility, and none is more informative than John R. Brodhead, *History of the State of New York* (2 vols., New York, 1853–71), which provides a virtual calendar of the province's colonial records before 1689, and so becomes as useful as it is unreadable. Mrs. Schuyler van Rensselaer, *History of the City of New York in the Seventeenth Century* (2 vols., New York, 1909), is another work to which more recent students turn with gratitude for the information it provides. Wilbur C. Abbott, *"Colonel" John Scott of Long Island, 1634?–1696* (New Haven, 1918), seems to have put a block in the way of any later attempt to rescue the "Colonel's" reputation. Henry L. Schoolcraft, "The Capture of New Amsterdam," *English Historical Review,* XXII (1907), 674–693, and Albert E. McKinley, "The Transition from Dutch to English Rule in New York," *American Historical Review,* VI (1900–1901), 693–724, are both informative. Nowhere perhaps are the special talents of J. Franklin Jameson as an editor better displayed than in his *Narratives of New Netherland, 1609–1664* (New York, 1909).

What is lacking is a persuasive synthesis of the full story. Possibly the main trouble has been the inclination to write of the subject in the basic context of a provincial history, when actually the New York jurisdiction of the seventeenth century was both much more and much less than a distinct province. Hurtful for a long time was the desire to perpetuate the tradition of the state's Dutch origins, and more recently its history has suffered on occasion from a dependence upon themes more appropriate to our later history than to a reading of the seventeenth century, as in

Jerome R. Reich, *Leisler's Rebellion: A Study of Democracy in New York, 1664–1720* (Chicago, 1953). Alexander C. Flick (ed.), *History of the State of New York* (10 vols., New York, 1933–37), is topical in its arrangement, and for this early period the discussions are usually disappointingly scanty.

New Jersey

All students of New Jersey's early history remain indebted to Aaron Leaming and Jacob Spicer for *The Grants, Concessions and Original Constitutions of the Province of New Jersey* (Philadelphia, [1752]), as also to William A. Whitehead for, among other services, his *East Jersey under the Proprietary Governments* (Newark, 1875). Also still useful is Edwin P. Tanner, *The Province of New Jersey, 1664–1738* (New York, 1908). More recent studies pertinent to the period here under discussion have been Donald L. Kemmerer, *The Path to Freedom: The Struggle for Self-Government in Colonial New Jersey, 1703–1776* (Princeton, 1940); and especially the contributions from the pen of John E. Pomfret, which include *The Province of West Jersey, 1609–1702: A History of the Origins of an American Colony* (Princeton, 1956); *The Province of East Jersey, 1609–1702: The Rebellious Proprietary* (Princeton, 1962); "The Proprietors of the Province of East Jersey, 1682–1702," *Pennsylvania Magazine of History and Biography*, LXXVII (1953), 251–293; "The Proprietors of the Province of West Jersey, 1674–1702," *ibid.*, LXXV (1951), 117–146; and his contribution to the New Jersey Tercentennial Series, *The New Jersey Proprietors and Their Lands, 1664–1776* (Princeton, 1964).

Other volumes in this last mentioned series include Julian P. Boyd (ed.), *Fundamental Laws and Constitutions of New Jersey, 1664–1964* (Princeton, 1964); Richard P. McCormick, *New Jersey from Colony to State* (Princeton, 1964), possibly the most illuminating short history any state in the Union has of its provincial period; and Wesley Frank Craven, *New Jersey and the English Colonization of North America* (Princeton, 1964).

Pennsylvania

The early history of Pennsylvania has been written mainly, and understandably, as the history of William Penn's "Holy Experiment." No other man identified with our colonial origins has attracted so many biographical studies as has Penn. The latest and fullest is Catherine O. Peare, *William Penn: A Biography* (Philadelphia and New York, 1957); other modern biographies have been listed in footnote 21 of Chapter 6, and the list need not be repeated here. Studies of special aspects of his career include Edward C. O. Beatty, *William Penn as Social Philosopher* (New York,

1939) ; William I. Hull, *William Penn and the Dutch Quaker Migration to Pennsylvania* (Swarthmore, 1935) ; Mary Maples, "William Penn, Classical Republican," *Pennsylvania Magazine of History and Biography,* LXXXI (1957), 138–156, and her unpublished Ph.D. dissertation, "A Cause to Plead: The Political Thought and Career of William Penn" (Bryn Mawr College, 1959) ; and the more recent development of this thesis in Mary Maples Dunn, *William Penn: Politics and Conscience* (Princeton, 1967). Another recent contribution is Joseph E. Illick, *William Penn the Politician: His Relations with the English Government* (Ithaca, 1965). In the absence of a collected edition of Penn's many writings, Frederick B. Tolles and E. Gordon Alderfer, *The Witness of William Penn* (New York, 1957), provides easy access to some of the more important of his papers.

The history of Quakerism is as fundamental for an understanding of Pennsylvania's origins as is Puritanism for an understanding of New England, and fortunately the Quakers from an early date have been keenly alert to the importance of their history. Among modern studies, William C. Braithwaite, *The Beginnings of Quakerism,* as revised for a second edition by Henry J. Cadbury (Cambridge, Eng., 1955), and *The Second Period of Quakerism,* revised by Cadbury (Cambridge, Eng., 1961), are especially important. Arnold Lloyd's *Quaker Social History, 1669–1738* (London, 1950), through its attention to the development of the system of Quaker meetings, helps one to understand the opportunities the Quakers enjoyed for co-ordination of their plans for settlement in America. Rufus Jones *et al., The Quakers in the American Colonies* (London, 1911), continues to be rewarding.

Of outstanding importance is Frederick B. Tolles, *Meeting House and Counting House: The Quaker Merchants of Colonial Philadelphia, 1682–1763* (Chapel Hill, N.C., 1948). Helpful too are the earlier chapters of his *Quakers and the Atlantic Culture* (New York, 1960) ; and his *James Logan and the Culture of Provincial America* (Boston, 1957). A recent survey of the colony's early history is Edwin B. Bronner, *William Penn's "Holy Experiment": The Founding of Pennsylvania, 1681–1701* (New York, 1962). Robert L. D. Davidson, *War Comes to Quaker Pennsylvania, 1682–1756* (New York, 1957), discusses one of the colony's peculiar problems.

What is missing in the bibliography is a close study of one of the more successful colonizing ventures of the seventeenth century. There is help in William R. Shepherd, *History of Proprietary Government in Pennsylvania* (New York, 1896) ; Hope Francis Kane, "Notes on Early Pennsylvania Promotion Literature," *Pennsylvania Magazine of History and Biography,* LXIII (1939) ; John E. Pomfret, "The First Purchasers of

Pennsylvania, 1681–1700," *ibid.*, LXXX (1956), 137–163; Gary B. Nash, "The Free Society of Traders and the Early Politics of Pennsylvania," *ibid.*, LXXXIX (1965), 147–173; and Nash's unpublished Ph.D. dissertation, "Economics and Politics in Early Pennsylvania, 1682–1701" (Princeton University, 1964). Roy N. Lokken, *David Lloyd, Colonial Lawmaker* (Seattle, 1959), traces one of the important political careers of the colony's early history.

Virginia

Virginia has been fortunate in the historians who have been attracted to the study of its seventeenth-century history, and at no time more so than when Philip Alexander Bruce wrote his *Economic History of Virginia in the Seventeenth Century* (2 vols., New York, 1895), and his *Institutional History of Virginia in the Seventeenth Century* (2 vols., New York, 1910). Bruce was followed by Thomas J. Wertenbaker, whose *Patrician and Plebeian in Virginia; or, the Origin and Development of the Social Classes of the Old Dominion* (Charlottesville, 1910), established a reputation that was subsequently bolstered by *Virginia under the Stuarts, 1607–1688* (Princeton, 1914), and by *The Planters of Colonial Virginia* (Princeton, 1922).

Wertenbaker's *Torchbearer of the Revolution: The Story of Bacon's Rebellion and Its Leader* (Princeton, 1940) is the most readable narrative of the Rebellion and provides valuable biographical data on Bacon himself. The interpretation, which is well enough suggested by the title, has been vigorously challenged, with not a little additional information, by Wilcolmb E. Washburn in *The Governor and the Rebel: A History of Bacon's Rebellion in Virginia* (Chapel Hill, N.C., 1957). Also helpful are Washburn's "Governor Berkeley and King Philip's War," *New England Quarterly*, XXX (1957), 363–377, and "The Effect of Bacon's Rebellion on Government in England and Virginia," *United States National Museum Bulletin* 225 (Washington, 1962), pp. 137–152. A very suggestive essay on this much debated, and debatable, subject is Bernard Bailyn, "Politics and Social Structure in Virginia," in James M. Smith (ed.), *Seventeenth-Century America* (Chapel Hill, N.C., 1959), pp. 90–115. Mention belongs also to Neville Williams, "The Tribulations of John Bland, Merchant: London, Seville, Jamestown, Tangier, 1643–1680," *Virginia Magazine of History and Biography*, LXXII (1964), 19–41; and to Thomas P. Abernethy (ed.), *More News from Virginia* (Charlottsville, 1943).

Richard L. Morton, *Colonial Virginia* (2 vols., Chapel Hill, N.C., 1960), helpfully supplements the studies of Bruce and Wertenbaker, especially by the coverage it gives to the eighteenth century. The privately printed and often useful studies by Fairfax Harrison include *Proprietors of the Northern Neck: Chapters of Culpeper Genealogy* (Richmond, 1926), and *Virginia Land Grants: A Study of Conveyancing in Relation to Colonial Politics* (Richmond, 1925). George M. Brydon, *Virginia's Mother Church* (2 vols., Richmond, 1947), is informative, as also is William H. Seiler's excellent essay, "The Anglican Parish in Virginia," in Smith (ed.), *Seventeenth-Century America*, pp. 119–142. Susie M. Ames, *Studies of the Virginia Eastern Shore in the Seventeenth Century* (Richmond, 1940), is one of the few studies after those by Bruce to exploit the county records. Percy S. Flippin, *The Royal Government in Virginia, 1624–1775* (New York, 1919), and Elmer I. Miller, *The Legislature of the Province of Virginia* (New York, 1907), remain useful.

Of Louis B. Wright's many contributions to an understanding of this period, special mention belongs to *The First Gentlemen of Virginia: Intellectual Qualities of the Early Colonial Ruling Class* (San Marino, Calif., 1940, reissued in paperback at Charlottesville, 1964); his edition of Robert Beverley's *History and Present State of Virginia* (Chapel Hill, N.C., 1947); his "William Byrd's Defense of Sir Edmund Andros," *William and Mary Quarterly*, 3d. ser., II (1945), 47–62; and his edition of *An Essay upon the Government of the English Plantations on the Continent of America (1701)*, (San Marino, Calif., 1945), which the editor believes was probably written by Robert Beverley. Of comparable value is Hunter D. Farish (ed.), *The Present State of Virginia, and the College, by Henry Hartwell, James Blair, and Edward Chilton* (Williamsburg, 1940). Clifford Dowdey, *The Great Plantation: A Profile of Berkeley Hundred and Plantation Virginia, from Jamestown to Appomattox* (New York, 1957), is useful on the Harrison family. Richard Beale Davis (ed.), *William Fitzhugh and His Chesapeake World, 1676–1701* (Chapel Hill, N.C., 1963), brings together an unusually significant correspondence. Manning C. Voorhis, "Crown vs Council in the Virginia Land Policy," *William and Mary Quarterly*, 3d. ser., III (1946), 499–514, is an illuminating discussion of politics at the turn of the century.

Special Topics

Some of the more important modern studies of colonial America deal broadly with special topics, as in Richard B. Morris, *Studies in the History of American Law, with Special Reference to the Seventeenth and Eighteenth Centuries* (New York, 1930); the previously listed study by Nettels, *The Money Supply of the American Colonies*, which should be read together with E. James Ferguson's informative "Currency Finance: An Interpretation of Colonial Monetary Practices," *William and Mary*

Quarterly, 3d. ser., X (1953), 153–180; Carl Bridenbaugh, *Cities in the Wilderness: The First Century of Urban Life in America, 1625–1742* (New York, 1938); Leonard W. Labaree, *Conservatism in Early American History* (New York, 1948); or Chilton Williamson, *American Suffrage: From Property to Democracy, 1760–1860* (Princeton, 1960), which in its introductory chapters most usefully supplements the old standard, Albert E. McKinley, *The Suffrage Franchise in the Thirteen English Colonies in America* (Philadelphia, 1905).

The subject of the **franchise**, after many years of neglect, has recently come very much alive, as may be seen in Robert E. Brown, *Middle-Class Democracy and the Revolution in America, 1691–1780* (Ithaca, 1955); B. Katherine Brown, "Freemanship in Puritan Massachusetts," *American Historical Review*, LIX (1954), 865–883; David H. Fowler, "Connecticut's Freemen: The First Forty Years," *William and Mary Quarterly*, 3d. ser., XV (1958), 312–333; George D. Langdon, Jr., "The Franchise and Political Democracy in Plymouth Colony," *ibid.*, XX (1963), 513–526; or Richard P. McCormick, *The History of Voting in New Jersey: A Study of the Development of Election Machinery, 1664–1911* (New Brunswick, 1953).

Among studies of the **legislative assembly**, Jack P. Greene, *The Quest of Power: The Lower Houses of Assembly in the Southern Royal Colonies, 1689–1776* (Chapel Hill, N.C., 1963), is more informative than any other study that has been made. Until more studies have been undertaken, Greene's "The Role of the Lower House of Assembly in Eighteenth Century Politics," *Journal of Southern History*, XXVII (1961), 451–474, must remain a special dependence of any historian writing on the general topic. Labaree's *Royal Government in America*, listed above, has much to offer on the subject. Mary P. Clarke, *Parliamentary Privilege in the American Colonies* (New Haven, 1943), has an especially valuable chapter on the judicial functions of the assembly in the seventeenth century. Henry R. Spencer, *Constitutional Conflict in Provincial Massachusetts: A Study of Some Phases of the Opposition between the Massachusetts Governor and General Court in the Early Eighteenth Century* (Columbus, Ohio, 1905), can be read by modern students with respectful attention. Although J. R. Pole, *Political Representation in England and the Origins of the American Republic* (New York, 1966), is primarily concerned with a later period, the earlier chapters merit notice here.

Information on the fundamental problem of **land policy** is widely scattered, much of it in works previously listed, and, one suspects, seriously incomplete. Viola F. Barnes, "Land Tenure in English Colonial Charters of the Seventeenth Century," in *Essays . . . Presented to Charles McLean Andrews*, pp. 4–40, provides a helpful introduction to the subject. Beverley W. Bond, *The Quit-Rent System in the American Colonies* (New

Haven, 1919), is an indispensable guide on a subject as important for the political history of the colonies as for any other side of their history. Marshall Harris, *Origin of the Land Tenure System in the United States* (Ames, Iowa, 1953), is factual, heavily documented, and frequently a useful reference. For New England see especially Labaree's *Milford*, already mentioned, and for New York the chapter on land policy in Fox's *Caleb Heathcote*. Joseph N. Beale, Jr., "The Origin of the System of Recording Deeds in America," *The Green Bag*, III (1907), 335–339, has pertinence, as does the discussion of the same topic by Richard B. Morris in his *Studies in the History of American Law*.

On the **indentured servant**, Abbot E. Smith, *Colonists in Bondage: White Servitude and Convict Labor in America, 1607–1776* (Chapel Hill, N.C., 1947), is virtually definitive on the servant as a commodity in the trade between England and the colonies, and somewhat less satisfactory as a study of the servant's lot in America. On this last subject, a number of topics discussed by Richard B. Morris in his *Government and Labor in Early America* (New York, 1946) are especially helpful.

Of all members of the labor force, the **Negro** naturally has claimed from historians the closest attention. Older studies upon which Ulrich B. Phillips drew heavily in writing his *American Negro Slavery* (New York, 1918) continue to be indispensable for the information they provide, such as James C. Ballagh, *A History of Slavery in Virginia* (Baltimore, 1902); Jeffry R. Brackett, *The Negro in Maryland: A Study of the Institution of Slavery* (Baltimore, 1889); or John H. Russell, *The Free Negro in Virginia* (Baltimore, 1902). Indispensable too are W. E. B. DuBois, *The Suppression of the African Slave-Trade to the United States of America, 1638–1870* (New York, 1896), and Elizabeth Donnan (ed.), *Documents Illustrative of the Slave Trade to America* (4 vols., Washington, 1930–35).

Among more recent studies, David B. Davis, *The Problem of Slavery in Western Culture* (Ithaca, 1966), is an unusually successful effort to place the story of American Negro slavery in its full context. The previously cited Davies, *The Royal African Company*, is also of fundamental importance. Others helping to fill gaps in our knowledge have been Herbert Aptheker, *American Negro Slave Revolts* (New York, 1943); Lorenzo J. Greene, *The Negro in Colonial New England* (New York, 1942); Edgar J. McManus, *A History of Negro Slavery in New York* (Syracuse, 1966); Frank J. Klingberg, *Anglican Humanitarianism in Colonial New York* (Philadelphia, 1940), and *An Appraisal of the Negro in Colonial South Carolina* (Washington, 1941). Frank Tannenbaum's *Slave and Citizen: The Negro in the Americas* (New York, 1947) is helpfully suggestive, but it should be read with the study by Professor Davis that has been cited at the beginning of this paragraph. James H. Brewer, "Negro Property

Owners in Seventeenth Century Virginia," *William and Mary Quarterly*, 3d. ser., XII (1955), 575–580, and Benjamin Quarles, "The Colonial Militia and Negro Manpower," *Mississippi Valley Historical Review*, XLV (1958–59), 643–652, are useful additions to the bibliography.

Oscar and Mary F. Handlin, "Origins of the Southern Labor System," *William and Mary Quarterly*, 3d. ser., VII (1950), 199–222, has served to stimulate a vigorous discussion of fundamental issues in which the rejoinder by Carl N. Degler in *Out of Our Past: The Forces that Shaped Modern America* (New York, 1959) holds an important place. Stanley Elkins, *Slavery: A Problem in American Institutional and Intellectual Life* (Chicago, 1959), contains an excellent summary of the debate, which is also helpfully commented upon by Winthrop D. Jordan in "Modern Tensions and the Origins of American Slavery," *Journal of Southern History*, XXVII (1962), 18–30. More substantive contributions by Jordan to the discussion are his unpublished Ph.D. dissertation, "White over Black: The Attitudes of the American Colonists toward the Negro, to 1784," (Brown University, 1960); "The Influence of the West Indies on the Origins of New England Slavery," *William and Mary Quarterly*, 3d. ser., XVIII (1961), 243–250; and "American Chiaroscuro: The Status and Definition of Mulattoes in the British Colonies," *ibid.*, XIX (1962), 183–200. M. Eugene Sirmans, "The Legal Status of the Slave in South Carolina, 1670–1740," *Journal of Southern History*, XXVIII (1962), 462–473, should be added. John Hope Franklin, *From Slavery to Freedom: A History of American Negroes* (New York, 1950), is the standard study.

Encouraging evidence of a reviving interest in the **Indian** among historians is found in a number of modern studies: George T. Hunt, *The Wars of the Iroquois: A Study in Intertribal Relations* (Madison, Wis., 1940); the especially valuable, and previously cited, study by Trelease, *Indian Affairs in Colonial New York;* Douglas E. Leach, *Flintlock and Tomahawk: New England in King Philip's War* (New York, 1958), a skillful narrative of New England's great tragedy; Alden T. Vaughan, *New England Frontier: Puritans and Indians, 1620–1675* (Boston, 1965), which is primarily concerned to defend the Puritan's record in this regard; William Kellaway, *The New England Company, 1649–1776: Missionary Society to the American Indians* (New York, 1961), which rounds out our information on the New England missions; and Richmond P. Bond, *Queen Anne's American Kings* (Oxford, 1952), which provides an entertaining account of a visit to London by New York chieftains during the second Anglo-French war. Helpful to any historian venturing into this difficult subject is William Nelson Fenton, *American Indian and White Relations to 1830, Needs & Opportunities for Study: An Essay. A Bibliography by L. H. Butterfield, Wilcomb E. Washburn, and William N.*

Fenton (Chapel Hill, N.C., 1957) . Helpful articles are Paul A. W. Wallace, "The Iroquois: A Brief Outline of Their History," *Pennsylvania History,* XXIII (1956) , 15–28; and A. F. C. Wallace, "Origins of Iroquois Neutrality: The Grand Settlement of 1701," *ibid.,* XXIV (1957) , 223–235.

Among older studies by historians, first mention undoubtedly belongs to Charles H. McIlwain's introduction to *An Abridgement of the Indian Affairs Contained in Four Folio Volumes, Transacted in the Colony of New York, from the Year 1678 to the Year 1751, by Peter Wraxall* (Cambridge, Mass., 1915) for its extraordinarily influential suggestion that a critical factor in the over-all story was a struggle among the Indians for the advantage of acting as the middleman in the trade between the European settlements and the more distantly situated tribes. Anthropologists seem to have found the suggestion as attractive as have historians, but Professor Trelease has raised important questions which are summed up in his "The Iroquois and the Western Fur Trade: A Problem in Interpretation," *Mississippi Valley Historical Review,* XLIX (1962) , 32–51.

Except for the discussion in Verner Crane's *Southern Frontier,* listed above, the United States has yet to produce a comprehensive study of any part of the fur trade that is at all comparable to Harold A. Innis, *The Fur Trade in Canada* (New Haven, 1930; rev. ed., Toronto, 1956) . Two articles by Arthur H. Buffinton are especially helpful: "New England and the Western Fur Trade, 1629–1675," in *Publications of the Colonial Society of Massachusetts,* XVIII (1917) , 160–192; and "The Policy of Albany and English Westward Expansion," *Mississippi Valley Historical Review,* VIII (1922) , 327–366. Carl P. Russell, *Guns on the Early Frontiers: A History of Firearms from Colonial Times through the Years of the Western Fur Trade* (Berkeley and Los Angeles, 1957) , has interest; and still useful is Almon W. Lauber, *Indian Slavery in Colonial Times within the Present United States* (New York, 1913) .

Anthropological studies which have proved to be especially helpful are A. L. Kroeber, *Cultural and Natural Areas of Native North America* (Berkeley and Los Angeles, 1947) ; John R. Swanton, *The Indian Tribes of North America* (Washington, 1952) , and *The Tribes of the Southeastern United States* (Bureau of Ethnology Bulletin 137, Smithsonian Institution, Washington, 1946) ; James Mooney, *The Aboriginal Population of America North of Mexico* (*Smithsonian Miscellaneous Collections,* LXXX, No. 7, Feb. 1928) ; Alfred G. Bailey, *The Conflict of European and Eastern Algonkin Cultures, 1504–1700* (Saint John, New Brunswick, 1937) ; and the sources cited in Chapter 4, n. 16, above.

On the difficult subject of colonial population, the chief dependence continues to be Evarts B. Greene and Virginia D. Harrington, *American Population before the Federal Census of 1790* (New York, 1932) . Stella H. Sutherland, *Population Distribution in Colonial America* (New York,

1936), is a helpful supplement. Also useful is Herman R. Fries, "A Series of Population Maps of the Colonies and the United States, 1625–1790," *Geographical Review*, XXX (1940), 463–470. Richard L. Bowen, *Early Rehoboth* (Rehoboth, Mass., 1945), I, 1–24, and Arthur E. Karinen, "Maryland Population, 1631–1730," *Maryland Historical Magazine*, LIV (1959), 365–407, have helped persuade me that conventional estimates, especially for the earlier years of the period, may be greatly exaggerated. Kenneth A. Lockridge's venturesome study of "The Population of Dedham, Massachusetts, 1636–1736," *Economic History Review*, XIX (1966), 318–344, offers assistance in reconciling a rejection of conventional estimates for 1660 and an acceptance of them for the end of the century. See also Philip J. Greven, Jr., "Family Structure in Seventeenth-Century Andover, Massachusetts," *William and Mary Quarterly*, 3d. ser., XXIII (1966), 234–256, for data pertinent to the problem.

Specialized studies of the church and state relationship have a very sharp and understandable focus on the Church of England, its influence with the imperial government, and its growing activity in the colonies after the Revolution of 1688. Wilbur L. Cross, *The Anglican Episcopate and the American Colonies* (New York, 1902), was a pioneer study of great value, to which Carl Bridenbaugh recently has added a helpful supplement in *Mitre and Sceptre: Transatlantic Faiths, Ideas, Personalities, and Politics, 1689–1775* (New York, 1962). For the church settlement at the time of the Restoration, see especially Robert S. Bosher, *The Making of the Restoration Settlement: The Influence of the Laudians, 1649–1662* (London, 1951); for the colorful and significant career of Bishop Compton, Edward F. Carpenter, *The Protestant Bishop, Being the Life of Henry Compton, 1632–1713, Bishop of London* (London, 1956); and for the founder of the S.P.G., H. P. Thompson, *Thomas Bray* (London, 1954). Elizabeth H. Davidson, *The Establishment of the English Church in Continental American Colonies* (Durham, N.C., 1936), provides a convenient summary for the several provinces. Evarts B. Greene, *Religion and the State: The Making and Testing of an American Tradition* (New York, 1941), deals broadly with the theme indicated by its title. Jacob R. Marcus, *Early American Jewry* (2 vols., Philadelphia, 1951–53), is an especially well-informed and interesting discussion of the Jew in seventeenth- and eighteenth-century America.

Index

Acadia, 238, 248, 305, 311, 312, 314
Adams, John, quoted, 23
Admiralty courts, 254–255, 259
Africa, 35, 36, 59, 61, 292, 297
Albany, 72, 73, 79, 201, 207, 225, 227, 228, 229, 243, 244, 280, 282, 287, 305, 316, 317; defense of, 237, 240, 241, 248, 306; its fur trade, 205, 206, 306
Albemarle, George Monk, Duke of, 1, 56, 176
Albemarle County, 91, 232
Albemarle Sound, 16–17; early settlement of, 43, 96–97
Algonkin Indians, 108, 113, 136
Allen, Samuel, 244
Amsterdam, 61, 72
Andros, Sir Edmund, early career of, 202–203; governor of New York, 78, 79, 106, 188, 201, 202, 203, 204, 207, 208; of the Dominion of New England, 215–222, 225, 236; of Virginia, 236, 270
Annapolis, Md., 277
Anne Arundel County, Md., 9n.
Appomattox River, 114
Archdale, John, 178, 278; Laws, 278
Arlington, Henry Bennett, Earl of, 152
Arthur, Gabriel, 115
Ash, John, 278
Ashley River, 99
Ashurst, Sir Henry, 245, 321
Asia, 33, 35
Assembly (or Court), the General, 28–29, 53, 91–92; as consultative body, 25–27, 146, 152, 199, 263; the bi-cameral, 27, 263; its judicial func-

tions, 154–155, 263, 283; its development, 262–265, 283–284, 325; lower houses of, 164, 199, 263, 264, 320–322, 325–327; see entries under the several colonies
Assiento, the, 319
Assize, court of, 76, 77–78
Augsburg, War of the League of, see King William's War
Azores, the, 38

Bacon's Assembly, 133, 140
Bacon's Laws, 137–138, 140, 146
Bacon, Nathaniel, 127, 130–131, 134, 139–141, 143, 145–146, 149
Bacon, Nathaniel, Sr., 131
Bacon's Rebellion, 107, 108, 126–134, 137, 148, 160, 167; its interpretation, 138–146; its sequel, 134, 142, 146, 149–153
Badcock, Nicholas, 164
Bahama Islands, proprietors of, 56
Baltimore, Cecelius Calvert, 2d. Lord, 9, 17, 22, 40, 43, 64, 72, 160, 191; Charles, 3d. Lord, 27, 160–165, 190–191, 198, 199, 230–231, 241, 274, 275
Baltimore County, Md., 17
Baptists, 95
Barbados, 3, 39, 55, 98, 99, 202, 233, 237, 290, 292, 309; and settlement of Carolina, 88–89, 96, 101, 135
Barclay, Robert, 190
Barnegat Bay, 82
Basse, Jeremiah, 260
Batts, Thomas, 115
Bayard, Nicholas, 227, 230

353

hARpER ⚡ ꓔORChbOOKS

HUMANITIES AND SOCIAL SCIENCES

American Studies: General

HENRY STEELE COMMAGER, Ed.: The Struggle for Racial Equality   TB/1300
CARL N. DEGLER, Ed.: Pivotal Interpretations of American History   TB/1240, TB/1241
A. S. EISENSTADT, Ed.: The Craft of American History: Recent Essays in American Historical Writing
Vol. I TB/1255; Vol. II TB/1256
CHARLOTTE P. GILMAN: Women and Economics. ‡ Ed. with an Introduction by Carl N. Degler   TB/3073
MARCUS LEE HANSEN: The Atlantic Migration: 1607-1860. Edited by Arthur M. Schlesinger   TB/1052
MARCUS LEE HANSEN: The Immigrant in American History   TB/1120
JOHN HIGHAM, Ed.: The Reconstruction of American History △   TB/1068
ROBERT H. JACKSON: The Supreme Court in the American System of Government   TB/1106
JOHN F. KENNEDY: A Nation of Immigrants. △ Illus.   TB/1118
LEONARD W. LEVY, Ed.: American Constitutional Law: Historical Essays   TB/1285
LEONARD W. LEVY, Ed.: Judicial Review and the Supreme Court   TB/1296
LEONARD W. LEVY: The Law of the Commonwealth and Chief Justice Shaw   TB/1309
RALPH BARTON PERRY: Puritanism and Democracy   TB/1138
ARNOLD ROSE: The Negro in America   TB/3048

American Studies: Colonial

BERNARD BAILYN, Ed.: The Apologia of Robert Keayne: Self-Portrait of a Puritan Merchant   TB/1201
BERNARD BAILYN: The New England Merchants in the Seventeenth Century   TB/1149
JOSEPH CHARLES: The Origins of the American Party System   TB/1049
CHARLES GIBSON: Spain in America†   TB/3077
LAWRENCE HENRY GIPSON: The Coming of the Revolution: 1763-1775. † Illus.   TB/3007
PERRY MILLER: Errand Into the Wilderness   TB/1139
PERRY MILLER & T. H. JOHNSON, Eds.: The Puritans: A Sourcebook   Vol. I TB/1093; Vol. II TB/1094
EDMUND S. MORGAN, Ed.: The Diary of Michael Wigglesworth, 1653-1657: The Conscience of a Puritan   TB/1228
EDMUND S. MORGAN: The Puritan Family   TB/1227
RICHARD B. MORRIS: Government and Labor in Early America   TB/1244
KENNETH B. MURDOCK: Literature and Theology in Colonial New England   TB/99
WALLACE NOTESTEIN: The English People on the Eve of Colonization: 1603-1630. † Illus.   TB/3006
JOHN P. ROCHE: Origins of American Political Thought: Selected Readings   TB/1301

JOHN SMITH: Captain John Smith's America: Selections from His Writings. Ed. with Intro. by John Lankford   TB/3078
LOUIS B. WRIGHT: The Cultural Life of the American Colonies: 1607-1763. † Illus.   TB/3005

American Studies: From the Revolution to 1860

JOHN R. ALDEN: The American Revolution: 1775-1783. † Illus.   TB/3011
MAX BELOFF, Ed.: The Debate on the American Revolution, 1761-1783: A Sourcebook △   TB/1225
RAY A. BILLINGTON: The Far Western Frontier: 1830-1860. † Illus.   TB/3012
EDMUND BURKE: On the American Revolution. ‡ Edited by Elliott Robert Barkan   TB/3068
WHITNEY R. CROSS: The Burned-Over District: The Social and Intellectual History of Enthusiastic Religion in Western New York, 1800-1850   TB/1242
GEORGE DANGERFIELD: The Awakening of American Nationalism: 1815-1828. † Illus.   TB/3061
CLEMENT EATON: The Growth of Southern Civilization: 1790-1860. † Illus.   TB/3040
LOUIS FILLER: The Crusade Against Slavery: 1830-1860. † Illus.   TB/3029
WILLIAM W. FREEHLING, Ed.: The Nullification Era: A Documentary Record‡   TB/3079
FELIX GILBERT: The Beginnings of American Foreign Policy: To the Farewell Address   TB/1200
FRANCIS GRIERSON: The Valley of Shadows: The Coming of the Civil War in Lincoln's Midwest: A Contemporary Account   TB/1246
JAMES MADISON: The Forging of American Federalism. Edited by Saul K. Padover   TB/1226
BERNARD MAYO: Myths and Men: Patrick Henry, George Washington, Thomas Jefferson   TB/1108
JOHN C. MILLER: Alexander Hamilton and the Growth of the New Nation   TB/3057
RICHARD B. MORRIS, Ed.: The Era of the American Revolution   TB/1180
R. B. NYE: The Cultural Life of the New Nation: 1776-1801. † Illus.   TB/3026
FRANCIS S. PHILBRICK: The Rise of the West, 1754-1830. † Illus.   TB/3067
TIMOTHY L. SMITH: Revivalism and Social Reform: American Protestantism on the Eve of the Civil War   TB/1229
ALBION W. TOURGÉE: A Fool's Errand. ‡ Ed. by George Fredrickson   TB/3074
A. F. TYLER: Freedom's Ferment   TB/1074
GLYNDON G. VAN DEUSEN: The Jacksonian Era: 1828-1848. † Illus.   TB/3028
LOUIS B. WRIGHT: Culture on the Moving Frontier   TB/1053

American Studies: The Civil War to 1900

W. R. BROCK: An American Crisis: Congress and Reconstruction, 1865-67 ° △   TB/1283

---

† The New American Nation Series, edited by Henry Steele Commager and Richard B. Morris.
‡ American Persectives series, edited by Bernard Wishy and William E. Leuchtenburg.
* The Rise of Modern Europe series, edited by William L. Langer.
** History of Europe series, edited by J. H. Plumb.
¶ Researches in the Social, Cultural, and Behavioral Sciences, edited by Benjamin Nelson.
§ The Library of Religion and Culture, edited by Benjamin Nelson.
Σ Harper Modern Science Series, edited by James R. Newman.
° Not for sale in Canada.
△ Not for sale in the U. K.

1

W. A. DUNNING: Reconstruction, Political and Economic: 1865-1877 TB/1073
HAROLD U. FAULKNER: Politics, Reform and Expansion: 1890-1900. † Illus. TB/3020
ROBERT GREEN MC CLOSKEY: American Conservatism in the Age of Enterprise: 1865-1910 TB/1137
ARTHUR MANN: Yankee Reformers in the Urban Age: Social Reform in Boston, 1880-1900 TB/1247
CHARLES H. SHINN: Mining Camps: A Study in American Frontier Government. ‡ Ed. by R. W. Paul TB/3062
VERNON LANE WHARTON: The Negro in Mississippi: 1865-1890 TB/1178

American Studies: 1900 to the Present

A. RUSSELL BUCHANAN: The United States and World War II. † Illus. Vol. I TB/3044; Vol. II TB/3045
FOSTER RHEA DULLES: America's Rise to World Power: 1898-1954. † Illus. TB/3021
JOHN D. HICKS: Republican Ascendancy: 1921-1933. † Illus. TB/3041
SIDNEY HOOK: Reason, Social Myths, and Democracy TB/1237
WILLIAM E. LEUCHTENBURG: Franklin D. Roosevelt and the New Deal: 1932-1940. † Illus. TB/3025
ARTHUR S. LINK: Woodrow Wilson and the Progressive Era: 1910-1917. † Illus. TB/3023
GEORGE E. MOWRY: The Era of Theodore Roosevelt and the Birth of Modern America: 1900-1912. † TB/3022
RUSSEL B. NYE: Midwestern Progressive Politics: 1870-1958 TB/1202
JACOB RIIS: The Making of an American. ‡ Edited by Roy Lubove TB/3070
PHILIP SELZNICK: TVA and the Grass Roots: A Study in the Sociology of Formal Organization TB/1230
IDA M. TARBELL: The History of the Standard Oil Company: Briefer Version. ‡ Edited by David M. Chalmers TB/3071
GEORGE B. TINDALL, Ed.: A Populist Reader ‡ TB/3069

Anthropology

JACQUES BARZUN: Race: A Study in Superstition. Revised Edition TB/1172
JOSEPH B. CASAGRANDE, Ed.: In the Company of Man: Portraits of Anthropological Informants TB/3047
W. E. LE GROS CLARK: The Antecedents of Man: Intro. to Evolution of the Primates. ° △ Illus. TB/559
CORA DU BOIS: The People of Alor. New Preface by the author. Illus. Vol. I TB/1042; Vol. II TB/1043
DAVID LANDY: Tropical Childhood: Cultural Transmission and Learning in a Puerto Rican Village TB/1235
L. S. B. LEAKEY: Adam's Ancestors: The Evolution of Man and His Culture. △ Illus. TB/1019
ROBERT H. LOWIE: Primitive Society. Introduction by Fred Eggan TB/1056
EDWARD BURNETT TYLOR: The Origins of Culture. Part I of "Primitive Culture." § Intro. by Paul Radin TB/33
EDWARD BURNETT TYLOR: Religion in Primitive Culture. Part II of "Primitive Culture." § Intro. by Paul Radin TB/34
W. LLOYD WARNER: A Black Civilization: A Study of an Australian Tribe. ¶ Illus. TB/3056

Art and Art History

WALTER LOWRIE: Art in the Early Church. Revised Edition. 452 illus. TB/124
EMILE MÂLE: The Gothic Image: Religious Art in France of the Thirteenth Century. § △ 190 illus. TB/44
MILLARD MEISS: Painting in Florence and Siena after the Black Death. 169 illus. TB/1148
ERICH NEUMANN: The Archetypal World of Henry Moore. △ 107 illus. TB/2020
DORA & ERWIN PANOFSKY: Pandora's Box: The Changing Aspects of a Mythical Symbol TB/2021
ERWIN PANOFSKY: Studies in Iconology: Humanistic Themes in the Art of the Renaissance △ TB/1077

ALEXANDRE PIANKOFF: The Shrines of Tut-Ankh-Amon. Edited by N. Rambova. 117 illus. TB/2011
JEAN SEZNEC: The Survival of the Pagan Gods △ TB/2004
OTTO VON SIMSON: The Gothic Cathedral △ TB/2018
HEINRICH ZIMMER: Myths and Symbols in Indian Art and Civilization. 70 illus. TB/2005

Business, Economics & Economic History

REINHARD BENDIX: Work and Authority in Industry TB/3035
GILBERT BURCK & EDITORS OF FORTUNE: The Computer Age: And Its Potential for Management TB/1179
ROBERT DAHL & CHARLES E. LINDBLOM: Politics, Economics, and Welfare TB/3037
PETER F. DRUCKER: The New Society: The Anatomy of Industrial Order △ TB/1082
EDITORS OF FORTUNE: America in the Sixties: The Economy and the Society TB/1015
ROBERT L. HEILBRONER: The Great Ascent: The Struggle for Economic Development in Our Time TB/3030
ROBERT L. HEILBRONER: The Limits of American Capitalism TB/1305
FRANK H. KNIGHT: The Economic Organization TB/1214
FRANK H. KNIGHT: Risk, Uncertainty and Profit TB/1215
ABBA P. LERNER: Everybody's Business TB/3051
PAUL MANTOUX: The Industrial Revolution in the Eighteenth Century ° △ TB/1079
HERBERT SIMON: The Shape of Automation: For Men and Management TB/1245
PERRIN STRYKER: The Character of the Executive: Eleven Studies in Managerial Qualities TB/1041

Contemporary Culture

JACQUES BARZUN: The House of Intellect △ TB/1051
CLARK KERR: The Uses of the University TB/1264
JOHN U. NEF: Cultural Foundations of Industrial Civilization △ TB/1024
NATHAN M. PUSEY: The Age of the Scholar: Observations on Education in a Troubled Decade TB/1157
PAUL VALÉRY: The Outlook for Intelligence △ TB/2016

Historiography & Philosophy of History

JACOB BURCKHARDT: On History and Historians. △ Intro. by H. R. Trevor-Roper TB/1216
J. H. HEXTER: Reappraisals in History: New Views on History & Society in Early Modern Europe △ TB/1100
H. STUART HUGHES: History as Art and as Science: Twin Vistas on the Past TB/1207
ARNALDO MOMIGLIANO: Studies in Historiography ° △ TB/1288
GEORGE H. NADEL, Ed.: Studies in the Philosophy of History: Essays from History and Theory TB/1208
KARL P. POPPER: The Open Society and Its Enemies △ Vol. I: The Spell of Plato TB/1101; Vol. II: The High Tide of Prophecy: Hegel, Marx and the Aftermath TB/1102
KARL R. POPPER: The Poverty of Historicism ° △ TB/1126
G. J. RENIER: History: Its Purpose and Method △ TB/1209
W. H. WALSH: Philosophy of History △ TB/1020

History: General

L. CARRINGTON GOODRICH: A Short History of the Chinese People. △ Illus. TB/3015
DAN N. JACOBS & HANS H. BAERWALD: Chinese Communism: Selected Documents TB/3031
BERNARD LEWIS: The Arabs in History ° △ TB/1029
BERNARD LEWIS: The Middle East and the West ° △ TB/1274

History: Ancient

A. ANDREWES: The Greek Tyrants △ TB/1103
ADOLF ERMAN, Ed.: The Ancient Egyptians TB/1233
MICHAEL GRANT: Ancient History ° △ TB/1190
SAMUEL NOAH KRAMER: Sumerian Mythology TB/1055
NAPHTALI LEWIS & MEYER REINHOLD, Eds.: Roman Civilization. Sourcebook I: The Republic TB/1231; Sourcebook II: The Empire TB/1232

2

CARL J. FRIEDRICH: The Age of the Baroque, 1610-1660. *
Illus. TB/3004
RENÉ FUELOP-MLILER: The Mind and Face of Bolshevism TB/1188
M. DOROTHY GEORGE: London Life in the Eighteenth Century △ TB/1182
C. C. GILLISPIE: Genesis and Geology: The Decades before Darwin § TB/51
ALBERT GOODWIN: The French Revolution △ TB/1064
ALBERT GUÉRARD: France in the Classical Age △ TB/1183
CARLTON J. H. HAYES: A Generation of Materialism, 1871-1900. * Illus. TB/3039
J. H. HEXTER: Reappraisals in History △ TB/1100
STANLEY HOFFMANN et al.: In Search of France TB/1219
A. R. HUMPHREYS: The Augustan World: Society and and Letters in 18th Century England o △ TB/1105
DAN N. JACOBS, Ed.: The New Communist Manifesto & Related Documents. Third edition, revised TB/1078
LIONEL KOCHAN: The Struggle for Germany: 1914-45 TB/1304
HANS KOHN: The Mind of Germany △ TB/1204
HANS KOHN, Ed.: The Mind of Modern Russia: Historical and Political Thought of Russia's Great Age TB/1065
WALTER LAQUEUR & GEORGE L. MOSSE, Eds.: International Fascism, 1920-1945 o △ TB/1276
WALTER LAQUEUR & GEORGE L. MOSSE, Eds.: Left-Wing Intellectuals Between the Wars, 1919-1939 o △ TB/1286
WALTER LAQUEUR & GEORGE L. MOSSE, Eds.: 1914: The Coming of the First World War o △ TB/1306
FRANK E. MANUEL: The Prophets of Paris: Turgot, Condorcet, Saint-Simon, Fourier, and Comte TB/1218
KINGSLEY MARTIN: French Liberal Thought in the Eighteenth Century TB/1114
L. B. NAMIER: Facing East: Essays on Germany, the Balkans, and Russia △ TB/1280
L. B. NAMIER: Personalities and Powers △ TB/1186
L. B. NAMIER: Vanished Supremacies: Essays on European History, 1812-1918 o △ TB/1088
JOHN U. NEF: Western Civilization Since the Renaissance: Peace, War, Industry, and the Arts TB/1113
FRANZ NEUMANN: Behemoth: National Socialism, 1933-1944 o △ TB/1289
FREDERICK L. NUSSBAUM: The Triumph of Science and Reason, 1660-1685. * Illus. TB/3009
DAVID OGG: Europe of the Ancien Régime, 1715-1783 ** o △ TB/1271
JOHN PLAMENATZ: German Marxism and Russian Communism o △ TB/1189
RAYMOND W. POSTGATE, Ed.: Revolution from 1789 to 1906: Selected Documents TB/1063
WILLIAM PRESTON, JR.: Aliens and Dissenters: Federal Suppression of Radicals, 1903-1933 TB/1287
PENFIELD ROBERTS: The Quest for Security, 1715-1740. * Illus. TB/3016
PRISCILLA ROBERTSON: Revolutions of 1848: A Social History TB/1025
GEORGE RUDÉ: Revolutionary Europe, 1783-1815 ** o △ TB/1272
LOUIS, DUC DE SAINT-SIMON: Versailles, The Court, and Louis XIV △ TB/1250
A. J. P. TAYLOR: From Napoleon to Lenin: Historical Essays o △ TB/1268
A. J. P. TAYLOR: The Habsburg Monarchy, 1809-1918 o △ TB/1187
G. M. TREVELYAN: British History in the Nineteenth Century and After: 1782-1919 o △ TB/1251
H. R. TREVOR-ROPER: Historical Essays o △ TB/1269
ELIZABETH WISKEMANN: Europe of the Dictators, 1919-1945 ** o △ TB/1273
JOHN B. WOLF: The Emergence of the Great Powers, 1685-1715. * Illus. TB/3010
JOHN B. WOLF: France: 1814-1919: The Rise of a Liberal-Democratic Society TB/3019

Intellectual History & History of Ideas

HERSCHEL BAKER: The Image of Man TB/1047
R. R. BOLGAR: The Classical Heritage and Its Beneficiaries △ TB/1125
J. BRONOWSKI & BRUCE MAZLISH: The Western Intellectual Tradition: From Leonardo to Hegel △ TB/3001
NORMAN COHN: Pursuit of the Millennium △ TB/1037
C. C. GILLISPIE: Genesis and Geology: The Decades before Darwin § TB/51
ARTHUR O. LOVEJOY: The Great Chain of Being: A Study of the History of an Idea TB/1009
FRANK E. MANUEL: The Prophets of Paris: Turgot, Condorcet, Saint-Simon, Fourier, and Comte TB/1218
RALPH BARTON PERRY: The Thought and Character of William James: Briefer Version TB/1156
BRUNO SNELL: The Discovery of the Mind: The Greek Origins of European Thought △ TB/1018
PAUL VALÉRY: The Outlook for Intelligence △ TB/2016
W. WARREN WAGAR, Ed.: European Intellectual History since Darwin and Marx TB/1297
PHILIP P. WIENER: Evolution and the Founders of Pragmatism. △ Foreword by John Dewey TB/1212

Literature, Poetry, The Novel & Criticism

JACQUES BARZUN: The House of Intellect △ TB/1051
W. J. BATE: From Classic to Romantic: Premises of Taste in Eighteenth Century England TB/1036
JAMES BOSWELL: The Life of Dr. Johnson & The Journal of a Tour to the Hebrides with Samuel Johnson LL.D.: Selections o △ TB/1254
ERNST R. CURTIUS: European Literature and the Latin Middle Ages △ TB/2015
ALFRED HARBAGE: As They Liked It: A Study of Shakespeare's Moral Artistry TB/1035
A. R. HUMPHREYS: The Augustan World: Society in 18th Century England o △ TB/1105
ALDOUS HUXLEY: Antic Hay & The Giaconda Smile. o △ Introduction by Martin Green TB/3503
ALDOUS HUXLEY: Brave New World & Brave New World Revisited. o △ Introduction by Martin Green TB/3501
HENRY JAMES: The Tragic Muse TB/1017
ARNOLD KETTLE: An Introduction to the English Novel. △ Volume I: Defoe to George Eliot TB/1011
Volume II: Henry James to the Present TB/1012
RICHMOND LATTIMORE: The Poetry of Greek Tragedy △ TB/1257
J. B. LEISHMAN: The Monarch of Wit: An Analytical and Comparative Study of the Poetry of John Donne o △ TB/1258
J. B. LEISHMAN: Themes and Variations in Shakespeare's Sonnets o △ TB/1259
SAMUEL PEPYS: The Diary of Samuel Pepys. o Edited by O. F. Morshead. Illus. by Ernest Shepard TB/1007
ST.-JOHN PERSE: Seamarks TB/2002
V. DE S. PINTO: Crisis in English Poetry, 1880-1940 o △ TB/1260
ROBERT PREYER, Ed.: Victorian Literature TB/1302
GEORGE SANTAYANA: Interpretations of Poetry and Religion § TB/9
C. K. STEAD: The New Poetic o △ TB/1263
HEINRICH STRAUMANN: American Literature in the Twentieth Century. △ Third Edition, Revised TB/1168
PAGET TOYNBEE: Dante Alighieri: His Life and Works. Edited with Intro. by Charles S. Singleton TB/1206
DOROTHY VAN GHENT: The English Novel TB/1050
E. B. WHITE: One Man's Meat. TB/3505
BASIL WILLEY: Nineteenth Century Studies: Coleridge to Matthew Arnold o △ TB/1261
BASIL WILLEY: More Nineteenth Century Studies: A Group of Honest Doubters o △ TB/1262
RAYMOND WILLIAMS: Culture and Society, 1780-1950 o △ TB/1252
RAYMOND WILLIAMS: The Long Revolution o △ TB/1253
MORTON DAUWEN ZABEL, Editor: Literary Opinion in America Vol. I TB/3013; Vol. II TB/3014

Myth, Symbol & Folklore

JOSEPH CAMPBELL, Editor: Pagan and Christian Mysteries. *Illus.* TB/2013
MIRCEA ELIADE: Cosmos and History: *The Myth of the Eternal Return* § △ TB/2050
MIRCEA ELIADE: Rites and Symbols of Initiation: *The Mysteries of Birth and Rebirth* § △ TB/1236
THEODOR H. GASTER: Thespis: *Ritual, Myth & Drama in the Ancient Near East* △ TB/1281
DORA & ERWIN PANOFSKY: Pandora's Box: *The Changing Aspects of a Mythical Symbol. △ Revised Edition. Illus.* TB/2021
HELLMUT WILHELM: Change: *Eight Lectures on the I Ching* △ TB/2019

Philosophy

G. E. M. ANSCOMBE: An Introduction to Wittgenstein's Tractatus. *Second edition, Revised* ° △ TB/1210
HENRI BERGSON: Time and Free Will ° △ TB/1021
H. J. BLACKHAM: Six Existentialist Thinkers ° △ TB/1002
CRANE BRINTON: Nietzsche TB/1197
ERNST CASSIRER: The Individual and the Cosmos in Renaissance Philosophy △ TB/1097
FREDERICK COPLESTON: Medieval Philosophy ° △ TB/376
F. M. CORNFORD: Principium Sapientiae: *A Study of the Origins of Greek Philosophical Thought* TB/1213
F. M. CORNFORD: From Religion to Philosophy § TB/20
WILFRID DESAN: The Tragic Finale: *An Essay on the Philosophy of Jean-Paul Sartre* TB/1030
A. P. D'ENTRÈVES: Natural Law △ TB/1223
MARVIN FARBER: The Aims of Phenomenology: *Husserl's Thought* TB/1291
MARVIN FARBER: Phenomenology and Existence: *Towards a Philosophy Within Nature* TB/1295
PAUL FRIEDLÄNDER: Plato: *An Introduction* △ TB/2017
J. GLENN GRAY: The Warriors: *Reflections on Men in Battle. Intro. by Hannah Arendt* TB/1294
W. K. C. GUTHRIE: The Greek Philosophers: *From Thales to Aristotle* ° △ TB/1008
G. W. F. HEGEL: The Phenomenology of Mind ° △ TB/1303
F. H. HEINEMANN: Existentialism and the Modern Predicament △ TB/28
EDMUND HUSSERL: Phenomenology and the Crisis of Philosophy TB/1170
IMMANUEL KANT: The Doctrine of Virtue, *being Part II of the Metaphysic of Morals* TB/110
IMMANUEL KANT: Groundwork of the Metaphysic of Morals. *Trans. & analyzed by H. J. Paton* TB/1159
IMMANUEL KANT: Lectures on Ethics § △ TB/105
IMMANUEL KANT: Religion Within the Limits of Reason Alone. § *Intro. by T. M. Greene & J. Silber* TB/67
QUENTIN LAUER: Phenomenology TB/1169
GABRIEL MARCEL: Being and Having △ TB/310
GEORGE A. MORGAN: What Nietzsche Means △ TB/1198
MICHAEL POLANYI: Personal Knowledge △ TB/1158
WILLARD VAN ORMAN QUINE: Elementary Logic: *Revised Edition* TB/577
WILLARD VAN ORMAN QUINE: From a Logical Point of View: *Logico-Philosophical Essays* TB/566
BERTRAND RUSSELL et al.: The Philosophy of Bertrand Russell Vol. I TB/1095; Vol. II TB/1096
L. S. STEBBING: A Modern Introduction to Logic △ TB/538
ALFRED NORTH WHITEHEAD: Process and Reality: *An Essay in Cosmology* △ TB/1033
PHILIP P. WIENER: Evolution and the Founders of Pragmatism. *Foreword by John Dewey* TB/1212
WILHELM WINDELBAND: A History of Philosophy
Vol. I: *Greek, Roman, Medieval* TB/38
Vol. II: *Renaissance, Enlightenment, Modern* TB/39
LUDWIG WITTGENSTEIN: The Blue and Brown Books ° TB/1211

Political Science & Government

JEREMY BENTHAM: The Handbook of Political Fallacies. *Introduction by Crane Brinton* TB/1069
KENNETH E. BOULDING: Conflict and Defense TB/3024
CRANE BRINTON: English Political Thought in the Nineteenth Century TB/1071
ROBERT CONQUEST: Power and Policy in the USSR: *The Study of Soviet Dynastics* △ TB/1307
ROBERT DAHL & CHARLES E. LINDBLOM: Politics, Economics, and Welfare TB/3037
F. L. GANSHOF: Feudalism △ TB/1058
G. P. GOOCH: English Democratic Ideas in Seventeenth Century TB/1006
SIDNEY HOOK: Reason, Social Myths and Democracy △ TB/1237
DAN N. JACOBS & HANS BAERWALD, Eds.: Chinese Communism: *Selected Documents* TB/3031
HANS KOHN: Political Ideologies of the 20th Century TB/1277
KINGSLEY MARTIN: French Liberal Thought in the Eighteenth Century △ TB/1114
BARRINGTON MOORE, JR.: Soviet Politics—The Dilemma of Power ¶ TB/1222
BARRINGTON MOORE, JR.: Terror and Progress—USSR ¶ TB/1266
JOHN B. MORRALL: Political Thought in Medieval Times △ TB/1076
KARL R. POPPER: The Open Society and Its Enemies △
Vol. I: *The Spell of Plato* TB/1101
Vol. II: *The High Tide of Prophecy: Hegel, Marx, and the Aftermath* TB/1102
BENJAMIN I. SCHWARTZ: Chinese Communism and the Rise of Mao TB/1308
PETER WOLL, Ed.: Public Administration and Policy: *Selected Essays* TB/1284

Psychology

ALFRED ADLER: The Individual Psychology of Alfred Adler △ TB/1154
ARTHUR BURTON & ROBERT E. HARRIS, Eds.: Clinical Studies of Personality
Vol. I TB/3075; Vol. II TB/3076
HADLEY CANTRIL: The Invasion from Mars: *The Psychology of Panic* TB/1282
HERBERT FINGARETTE: The Self in Transformation ¶ TB/1177
SIGMUND FREUD: On Creativity and the Unconscious § △ TB/45
WILLIAM JAMES: Psychology: *Briefer Course* TB/1034
RICHARD M. JONES, Ed.: Contemporary Educational Psychology: *Selected Readings* TB/1292
C. G. JUNG: Symbols of Transformation △
Vol. I: TB/2009; Vol. II TB/2010
JOHN T. MC NEILL: A History of the Cure of Souls TB/126
KARL MENNINGER: Theory of Psychoanalytic Technique TB/1144
ERICH NEUMANN: Amor and Psyche △ TB/2012
ERICH NEUMANN: The Origins and History of Consciousness △ Vol. I *Illus.* TB/2007; Vol. II TB/2008
JEAN PIAGET, BÄRBEL INHELDER, & ALINA SZEMINSKA: The Child's Conception of Geometry ° △ TB/1146
JOHN H. SCHAAR: Escape from Authority: *The Perspectives of Erich Fromm* TB/1155
MUZAFER SHERIF: The Psychology of Social Norms TB/3072

Sociology

JACQUES BARZUN: Race: *A Study in Superstition* TB/1172
BERNARD BERELSON, Ed.: The Behavioral Sciences Today TB/1127
LEWIS A. COSER, Ed.: Political Sociology TB/1293
ALLISON DAVIS & JOHN DOLLARD: Children of Bondage ¶ TB/3049
ST. CLAIR DRAKE & HORACE R. CAYTON: Black Metropolis Vol. I TB/1086; Vol. II TB/1087
ALVIN W. GOULDNER: Wildcat Strike ¶ TB/1176

5

6